THOMAS G

HISTORY

OF THE

GREEK REVOLUTION

Volume 1

Elibron Classics
www.elibron.com

HISTORY

OF

THE GREEK REVOLUTION.

EDINBURGH: PRINTED BY BALLANTYNE AND COMPANY, PAUL'S WORK.

HISTORY

OF THE

GREEK REVOLUTION.

BY

THOMAS GORDON, F.R.S.

IN TWO VOLUMES.

VOL. I.

WILLIAM BLACKWOOD, EDINBURGH; AND
T. CADELL, STRAND, LONDON.
MDCCCXXXII.

PREFACE.

THE contest betwixt the Greeks and Turks has employed so many pens, that he who now ventures to write on that hackneyed, and apparently exhausted subject, must begin by explaining his reasons for travelling over a beaten road, to which he cannot hope to attract public curiosity, since it is either satiated by preceding narratives, or drawn away towards more recent and important transactions : these reasons may be summed up in a few words. That momentary interest, which induced a number of persons hastily to publish what they had seen or heard in Greece, exists no longer ; but there is, and ever will be, a grave class of readers loving truth more than novelty, and desirous of becoming acquainted with the exact details of a revolution, that must take its place in the history of the world. As yet there is nothing calculated to satisfy their taste, for of the forty authors whom the struggle in Greece has called forth, three or four alone have any claims to accuracy, and their labours were confined to short and isolated periods, and detached scenes of the war;* neither are they always free from the influence of strong prejudices. Conceiving that a day would come when a work more connected, and written on a larger basis, will be acceptable to literary men, the author of the following pages has presumed to take upon himself the task of composing it; because having served in the Greek army, and lived several years in close intimacy with the people of Hellas, he is indebted to the friendship of numerous individuals who bore a distinguished part in their country's affairs, as well as to the kindness of his Philhellenic comrades, for authentic materials, which are not likely either to survive the present generation, or to fall in the way of others.

---

* As an example we shall pitch upon the campaign of 1821, certainly better described hitherto, than any subsequent epoch. Of four authors who have treated it in detail, Messrs Raybaud, Blaquiere, Pouqueville, and Green, the first served in Greece, and may be implicitly trusted for every thing that happened under his own eyes; the second, though partial, is a lover of truth, and derived his information from a Philhellene serving in the Morea; the third (long a resident in the East, and brother to the French Consul at Patrass) and the fourth, (himself Consul at that port,) had very good means of sifting out the real progress of events, but were both unfortunately wedded to violent prejudices on opposite sides, and both wrote for a political purpose. By comparing their accounts, a reader of judgment may obtain an accurate knowledge of the insurrection at Patrass, the siege of Tripolizza, and generally of the campaign in Peloponnesus: but with regard to the contemporaneous operations in Northern Greece, and beyond the Danube, he will either be left in the dark or led astray.

At the same time he has thought it his duty carefully to peruse all former publications on the topic of Greece, neither affecting to differ from his predecessors, where they are correct, nor admitting any thing upon their authority, unless when assured of its exactitude by his own observations, or by collating oral and MS. evidence worthy of credit. His study, in short, has been, by clearing away exaggeration, rectifying errors and anachronisms, and supplying omissions, to represent the Greek Revolution as it really was.

CAIRNESS, *Nov.* 1, 1832.

CONTENTS

OF

VOLUME FIRST.

DIRECTIONS TO THE BINDER.

VOL. I.

VOL II.

INTRODUCTION.

THE glory of the ancient Greeks, their proficiency in the arts of war and peace, and the profound misery and degradation of their modern descendants, are historical facts so well known and established, that any attempts to prove or dilate upon them, might justly be considered a waste of words : nevertheless, in order properly to introduce our subject, we may be allowed to take a short retrospect of the different phases which that celebrated and unfortunate people has presented, from the beginning of history to our own time, a space of two thousand five hundred years.

Placed, as it is, at the south-eastern extremity of Europe, it was through Greece that the first rays of light and civilisation penetrated the darkness of our continent, and there it was that the seeds of knowledge, imparted from Asia and Africa, found an intellectual soil, so admirably fitted to receive them, that the Greeks, but just emerged from a savage life, vastly surpassed their Phœnician and Egyptian instructors, and stationed themselves at the head of the human race. At the very commencement of their career, when tradition is taken up by regular history, we see that this restless and enterprising people (after producing a Homer and a Hesiod) had, although poor and divided at home, covered with flourishing colonies the shores of Asia Minor, Sicily, Italy, Thrace, and Northern Africa, thus extending the domain of their name and language, and had even planted some advanced posts of civilisation on the remote and barbarous coasts of Gaul, Spain, and Scythia. Next comes the most splendid page of their annals, when the military skill, and enthusiastic love of liberty, evinced by a part of their nation, overthrew in a series of brilliant exploits the brute force of despotism, and the gigantic might of Persia; when their patriotic warriors acquired in the immortal battles of Marathon, Thermopylæ, Salamis, and Platæa, laurels which the voice of fame has kept, and will ever keep fresh and verdant; when the most complete victory crowned the justest cause.

Well had it been for Greece, if the unquiet spirit of her sons, their romantic fondness for adventure, and overweening ambition, could have fully vented themselves in contests with the surrounding mass of barbarism; for some consolation may be derived amidst the miseries of war, when each triumph of a polished people adds to the sphere of light and letters. But unfortunately the Greeks, however much inclined to roam abroad in quest of wealth and martial renown, to subdue and pillage their ruder neighbours, had a still stronger disposition to oppress their own countrymen—to engage in civil broils—and to assert the preeminence of their petty republics and jarring factions. Hence sprung a deplorable succession of political crimes, domestic turmoil, discord, and hostility; the leading

states, such as Athens, Sparta, Thebes, Argos, and Sy-
racuse, exerting all their energies in a fruitless struggle
for permanent superiority, and drawing the lesser communities into the vortex; while in every city, either
individual tyrants, or oligarchical and democratical factions, not less tyrannical, were aiming to subvert the
existing constitution, and to destroy the lives and fortunes of their fellow-citizens; so that the face of the
country was overspread with devastation, and the number of exiles almost equalled those residing at home.
For a century and a half, however, the soil of Hellas
was untrodden by the foot of a foreign invader; but the
colonies, besides being afflicted by the same intestine
disorders, had to make head against the Persians, Car-
thaginians, and the barbarians of Italy and Thrace.
In spite of their unrivalled qualities as soldiers, the
successful campaigns of Agesilaus in Asia, and some
memorable victories of the Sicilian Greeks, the bounds
of Hellenic domination rather receded, until the first
Philip, skilfully availing himself of the balance of parties, and the weakness to which continual revolutions
had reduced the principal republics, gave to the rising
kingdom of Macedonia a clear ascendency over the
whole confederation. So confused and calamitous a
period seems ill fitted for the cultivation of learning
and the fine arts; but this is not the only instance
where the energy of men naturally ingenious and aspiring, being called into action by all that was passing around them, hath, under the influence of liberty,
shot forth branches in many different directions; and
it was precisely betwixt the epoch of the Persian inva-
sions and the reign of Alexander, that the most cele-

brated poets, historians, orators, and philosophers of
Greece flourished, and that painting, sculpture, and
architecture, attained a pitch that has never been surpassed.

The conquests of Alexander, wonderful alike for
their extent and the rapidity with which they were
effected, the partition of his empire, and the long wars
of his successors, gave fresh scope to the ambition and
active talents of the nation; an unceasing stream of
adventurers poured into the East, where wealth and
honours, such as before they had hardly conceived in
imagination, were offered as a ready prize to their
valour and ability. For another century, Macedonians
and Greeks ruled over all Western Asia, Syria, and
Egypt, and, establishing colonies in every province,
rooted there their own language, manners, and institutions. But that same buoyant and restless character,
which had led them by so many paths to the temple
of glory, displayed itself in yet more striking colours
on a larger theatre, and, banishing peace and repose,
involved the conquered countries in perpetual convul-
sions. Corrupt as the victors were before, their native
vices were aggravated by Oriental softness, and by
mingling with subjects still more corrupt than themselves; and it would be difficult to find any portion of
history so deformed by the blackest villainy, as that of
Alexander's successors. The treasures that were at
the disposal of those princes, enabled them to form
parties, and interfere in the domestic affairs of the
republics; while the flower of the European Greeks,
whose courage and prowess were in the highest repute,
left their homes to serve in the armies of Syria and

Egypt; and those circumstances caused the parent country to decline more and more, enfeebled first by domestic wars, and then by the shock of the Macedonians.

Even Macedon, when left to itself, was a kingdom possessing but moderate resources. Its sovereigns, aware, therefore, that force alone could not maintain their influence, took advantage of that factious spirit and proneness to division which some ancient authors * considered as a natural and incurable malady belonging to the Grecian temperament, and embraced the policy of supporting the petty tyrants, who, under their protection, set themselves up in almost every state. Some generous attempts were indeed made to retrieve their independence, and check the torrent of abuses. The union of Peloponnesian cities, called the League of Achaia, held out a hope of improvement, blasted by the jealousy and rapacity of the Spartans and Etolians. In this uneasy and troubled condition the Hellenic nation † was found by the Romans, who,

---

* Pausanias and Herodian.

† Polybius clearly sets forth the distress and poverty to which Peloponnesus was reduced during the Macedonian ascendency, by civil war, anarchy, and the depredations of robbers and pirates, especially the Illyrians and Etolians. He states, that the whole property of the peninsula, of every description, excepting only the bodies of its inhabitants, if sold into slavery, did not at the time he wrote (when things were better than they had been) amount to the sum of 6000 talents ; that is to say, did not equal the value of Attica at the beginning of the Peloponnesian war ; and yet, what comparison could ever be instituted between the extent and fertility of Attica and Peloponnesus?

The prosperity of Greece appears to have augmented at first after its conquest by the Romans; we deduce, however, sufficient proof from Strabo and Pausanias that it soon declined again. Nero's enthusiasm

far behind the Greeks in taste and genius, vastly excel-
led them in cool judgment and steady policy. The
maxims of the former tended to knit together and con-
solidate their acquisitions, while the levity of the latter led to eternal division and subdivision. Had it
been possible for Greece and Macedonia, following the
advice of Agelaus of Naupactus, to combine a resistance to Italian encroachment, the issue of the contest
might have been doubtful; but the Romans had no
such hard trial, for the republics that were then most
considerable, Rhodes, Etolia, and Achaia, joined their
standard, and lent very efficacious aid, first in over-
throwing the monarchies, and then in subjugating each
other. Before the era of Augustus, the Roman world
had swallowed up Hellas, its colonies, and the last
fragments of Alexander's empire, previously impaired
and shaken by the barbarians of Parthia, Pontus, and
Armenia, who, through the quarrels and imbecility of
the later Macedonian princes, had been able to form
new and powerful dynasties. For several hundred
years after the period to which we have just alluded,
Greece is lost to political history; but she continued to
reign pre-eminent over the departments of art and
science, and from the schools of Athens and Alexandria, to extend the peaceful conquests of her language
and literature both in the East and West, as well
amongst her masters, as the ruder nations her companions in servitude. Meanwhile the wheel of fortune
was accomplishing its revolution, and Rome herself,

went so far, that he allowed its states to govern themselves; but their
old dissensions broke out anew, and Vespasian was forced to revoke
the boon of liberty.

yielding to a foreign enemy, shared that lot which she had inflicted on the inhabitants of half the earth. Upon the fall of the Western empire, the Eastern might be looked upon as wholly a Grecian monarchy ; all vestige of the Latin tongue and manners gradually disappeared from the court of Constantinople ; and in the list of its Themes, we can hardly find one where Greek had not entirely, or to a great degree, supplanted the original dialects of the people.

Six centuries of despotism had now, however, fully done their work; instead of the aspiring though ill-regulated vigour of ancient Greece, history displays to us only Greekicized Asia, torpid, effeminate, and weighed down by tyranny and monastic superstition : genius, neither cherished by liberty, nor fostered by patronage, could no longer bear up against public calamity ; and learning, if not altogether lost, became at least silent and unprofitable. As invariably happens, arts and arms kept pace with it in decline, and a love of intrigue, and of vain and noisy disputation, was all the Byzantines retained of the Hellenic character. The inert mass of the empire stood, nevertheless, for a thousand years, hating and contemning, hated and despised by the rest of the human race : one service, indeed, it rendered to the world, in preserving some seeds of classic lore, which, being scattered over Europe, when Constantinople sunk before the Turks, ultimately produced a glorious harvest.

From the chronicles of those dark and gloomy ages, we can extract but little information regarding the country to which our attention is more immediately directed. We only know that proper Greece was re-

peatedly and cruelly wasted by Goths, Saracens, and
Bulgarians, that her cities were mostly ruined, great
part of the population exterminated, and [that to fill
up the void, the emperors planted there, at various periods, colonies of Mardaites and Sclavonians. In 1202,
the French and Venetian crusaders took Constantinople,
and dismembered the western provinces of the empire.
Peloponnesus was conquered by a brother of the Count
of Champagne; other adventurers again, of Frankish
race, seized several districts of the mainland, while
Venice occupied the Archipelago; and a Greek prince
set up an independent sovereignty in Epirus. Before,
however, a century had elapsed, the Latins were chased
from Byzantium, and the second Greek empire recovered Thrace, Etolia, some of the islands, and Peloponnesus, which last remained attached to it until its final
catastrophe. Pressed by the Ottoman Sultans on their
eastern border, the later Byzantine monarchs could
never perfectly regain their ascendency in the wide
region betwixt the Adriatic and Egean seas, and this
served as a bone of contention, and a field of battle
for Greeks, Franks, Sclavonians, and Albanians. These
last sprung from the Illyrians, rose into notice during
that epoch of confusion, and pushed their predatory
bands over the adjacent countries. Received into the
Morea, at first as auxiliaries, they committed dreadful
ravages there, and would probably have taken entire
possession of the peninsula, if the Turks, under Mohammed the Second, had not crushed alike all the competitors who disputed with each other a precarious dominion over those few fragments of Constantine's heri-
tage, that still hung together by a thread. But neither

were the Moslems long allowed the undisturbed enjoyment of their new acquisitions. Venice courageously asserted her claim, and sustained reiterated contests, with varying result, for above two hundred years; being sometimes mistress of the best parts of Greece, and at other periods nearly expelled from the whole, until, in 1717, the banner of St Mark, driven finally from the Morea and the Archipelago, continued henceforth to float in the Ionian islands alone. The Greeks, oppressed by both parties, and turned over like cattle from one to the other, as suited the circumstances of the moment, do not seem to have felt much interest in the Venetian cause, nor to have regretted its defeat. The maxims of the republic towards them were ill calculated to gain their affection; her policy consisted in keeping them debased and ignorant; and the bigotry of the Catholic priests was little less displeasing to those zealous sectarians than Mohammedan fanaticism.*

Leaving for an instant the subject of Greece, now sunk to the nadir of her fortunes, we shall briefly consider that infidel state, whose sudden rise and dazzling progress seriously threatened the religion and liberties of Europe. The foundations of Ottoman power were laid in the 13th century, by Ortogrul, the chief of a Turkoman tribe, residing in tents, not far from Dorylæum, in Phrygia, at a time when the Moghols of Jenghiz and his successors had, by continual inroads, overturned the Seljukian dynasty, the first Mussulman lineage that subdued and ruled a large portion of Asia

---

* " Feed a negro well, and flog him well," is the maxim of the Arab slave-merchants; that of the Venetians, in regard to their Greek subjects, was " a little bread, and abundant use of the stick;" the same measure the Austrians now mete to themselves.

Minor. His son, Osman, assumed the title of Sultan, and reducing, in 1300, the city of Prusa, in Bithynia, made it the capital of his dominions, which he extended daily, at the expense of the Byzantine emperors.

The Sultans that followed for some generations, almost all men of vigour and talent, passed the Hellespont, conquered Thrace, and the countries as far as the Danube, defeating at Nicopolis, Cossova, and Varna, the efforts of the Poles, Hungarians, and the Sclavonic princes of Bulgaria, Servia, Bosnia, &c.; and, in 1453, Mohammed the second, by storming Constantinople, extinguished the last vestige of the Roman world, and before his death gave to European Turkey nearly the same limits that bounded it in 1821. When we seek for the causes that led to so brilliant a career, we find them partly in the qualities of the victorious nation, and still more in the defects of its adversaries, the dotage and rottenness of the Byzantine empire, and the anarchical irregularity of the bordering kingdoms.

The Turkish armies that achieved such exploits, under the early Sultans, were formed purely on the Asiatic model, and as ignorant of tactics as those of Darius and Xerxes: like them, they would have failed if brought into contact with Grecian or Macedonian troops, commanded by a Miltiades or an Alexander. But they were numerous, intoxicated with the double enthusiasm of success and fanaticism, blindly obedient to their chiefs, and sure of pay and plunder; while the European states could only oppose to them, soldiers as undisciplined, raised by the voluntary service of the nobility, incapable of subordination, and always ready to disband themselves at the end of a short campaign.

The institution of the corps of Janissaries proved also a vast advantage to the Sultans, in an age when the infantry of other nations presented merely hasty levies of raw and spiritless peasants ; and in point of finance they were equally superior, since they disposed of a fixed revenue regularly collected, while the Christian sovereigns depended altogether on the spontaneous gifts of their vassals and the clergy.* The Ottomans, too, solely busied with warlike affairs, were the first to derive important results from the discovery of gunpowder ; they first brought formidable battering trains against the walls of cities ; and it was to his artillery, and the musketry of his Janissaries, that Sultan Selim the Ferocious† owed the victories he gained over the Mamelukes and Persians. It was well for Europe that this bloodthirsty prince, the grandson of Mohammed the Second, was occupied during his whole reign in eastern wars, and the conquest of Syria and Egypt.

Previous, however, to the close of the fifteenth century, a change began to appear in those matters ; the revival of learning in the west, brought with it the revival of military skill ; the turbulent nobility lost their independence ; and the chaos of European polity

---

* All the earlier travellers who visited Turkey, were forcibly struck with the order and obedience that prevailed in its provinces ; and the silence and modesty of the soldiery, so different from what they saw at home. The contrast between despotism and anarchy seemed to be in favour of the former ; and there is reason to suspect, that however much the Christian subjects of the Porte were harassed and insulted, the industrious classes in the west sometimes envied their condition. We are assured, that in Italy, the natives, goaded to despair by the Imperialists and French contending for its possession, desired to repose under the shade of the Crescent.

† Sultan Selim the First is surnamed by Turkish historians Yaveuz, or the Fierce.

subsided into regular monarchies, which advanced in a race of improvement, while the Turks, wedded to their original customs, remained stationary. The effect of this alteration became visible when the Ottoman empire was at its zenith, under Sulyman the Magnificent, who, after overrunning Hungary, failed in his attempts to take Vienna and Malta, and expired at length in a fit of rage, occasioned by witnessing the glorious stand made by a handful of Austrians, at Sigeth, against his immense army.

During the sway of his son and successor, Selim the Second, the battle of Lepanto, fought in 1571, gave a blow to the Turkish marine, from which it never entirely recovered. Nevertheless, for above an hundred years after that event, Christendom, distracted by religious and political wars, trembled at the name of those Mohammedans, who persisted in the design they had conceived of universal subjugation. Not only Poland and Venice, but even the German emperors, chose frequently to purchase a precarious truce by humiliating concessions, rather than risk expensive hostilities against an enemy whose resources appeared prodigious. The complete and bloody overthrow that Montecuculi gave the Turks at St Gothard, in 1664, first showed the inferiority of their troops to the disciplined armies of Europe, and dispelled the idea before generally entertained, that by land they were invincible. Yet, supported by their ancient reputation, they made peace on favourable terms, and indemnified themselves for their late disaster by the final reduction of Candia, accomplished in 1669. According to a principle they acted on, of commencing a new war against a fresh adversary

as soon as they had brought a former one to a conclusion, they next turned their arms against the Poles and
Muscovites ; and although experiencing another terrible defeat near Chotin, in 1673, from Sobieski, who
destroyed 25,000 of them, the end of the struggle was
to their advantage, as they gained by it Kaminiek and
the Ukraine. Thus the balance hung doubtful, or
rather inclined to the side of the Infidels, when, in
1681, the haughty and ambitious Grand Vizier, Kara
Mustafa, persuaded Sultan Mohammed the Fourth to
break his treaty with the Emperor Leopold ; and two
years after, laid siege to Vienna, with above 150,000
men. On the 12th September, 1683, 70,000 Poles and
Germans, under Sobieski, dispersed this mighty host,
like chaff before the wind ; and from that memorable
day we may date the decline of Ottoman power. The
Christians, now aware of their own military superiority, instead of seeking peace, combined their enterprises,
and vigorously pressed the common enemy, until the
Porte, after great exertions and great reverses, confessed itself vanquished, by subscribing to the pacification
of Carlovitz, which stripped it of Hungary, the Morea,
Podolia, and the Ukraine. Henceforth Europe ceased
to dread the Turks, and began even to look upon their
existence as a necessary element of the balance of power
among its states. Throughout the former half of the
eighteenth century, the court of Constantinople, abandoning its extensive schemes of conquest in the west,
maintained, however, a respectable attitude,—repelled
the invasion of the Czar, Peter the Great, compensated
the loss of the Bannat, in the war of 1715, by recovering Peloponnesus, and opposed an honourable resist-

ance to the united aggression of Austria and Russia in 1737. Russia was then shaking off her pristine barbarism; and that immense and growing empire had hitherto caused little apprehension to the Ottomans, who were destined to receive from thence the most fatal blows.

The campaigns of Marshal Munich—glorious, indeed, but costing an excessive waste of his troops, few of whom fell by the sword—proved, that the best bulwark of Turkey lay in the wide and uncultivated plains to the north of the Black Sea, and in the habits of the Tartar tribes that roamed over them. The bold and judicious policy of Catharine the Second cleared away those obstacles; and the signal discomfitures which the Turks sustained in their two wars with that empress, as well as the events of the French expedition to Egypt, demonstrated to the wisest amongst them, that old institutions no longer sufficed for their defence. At the commencement of the present century, Sultan Selim the Third endeavoured to reform their military discipline; but his project wounding the interest of the Janissaries, and the prejudices of the bulk of his people, led to his deposition and death. His successor, Mustafa, in a few months shared the same fate; and such tumults arose, as might probably have caused the dissolution of the monarchy, had the sceptre passed to the hands of a less firm and able prince than Mahmoud the Third.

Mounting the throne at a very early age, Mahmoud saw himself environed by dangers and difficulties. In November 1808, the year that he began to reign, a furious civil war raged in the heart of Constantinople;

the Grand Vizier, Mustafa Bairactar, lost his life, and
the victorious Janissaries, giving the law to their sovereign, forced him to sanction their rebellion, to abolish
the new institution of the Nizami'jedid, and to sacrifice to their vengeance his most faithful servants. The
youthful Sultan, thus left to his own guidance, was
farther embarrassed by foreign and domestic hostilities
with Russia and Servia ; many provinces set his authority at nought, and it required the shoulders of an
Atlas to support the sinking empire.

Endowed by nature with a mind singularly cool,
vigorous, and undaunted, Mahmoud had received an
excellent Oriental education, from the paternal care of
his uncle Selim, whose plans of reform he was determined to follow up ; but circumstances obliged him
long to dissemble, and proceed with extreme caution
in curbing the mutinous soldiery, until he should extricate himself from the pressure of external war.

Napoleon's invasion of Russia in 1812 having forced
the Emperor Alexander to concentrate his means for
the defence of his own dominions, Turkey obtained
peace on better conditions than the events of the contest entitled her to expect. The treaty of Bukorest
stipulated the cession to Russia of Bessarabia, and half
Moldavia ; but being patched up in haste, it left numerous points open to future discussion, and not least so
the affairs of Servia, which had figured for five years
as a Russian ally. The Sultan lost no time in seizing
the favourable moment to turn his arms against that
nation, weakened through faction fomented by the
intrigues of Caradja, the new Prince of Wallachia, (a
devoted slave to the Porte,) and tired of the tyranny

of its chief, Czerni George. In the summer of 1813, a powerful Turkish army, led by the Grand Vizier, Khourshid Pashá, overran Servia with very little opposition. Czerni George, withdrawing into Russia, lived at Kief, on a pension assigned him by the Emperor, and a multitude of the people escaped death or captivity by flying to the Austrian states. At the same period, the Pasha of Vidin, and several other rebels of minor importance in Roumelia, were suppressed, and most of their heads exposed at the Seraglio gate. When Ottoman vengeance was fully satiated by the devastation of Servia, its fugitive inhabitants were allowed to return under favour of an amnesty, and to resume the cultivation of their soil. But having once broken the Mussulman yoke, they could not again tamely submit to it ; a fresh insurrection broke out in 1815, and some blood was spilt on both sides. Europe was then at peace, and Russia having leisure to interfere, the Porte appeased these troubles, by granting the Servians an accommodation on fair terms, and suffering them to administer their own internal affairs, under the presidency of Milosh, brother-in-law to Czerni George. He was permitted to keep on foot a body of troops for the purposes of police, and the tribute was fixed at an annual sum of 3,000,000 of piastres ;* it was moreover agreed, that the Turkish garrisons in the Danubian fortresses should not be augmented beyond a certain number.

Having pacified his European dominions, Mahmoud directed his attention to Asia, the larger division of the

---

* At that time about £120,000 sterling.

empire, where the tenets of Islamism are supposed to flourish in greater purity, and the Mohammedan infinitely exceeds the Christian population.

There he was equally successful in putting down open revolt, and sapping the authority of those great families, that from generation to generation inherited extensive domains in Anatolia. His constant good fortune in crushing domestic enemies became a matter of popular remark, especially after the ruler of the Vechabys had been vanquished by the armies of Egypt, led captive to the foot of his throne, and publicly executed at Constantinople, and the holy cities of Mecka and Medina again brought within the Ottoman pale. The design he had conceived of military reform was never allowed to slumber entirely, but he pursued it with so much caution, that the steps he took were almost imperceptible. As it was necessary to have some force on which he could rely as a counterpoise to the Janissaries, he selected for that end the corps of Topjees, or artillerymen, greatly increasing their strength, and endeavouring to gain their attachment. Three qualities appeared conspicuous, as the Sultan's character developed itself; inflexible steadiness of purpose, unrelenting cruelty, and an excessive love of amassing money, which induced him to debase the coin of the empire to such a degree, that he brought it down to one-third of its former value, and thereby occasioned heavy distress to his subjects. Neither were the people better satisfied with the system he introduced of abrogating those inferior and milder jurisdictions, which during preceding reigns had taken root in many provinces, and setting up in their stead griping and ephemeral Pashas, who, purchasing their posts from one year to another, thought only of enriching themselves by extortion. Such were the principal features of the first twelve years of Sultan Mahmoud's reign: his government was highly unpopular, but it was strong, stern, and uniform, and he had certainly removed many impediments to the execution of his ulterior projects.

With regard to the foreign relations of the Porte, the only thing worth notice was a prolonged and seemingly interminable negotiation with Russia, touching the fulfilment of the articles of the treaty of Bukorest, and the restitution of some Asiatic fortresses.

On the 1st of January 1821, Turkey in Europe still comprehended almost all those territories within our continent, which, in the division of the Western and Eastern empires, were allotted to the latter. Its northern frontier had indeed gradually receded from the Dnieper to the Pruth, but the Mussulmans did not in those days attach much importance to the distant extremities that they found themselves unable to defend; content if they might be permitted for a few years longer to draw a tribute from the Christian principalities beyond the Danube. The vitals of the monarchy lay within that vast triangle circumscribed by the Danube, the Save, the Adriatic, Euxine, and Egean Seas, whose altitude may be computed at 500, and the length of its base at 700 geographical miles. It was covered by two formidable lines of defence; first, the Danube, whose banks were studded with fortified places, and, second, that long and lofty chain of mountains running in a waving line from the Carnian Alps to the promontory of Eminch Bournou, where Hœmus (the modern Balkan) projects abruptly into the waves of the Black Sea. The interior of the country is intersected by great ridges of hills, discharging on each side copious rivers, and enclosing spacious and very fertile plains, capable of nourishing a population infinitely more numerous than that actually existing there, and which has generally been reckoned at about eight millions, a calculation, as we presume, rather above than below the truth.

Were European Turkey thoroughly civilized and well cultivated, it would alone make a powerful kingdom ; but besides being semi-barbarous, and thinly peopled, the diversity of race, language, and religion among its inhabitants, constituted such an element of weakness, that it could not have stood at all, unless backed by its extensive territories in Asia.

Along the southern banks of the Danube and the Save, is a great body of pure Sclavonians, who, like their kinsmen the Croats, descending in the middle ages from the forests of Poland and Russia, founded the realms of Bosnia, Servia, and Bulgaria : they have retained to this day their original language and manners, and are men noted for strength and stature, their ignorance, rudeness, and warlike disposition.* The Bosniaks have partly apostatized to the Mohammedan faith ; there are likewise many Mussulmans amongst the Bulgarians, but the majority of that people has

* According to the most authentic accounts, one-third of the Bosniaks are Mohammedans, and the remaining two-thirds pretty equally divided between the Greek and Latin Churches.

remained attached to the Greek church; they are expert horsemen, and industrious cultivators, and have pushed their colonies far into Macedonia and Thrace. The Servians, who, during the reign of the Emperor Heraclius, occupied the mountainous province of Upper Mœsia, and were finally given over by Austria to the Porte in 1739, deserve to be mentioned with respect, since, after a gallant and sanguinary struggle of fifteen years, they gained partial independence, and thus set an example to the Greeks.

Moslems of genuine Turkish blood, the progeny of those conquerors that overturned the Eastern empire, are chiefly to be found in the upper districts of Roumelia, a central province of extended dimensions, including Thrace, Macedonia, and Northern Greece, as far as the Isthmus of Corinth. Next on the list come the Albanians, unquestionably the most barbarous people in Europe. Their origin has given rise to a good deal of discussion, some bringing them from Asiatic Albania, and the coasts of the Caspian Sea. It appears, however, more natural and probable, to derive them from the old Illyrians, and deduce their modern appellation from the town of Albanopolis, or Elbassan. They call themselves Skypetars in their own peculiar tongue, a harsh and guttural jargon, full of borrowed terms; alphabet they have none, but the few amongst them who can write, use either Greek or Turkish letters. They are bold and enterprising, but at the same time cruel, treacherous, greedy, and avaricious. War and robbery are the only employments they esteem honourable, and to these they addict themselves from the moment they are able to carry a musket, either infesting the roads, or hiring out their military services to whatever party is willing to engage them as mercenaries in Europe, Asia, or Africa. The Albanians are generally middle-sized, fair-haired, spare and even haggard in person ; nimble, active, patient of hardships to the last degree ; they have a remarkable tact in mountain warfare, skirmishes, guarding posts, and planning ambuscades, but are not equal in steady courage to the Bosniaks and other Sclavonians we have just been speaking of. The elegant and truly Roman dress of their soldiery has since the revolution been generally adopted in Greece. As is often the case in poor and barren lands, they have an excessive attachment to their native hills ; and when serving in the neighbouring provinces, it is not easy to retain them during winter.* We have stated above, that the decay of the Byzantine monarchy enabled them to issue from their own proper country, (the Illyria of the Greeks,) and to spread themselves over Epirus and Greece, where their descendants, preserving their identity of speech and feature, still tenant nearly half the soil.

They are divided into many tribes, of which the following are the most considerable. The Ghegs about

---

* No nation is dirtier than the Albanians ; they are always covered with vermin, and esteem cleanliness unworthy of a soldier; a single shirt, dipped in hot grease, serves them for an expedition, and on their return home, they find a new one made by their wives, which goes through a campaign in its turn. The Ghegs and Mirdites differ somewhat from the others, and bear a better character for fidelity ; the latter are governed by a prince of their own, and wear black tunics as a distinctive mark, while the Mohammedan Ghegs are decked in red or green jerkins.

Scodra, and on the northern frontier, who are evidently mingled with the adjoining Sclavonians ; in the interior, about Tepeleni, the Toshke, or Toxides, a sept to which Ali Pasha belonged ; the Chameides in Thesprotia, the Chimariotes on the Acroceraunian shore, and behind them the Lyapis, the most squalid, brutish, and barbarous of all. A variety of religions prevails among them ; the Chimariotes, like the Souliotes, profess the Greek ritual ; the Mirdites, settled in Upper Albania, along the Adriatic Sea, (a branch of the Ghegs, and countrymen of Scanderberg,) are zealous Catholics : the larger portion has, however, since the Ottoman conquest, outwardly conformed to Islamism ; but religion sits very light upon them, and a change of circumstances would probably superinduce a fresh change of faith. Those settled in Greece have continued Christians, with the exception of two tribes in the Morea, at Bardounia and Lalla.   When we add to this catalogue some colonies of Wallachians, Armenians, and Jews, we shall have enumerated every race of men that peoples the Sultan's European dominions, save the Greeks, to whom a separate place is reserved.*

During the last thirty years of the eighteenth century, the decline of Turkish power had been marked and rapid ; but the empire, although little capable of offensive operations, appeared yet to possess within itself no contemptible means of resistance, in the extent and natural strength of the country, the fortresses which guarded its confines—the want of roads embarrassing

---

* It has not been thought worth while to mention in the text, the Zinganies, or gipsies, numbers of whom are scattered about the Balkan.

an invader—and above all, from the haughty and un-
bending temper of its Mussulman subjects, who regarded with horror the idea of submitting to a foreigner.
Pride and stupid self-conceit are the distinctive characteristics of the Turks of every class ; slaves themselves, yet accustomed from infancy to domineer over
the Rayahs ; they looked upon the rest of the human
species, and especially the part of it that was not Mohammedan, as beings of an inferior order. Each individual, however low his sphere of existence, identified
himself with the glory of the monarchy and the prosperity of Islam, and considered the person of the Sultan, in his quality of successor to the Khalifat, as something almost divine. Habitually slow, heavy, and indolent, they can, when roused, make extraordinary exertions, and bear suffering and adversity with unexampled
patience and apathy. The well-known disaffection of
their Christian serfs had the effect of inducing them
to go always armed, and prepared for war ; courage
and a sense of military honour were not wanting, and
their fancied superiority raised a feeling sometimes
bordering on magnanimity. Their imperfect civilisation giving an immense advantage over them in the
field to a well ordered enemy, removed that facility of
composition with the victors, so common to polished
nations, and rendered their defence of fortified places
singularly obstinate and bloody. In physical endowments nature has been sufficiently bountiful to them.
The organization of the Turkish forces was still founded on the Suleyman Canuni, an old set of regulations
laid down by Suleyman the Magnificent, and upheld
by the prejudices of the people, in spite of repeated

attempts to introduce a better system. The regular Janissaries, the Kapou Couly, or slaves of the Porte, did not exceed 25,000 quartered at Constantinople, and some thousands disseminated in distant garrisons. In time of war levies of provincial militia, marching under the banners of their Pashas, Beys, and Ayans, composed the bulk of the army. The cavalry was splendid in appearance, and dangerous from its numbers and swiftness; the undisciplined infantry useful only in defending posts and strongholds. Before the time of Sultan Selim, the Turks, though dragging after them unwieldy battering trains, had nothing that could with propriety be termed field artillery. Selim made great improvements, and his nephew Mahmoud, following them up, augmented the gunners to at least 60,000, and rendered them the first corps in the army for spirit, discipline, and equipment. However, those ameliorations, which made the Ottoman field artillery very respectable, do not seem to have been effectually extended to the fortresses, with the exception perhaps of a few important towns on the Danube; in most of them, from the negligence of their commandants, the ordnance was left in a highly defective state.

By an appeal to the fanaticism of his subjects, the Sultan could assemble large masses of armed men, but it was not so easy to keep them together, owing to the modicity of the public revenue, and the vicious administration of a realm where industry was discouraged.

Kutchuk Hussein Pasha, brother-in-law to Sultan Selim, being intrusted with the marine when the French invaded Egypt, closely observed the European squadrons that he frequently came into contact with, and made many changes for the better, in the methods of building, rigging, and working ships of war. As the native Turks have rarely shown any aptitude for navigation, the latter branch was committed altogether to Greek contingents from the Archipelago, and some renegadoes, the scum of Europe. Nevertheless, the navy, strong in beautiful vessels of every class, could still struggle against that of Russia, until the revolution of 1821 deprived it of its sailing masters, and only real mariners.

It does not fall within our scope to treat of the Asiatic dominions of the Porte, the more considerable and certainly the finest portion of Turkey ; more varied in productions, more abundant in resources, and containing probably a population of ten millions of Mussulmans. From thence the Sultans have always drawn the largest bodies of their troops, but, on the other hand, its inhabitants are acknowledged to be, as soldiers, far inferior to the European Turks.

Seated on the borders of three continents, the Ottomans, for several ages, saw themselves involved by ambition and necessity in a double line of action, and their attention was perpetually fluctuating betwixt Germany and Venice to the west, and Persia and Arabia on the east. This, no doubt, may be counted as one reason why they succeeded badly on both sides. Muscovy entered the lists at the commencement of the last century, but she became suddenly terrible to the Porte, which for fifty years has thought only of parrying the blows aimed at her existence by that youthful power. It was long ago predicted, that the northern eagle would devour the crescent ; the prophecy is hastening to its accomplishment, and it seems evident, that Russia (herself as yet unpolished) is the instrument chosen by Providence to civilize the middle regions of Asia, and overturn the superstition of Mohammed, which cannot be extinguished otherwise than by subjugating the countries where it is rooted. Such a consummation is to be desired by cosmopolites, who look beyond the present hour, and elevate their ideas above mean jealousies and puerile fears. Besides the steady and admirable sagacity that has guided the councils of Russia, and the advantageous positions for attack she has gradually occupied in Europe and Asia, she possessed in her religion a lever fitted to shake Turkey to its foundations, and stir up the enthusiasm of the Porte's Christian subjects, ever the secret and irreconcilable enemies of their own government, but almost equally repelled by the Romish tenets of the Germans and Italians.

The first body of tributary subjects that asserted and maintained their liberty by force of arms were the Sclavonians of Montenegro, at the period of the Czar Peter's unfortunate expedition to the Pruth in 1711. For near a century, no other instance occurred of successful revolt, until, in 1800, Czerni George proclaimed himself the champion of Servian independence, and fairly drove the Ottomans out of his native province. That singular, cruel, and energetic barbarian, would have shone as a great hero in the dark ages; his exploits were at the time almost unheard of in Europe, or at least considered as an ebullition of discontent, to which no importance was to be assigned; in fact, however, he sapped the basis of Turkish domination, and sowed the seeds of a mighty convulsion.* The end of Czerni George's career was unhappy, but the spirit he had evoked survived him, and the emancipated Servians gave the unwonted spectacle of a brave and armed Christian nation, living under its own laws in the heart of Turkey, ready, in case of foreign war, to act as a check upon Bosnia, to hold out help to their brethren the Bulgarians, and affording encouragement to all who dared to imitate them. The Sultan sorely felt that this disgrace was ill compensated by a slender tribute and a nominal recognition of sovereignty. He awaited an opportunity to exact signal vengeance, and fill up the incipient chasm, without knowing that he was already placed on the very edge of a precipice.

We now turn back to the Greeks, whom we left in the lowest depths of adversity, condemned at length to wear the chains of a barbarous Oriental despotism. It is well to premise, that under the same appellation we include, not only all those quondam subjects of the Eastern empire, who speak the modern Greek tongue, and owning spiritual obedience to the Byzantine church, are spread over Hellas, Macedonia, Thrace, the islands, and Asia Minor; but, likewise, the Christian Albanians of Roumelia and the Morea, who, differing from the former in language, physiognomy, and character, are allied to them by similarity of faith and suffering,

---

* He shot his father when he found that the old man, deaf to his son's entreaties and remonstrances, intended to betray him to the infidels. He caused one of his brothers to be hanged, and a priest to be buried alive, but it was from a rude and savage notion of justice. He combated, with equal valour and success, the fierce Bosniaks, the Albanians, and all the forces of European Turkey. He manifested an impatience of Russian interference in the affairs of Servia, and to this latter cause we may attribute his downfall.

and have borne a very active part in the contest for
freedom. Any attempt accurately to estimate the total
amount of this class of mankind would be fruitless.
They are naturally most numerous in Proper Greece,
Epirus, Constantinople and its vicinity, the Archipelago, and the maritime cities and districts of Anatolia.
An inconsiderable Greek population languishes in the
interior Asiatic provinces, where they have forgotten
their own and adopted the Turkish language. On that
continent the great body of Rayahs consists of Armenians, and those, of course, we do not take into account,
any more than the Sclavonians of Europe, who have
no affinity with the Greeks, except in religious com-
munion.

For near three hundred years after the middle of
the fifteenth century, the very existence of modern
Greece would have almost been erased from the memory of the western nations, had she not been connected with the history of Venice, and if some adventurous
travellers, penetrating thither from time to time in
search of antiquities, had not given an insight into her
mournful condition.

The Turks remaining, from the epoch of Mohammed the Second, undisputed masters of the northern
part of the country, did not (unless in Thessaly)
generally settle there. Beyond Mount Oeta, although
they seized the best lands, the Mussulman inhabitants
were chiefly composed of the garrisons of towns with
their families. Finding it impossible to keep in subjection with a small force so many rugged cantons,
peopled by a poor and hardy race, and to hold in check
the robbers of Albania, the Sultans embraced the same

policy, which has induced them to court the Greek hierarchy and respect ecclesiastical property, by enlisting in their service the armed bands that they could not destroy. Fourteen capitanerias, or companies of Christian Armatoles, (literally gendarmes,) sanctioned by imperial diplomas, were fixed among the mountains of Olympus, Othryx, Pindus, and Oeta ; certain revenues were allotted for their support, and the command seems to have been for the most part hereditary in the same families.*

The appearance of armed Christians being a scandal in the eyes of true Mussulmans, frequent causes of offence could not fail to occur, especially when the Albanians had by degrees, and contrary to the old maxims of the Porte, attained to rank and influence. When wronged or insulted, the Armatoles threw off their allegiance, infested the roads, and pillaged the country ; while such of the peasants as were driven to despair by acts of oppression, joined their standard to avenge the wrongs they had suffered ; the term Armatole was then exchanged for that of Klefthis or Thief, a profession which the Greeks esteemed highly honourable, when it was exercised sword in hand at the expense of the Moslems. Even in their quietest mood these sol-

* The following is a list of the capitanerias in Macedonia and Thessaly: Karaverria, Servia, Alasson, Grevino, Milias, Elymbo, Mavrovouni, Kakhia, Agrafa, Malacassis, and Patradjik; in Etolia and Acarnania, Venetico, Lidoriki, and Xeromeros. It appears, however, that latterly the number of Armatoliks was increased; since a militia of that kind existed in Livadia, Talanta, Vrachori, Vonizza, Arta, and in almost every district of Northern Greece. Pouqueville reckons the strength they could bring into the field in 1814, at 10,000 combatants.

diers curbed Turkish tyranny; for the captains and Christian primates of districts understanding each other, the former by giving to some of their men a hint to desert and turn Klefts, could easily circumvent Mohammedans, who came on a mission disagreeable to the latter. The habits and manners of the Armatoles, living among forests and in mountain passes, were necessarily rude and simple; their magnificence consisted in adorning with silver their guns, pistols, and daggers; their amusements, in shooting at a mark, dancing, and singing the exploits of their most celebrated chiefs. Extraordinary activity, and endurance of hardships and fatigue, made them formidable light troops in the native fastnesses; wrapped in shaggy cloaks they slept on the ground, defying the elements, and the pure mountain air gave them robust health. Such were the warriors, that, in the very worst times, kept alive a remnant of Grecian spirit. Although the Turks committed to the armed population of Megaris the defence of those defiles that lead into the Morea, they never organized any Armatoles within the Peninsula itself. But as far as the example of resistance went, their place was supplied by parties of outlaws always lurking in its more inaccessible regions, and by the warlike and virtually independent Mainats of Laconia.

At the period of its final subjugation in 1717, Peloponnesus was supposed to contain 200,000 inhabitants; the effect of a long peace considerably augmented that number, when in 1756 a dreadful plague swept away one half of them. Before they fully recovered from this calamity, the ill concerted and ill conducted expe-

dition of Orloff, in 1770, occasioned heavier misfortunes ; the Russian troops, few in number, badly commanded, and constantly abandoned by their Greek
auxiliaries, evacuated the Morea with disgrace, and the
hordes of Albania, pouring into that province, exercised
there for ten years unbounded cruelty and rapacity.
By sending her fleet into the Mediterranean, the Empress Catharine made a diversion favourable to Russia,
but extremely fatal to the Peloponnesians and islanders,
whom the Turks punished with the utmost severity,
for their demonstrations of attachment to Muscovy.
When the famous Capitan Pasha, Hassan Gazi, had at
length exterminated the Arnauts, the country, ruined
and depopulated, was again visited by pestilence in
1781. Instead of alleviating public distress, by diminishing the taxes, the Ottoman government augmented them, although, even before the last plague, the population scarcely amounted to 100,000 souls ; an extensive emigration began, and Peloponnesus was in
danger of losing its Christian inhabitants, when the
events of Western Europe, turning trade into new
channels, opened to them a more advantageous prospect, and caused past miseries to be forgotten.

During the war of 1789, the Empress again endeavoured to excite disturbances in Greece, but her agents
neglecting the Morea, still smarting from former
wounds, transferred their intrigues to Epirus, where
the Souliotes gained a brilliant victory over Ali Pasha.
In the Archipelago, a small Grecian squadron, commanded by Lambro, carried on for some months a very
spirited contest against the Mohammedan fleets.

From an attentive consideration of ancient and modern history, and a close inspection of those particular shades of virtue, folly, and vice, that distinguish the various families into which the human race is divided, we may be led to suspect, that there belong to climates, and countries, certain hidden influences strongly affecting the character of nations ; but favourable or adverse political circumstances fashion the courses by which that character is brought to light. Those who are best acquainted with the Greeks, cannot fail to remark the numerous and striking features of resemblance that connect them with their ancestors : they have the same ingenious and active bent of mind, joined to a thirst of knowledge and improvement ; the same emulation in their pursuits, love of novelty and adventure, vanity and loquacity, restless ambition and subtlety. The Grecian character was, however, so long tried in the furnace of misfortune, that the sterling metal had mostly evaporated, and little but dross remained; having obliterated whatever was laudable in the institutions of their forefathers, their recent masters had taught them only evil. It would, no doubt, be possible to cite a more cruel oppression than that of the Turks towards their Christian subjects, but none so fitted to break men's spirit, or less mitigated by those sympathies which in ordinary cases bind the people to their rulers. To the Moslems themselves, the Sultan's tyranny is a common form of Oriental despotism, but his sway is far more intolerable to the Rayahs, exposed to the caprices not of one or of a few persons, but of a whole dominant nation, the slaves, in fact, of slaves.

In Constantinople and other great cities, immediately under the eye of government, (although looked down upon with haughty contempt,) they were indeed protected and occasionally favoured; and in some secluded or insular situations, seem to have almost escaped the observation of their masters, and this was the happiest lot that could befall them. But in general throughout the empire, they were, in the habitual intercourse of life, subjected to vexations, affronts, and exactions from Mohammedans of every rank : spoiled of their goods, insulted in their religion and domestic honour, they could rarely obtain justice ; the slightest flash of courageous resentment brought down swift destruction on their heads, and cringing humility alone enabled them to live in ease, or even safety. The insolent superiority assumed by the Turks was the more galling, that it arose entirely out of a principle of fanatical intolerance, which renders Mussulman superiority singularly bitter, and odious to people of a different faith. We ought not to be surprised at detecting in a majority of Greeks, meanness, cunning, cowardice, and dissimulation, but rather to wonder that they had firmness enough to adhere to their religion, and eat the bread of affliction, since an act of apostasy opened the road to employment and wealth, and from the meanest serfs aggregated them to the caste of oppressors. Amongst themselves certain shades of distinction are drawn ; the Roumeliotes being reckoned brave and hardy, the Moreotes timid and deceitful, the islanders of the Archipelago, and natives of the shore of Asia, acute and dexterous, but inclined to indolence and frivolity. A considerable difference also exists between the Greeks and Christian Albanians ; the latter are less ingenious, less disposed to learn, graver, more taciturn, more

industrious, and of a sterner temper.*   Until the 18th
century was near its conclusion, the whole nation lay
plunged in the grossest ignorance, their keen intellects
being stimulated only by the pursuit of petty profits in
local trade, and by devising shifts to evade the rapacity
of their governors. Occasionally at distant intervals, a
Grecian name appeared in the world of letters ; but
these few authors, almost unknown beyond the walls of
Constantinople, belonged either to the higher clergy or
the Phanariotes, a fictitious and servile noblesse, the
instruments of the Porte, and frequently its victims.
In spite of the enthusiastic attachment of the people to
their form of worship, the Church had sunk very low ;
the priests and monks, nay, even most of the bishops,
were but blind guides ; fasting usurped the place of
morality, and religion was deformed by innumerable
superstitions, whose objects had been often under a new
nomenclature transferred from the heathen to the Christian Calendar. While such was the social condition of
their tributary subjects, the Turks had no great reason
to fear their despair ; and the lazy and voluptuous
tyranny in which the Moslems indulged, was merely

* Attica, Argolis, Bœotia, Phocis, and the isles of Hydra, Spezzia,
Salamis, and Andros, are inhabited by Albanians. They likewise pos-
sess several villages in Arcadia, Achaia, and Messenia. In the rest of
Peloponnesus, all the other islands, Etolia, Acarnania, a great part of
Thessaly, and Lower Macedonia, the population is exclusively Greek.
Some late authors have run into a grievous mistake, in supposing that
the Albanian colonies had forgotten their native tongue, and that they
could in the Morea discover traces of Sclavonians : the blue eyes, fair
complexion, and sandy hair they refer to, are essentially Albanian.
Among themselves those people always converse in their own language ;
many of them do not understand Greek, and they pronounce it with
a strong accent.

broken in upon now and then, by the incursions of predatory bands of mountaineers, whom they were too indolent to exterminate.

The thirty years that elapsed from 1790 to 1820, made, in the ideas and prospects of the Greeks, a wonderful alteration, proceeding chiefly from two causes; the growing influence acquired by Russia in Eastern affairs after the peace of Yassy, and the consequences of the French revolution. The first afforded them hopes of future liberation, as well as ready means of exchanging obedience to Ottoman authority, individually, for the protection of the court of St Petersburgh, through the medium of the Russian embassy at Constantinople. The second, by creating a demand for corn in the ports of the West, sharpened their instinctive love of commerce and navigation, and, for a paltry coasting traffic in small barks, substituted strong and lofty vessels, distant voyages, and extensive speculations. By unlocking the straits between the Euxine and the Mediterranean, the Empress Catharine had procured an outlet for the harvests of Poland and southern Russia. The new town of Odessa, built on a Tartarian steppe, attracted a multitude of Greeks, all occupied in commercial pursuits. War had paralysed the merchant marine of France ; while that of Austria, now so flourishing, did not as yet exist. Thus the trade of the Black Sea fell, without competition, into the hands of some islanders of the Egean. The impulse once given was followed up with singular alacrity : at Constantinople, Smyrna, Salonika, and every great city of the Turkish empire—at Odessa, Trieste, Leghorn, and all the principal ports of Europe, were established opulent

Greek houses, whose rising prosperity casting into shade that of the foreign Levant merchants, excited too commonly in the breasts of the latter a rancorous feeling of hostility, which has been its own punishment. In 1816, the number of vessels belonging to the Christian subjects of the Porte, and fitted out from the havens and islands of Thrace, Macedonia, and Greece, (many of them, however, carrying the Russian flag,) amounted to upwards of 600, employing 17,000 seamen, and armed with 6000 pieces of cannon. Nor was it on the coasts alone that trade gained ground, the movement communicated itself to the secluded valleys of Pindus, Ossa, and Cyllene; and the woollen manufactures of Thessaly and Epirus, the exportation of oil from Crete, of currants, silk, and other commodities from Peloponnesus, brought in considerable sums, and vivified countries hitherto poor and neglected. It is universally admitted, that commerce essentially contributes to the progress of knowledge and refinement, and that the Greeks are as anxious as they are apt to learn. On this head we shall touch very briefly, because of late the subject has been so fully and ably handled, that we can only repeat what preceding authors have said before us. In general, the march of information is slow and gradual; but amongst this people it resembled a sudden explosion—it was something almost miraculous, producing a revulsion of ideas, that contrasted singularly with the phlegm and patient immobility of the other Rayahs. Scarcely had the example been given by some considerable families at Constantinople, scarcely was a signal hung out, and assistance proffered by a few opulent merchants set-

tled abroad, who took a warm interest in the improvement of their benighted countrymen, when schools, colleges, and libraries, sprung up on every side. In the
capital, at Smyrna, Chios, Kidonia, Yannina, and every
town of the least note, the Grecian youth eagerly courted
learning under the auspices of able professors ; instruction penetrated even to the villages, and knowledge,
hitherto imprisoned in the palaces of the Fanar, and the
cloisters of Mount Athos, pervaded the provinces with
rapid strides ; insomuch that (we use the words of a
recent work)* those who saw Greece in one year, could
hardly recognise her in the next. Amid the influx of
wealth and the spreading of education, the long lost
voice of patriotism began to be heard, and the past
glories of Hellas were a theme not alone familiar to
the scholar in his closet, but which tingled in the ears
of the Kleft on the mountain side, of the mariner on
the main, and the tradesman behind his counter. The
study of ancient classic writers, drew the attention of
young men entering the world to the history of their
forefathers, and roused a train of sentiments, promoted
no doubt by the visits and researches of European travellers. Many of these, indeed, looked down with cold
disdain upon the forlorn condition of a people, for
whose ancestors they professed an extravagant veneration ; but others addressed to them words of hope and
comfort, and endeavoured to foster their regeneration.
Among their friends, the most honourable place is due
to that excellent and lamented nobleman who first presided over the Ionian university, and sunk into the

* A treatise on modern Greek literature, by Jackovacki Rizo.

grave amid the tears and blessings of a grateful nation.

Nearly coeval with the revival of letters and commerce in Greece, was the elevation of Ali of Tepeleni, the Tissaphernes of modern Hellas ; a satrap who, by his talents and crimes, acquired unbounded sway over the western parts of the Turkish empire, and crushing the wild independence and innumerable factions of his native Albania, converted her sons into engines of his ambition and rapacity.   Indissolubly connected as his name must be with Grecian affairs, it is worth while to consider whether he did more to accelerate, or retard the revolution destined to give a new complexion to the East.   He rooted out of Epirus, after a long and obstinate contest, the Souliotes, a valiant tribe of Christian Albanians, that defended with heroic courage their rocks, their liberty, and the exercise of their worship ; but who, from their pride, barbarism, and exclusive selfishness, were incapable of conceiving or directing any general plan of emancipation, and served the cause of Greece more effectually as exiles, than when entrenched at Souli.   He persecuted with persevering animosity the refractory Armatoles, and broke their strength, while his son, Veli Pasha, chased from the Morea, Colocotroni, Anagnostoras, and the other Kleftic chiefs who kept that province in a state of ferment ; but then he annihilated the power of the Turkish and Albanian Beys, blended the distinction of castes, and admitted indifferently into his troops Christians and Moslems, caring nothing for the prejudices of Islamism, and wishing, from a cunning system of policy, to hold the balance even betwixt the two religions.   His secretaries were Greeks, and artful enough, notwithstanding his natural sagacity, frequently to defeat in secret the plans he formed for establishing his authority on a permanent basis. His avarice pressed heavily on trade and agriculture, but he maintained a strict police, and cleared the roads of robbers. It was better for the merchant and cultivator, in so melancholy and inevitable a choice of evils, to sacrifice a part of their gains in buying protection, rather than to lose all by lawless outrage.

In fine, we may conclude, that whilst Ali Pasha lived and reigned in amity with the Porte, any revolutionary movement must have failed, but that the sudden breaking up of his system, at a critical moment, opened a way to its probable success. The worst injury he inflicted on the Greeks was, by demoralizing all that surrounded him, propagating corrupt and selfish principles as the only measure of action, and thus infusing his own poison into the minds of his subjects. However, the establishment of schools and colleges caused no umbrage to Ali, as long as the Rayahs paid their taxes. Most of their thriving seats of maritime trade and education were beyond the limits of his rule ; and as the Ottoman Porte, slow in perceiving innovation—too proud to be easily alarmed—occupied in important affairs, and a good deal influenced by the Phanariotes, threw no obstacles in the way, commercial prosperity and intellectual improvement continued to advance hand in hand. As their knowledge and opulence increased, the Greeks felt more keenly the disgrace of being trampled on by infidels, remarkable only for arrogance and intolerance, and saw with undisguised joy the gradual decrepitude of the Turkish monarchy.

Riga, as early as 1796, fell a martyr to his enthusiasm. That zealous poet and patriot planned an insurrection, and found some associates among his countrymen at Vienna; but just on the point of making a rash and premature attempt, he was arrested by the Austrian government, delivered to the Turks, and put to death at Belgrade. His memory, however, lived in the breasts of his countrymen, who at their festive meetings seldom failed to sing his celebrated Ode to Liberty.

A few years later, the expatriated Souliotes, and the captains of freebooters, expelled out of the Morea, kept up a constant intercourse from the Ionian islands with the Armatoles and Klefts remaining in the mountains, and agitated projects of insurrection. Colocotroni formed, in concert with an Albanian chief of Lalla, named Ali Pharmaki, a scheme for seizing Peloponnesus, and had the Russians (then at war with the Porte) embraced it, success was infallible. In 1806, a revolt actually broke out in Thessaly, headed by a Captain of Armatoles, called Evthymos Vlachavas, but it was soon suppressed by Ali Pasha, and for the six following years, the Greeks, apparently tranquil and submissive, waited vainly the approach of the Muscovite armies, which never crossed Mount Hæmus. It would have been long perhaps ere they had been able, within their own territory, and under the eye of their masters, to organize a general rising, if the famous association of the Hetœria had not furnished a proper medium of communication, and extended its ramifications into each city, isle, and district, where Greeks were to be met with. The birth of that society is enveloped in mystery. Some persons assert that the ex-hospodar of Wallachia, Alexander Mavrocordato, long an exile in Russia, founded it about the commencement of the present century, with the ostensible view of promoting education; while others give the merit to Riga, and consequently carry its origin farther back. What appears certain, is, that from the epoch of the French Revolution, a few Greeks busied themselves in imagining plans for the liberation of their country; of this number were Alexander Ypsilanti's father, (who privately stirred up and supported with money the Servians,) and Anthymos Gazi, a Thessalian, and a distinguished scholar, one of Riga's associates, and editor of a literary journal published at Vienna in the Romaic tongue. It was not, however, until 1815 that the Hetœria assumed form and consistence as a political society, when the Greeks, who had expected that the Congress of Vienna would work a change in Eastern affairs, finding their hopes disappointed in that respect, resolved to take measures for emancipating themselves. The most distinguished personage of their nation, at the period we are treating of, was the Count Capodistria of Corfu, who, entering the Russian service in 1812, in the humble capacity of private secretary to Admiral Tchitchagoff, speedily became a Cabinet Minister, and Secretary to the Emperor Alexander. It would be paying that statesman a bad compliment to suppose that he did not lament the depression of Hellas, and wish to dissever her from Turkey, and we cannot be astonished that the method he proposed to

himself of effecting his object, was by converting her
into a dependency of Muscovy, through the influence
of the priests, which he endeavoured to strengthen,
and the bigotry of the people. He proceeded in the
business with address and caution, apparently limiting,
for the moment, his exertions to encouraging science,
and raising up a higher tone of moral feeling. Dis-
avowing all projects of open resistance to the Porte, he
set on foot a benevolent association called the Philomuse Society, whose declared aim was to cherish the
culture of letters among the Greeks, and obtained for
it the patronage of kings and princes. Having thus
launched a Hetœria, and well knowing the course it
must inevitably steer, he ceased all public superintendence, and retired behind a curtain, whence he watched
its movements. Of course it immediately underwent
a total alteration, but we have not information exact
enough to enable us positively to name all the individuals that brought it about, invented the new oath, and
laid down its new statutes. The following is a summary account of the Society's maxims and regulations,
as well as of the five degrees into which it was divided.

Each member had the right to initiate others, but
not without a rigid scrutiny into their characters. The
neophyte, after going through a long previous examination, touching the most minute points connected
with his former life, disposition, age, prospects, place
of nativity, &c., swore on his knees at the dead of
night, to be faithful to his afflicted country, to labour
for her regeneration, not to disclose either the secrets
of the institution, or the name of the person who initiated him, and to put to death even his nearest and

dearest relations should they be guilty of treachery. He was then admitted into the first class of Ἀδελφόιωιτοι, or Adopted Brethren, to which all Greeks were eligible,* but which was only permitted to learn that a design was on foot to ameliorate the condition of Greece. The next step was that of Σνϛιμὲνοι, (Systimenoi,) or Bachelors; these, selected with somewhat more discrimination, were apprised that the intention of the Society was to effectuate a revolution. The third class, termed Priests of Eleusis, was drawn from the better orders, and to them it was imparted, that the period of the struggle approached, and that there existed in the Hetœria higher ranks than their own. The fourth grade, that of Prelates, never exceeded the number of an hundred and sixteen, but included some of the most distinguished men in the nation, who, possessing full information, were appointed to superintend different districts, and correspond directly with the Grand Arch, or managing committee. This last was said to contain sixteen mysterious and illustrious names; those of the Russian Autocrat, the Crown Princes of Bavaria and Wurtembergh, Count Capodistria, Caradja hospodar of Wallachia, &c., were whispered among the prelates, but it really comprehended persons of quite a different stamp. The orders of the Grand Arch, written in cipher, were signed with a seal, bearing in sixteen compartments as many initial letters.

Every Hetœrist was expected, according to his means, and the degree he assumed, to contribute to the So-

---

* There was an order that no Wallachians or Sciotes should be initiated, as not being deemed trustworthy; but the exception was latterly dispensed with.

ciety's funds, which were at the disposal of the Grand
Arch. A neophyte could hardly give less than 50
piastres, and from 300 to 1000 were ordinary donations of the higher grades.* It may be conceived that
a portion of these gifts never reached their destination,
having been embezzled before flowing into, or after
issuing from, the provincial chests. The whole sum
collected must, nevertheless, have been very considerable, since 600,000 piastres, or 20,000 pounds sterling,
a quota only of the Moreote contributions, were transmitted through one individual at Hydra, to a mercantile house at Constantinople, which acted as the Society's bankers, and lies under a heavy charge of peculation.

In order to recognise each other, the Hetœrists, like
the Free Masons, used certain private signs and words,
differing for the different classes ; and each member
knowing those alone allotted to his own, and to the inferior degrees. The symbols and words of recognition
were as follows :—For the first class (Adelphoi, or
Adelphoipitoi,) a pressure of the hand on the breast,
and the words " Sipsi," (an Albanian term for a pipe,)
and " Sarroukia," or sandals ; the interrogating party
taking an opportunity in conversation to introduce
the first word, and the other answering with the second.
For the degree of Systimenoi, it was usual to require
the name of the respondent's mother, which was put
down in cipher on the back of the letter of recom-
mendation they carried from the provincial superintendent, as a guarantee that they were true brethren ;

---

* It was not always necessary to pass in succession through the
inferior grades ; some favoured individuals became at once prelates.

they then pronounced alternately the two syllables
forming the word Lon-don. The mystical terms of
the Eleusinian priests were " Pos echeis," and " Os
echeis." These phrases have a double meaning in
Greek, according as they are written with an *omega* or
omikron, but their pronunciation is nearly the same.
Πῶς ἔχεις signifies " how do you do ?" and ὡς ἔχεις " as
well as you are ;" but πόσ' ἔχεις means " how many
have you ?" and ὅς ἔχεις " as many as you have." The
interrogator then repeated " Pos," and the respondent
answered " sixteen ;" the first rejoined, " have you no
more ?" and the other replied, " tell me the first and I
will tell you the second ;" they then alternated the
syllables composing the Turkish word Hakykè, or justice. Their signs were a particular touch of the right
hand, and making the joints of the two fingers creak,
then folding the arms and wiping the eyes ; the signs,
of course, always preceded the words. The prelates
recognised each other by pressing the wrist in shaking
hands with the forefinger, and reclining the head on
the left hand, and pressing the right on the heart ; to
this a reply was made, by rubbing gently the forehead.
The enquiring party then went over the words assigned
to the three first classes, and if the other answered
right, they completed their recognition, by repeating
alternately the syllables Va-an-va-da. All the degrees
except the lowest received letters patent. We sub-
join a fac-simile of the diploma given to the prelates,
with the cipher of the Hetœria. When a novice was
admitted, he delivered to his initiator a sum of money
for the common fund, and a letter written in ordinary
characters, and couched in the following, or similar

terms :—" I, named X., a native of N., exercising the profession of M., although now arrived at the age of — years, have not yet had time to dedicate a gift to some useful purpose ; I now therefore consign to you A—A, the sum of piastres —, to be paid over to the monastery, or school of B—B."

To the signature was attached a cipher, serving afterwards to verify letters to the directing committee, which kept a list of names with their annexed marks, as well as the vouchers of sums paid. Besides this, the neophyte affixed a private sign on the inside of the paper, that the initiator was not to see, and which the Arch employed to authenticate any posterior communications to the person initiated. The money, the letter, and the consignee's receipt, passed through the hands of the provincial superintendent, who sent them to the fountain-head.

As the political atmosphere of Vienna is ill fitted for hatching conspiracies, the Grand Arch fixed its lodge at Moscow, and from thence held intercourse with every part of Europe, by means of itinerant emissaries called Apostles, who cloaked the real purpose of their frequent journeys, by pretending to be engaged in works of charity, and in seeking subscriptions for founding and maintaining places of education, under the patronage of the Philomuse Society. That parent trunk, after pushing out the vigorous shoot of the Hetœria Philiki, or friendly society, quickly began to wither, and died away about the middle of the year 1817, at Munich, whither its chest, papers, and secretary, had been removed from Vienna. Its name, however, was of great use in screening the operations of the Apostles, and disguising the true object for which so much money was collected. The people invariably confounded the two associations, and therefore interpreted amiss the motives of those crowned heads, that had generously assisted in establishing the first, and were ignorant of the second's existence. The mistake is not surprising, if we consider that the teachers paid by the Philomuse were often active though concealed agents of the political Hetœria. The majority of that large body of Greeks residing in Southern Russia, and other foreign countries, seems to have become in a short time zealous proselytes, and the patriotic association rooted itself firmly in the cities of Odessa, Yassy, and Bukorest. In the latter lived a very bustling and indefatigable member, one, indeed, of its Coryphæi, named Count Galati, a native of Ithaca, but long trading as a jeweller at Moscow. In 1816, Anthymos Gazi, and some select Apostles, made a progress through proper Greece, appointing prelates and superintendents of districts, and initiating such persons of note as full reliance might be placed in. Among these was the Bey of Maina, who had received his investiture from the Porte two years before, and whom they flattered with hopes of reigning over all Peloponnesus. Prudence was requisite within the Ottoman dominions, and consequently there the society went on slowly for three or four years. It was not till 1819 that it admitted most of the Moreote primates, and the Phanariotes, who could not be trusted, remained generally to the last moment in utter ignorance.

No description of men embraced the doctrines of regeneration with greater enthusiasm than the Greek soldiers of fortune, in the pay of England, France, and Russia. The first named power disbanded, in 1815, two fine battalions of light infantry, recruited from the mountaineers of Souli and Maina, the Klefts of Peloponnesus, and Armatoles of Roumelia; and the French, on evacuating Corfu, let loose a corps of Christian Albanians. The bulk of these troops returning home, bore with impatience a renewed subjection to Turkish authority, ready to throw themselves into the arms of any party that spoke to them of freedom and vengeance: some who were proscribed, continued to inhabit the Ionian islands, and laboured, as strenuous disciples, to enlarge the circle of the Hetœria.

Reflecting on the usual levity of the Grecian character, we cannot but admire the secrecy that shrouded so extensive a conspiracy. The stupid Moslems never entertained the least suspicion of a plot hatching in the midst of them; and the lynx-eyed police of the Russian empire (from a different cause, doubtless), was as blind as a mole on all matters connected with the Society; the few Hetœrists that resided elsewhere, easily escaped observation. Nevertheless, their projects were at one time in imminent danger of shipwreck, through the treachery of a false brother. A Zantiote butcher, actuated by private pique against Colocotroni, went expressly to Prevesa, in order to disclose to Ali Pasha the intentions and symbols of the association, into whose ranks he had been admitted. Ali, however, who foresaw a gathering storm from Constantinople, concluding that the scheme emanated from the Court of St Petersburgh, and that the Emperor Alexander was at the head of the Hetœria, instantly conceived an idea of rendering it conducive to his own interests.*

It is certain, that nearly all the Hetœrists were warm partisans of Russia, not so much from community of religion, as because they knew her to be the natural enemy of their oppressors; whereas, England, France, and Austria, showed an evident disposition to uphold Turkey, and thus perpetuate the slavery of Greece. An eager anxiety to cast off the Mussulman yoke, peeped forth in a vague inquietude, particularly at Bukorest and Yassy; and in constant reports of approaching hostilities betwixt the Czar and the Sultan. Several discreet persons, unwilling to yield entire credit to the promises of the apostles, undertook at vari-

---

* When Ali Pasha received this information, there was at his Court, an officer, belonging to a distinguished Armatolic family, who had commanded a company in the Greek corps raised by England, and has since made a considerable figure in the revolution. The Pasha had engaged him to come to Prevesa, in order to discipline some regular troops that he wished to form; but learning from the Zantiote traitor, that he was a member of the Society, in the first burst of rage threatened to put him to death. The other thus involved in unexpected peril, conducted himself with so much address and coolness, that the tyrant began to doubt the veracity of his informant, whose manner and character were not calculated to add weight to his testimony. Desirous of prying farther into the affair, and hoping to open a correspondence with the mysterious Arch, he detained the Captain; but the latter fled at the commencement of the siege of Yannina.

In 1818, Ali Pasha ordered his agent in Moldavia, to wait upon the Russian Emperor at Kishneff, and solicit his protection. Alexander replied, that Ali was not a Russian subject, but a Turk; that he would not countenance rebellion against his lawful sovereign, the Sultan, but would, if he thought proper to retire to his dominions, afford him an asylum.

It is to be remarked, that the Zantiote was able to disclose only so much of the secret as was known to the lowest class, and this might be vaguely interpreted.

ous periods journeys to St Petersburgh, and applied to
Count Capodistria for a solution of the question. He
received them courteously, and, if reports be true, gave
them presents in the Autocrat's name, but declared
that they had no aid to expect in case of rebellion; at
the same time he, through his secret emissary, and
former valet-de-chambre, Candiotti, counselled the leaders in Greece to avoid an explosion, as long as Russia
was at peace with the Porte. The advice was good,
and probably sincere, but altogether lost on a volatile
nation, prone to run after flattering delusions, and persuaded that no vast importance ought to be attached
to the official words of a minister, when opposed to the
scope of his policy. It has been asserted, that Czerni
George, the exiled chief of Servia, took a prominent
part in these machinations; and that his clandestine
return to the neighbourhood of Semendria, in 1817,
had reference to a project of insurrection. If such a
plan existed, his brother-in-law, Milosh, defeated it by
causing him to be murdered, and sending his head to
the Pasha of Belgrade. Russia publicly condemned
his evasion from Kief, and it was given out, perhaps
by his confederates, that he had gone back to Servia,
in quest of a hidden treasure.

Many Hetœrists believed that the year 1825 had
been pitched on as a proper period for executing their
design, since according to their calculation, the necessary preparations would then have been completed.
Others, with more show of reason, pretend that no precise time was fixed, and that they waited in hopes of
a war growing out of the tedious negotiation respecting the articles of the treaty of Bukorest. However,

such circumstances took place in 1820, as seemed to leave no room for ulterior delay.

That tract of sea and land to which the name of Greece peculiarly appertains, lies within the 40th and 35th degrees of north latitude, the first passing a few miles to the northward of Corfu, and intersecting the Eastern shore of Thessaly, near the Straits of Tempe, the second running through the Island of Crete, and between the 20th and 27th parallels of east longitude. The space thus circumscribed is singularly broken and indented by isles, bays, gulfs, and mountains, presenting every where a picture of romantic beauty, which those who have once seen it cannot easily forget.* In casting a rapid survey over its principal features, the first that strikes our attention is the multiplicity of high mountainous chains, some stretching from north to south, some from east to west, crossing each other, and dividing the country as it were into squares. Extremely deficient in mineralogical treasures, the Grecian hills cannot be compared to the Alps and Pyrenees; nevertheless their dominant peaks range at an altitude of from six to eight thousand feet above the level of the sea ; the loftiest are those of Pindus, Parnassus, Taygetus, Cyllene, Erymanthus, and Lycæus. It follows from what we have just stated, that a large portion of its superficies is incapable of cultivation, but

---

* It has been remarked, that classical travellers in Italy do not experience all the delight they anticipated ; there nature is often tame, and the monuments of antiquity are eclipsed by the bustle and splendour of modern civilisation. In Greece it is otherwise ; her lonely ruins, frowning amidst desolation, call up the idea of distant ages, and a feeling of awe is excited by the still majesty of the surrounding scenery.

this disadvantage is balanced by the rich fertility of the wide plains of Thessaly and Bœotia, those of Elis and Messenia, of Argos, of Helos, of Mistra in Laconia, and the flat shore of Achaia, as well as numberless beautiful and sequestered valleys in Arcadia and Western Greece.

There are few rivers really deserving that appellation, except the Achelous, Alpheus, Eurotas, Pamisus, and some of their more considerable affluents; the others are almost universally dried up during the hot season, but after rain become impetuous torrents. The eastern side of the country, especially Argolis, may be justly taxed with aridity, wood being scarce, and fountains rarely to be met with; but the western regions, from the Gulf of Ambracia to the Coryphasian promontory, abounding in sources of water, are clothed with magnificent forests of oak, pine, &c. Although the summer heats are excessive, and the rigours of winter occasionally severe amongst the hills, yet for above half the year Greece enjoys a serene and delicious climate. Unfortunately, however, in many maritime districts, the vicinity of neglected swamps renders the air highly insalubrious from the month of June to that of November.

In general the mainland is a pleasant and plentiful territory, yielding exuberant crops of grain, wine, oil, fruit; and in Peloponnesus, silk and cotton. The islands, on the contrary, are mostly rough and barren rocks, although we must except from such reproach Chios, Tinos, Naxos, and the superb Crete. In one respect Hellas surpasses any part of Europe, namely, in the number and excellence of her havens and roadsteads, and her deep and placid gulfs, sheltered by mountains, and favoured with a regular vicissitude of sea and land breezes, making their navigation safe and sure, and offering no common facilities to commerce.

Under a government disposed to smile upon industry, the amount of produce would be very great ; but the fiscal system of Turkey, where improvements were certainly rewarded with a heavier contribution, the exactions of Ali Pasha and the insecurity of fixed property had ruined agriculture. While the islanders naturally looked to the sea for subsistence, the people of the continent applied themselves to the breeding of cattle, a species of wealth which they could more easily remove out of the way of spoliators. This was particularly the case in Northern Greece, betwixt Mount Oeta and the Isthmus of Corinth. In Thessaly and Peloponnesus, tillage, though languishing, had not so generally given place to pasture ; but the possession of land appeared so precarious, that it could not be sold for more than three years' purchase. With regard to statistics and population, we are very much in the dark ; neither can correct details be got at, until an enlightened government, permanently established, shall have inclination and leisure to make the necessary enquiries. For the period that preceded the revolution, M. de Pouqueville's calculations seem most worthy of credit, since he resided long in European Turkey, and held the office of consul-general at Yannina and Patrass. If we may believe him, the number of smaller cattle paying a poll-tax, in the provinces of Epirus, Macedonia, and northern Greece, ruled by the Satrap of Yannina, was, in 1815, estimated by the tribute-gatherers at five millions of sheep, and seven millions of goats, besides a million of each kind possessed by the Pasha and his family. There is reason to think that in 1821 Peloponnesus contained at least half as many, for innumerable flocks covered the hills and plains of the peninsula; a single village could often boast of 20,000 head, and there were far more than a thousand villages. The French author whom we have quoted, valued the territorial productions of the Morea brought into the market in the year 1814 at 30,698,000 Turkish piastres, then equal to the same number of francs, or L.1,230,000 sterling.* Of this revenue, 14,000,000 were absorbed by taxes, maintenance of troops, fortresses, clergy, &c., and two-thirds of the remainder passed into the hands of Mussulman proprietors. The exports of Maina, consisting of oil, silk, and vallonia, and supposed to be worth a million and a half of piastres, are not included in the above calculation. According to the Greeks, only one-fifth of the surface of Peloponnesus was under cultivation, and of that portion four-fifths belonged to Turks.

The population of the peninsula was usually reckoned at above 400,000 souls, although M. Pouqueville will allow no more than 240,000 Christians and 40,000 Mohammedans. In respect of the latter he is probably right, but his calculation of the former is surely too small, for the Morea contained upwards of 1400 towns

---

* According to some Greek accounts, the annual value of the products of the Morea amounted to about 45,000,000 of piastres, or one-third more than Pouqueville reckons, and the number of small cattle to six millions. Vide Appendix, for a table of statistics.

and villages, which, at the moderate average of from 60 to 80 houses each, would give half a million of people; while we may not unreasonably assign to it a million in the flourishing times of Hellas.

It is easy to form an idea of the terrible depopulation of Greece, by reflecting that Attica, which once numbered 400,000 inhabitants, was not thought to possess, at this latter period, above 25,000; that the territory of Argos, formerly able to lose in one battle 6000 citizens, had not in all more than 10,000 persons; and that in Acarnania, Etolia, Phocis, and Locris, there were only about fourscore thousand Christians. In choosing a round number, and stating at one million the whole insurgent Greek population of the continent and isles, we shall not, perhaps, be far from the truth; of these, from 20 to 30,000 Armatoles, Mainatts, Megarians, Souliotes, Sphakiotes, and the merchant crews of Hydra, Spezzia, and Psarra, were well-armed and practised soldiers and seamen. By adding the hasty levies of peasants, the Cretans, and other islanders, we shall make up a mass of 50,000 combatants; a feeble array, when it is considered, that they had not only to contend against an empire reaching from the Adriatic to the Gulf of Persia, but were bridled by a dozen fortresses, and 10 or 12,000 Turkish militia, living amongst the Rayahs. Indeed, had Greece been a country where large armies could move with facility, and force their enemies to pitched battles, her revolution must soon have been extinguished; but she is fortified by nature, and admirably adapted for that defensive and desultory system of operations which alone suited the habits and genius of the people. A short topographical sketch will show the difficulties awaiting an invader, who is not entirely and permanently master of the sea ; difficulties to which the ancient Hellenes were indebted, as much as to their skill in war, for repelling the Persians. Although the insurrection embraced at its commencement, Athos, Olympus, and part of Macedonia and Epirus, yet it quickly rolled back within the true military frontier of Hellas—namely, the line of mountains branching off from each side of the main chain of Pindus, and stretching from the Ambracic to the Malian gulf. In front of Oeta, in a hollow valley formed by that mountain and the opposite side of Othryx, flows the deep and narrow Sperchius, and beyond it is the famous pass of Thermopylæ, whence three roads lead into Eastern Greece*—one along the Eubœan strait by Talanta or Opus ; a second passing Oeta at Fontana, and descending the Cephisus, by Elatæa and Cheronæa, to the city of Livadia ; a third crossing the same river near its source, winding through rocks and forests, and skirting

---

* On the main roads of Eastern Greece, the distances are as follows :—from Zeitouni to Mola, in the Straits of Thermopylæ, 4 hours or leagues ; from Mola to Livadia, 18 hours ; from Mola to Salona, about the same distance ; from Mola to Livadia by Talanta and Topolias (the ancient Copæ), 22 hours ; from Salona to Livadia by Delphi, 10 hours ; from Livadia to Thebes, 6 hours ; from Thebes to Negropont, 6 hours ; from Thebes to Athens by Mount Parnes, 9 hours ; from Thebes to Megara by Cythæron, 9 hours ; fiom Megara to Athens by Eleusis, 9 hours ; from Megara to Corinth, 12 hours.

In Western Greece, there are 24 hours from Arta to Vrachori, or Thermus, and as many from Loutrachi to Missolonghi ; and again, from the latter town to Salona, 24 hours.

the western side of Parnassus to Salona. Once over
Oeta, the Turkish cavalry could occupy at pleasure the
Bœotian plains around the marsh of Copais, but the
double line of Mounts Cythæron and Geranion defended the approach to the Isthmus, while Parnes covered
Attica. On the opposite coast of the continent, a path
leads from Arta, turning the head of the gulf, into
Acarnania and Etolia. Those, however, who go that
way, must surmount, with much fatigue and labour,
the hills and woods of Makrynoros, where a handful
of men can stop an army ; and ford the Achelous, or
Aspropotamos, the largest and most rapid of the Grecian rivers.

There is likewise a central tract, diverging from the
bridge of Alamanna, on the Sperchius—climbing Mount
Corax—threading the defiles of Etolia—traversing
Patradjik and Carpenizza, and falling down on Vrachori. By this route, of which Livy has left a description, the consul Fulvius marched from Thessaly to
Naupactus. A transverse road, always dangerous, and
often impassable when the Evenus is flooded by rain,
conducts from Missolonghi to Salona, and from thence,
under the southern cliffs of Parnassus, by Delphi to
Livadia.

Peloponnesus presents to an enemy as many obstacles
as Northern Greece. From the Isthmus to Modon are
five very long and harassing days' journeys for a horseman, and four natural barriers, rising one behind the
other. First, the hills betwixt Corinth and Argos,
pierced by the passes of Dervenaki and Klissoura ;
second, the Arcadian chain of Parthenius and Artime-

sion, separating the plain of Argos from that of Tripolizza; third, Mount Mœnalion, between the latter and the valley of the Alpheus; fourth, the defiles of Makryplai, dividing that valley from the Messenuàn flats of Stenyclaros. It is easier to march along the western and northern coast, although even there steep and rocky ridges running into the sea, frequently render the road narrow and perilous. Excessive difficulties await hostile troops that endeavour, by ascending Mounts Olenos, Pholoe, or Cyllene, to penetrate into the interior from the shores of Elis or Achaia; and, with the exception of the valley of the Eurotas, Laconia may be looked upon as altogether impracticable.

We shall conclude with a few remarks on the general structure of the country.—The mountains are extremely steep, covered either with forests, sharp-pointed stones, or a brake of thorny plants, and intersected by numberless deep ravines, the beds of winter torrents. The roads, commodious enough on the plain, from the moment they enter the hills become merely rugged pathways, bordered by precipices, and continually commanded from above. An invading army must either weaken itself at every step by detachments, or expose its communications to be cut off by the inhabitants, who retire from before its advance into sequestered caverns, and monasteries of solid construction, placed in almost inaccessible situations, and against which cannon can rarely be brought to bear. To transport artillery or heavy equipages is a prodigious labour, and all that straggles is destroyed by the armed peasants, whose ordinary mode of life, and endurance

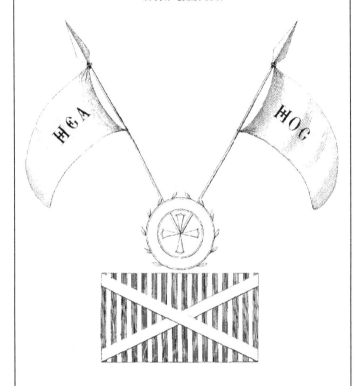

Зα ba 8786η b3α 6ω5εα3α α8b3o3ηα

4η23ωο878 3ωοαη γ353487 4ω η-γ3ωο878 3α b37 ηνη237 b3α γ35343α

ωbωο3ηα 4ω 3α b37 39ωοηα93α37 b87 6ωνη587 3ωοω87 b87 ω5ωγα3

7387 b87 α369853b37 38ηαην νωθον3ε 5ο8787 bο3η487bη 8α 2ωα687

39ωοηα93αb37 b3α ωξↄω687зηα b3α 9ηbо343α 4ηb3838ω7bη 4ω

8о482ω7bη 9ηοωbε Ⅲ ↄ78ω6ξο3ε. u. 3α 3ηοη7: 16: bο7 γ353487.

Drawn by J. Moffat

of privations, make them excellent guerillas. By commanding the sea, most of these difficulties may be got rid of ; but, in the whole course of history, it is perhaps impossible to find examples of such cowardice and incapacity as the Ottoman admirals betrayed throughout the war.

APPENDIX

THE INTRODUCTION.

STATISTICAL TABLES *of Northern Greece (except Acarnania) and Peloponnesus.**

ATTICA.

As the greater part of the soil of Attica is mountainous and rough, its productions are not abundant, except in the article of olives; it grows, moreover, wheat and barley enough for its scanty population, wine and figs of the best quality, and its grapes and pomegranates are excellent.

Products.			Value in Turkish piastres.†
Wheat,	.	100,000 kiloes of 22 okes,	800,000
Barley,	.	50,000 do. .	200,000
Oil,	.	500,000 okes (each = $2\frac{7}{9}$),	500,000
Honey,	.	40,000 do. .	40,000
Wax,	.	4,000 do. .	20,000
Cheese,	.	90,000 do. .	90,000
Butter,	.	5,000 do. .	10,000
Wool,	.	50,000 do. .	40,000
Rice,	.	60,000 do. .	15,000
Nitre,	.	30,000 do. .	30,000
Soap,	.	600,000 do. .	900,000
Cotton,	.	10,000 do. .	10,000
Goat skins,	.	60,000 . . .	180,000
Ox hides,	.	6,000 . . .	180,000
Total,	. . . . .		3,015,000

Population of Attica, 22,000, Greeks and Turks in the city, Albanians in the villages.

* Communicated to the author by a Greek priest, physician, and man of letters, who travelled through those countries, and carefully examined them, in the years 1815-16.

† Five piastres were then equal to a Spanish dollar.

BŒOTIA.

Bœotia, having large and rich plains, is very fertile; its wheat, wine, melons, and water-melons, are excellent.

DISTRICT OF THEBES.

Products.				Value in piastres.
Wheat,	.	100,000 kiloes,	.	800,000
Barley,	.	60,000 do.	.	160,000
Oats,	.	40,000 do.	.	120,000
Maize and millet,		70,000 do.	.	80,000*
Beans,	.	6,000 okes,	.	1,500
Lentiles,	.	15,000 do.	.	5,625
Cheese,	.	220,000 do.	.	100,000
Butter,	.	80,000 do.	.	160,000
Wool,	.	66,000 do.	.	66,000
Wax,	.	1,760 do.	.	10,560
	Total,	. . .	.	1,503,685

Population, 18,000; Greeks, Turks, and Jews in the towns, Albanians in the villages.

DISTRICT OF LIVADIA.

Products.				Value in piastres.
Wheat,	.	250,000 kiloes,	.	2,000,000
Barley,	.	60,000 do.	.	280,000
Oats,	.	25,000 do.	.	125,000
Maize or millet,		65,000 do.	.	480,000
Beans,	.	15,000 do.	.	90,000
Lentiles,	.	6,000 do.	.	60,000
Rice,	.	7,000 kiloes of 10 okes,		105,000
Cotton,	.	300,000 okes,	.	300,000
Wool,	.	88,000 do.	.	88,000
Cheese,	.	18,000 do.	.	16,000
Wax,	.	5,000 do.	.	50,000
Honey,	.	20,000 do.	.	10,000
Dried figs,	.		.	80,000
Wine,	.	100,000 do.	.	50,000
				3,734,000
District of Thebes,	.	.	.	1,503,685
Total value of the products of Bœotia,				5,237,685

* A mistake seems to have crept in here, although much of it was of a very inferior quality.

Population, 17,000; all Greeks, except a few Turkish and Albanian families.—Total population of Bœotia, 35,000.

OPUNTIAN AND EPIKNEMIDIAN LOCRIS.

This country, as well in the district of Talanta as in that of Boudounizza, is fruitful, especially in wheat, barley, cotton, maize, wine, and figs. What the inhabitants do not consume they sell to the people of Livadia. Population, 10,000. No table of products.

PHOCIS AND OZOLIAN LOCRIS.

DISTRICT OF SALONA,

Being stony and barren, does not produce much. Its olives are the best in Greece, and the cheese and butter of Mount Parnassus much esteemed.

Products.				Value in piastres.
Wheat,	.	80,000 kiloes,	.	640,000
Barley,	.	80,000 do.	.	320,000
Maize,	.	20,000 do.	.	80,000
Oil,	.	380,000 okes,	.	308,000
Cotton,	.	143,000 do.	.	214,500
Wool,	.	56,000 do.	.	54,000
Cheese,	.	25,000 do.	.	24,375
Butter,	.	18,000 do	.	36,000
Silk,	.	4,400 do.	.	44,000
Wax,	.	3,520 do.	.	22,080
Red berries,		1,320 do.	.	17,160
Vallonia,	.	26,000 do.	.	1,980

District of Salona,   .   1,762,095

Population, 20,000; mostly Greeks.

DISTRICT OF LEPANTO,

On account of the scarcity of inhabitants, has few productions, but of good quality.

Products.				Value in piastres.
Wheat,	.	5,000 kiloes,	.	40,000
Maize,	.	8,000 do.	.	40,000

Carry over,   80,000

Products.				Value in piastres.
		Brought over,		80,000
Currants,	.	88,000 kiloes,	.	44,000
Silk,	.	880 do.	.	35,000
Fustic,	.	88,000 do.	.	2,200
Oil,	.	12,000 do.	.	12,000
Dried fish,	.	10,000 do.	.	5,000
Rice,	.	3,000 do.	.	2,000
Wool,	.	2,200 do.	.	2,000
Red berries,		500 do.	.	6,500
				188,700
		District of Salona,	.	1,762,095

Total value of products of Phocis and Ozolian Locris, 1,950,795

Population, 8500.—Total population of Phocis and Locris, 28,500.

ETOLIA.

Products.				Value in piastres.
Wheat,	.	40,000 kiloes,	.	320,000
Maize,	.	60,000 do.	.	240,000
Oil,	.	144,000 okes,	.	144,000
Wine,	.	3,000,000 do.	.	800,000
Currants,	.	100,000 do.	.	86,000
Red berries,		500 do.	.	10,000
Silk,	.	1,700 do.	.	70,400
Cotton,	.	50,000 do.	.	25,000
Wool,	.	10,000 do.	.	10,000
Cheese.	.	6,000 do.	.	4,000
Salt,	.	5,000,000 do.	.	120,000
Fish,	.	500,000 do.	.	250,000
Botaraga,*		5,000 do.	.	7,500
Vallonia,	.	55,000 do.	.	6,000
				2,092,900

Population, 20,000. Total population of Attica, Bœotia, Phocis, Locris, and Etolia, 115,500.

* Salted roes of grey mullet.

PELOPONNESUS.

CORINTHIA, SYCRONIA, AND MEGARIS.*

Products.					Value in piastres.
Wheat,	.	100,000	kiloes	.	1,000,000
Barley,	.	60,000	do.	.	300,000
Oats,	.	30,000	do.	.	120,000
Currants,	.	202,400	okes	.	202,400
Cheese,	.	220,000	do.	.	165,000
Wool,	.	44,000	do.	.	44,000
Silk,	.	1,760	do.	.	61,600
Wax,	.	968	do.	.	9,680
Oil,	.	132,000	do.	.	132,000
Red berries,		1,980	do.	.	39,600
Rosin,	.	308,000	do.	.	77,000
Pitch,	.	264,000	do.	.	79,200
Turpentine,		10,400	do.	.	140,000
					2,370,280
According to Pouqueville, in 1814,				.	2,725,000

Population, 23,760 ; Albanians, Greeks, and a few Turks in the towns.

ACHAIA.

DISTRICT OF PATRASS.

Products.					Value in piastres.
Wheat,	.	64,000	kiloes	.	640,000
Barley,	.	12,000	do.	.	60,000
Maize,	.	300,000	do.	.	1,500,000
Currants,	.	3,740,000	okes	.	3,740,000
Cotton,	.	69,600	do.	.	39,600
Cheese,	.	935,000	do.	.	926,250
Butter,	.	220,000	do.	.	440,000
Wool,	.	528,000	do.	.	528,000
Silk,	.	500	do.	.	17,500
Flax,	.	17,600	do.	.	16,700
Red berries,		5,280	do.	.	105,600
Yellow berries,		4,400	do.	.	88,000
Gum Dragacanth,		5,000	do.	.	50,000
Carry over,	.	.	.	.	8,151,650

* Included here because it belonged to the government of Corinth.

2

Products.				Value in piastres.
		Brought over,		8,151,650
Fustic,	.	66,000 okes	.	33,000
Dressed goat skins,	4,520		.	43,560
Raw hides,	24,000		.	24,000
Lamb skins,	72,000		.	18,000
Hare skins,	8,400		.	8,400
Oil,	.	52,800 okes,	.	52,800
Wine,	.	176,000 do.	.	88,000
Brandy,	.	26,400 do.	.	28,400
Wax,	.	5,000 do.	.	50,000
Vallonia,	.	374,000 do.	.	93,500
Honey,	.	15,000 do.	.	15,000
				8,606,310

According to Pouqueville, in 1814, 1,689,500

DISTRICT OF VOSTIZZA.

Products.				Value in piastres.
Wheat,	.	6,000 kiloes,	.	60,000
Maize,	.	4,000 do.	.	20,000
Currants,	.	528,000 okes.	.	528,000
Wine,	.	198,000 do.	.	98,000
Oil,	.	52,800 do.	.	52,800
Silk,	.	4,000 do.	.	140,000
Tobacco,	.	5,000 do.	.	10,000
Onions,	.	40,000 do.	.	20,000
				928,800*
District of Patrass,		. . .		8,606,310

Total value of the products of Achaia, 9,535,100
Population of Achaia, 48,885 ; all Christians, except a few
Turks at Patrass.

ELIS.

DISTRICT OF GASTOUNI.

Products.				Value in piastres.
Wheat,	.	200,000, kiloes,	.	2,000,000
Barley,	.	15,000 do.	.	75,000
		Carry over,	.	2,075,000

* According to Pouqueville, the value of the productions of Vostizza and
Calarryta amounted to 1,286,000 piastres, according to this table to 2,761,580.

Products.				Value in piastres,
			Brought over,	2,075,000
Oats,	.	10,000	kiloes, .	50,000
Maize,	.	100,000	do. .	500,000
Vetches,	.	100,000	do. .	500,000
Currants,	.	88,000	okes, .	88,000
Silk,	,	1,540	do. .	53,900
Flax,	.	66,000	do. ,	132,000
Cotton,	.	110,000	do. .	110,000
Cheese,	.	660,000	do. .	660,000
Butter,	.	2,200	do. .	4,400
Wool,	.	88,000	do. .	88,000
Linseed,	.	44,000	do. .	88,000
Tobacco, in leaf,		88,000	do. .	88,000
Oxen,	.	1,500	do. .	150,000
Swine,	.	8,000	do, .	80,000
Fowls,	.	50,000	do. .	25,000
Geese,	.	10,000	do. .	20,000
Turkeys,	.	20,000	do. ,	40,000
				4,752,300

DISTRICT OF PYRGOS.

Products.				Value in piastres,
Wheat,	.	20,000	kiloes, .	1,500,000
Barley,	.	88,000	do. .	400,000
Oats,	.	70,000	do. .	350,000
Maize and millet,		190,000	do. ,	950,000
Silk,	.	500	okes, .	17,500
Butter,	.	3,080	do. .	6,160
Cheese,	.	8,800	do. ,	8,800
Wine,	.	176,000	do. .	44,000
Brandy,	.	44,000	do. .	44,000
Oxen,	,	100	. .	10,000
Swine,	,	2,000	. .	20,000
Sheep	.	30,000	. .	30,000
Goat skins,		1,760	, .	3,620
Dried fish,		, .	. .	300,000
Eels,		. .	, ,	200,000
				3,884,080
District of Gastouni,			. .	4,752,300
				8,636,380
Total Products of Elis,			.	
According to Pouqueville, in 1814,			.	5,739,500
Population of Elis, 30,000.				

ARCADIA.

Arcadia being a mountainous country, its chief wealth consists in its numerous flocks, herds of oxen and horses, cheese and butter, wheat, maize, and red berries. As the air is excellent, it is the most populous division of Peloponnesus.

ARCADIA.—DISTRICTS OF ANDRIZZENA AND LEONDARI.

Products.				Value in piastres.
Wheat	.	200,000	kiloes, .	2,000,000
Maize,	.	200,000	do. .	1,000,000
Silk,	.	2,420	okes, .	72,600
Red berries,		4,400	do. .	88,000
Cheese,	.	44,000	do. .	33,000
Butter,	.	4,400	do. .	8,800
Cotton,	.	8,800	do. .	8,800
Dried fish,*		74,800	do. .	37,000
Horses,	.	1,000	. .	80,000
				3,328,200

According to Pouqueville, in 1814, . 1,447,502
Population, 17,000.

DISTRICT OF CARITENA.

Products.				Value in piastres.
Wheat,	.	50,000	kiloes, .	500,000
Barley,	.	72,000	do. .	350,000
Oats,	.	8,000	do. .	40,000
Maize and millet,		60,000	do. .	300,000
Silk,	.	1,100	okes, .	22,000
Red berries,	.	4,840	do. .	96,800
Honey,	.	17,600	do. .	17,600
Wax,	.	4,400	do. .	44,000
Cheese,	.	220,000	do. .	165,000
Butter,	.	101,000	do. .	202,000
Wool,	.	220,000	do. .	220,000
				1,957,400

According to Pouqueville, in 1814, . 2,019,000
Population, 44,000.

* From the River Alpheus and Lake of Agholinizza.

DISTRICT OF TRIPOLIZZA.

Products.				Value in piastres.
Wheat,	.	80,000	kiloes,	. 880,000
Barley,	.	20,000	do.	. 100,000
Cheese,	.	352,000	okes,	. 264,000
Butter,	.	88,000	do.	. 176,000
Honey,	.	88,000	do.	. 88,000
Wax,	.	1,936	do.	. 19,360
Red berries,	.	3,080	do.	. 61,600
Yellow berries,	.	1,056	do.	. 21,120
Goat skins,	.	9,680	do.	. 19,360

1,629,440

According to Pouqueville, in 1814, . 2,027,000
Population, 30,000.

DISTRICT OF CALARRYTA.

Products.				Value in piastres.
Wheat,	.	80,000	kiloes,	. 880,000
Barley,	.	30,000	do.	. 150,000
Maize,	.	20,000	do.	. 100,000
Currants,	.	308,000	okes,	. 308,000
Silk,	.	11,000	do.	. 330,000
Red berries,	.	2,200	do.	. 44,000
Wax,	.	3,520	do.	. 35,200
Butter,	.	1,400	do.	. 2,800
Wool,	.	1,400	do.	. 2,200
Cotton,	.	3,080	do.	. 3,080
Rice,	.	10,000	do.	. 7,500

1,862,780

Population, 18,000.   Total population of Arcadia, 109,000.

MESSENIA,

Being extensive and mostly flat, abounds in excellent productions.

DISTRICT OF NEW ARCADIA.

Products.					Value in piastres.
Wheat,	.	40,000	kiloes,	.	400,000
Maize and millet,		55,000	do.	.	275,000
Oil,	.	528,000	okes,	.	528,000
Soap,	.	220,000	do.	.	330,000
Wine,	.	440,000	do.	.	110,000
Silk,	.	880	do.	.	26,400
Honey,	.	440,000	do.	.	440,000
Wax,	.	1,980	do.	.	19,800
Butter,	.	220,000	do.	.	440,000
Cheese,	.	176,000	do.	.	132,000
Wool,	.	35,200	do.	.	35,200
Cotton,	.	17,600	do.	.	17,600
Red berries,	.	1,320	do.	.	26,400
Gall nuts,	.	44,000	do.	.	88,000
Vallonia,	.	.	.	.	99,000
Oxen,	.	2,000	.	.	100,000
Sheep,	.	5,000	.	.	25,000
Goats,	.	5,000	.	.	50,000
Goat skins,	.	10,000	.	.	10,000
Hare skins,	.	5,000	.	.	1,000
Lamb skins,	.	10,000	.	.	2,200

	3,155,600
According to Pouqueville, in 1814, only	1,767,000

DISTRICT OF CALAMATA.

Products.					Value in piastres.
Wheat,	.	100,000	kiloes,	.	1,000,000
Maize,	.	150,000	do.	.	750,000
Oil,	.	264,000	okes,	.	132,000
Figs,	.	.	.	.	132,000
Cheese,	.	3,520	.	.	2,640
Wool,	.	3,520	.	.	3,520
Silk,	.	7,040	.	.	264,000
Cotton,	.	22,088	.	.	22,088
Oranges and lemons,			.	.	500,000

	2,806,248
According to Pouqueville, in 1814,	1,732,500

DISTRICTS OF ANDROZUSSA AND NISSI.

Products.				Value in piastres.
Wheat,	.	20,000 kiloes,	.	200,000
Barley,	.	7,000 do.	.	35,000
Maize,	.	35,000 do.	.	175,000
Silk,	.	1,848 okes,	.	46,200
Wool,	.	26,400 do.	.	26,400
Oil,	.	26,400 do.	.	39,600
Figs,	.		.	66,600
Oxen,	.	600	.	36,000
Swine,	.	3,000	.	30,000
				654,800
According to Pouqueville, in 1814,				1,988,500

DISTRICT OF CORON.

Products.				Value in piastres.
Barley,	.	6,000 kiloes,	.	30,000
Oil,	.	440,000 okes,	.	440,000
Silk,	.	1,420 do.	.	48,700
Cheese,	.	6,600 do.	.	4,950
				523,650
According to Pouqueville, in 1814,				412,000

DISTRICT OF MODON.

Products.				Value in piastres.
White millet,		55,000 kiloes,	.	25,000
Oil,	.	352,000 okes,	.	352,000
Silk,	.	472 do.	.	16,520
Cheese,	.	79,200 do.	.	59,400
Honey,	.	8,800 do.	.	8,800
Wax,	.	1,100 do.	.	11,000
Red berries,		440 do.	.	8,800
				481,520
According to Pouqueville, in 1814,				393,000

DISTRICT OF NAVARIN.

Products.				Value in piastres.
Wheat,	.	6,000 kiloes,	.	60,000
Maize and millet,		10,000 do.	.	50,000
Oil,	.	264,000 okes,	.	264,000
			Carry over,	374,000

Products.				Value in piastres.
		Brought over,		
Cheese,	.	232,000 okes,	.	100,000
Silk,	.	308 do.	.	10,780
Red berries,		440 do.	.	8,800
Tobacco,	.	4,400 do.	.	4,400

	497,980
According to Pouqueville, in 1814,	302,300

Population of Messenia, 60,000.

LACONIA.

DISTRICT OF MISTRA.

Products.				Value in piastres.
Wheat,	.	60,000 kiloes,	.	600,000
Maize and millet,	200,000	do.	.	1,200,000
Silk,	.	19,000 okes,	.	669,000
Oil,	.	880,000 do.	.	880,000
Cheese,	.	17,600 do.	.	13,200
Figs,	.		.	11,000
Wax,	.	2,200 do.	.	22,000
Honey,	.	22,000 do.	.	22,000
Gall nuts,	.	8,800 do.	.	23,000
Red berries		264 kiloes,	.	72,800
Ox hides,	.	22,000	.	44,000
Oranges and Le-mons,		1,000,000	.	17,500

	3,574,500
According to Pouqueville, in 1814,	2,998,000

DISTRICT OF ST PETER.

Products.				Value in piastres.
Wheat,	.	15,000 kiloes,	.	150,000
Oil,	.	88,000 okes,	.	88,000
Silk,	.	2,420 do.	.	84,700
Cotton,	.	1,936 do.	.	1,936
Cheese,	.	132,000 do.	.	100,000
Wool,	.	22,000 do.	.	22,000
Wax,	.	2,904 do.	.	29,040

Carry over,	475,676

Products.			Value in piastres.
	Brought over,		475,676
Red berries,	2,400 okes,		24,000
Chestnuts,			
Charcoal,			
			499,676

According to Pouqueville, in 1814,   985,000
Population, 17,600.

DISTRICT OF MONEMVASIA.

Products.			Value in piastres.
Wheat,	10,000 kiloes,	.	100,000
Oil,	88,000 okes,	.	88,000
Honey,	35,200 do.	.	35,200
Wax,	3,520 do.	.	35,200
Cheese,	132,000 do.	.	100,000
Wool,	22,000 do.	.	22,000
Silk,	880 do.	.	3,080
Cotton,	22,000 do.	.	22,000
Red berries,	440 do.	.	8,800
Figs,			11,000
			425,280

According to Pouqueville, in 1814,   237,000
Population, 15,000.

MAINA.

Products.			Value in piastres.
Oil,	704,000 okes,	.	704,000
Wax,	1,672 do.	.	16,720
Honey,	44,000 do.	.	44,000
Silk,	1,320 do.	.	45,200
Cotton,	10,120 do.	.	10,120
Red berries,	792 do.	.	15,840
Gall nuts,	1,012 do.	.	3,036
Vallonia,	1,320,000 do.	.	44,000
Pickled Quails,	1,000,000 do.	.	100,000
			982,916

According to Pouqueville, in 1814,   1,450,000
Population, 55,000.

Total population of Laconia, 127,000, of whom 15,000
Mohammedans of Bardounia and Mistra.

ARGOLIS.

The wheat, maize, cotton, and wine of Argolis are excellent.

Products.			Value in piastres.
Wheat,	200,000 kiloes,		2,000,000
Barley,	80,000	do.	640,000
Maize,	100,000	do.	600,000
Rice,	100,000	do.	800,000
Lentils,	7,000	do.	70,000
Beans,	5,000	do.	50,000
Cotton,	100,000	okes,	140,000
Honey,	36,200	do.	36,200
Wax,	6,200	do.	62,000
Wine,	500,000	do.	250,000
Oil,	100,000	do.	200,000
Silk,	600	do.	24,000
Wool,	10,000	do.	10,000
Cheese,	61,000	do.	61,600
Butter,	10,000	do.	20,000
Red berries, .	880	do.	17,600
Goat skins, .	2,220		4,440
Sponges,	500,000		200,000
			5,185,840

Cantons of Argos and Nauplia, according to
Pouqueville, in 1814, ... 2,749,000
Population 34,800, mostly Albanians, who came from Bœotia in
1485.

Recapitulation of Statistical Tables.

Products of Northern Greece, within Thermopylæ,
  exclusive of Acarnania and Megaris, . . 12,296,380
Products of Peloponnesus and Megaris,* . . 48,119,500

        Total value, ... 60,415,880

Total population of Northern Greece, within Thermopylæ, exclusive of Acarnania and Megaris, 115,500
Population of Peloponnesus and Megaris, . 433,440

        Total, ... 548,940

Of whom about 500,000 were Christians.

* According to the last edition of Pouqueville's work, he makes the total
value of the products of Peloponnesus, brought into market, in the year 1814,
amount only to 32,148,000 piastres.

BOOK FIRST.

CHAP. I.

Rebellion of Ali Pasha, and its consequences.—Return to Epirus of the Souliotes, and their hostilities against the Turks.—Hopes and projects of the Hetærists.—Revolt of Theodore Vladimiresco in Wallachia, and Invasion of Moldavia by Ypsilanti.—Campaign in the Trans-Danubian Principalities.

SECTION I.

MANY friends and wellwishers to the Greek cause have said and written, that the insurrection was premature, and that another century should have been allowed to pass away before the Hellenes attempted to break their fetters. This opinion is founded on a belief that, in the course of an hundred years more, knowledge and civilisation would have been so widely diffused, as to render the road to emancipation safe and easy; we neither admit these premises nor join in the conclusion, and the following are our reasons of dissent. Although it be true, that education was steadily advancing, and that on certain points of the Archipelago, and the coasts of Asia, wealth and commerce had made a rapid progress; yet in continental Greece, where alone a successful stand could be maintained, the numbers of the people were rather diminishing; while the large trading cities presented an increase of Greek inhabitants, accustomed from their infancy to tremble at the sight of a Turk; ruin and depopulation were pressing on those hardy mountaineers, whose untamed hatred to their tyrants could alone support a revolutionary struggle. The effeminate Sciotes and Smyrniotes, enjoying the delights of Ionia, might extend their trade, form schools and libraries, nay even conspire; but on the day of trial, the European Greeks only were capable of wielding with effect the musket and sabre. In the province of Roumelia, distinguished for the high spirit of its natives, oppression was forcing the peasant to emigrate; the Souliotes, the flower of Albanian warriors, were driven from Epirus, the bravest Kleftic chieftains from the Morea, and the Armatoles were weakened and humiliated; another reign like that of Ali Pasha would have left on the mainland hardly any elements of resistance.

Universally in Asia, as well as in most of the larger islands, there was a Mussulman population sufficient to keep the Rayahs in subjection; in Crete, the finest of them all, intolerable persecution multiplied examples of apostasy, and Cyprus, the next in point of size, was fast losing its inhabitants.

Hydra, Spezzia, and Psarra, were flourishing indeed, and had risen into importance within a few years; yet on how precarious a tenure depended their prosperity, which had already begun to awaken the jealousy and avidity of their masters! A single fiat of the Sultan sufficed either to destroy the professors and capitalists of Greece, to shut up her seminaries of learning, and sweep away all local immunities, or else to oblige the Christians to take arms without previous preparation; it was time then to adopt measures for resistance, whilst the nation possessed some degree of information, joined to pecuniary resources, a respectable marine, and a body of men disposed to face the Ottomans in battle.*   At whatever period undertaken,

---

* Another political reason may be added for hastening the contest, although it occurred probably to few Greeks. Turkey in Europe had

the war must necessarily have been attended with massacres and excesses; which, however culpable in themselves, or declaimed against by party zeal, were not, in fact, of a deeper dye, than deeds perpetrated an hundred times in the civil wars of Great Britain, France, and Germany, as well as in the recent Spanish struggle against the ambition of Napoleon.

No event could have happened more propitious to the designs of the Hetœrists, than the rupture that broke out in the beginning of 1820, betwixt the Porte and its powerful vassal, the Satrap of Yannina; whose real strength, hanging as it did on the attachment of so faithless, venal, and inconstant a people as the Albanians, was not a little exaggerated, both by his partisans and enemies; but which, united to experience and cunning, would certainly have proved an overmatch for the Greeks.

The Sultan had long hated him, as much as he coveted his treasures, and had frequently meditated his destruction; however, he could not overlook the palpable expediency of rather waiting for the death of an infirm old man, than involving his empire in dangerous intestine warfare. Two acts of hasty passion, committed by the one and the other, hurled the Pasha from an almost regal seat to a bloody grave, and precipitated the ruin of European Turkey.

Ali had for some years past been pursuing with deadly rancour an Albanian named Ismael Pasho Bey, the confidential friend of his son Veli, and formerly attached to his own household. Flying from his wrath under various disguises, Pasho Bey at length reached Constantinople, leagued himself with Ali's enemies,

little chance of surviving half a century, and, in case of its sudden downfall, Greece must have become the conqueror's prey after assisting his triumph: such, no doubt, was Count Capodistria's calculation!

and obtaining the Sultan's good graces, was appointed
one of his Capoujee Bashees.   This promotion, and a
knowledge that Ismael was intriguing against him,
sharpened to such a degree the Pasha's animosity, that,
throwing aside all considerations of prudence and respect, he hired assassins to shoot the object of his
resentment in the midst of the imperial city.   They,
however, only wounded him, and being arrested, disclosed the name of their instigator.

The stern character of the Sultan could not brook
so outrageous an insult to his authority.   The Vizier
of Yannina, declared a rebel and traitor, was excommunicated by a solemn fetva, or sentence of the Sheikh
ul Islam, the head of the Mussulman law ; the Pashas
of Europe received orders to march against him, and
a squadron was fitted out from the port of Constantinople to attack him by sea.

Ali learned these violent resolutions of the divan in
the month of March 1820.   After endeavouring in
vain to allay the storm by craft and bribery, he bravely
took up the gauntlet, and prepared to defend himself.
Placing small confidence in his Mohammedan retainers,
he determined to court the Christians, for he seems to
have looked upon their disaffection towards Turkey as
a last resource, which he might employ when every
other failed.*   He therefore not only reorganized the
Armatoles, whom he had been so long labouring to
suppress, but convened also at Yannina an assembly of
bishops and primates, addressed them in the most flattering terms, and trusted so far to their credulity as to
throw out hints of his intention to give them a constitution.

On the other hand, Suleyman Pasha of Thessaly, who
led the Sultan's forces, circulated among the Rayahs

* It has been observed, that although, during his viceroyalty, he
built many churches, he never founded a single mosque.

numerous copies of a proclamation, written in Greek, exhorting them to rise in arms against their old tyrant and his Illyrian satellites.   It is supposed that this rash proclamation, which brought on the deposition and execution of Suleyman Pasha, was drawn up at the suggestion and by the pen of his secretary, Anagnosti, an ardent Hetœrist.   Thus the Greeks saw their alliance courted by two contending parties whom they equally abhorred : they could never forgive Ali's oppression, and distrusted his hypocrisy; while their inveterate hatred to the Turks, was fed with new fuel by the ravages of the imperial troops, who treated like a hostile territory the districts through which they passed, and wasted, out of a wanton spirit of destruction, the rich plains of Thessaly and Bœotia.

After the disgrace and decapitation of Suleyman Pasha, the task of reducing the rebel was confided to his old enemy Ismael Pasho, who received the titles of Serasker or generalissimo, and Pasha of Yannina and Delvino.   He advanced about the middle of summer towards the defiles of Pindus, while the celebrated Pehlevan Baba Pasha * invaded northern Greece, and Selim, Valeh of Roumelia,† penetrated through the Candavian mountains into Epirus.   From Upper Albania Mustai, Pasha of Scodra, invaded Ali's dominions with an army of Ghegs ; and an Ottoman fleet, under the Capitana Bey, appeared in the Ionian Sea, and threatened his coasts.   Those who had visited the Satrap's capital, and judged his power and resources in the hour of prosperity, generally imagined that the

* Baba Pasha was Janissary Aga when the English fleet appeared before Constantinople, and Sultan Selim's firmness is said to have been chiefly owing to his energetic representations.   He afterwards bravely defended Ismael against the Russians, who at length took him prisoner.   Pehlevan, in Turkish, means a wrestler.

† The title Valeh signifies a governor-general.

chances were in his favour, and that possessing, as he
did, an impervious country, vast treasures, strong fortresses, immense supplies of artillery and ammunition,
and above 15,000 excellent light troops, he would
easily baffle the Sultan's lieutenants. The following
are the dispositions he made for his defence :—Of his
two sons, Mukhtar and Veli, one administered Middle
Albania, residing at Berat, and the other commanded
in Lepanto, and on the shore of Epirus. The military
government of Phocis and Bœotia was committed to a
Greek, Odysseus, brought up among Ali's pages, and
son to a famous captain of Armatoles, named Andri-
seos ; Omer Bey Vriones, an Albanian chief of reputation,* Tahir Abbas, minister of police at Yannina, and
Alexis Nouzza, primate of Zagori, headed the principal
corps that guarded the passes of Pindus. The Satrap
himself remained at Yannina, from whence, as a common centre, he could direct every operation.

When hostilities began, it was quickly seen on how
frail a basis stands authority acquired and maintained
by perfidy and cruelty. The people, tired of Ali's long
reign, every where declared against him, although they
had little advantage to expect from a change, and, in
fact, in several provinces have since had reason to regret
his fall, which delivered them once more to the anarchical rule of a crowd of petty tyrants whom he had
overthrown. After a few skirmishes the Armatolic
bands joined the enemy. The inhabitants of Livadia
expelled from their city Odysseus, who with a small
corps retired to Yannina, and Baba Pasha occupied

---

* Omer Vriones, descended from the noble Byzantine family of
Bryennias, served long in Egypt, and defeated near Rosetta a party
of English troops—an exploit of which he always boasted highly.
Returning home with great wealth, he joined the faction of Ali Pasha ;
but the latter not only stripped him of his fortune, but even attempted
to poison him.

Lepanto without resistance. On the side of Pindus, Ali's three generals went over with their whole army to the imperial camp; meanwhile the Capitana Bey Kara Ali had only to show himself on the coast, to receive the submission of Prevesa and Parga; and, finally, Mukhtar and Veli Pashas surrendered to him their persons, families, and effects, and were sent as exiles to Kutaieh, in Phrygia, where for some time they lived unmolested. Besides a contingent from Hydra, another from Maina, and a body of Chimarriotes recently discharged from the service of Naples, the Ottoman vice-admiral was in this expedition assisted by the Souliotes, who, wearied of inactivity in the Ionian islands, offered their swords to the Capitana Bey, on condition that they should be allowed to reconquer Souli, and dwell there, as they had formerly done, independent in point of fact, but owning the Sultan's supremacy. The Turks having accepted these terms, without any intention of fulfilling them, the Souliotes, having at their head Mark Bozzaris, landed in Epirus to the number of 700 or 800, and took an active part in the war.

Although abandoned by most of his partisans, and surrounded by foes, Ali did not yet lose courage, but resolved to defend his capital to the last extremity, trusting that time, fortune, his own ability, and the faults of his adversaries, would work a favourable change in his affairs. The city of Yannina, beautifully situated on the banks of a large lake, was supposed to contain 30,000 inhabitants—including, however, in that reckoning the Satrap's court, and his Albanian soldiery; above one half of the population consisted of Greeks, respectable for their industry, love of letters, and civilisation. On a promontory running into the lake, six hundred yards long and three hundred in breadth, stood a spacious palace, separated from the town by a

wet ditch, and successive lines of bastioned works. To
the south of this, on the shore, the Vizier Ali had erected
a new and splendid residence, within the strong castle
of Litharizza, commanding both the town and promontory.   He had also constructed a third fortress, on an
island in the lake, where were several villages, and
with which he kept up his communication by means
of a flotilla of gunboats ; two hundred and fifty pieces
of cannon covered the ramparts, and he had filled his
magazines with a quantity of ammunition, and provisions sufficient for the consumption of several years.
The garrison, composed of Albanians and Ghegs, with
a small addition of Greeks and European adventurers,
did not fall far short of 3000 men, and for many months
it seems to have been kept up to this strength ; the
voids made by casualties and desertion, being more
than compensated by the number of Albanians, who,
allured by Ali's high pay, deserted into the place.
Caretto, a Neapolitan exile, was chief engineer. When
the rebel found himself under the necessity of standing
a siege, he determined to destroy the flourishing city,
that it might afford no shelter to his enemies.   He
therefore gave it up to be pillaged by his troops, and
then laid it in ashes, by a furious discharge of shot and
shells from his castles.

On the first day of September, 1820, the imperial
army pitched its tents in the plain of Yannina ; and
the Serasker, who was accompanied by more than
twenty other pashas, having soon after received cannon
and mortars from Prevesa, began to batter the fortress
of Litharizza, but made very little impression.   The
besieged returned his fire with spirit, and, by vigorous
sallies, occasionally penetrated into the hostile trenches.
Ismael Pasha was now able to judge of the difficulties
he would have to encounter ; provisions already became scarce in his camp, owing to the ravages of his

troops, and the approach of winter threatened to cover
the mountains with deep snow, and shut up the passes
of Pindus in his rear.   The soldiers disbanded, the
Ottoman generals quarrelled amongst themselves, and
the bravest of them, the intractable Baba Pasha, died
of poison administered by the Serasker.   The latter,
besides having to struggle against the disorders of his
own army, and the resistance of the besieged, soon saw
in his Christian auxiliaries a source of very serious
uneasiness.   Had no conspiracy, no plans of insurrection existed among the Greeks, the events that were
happening around them could not have failed to cause
a profound sensation, when both the belligerents invited
their assistance.   Ali offered any terms as the price of
their aid ; and the Sultan's lieutenants felt the necessity
of detaching from the rebel's cause, at least that portion
of them that had arms in their hands.

A natural love of change, the memory of past injuries, and the preference so commonly given to an uncertain and gloomy future, over an irksome present
state, led them at first to hearken to the latter ; but
the haughtiness and excesses of the Turks soon altered
this disposition, and made them forget the wrongs they
had suffered from the Satrap.   Ismael Pasha, although
long accustomed to the society of Rayahs, and speaking
with perfect facility several of their dialects, affected
great devotion, was a bitter enemy to Christians, and
did not conceal the dislike he entertained towards the
Armatoles who served under his orders : such sentiments he expressed in the most insulting way.   Encouraged by the example of their Serasker, the other
Turks seemed to take a pleasure in exasperating the
Greeks, plundering and burning their towns and villages, and carrying away their children into slavery ;
whole populations fled to the hills and woods, and those
who remained at home, or who were out of the Otto-

man line of march, were exposed to continual corvées,
and to requisitions of money, provisions, horses, &c.
&c. Ali, who had agents and correspondents in every
corner of the empire, from Moldavia to the Morea, had
foreseen this, and prepared to profit by it. A body of
Armatoles was shut up in his castles, whither they had
retired with Odysseus. Thinking they might be more
useful elsewhere, he engaged their leader to feign treachery, and go over to the imperialists, who welcomed
them with joy, but quickly treated them in such a
manner as to produce exactly the result that Ali expected. Odysseus suddenly withdrew to Ithaca, and
his soldiers, dispersing in small bands, and joined by
many of their countrymen, lurked in the defiles, and
infested the rear of the Ottoman army. The rebellious
Pasha executed another and a much deeper stroke of
policy, by converting into allies his most inveterate
foes, the Souliotes. It is true, that those warriors had
abundant cause of complaint against the Serasker, who
refused to ratify their convention with the Capitana
Bey, slighted their remonstrances, and drove their deputies from his presence. They were not of a humour
to bear such usage tamely ; like all Albanians, extremely
covetous, they were easily accessible to Ali's bribes ;
and indeed, under existing circumstances, they could
not, without changing sides, hope to succeed in the
object that had brought them to Epirus—namely, the
recovery of their native canton.

Mutual interests, and common necessity, thus rendering a reconciliation betwixt the Souliotes and the
Pasha equally desirable to both parties, his flotilla
wafted by night some deputies from their chiefs to the
castle of the lake, and after repeated conferences, a
treaty was agreed upon. It stipulated that they should
put into Ali's hands as hostages, the children of their
noblest families, and that he should deliver to them as

a counter-pledge, his grandson, the young Hussein
Pasha; that Souli, then held by a garrison of his forces,
should be given up to them as soon as they quitted the
Serasker; and, lastly, that he should provide them with
money and ammunition to act against the Turks—for
as long as the lake was open, he could either receive
or transmit supplies. The hostages having been exchanged, and half a million of piastres paid over to the
Souliotes, the latter, in November, marched away to
their mountains, and occupied all the posts about Souli,
except one impregnable citadel recently built by Ali,
and which his governor, acting on private instructions,
refused to evacuate. Although placed in a critical
situation by this breach of faith, they nevertheless executed their part of the treaty. The accession of Epirotes swelled their number from nine hundred to three
thousand musketeers; Nothi Bozzaris was chosen
polemarch, and his gallant nephew, Mark, opened the
campaign by seizing the Han of the five wells, a commanding position on the road from Arta to Yannina.
During the whole winter they prosecuted hostilities
with vigour, and gained some brilliant successes over
considerable bodies of Turks, led by the Roumeli Valchsi, the Pasha of Negropont, and Yussuf, Bey of Seres.
About the same period, Alexis Nouzza, who had deserted Ali's cause, disgusted at the treatment he met
with, returned to his former master, and not only excited an insurrection in Zagori, but persuaded Tahir
Abbas, and other Mohammedan beys, to take up arms
in the Satrap's defence against the imperialists.* So
embarrassing did the aspect of affairs appear to the
court of Constantinople, that it superseded the Serasker
Ismael, and ordered the veteran Khourshid Pasha, then
viceroy of the Morea, to assume the supreme command,

* Zagori is a mountainous province of Epirus, to the north-east of
the lake of Yannina, inhabited by Greeks.

and the post of Roumeli Valchsi. These appointments were conferred upon him at the end of 1820, but it was not till the commencement of the month of March 1821 that he arrived with a fresh army before Yannina. The most important action that happened in the intermediate lapse of time, was a grand sortie, executed by Ali on the 7th of February; his plan was to attack the imperial camp in front, while the Souliotes should assail it from behind; however, a messenger that he dispatched to them having been intercepted, he fell into an ambuscade, was defeated with loss, and had much difficulty in regaining his castles.

SECTION II.

THE Hetœrists, panting for an opportunity to liberate their country, could not behold with indifference these transactions in Epirus, so favourable to their views; transactions which obtained for them the support of that enemy whom they had chiefly dreaded, and employed the forces and attention of the Sultan; while the victories of a handful of Souliotes seemed a presage of future triumph, and raised the spirits of the Greek people. As they required a leader, uniting the qualifications of Russian connexion, a name known in Greece, and consideration from his rank in life, they cast their eyes on Prince Alexander Ypsilanti, son to that Hospodar of Wallachia, whose deposition by the Porte served as a pretext for the war of 1806. He was in the flower of his age, agreeable in person and manners, had risen to the rank of Major-General in the Russian service, and lost his right hand at the battle of Culm. Instead of an imaginary Grand Arch of sixteen illustrious names (the real patrons of the now extinct Philomuse Society), the business of the Patriotic

Association was conducted at that period by a committee of twelve members, consisting of Ypsilanti, Galati,
Pentidekas of Epirus, Sekeris of Tripolizza, Xanthos,
Amagnostopoulos, and others, mostly merchants, little
known or esteemed out of their own coterie. Its sittings were, early in the year 1820, transferred from
Moscow to Kishnoff, in Bessarabia, and a resolution
adopted, of carrying into effect without delay the project of a revolution. A swarm of apostles descended
from Southern Russia into Greece, visiting every isle
and every valley, and opening, with small discrimination, the doors of the Society to men of all descriptions.
In summer, Galati himself sailed from Galatz to Hydra, accompanied by a certain Foro ; his intention,
probably, was to head the insurrection in that quarter,
but his career was cut short by treachery ; his companion assassinated him amidst the ruins of Hermione,
and escaped to Italy, in spite of the exertions made to
apprehend him by the Russian consul at Hydra, in
whose house both had spent the preceding night.
There is no doubt that this murder was instigated by
the principal Hetœrists, and those are not wanting who
attribute it to Ypsilanti, because, according to their
version of the story, he saw in Galati a rival who
would not yield the superiority to him, and with whom
he had already quarrelled respecting the disposition of
the Society's funds. Others assign as a reason, that
Galati was a man of dissipated and intemperate habits;
and that they had no confidence in his discretion.
Perhaps, the true cause of his death was a suspicion on
the minds of the managing committee, that having been
a founder and prime mover of the Hetœria, he would
never consent to play a secondary part, under a new
member like Prince Alexander.* This last conjecture

* It was not till the spring of 1820 that Ypsilanti became a Hetœrist.

derives strength from the fact, that shortly afterwards
the provincial superintendents received a circular epistle
from the Grand Arch, recognising Ypsilanti as Procurator-general of the Hetœria, and desiring the prelates
to pay implicit obedience to his orders. Henceforth, he
corresponded with them in his own name, not in
cipher, but written characters, and without the proper
degree of precaution, enjoining them to provide ammunition, and make preparations for an approaching
conflict.   In his communications, he assumed the title
of Ἐπίτροπος των ἐπιτρόπων τῆς σεβαςῆς ἀρχῆς, " Steward of
the Stewards of the august Arch." During the autumn
and winter of 1820, the Patriotic Association was augmented by a vast influx of neophytes, and it was then
that the Primates of Hydra entered into its ranks, and
in consequence recalled their ships into port, and ceased
their commercial speculations; those of Spezzia had
been initiated some time before.   Meanwhile, even the
lower orders became aware that some great convulsion
was near at hand; the Greek population was agitated
by the insinuations of the apostles, the events of the war
in Epirus, and the misery which the continual passage
of Turkish troops occasioned; there prevailed a vague
but universal idea, that the hour of emancipation and
retribution was about to sound; and several monks
and hermits issuing from their cells, wrought on the superstition of the peasantry by visions and prophecies: it
needed but a spark to set the whole mass in combustion.
The conspiracy now proceeded in so open and undisguised a way, that it was hardly possible it should be
longer kept a secret. Ali Pasha was fully informed of
it, since he announced to the Souliotes, by letter, that
if they would serve his cause till the month of March,
they might assist at the funeral of the Ottoman Empire. The Lord High Commissioner of the Ionian
Islands had likewise an inkling of the affair; and in

the spring of 1821, dispatched an emissary, named Logotheti, to Hydra, to gain further intelligence, under
pretence of organizing a similar movement at Corfu ;
being detected, however, this spy was driven from the
place with blows and insult. Notwithstanding the natural sluggishness of the Turks, it may well be thought
incredible, that the Porte, the party chiefly interested,
should have had no intimation of the Society's machinations ; yet such appears to have been the case ; for
we attach no credit to pretended revelations of Ali Pasha, touching a scheme, said to be formed in the divan,
for exterminating the Rayahs of Europe, and planting
in their stead Mussulman colonies from Asia.   Two
circumstances occurred in the course of the winter,
which might have opened the eyes of the blindest government ; one of Ypsilanti's agents, proceeding to
Epirus, was assassinated at Naousta, in Macedonia,
by Zaphiris, a primate of that town ; another named
Aristides, setting out from Kishneff, in December,
charged with important letters to the Servians, was
seized and executed at the passage of the Danube, and
his papers laid before the Pasha of Vidin, who had
learned the purpose of his journey from the Prince of
Wallachia.   The Pasha, however, was so dilatory in
forwarding these documents to Constantinople, that
they did not arrive till the revolution had broken out ;
but the fear of inevitable detection, probably hurried
the measures of the patriots. Alexander Ypsilanti, thus
placed, without competition, at the head of an enterprise
so full of peril and glory, possessed neither the judgment nor firmness necessary for bringing it to a successful issue : he yielded too easy a belief to the reports of
the apostles, who are accused as well of embezzling large
sums of money, as of deceiving, by false and exaggerated statements, both those that sent them, and those
among whom they were sent. Buoyed up by their

flattering representations, he persuaded himself, that
not only Greece, but also Bulgaria, Servia, and Macedonia, were completely organized, and ready to fly to
arms, as soon as he should unsheath his sword on the
banks of the Pruth,-whence he proposed to begin his
attack upon the Ottoman power : at the same time
means had been devised for executing a simultaneous
insurrection at Constantinople itself. To set Ypsilanti
right on some of his mistaken ideas, a man of penetration, perfectly acquainted with the state of the Trans-
danubian principalities, addressed from Yassy a communication to the Arch, dated the first of February
1821, (*Vide* Appendix,) pointing out the little support
that he was likely to meet with in those provinces, and
the futility of his hopes from Bulgaria, and the northern
districts of European Turkey ; adding, that in Greece
alone could an effectual stand be made, and that any
attempt beyond the Danube ought only to be considered as a diversion, which might prove useful, if intrusted to proper hands, and if the natives could be induced to interest themselves heartily in the cáuse.
Ypsilanti paid no great attention to this exposé, and
persisted in his plan of conducting in person the campaign in Moldavia and Wallachia.

These two countries are alike remarkable for their
prodigious fertility, and the misfortunes under which
they have long groaned, arising out of a most corrupt
and defective system of government. Including a large
portion of the ancient Dacia, they extend in length
350, in breadth 160 miles ; are bounded by the Carpathian Mountains, the Danube, and the Pruth, and
watered by many noble streams, affluents of the Ister,
such as the Sireth, the Olta, Argish, Rimnik, &c.
These rivers, as well as an infinity of little lakes scattered over both provinces, yield an inexhaustible store
of fish. Wallachia may be divided into two distinct

regions; displaying, towards the Transylvanian frontier, romantic hills and tall forests; it has on the east one immense level track of alluvial soil, where not a stone can be discovered. Moldavia, smaller in extent, less productive, and of a drier, and more uneven surface, is nevertheless superior in the quality of its grain and timber. In spite of neglect and oppression, although much of the land lay waste and covered with brushwood, yet such is the excellence of the soil, that a starving peasantry gathered in very weighty harvests of wheat, maize, and millet; horses, cattle, and sheep were most abundant; and the principalities produced an immense quantity of the finest ship-timber, besides the minor articles of wax, honey, wine, fruit, cheese, butter, and dye-stuffs. From thence Constantinople was wont to draw its principal supply of food, not less than 1,500,000 bushels of wheat, and 250,000 sheep, being annually exported to that city from Galatz. The Carpathians contain veins of the precious metals, but policy forbade their being worked on the Ottoman side; however, the princes derived a considerable revenue from their salt mines. A recent author who favoured the public with an account of Moldavia and Wallachia, in most respects extremely accurate, seems, however, to have fallen into a gross error of excess, in stating their population at a million and a half. There are but five cities at all worthy of the name, viz. Bukorest, the metropolis of Wallachia, a straggling place on the banks of the slow and muddy river Dimborizza, with 400 churches and monasteries, and 70,000 people; Yassy, the Moldavian capital, containing from 30 to 40,000; Craiova, in Little Wallachia, inhabited by 15,000; Tergovisht, and Galatz, at the mouth of the Danube, their only maritime outlet. The towns are universally built of wood, and even paved with the same material.

It is now admitted by all those who have studied
the origin of the Wallachians, that they are descended
from a mixture of old Dacians, and Italian colonies,
settled beyond the Danube, by the Roman Emperors;
their language is a bastard Latin dialect, and their
national dress is precisely that worn by the Dacian
warriors, as represented on Trajan's column at Rome.

Dislodged from the flat country by Tartar and Sclavonic invaders, they retired into the Carpathian Mountains, dwelt there in obscurity for several hundred
years, paying tribute to their neighbours ; and in the
thirteenth century came down again to the plains from
Fogaratz in Transylvania.*

We find their Vayvodes, or native princes, continually embroiled in the wars of that turbulent period,
until the Turks acquired possession of Wallachia by
force of arms, and of Moldavia by capitulation. The
Sultans did not alter the form of government, but contented themselves with imposing a moderate tribute,
and obliging the princes to join their armies, with an
auxiliary contingent of light cavalry, which served like
the Cossacks and Tartars. When any attempt was
made to violate their privileges, the Vayvodes not
unfrequently rebelled, and called in the assistance of

* The very old anonymous history of the Dukes of Hungary in-
forms us, that in the ninth century, the Hungarians discovered in
Transylvania a Wallachian Prince, whose subjects were armed only
with bows and arrows, and had suffered many injuries from the Pet-
shinegars (or Patzinacæ), their Tartarian neighbours on the east. In
the Sclavonic tongue, Vlak signifies a Roman or Italian ; the Turks
and Albanians apply the same term to the Greek peasants ; and hence
comes the epithet of Velsh (Welsh), given by the Saxons to the pro-
vincials of Britain. That part of ancient Dacia belonging to the Austrian Empire, is still mostly inhabited by Wallachians ; they every
where call themselves Romans, and their language Romanisht. In
the Wallachian dialect, their princes are entitled Voda or Vayvode,
in Sclavonic, Hospodar, and by the Turks, Bey.

Christian powers. For this reason, the Porte, in 1716, ceased to appoint natives, and henceforth conferred the Hospodariates on Greeks of the Fanar, who being altogether pacific, anxious only to amass money, and consequently odious to their subjects, could inspire no apprehension. The tribute was gradually augmented ; and to gratify the cupidity of the Turkish ministers, as well as to provide for the future support of their own families and dependants, the greedy and unprincipled Fanariotes drained vast sums from the provinces during their short reigns ; the divan being always impatient to depose them, in order to put up their dignities to sale, utterly heedless of the ruin it inflicted, as long as a few Mussulman grandees filled their purses at the expense of those infidel countries. It is probably not too much to calculate at a million sterling, the annual burdens of the principalities. Neither did these heavy imposts exempt them from other vexations equally grievous ; they were compelled to replenish the magazines of the Ottoman fortresses on the Danube ; and that Constantinople might procure abundance of cheap food, their trade was annihilated by an ordinance prohibiting the exportation of almost every kind of produce, except to that city.* Russia, by three successive occupations, had tantalized them with hopes of being released from Turkish bondage, and at the close of each war had made in their favour stipulations which the Porte invariably eluded ; the people sighed for Muscovite domination, but they hated the Greeks almost as much as they did the Mohammedans. After the flight of Prince Caradja in 1818, Alexander

---

* Only three commodities were allowed to be exported, wool, yellow berries, and hare-skins, of which last 500,000 were annually shipped from Galatz ; for no part of Europe abounds in wild animals so much as Dacia.

Souzzo, an old man, well versed in Oriental diplomacy, was appointed Hospodar of Wallachia. He was, as we have already seen, accused of disclosing to the Turks the secret mission of Aristides. The Hetœrists, however, soon avenged themselves, and Souzzo died of poison on the 1st February 1821. Michael Souzzo, belonging to another branch of the same family, assumed the government of Moldavia in 1820, and in October of that year was initiated into the patriotic brotherhood.

Yassy and Bukorest being full of Greek and Sclavonic adventurers, many of whom had held commissions in the Russian and Servian armies, and the police being moreover extremely lax, the Hetœria counted there a numerous body of adepts of a class the best fitted to aid its designs. Formerly, the native force of the principalities was by no means despicable, consisting of Pandours, or militia, headed by the nobility, and enjoying considerable privileges. Since the sway of the Phanariotes began, however, military service was abolished, the Boyards (or nobles) sunk into sloth and effeminacy ; and the princes, wanting money and not swords, trampled under foot the franchises of the soldiery, and did all they could to depress the spirits of their subjects. Yet there was still a semblance of provincial militia arranged under the following denominations:—First, the Pandours of Little Wallachia, (the district between the Danube and the Olta,) where that institution, though languishing, had been suffered to exist ; they were estimated at 10,000. Secondly, the Playashes, or mountaineers, guarding the defiles toward the Austrian frontier, and on that account exempt from tribute. Thirdly, the Potokeshes, who are charged to watch over the security of the roads. Fourthly, the Vounatores, or huntsmen of the Boyards, whose only occupation is to provide their masters with game. All these together might amount to 20,000 men, wretchedly armed it is true, but at least accustomed to handle weapons, whereas the rest of the nation neither possessed any, nor had courage to use them. It was uncertain whether they would lend themselves to Ypsilanti's views, but he confidently reckoned on the support of a foreign description of troops introduced into Dacia during the Fanariote ascendency.

Included under the generic name of Arnauts, it was recruited from Roumeliote Greeks, Albanians, Bulgarians, and Servians, who acted as body-guards to the princes, the great functionaries, and even the simple Boyards ; for the country was so infested by robbers, that it was impossible for them either to travel or reside on their estates without military protection. Those mercenaries, computed at about 4000, although corrupted by the dissolute vices of the principalities, were perfectly well equipped, armed, and mounted, and held the native militia in contempt ; many of them were Hetœrists, and their leaders had engaged to bring over the whole of their troops to the cause of Hellenic regeneration.

A number of Greeks was besides dispersed abroad in Moldavia and Wallachia, in the capacity of Arundashes, or middle men, farming the lands of the nobles, who are in general too indolent to look after their own affairs ; the want of safety for persons and property obliged them to keep arms at hand, and their assistance was expected. Every thing being thus apparently in a fair train of preparation, a signal was, in January 1821, given from Kishneff to commence the revolution.

SECTION III.

ALTHOUGH the regular force at Yassy and Bukorest, paid by the two Hospodars, did not exceed five or six hundred horsemen, they had nevertheless an etat-major, with Turkish military titles, sufficient for ten times that amount. Under the administration of Alexander Souzzo, the troops of Wallachia were commanded by the Tufenkjee Bashee,* George, or as he was commonly called Yorgaki, a native of Mount Olympus, distinguished for prudence, valour, and patriotism, and enthusiastically wedded to the principles of the Hetœria. He would have been the most proper man to take the direction of the war beyond the Danube, but as Ypsilanti reserved that task to himself, George undertook to prepare the way for him. Just at the epoch of Souzzo's death, he sent into Little Wallachia a petty Boyard of that district, named Theodore Vladimiresko,† formerly a lieutenant-colonel of Pandours in the Russian service, accompanied by 150 soldiers, and instructed to raise disturbances there. With this band of followers, Theodore seized the small town of Czernitz, near the ruins of Trajan's Bridge, and addressed a proclamation to the people, announcing, that the moment was come to shake off the tyranny of the Greek princes and high noblesse, and restore their ancient constitution. Being himself a Wallachian, professing to have in view only the good of the province, and having begun by diminishing the taxes, the peasants hailed him with joy as a deliverer,

* General of Musketeers.

† Vladimiresko, was so called by the Wallachians, from the circumstance of his having received the Russian order of St Vladimir.

1

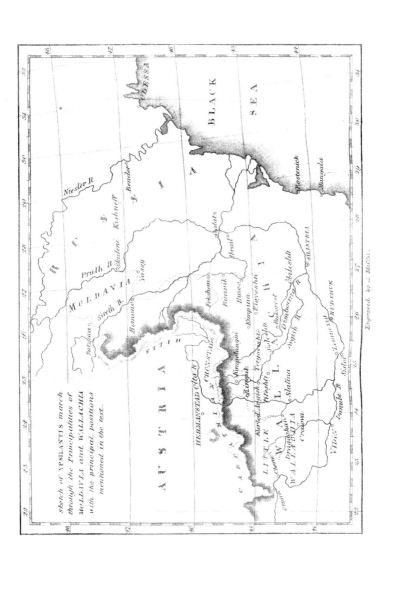

Sketch of YPSILANTIS march
through the Principalities of
MOLDAVIA and WALLACHIA
with the principal positions
mentioned in the text.

AUSTRIA

MOLDAVIA

Niester R.

Bender

Kishneff

Skuleni

Pruth R.

Sereth R.

Sutyawa

Romanez

Yassy

SITTH

HERMANSTAD or ROTH

CRONSTADT

CARPATHIAN

Kimpolungi

Argish

Kirickal Argish

Piteshti

Trigovishti

Fokshans

Rumnik

Buzeo

Kimpina

Bukorest

Ditesht

Elevesta

Dembovitza R.

Galatz

Ibrail

WALLACHIA

LITTLE WALLACHIA

Crajova

Dreidslan

Slatina

Aytish R.

VIDIN

Danube R.

Sistov

Lom

RATSCHUK

SILISTRIA

Karasu

ODESSA

BLACK

SEA

Kostenick

Mangala

Engraved by J. Moffat.

and the Pandours flocked to his standard. The Divan or Council of Great Boyards, who, as is usual in cases of interregnum, had, on the Hospodar's decease, taken the reins of government, alarmed at this novelty, successively despatched against him two corps of Arnauts, commanded by members of their assembly; but Captain George, who attended these expeditions, contrived to render them fruitless, by secretly inducing the soldiers to desert. The chiefs returned to Bukorest almost alone, while Theodore marched steadily on, protesting that he was the Sultan's devoted subject, and had no inclination to fight any one, but would defend himself if attacked. The Divan then proposed to have recourse to the Pashas beyond the Danube, but the Russian consul-general objected to such a measure, as being contrary to treaty, unless the consent of his court had been previously obtained. In this dilemma, the Boyards and the Kaimakan (or vicegerent) of Charles Callimachi, whom the Porte had appointed to the vacant principality, attempted to negotiate with Theodore ; the latter rejected their offers, took possession of the public money, and declared that the new prince should not cross the Danube without his permission, nor until the grievances of the people were redressed. Some of his detachments having shown themselves on the roads leading into Transylvania, the nobility of Bukorest was struck with panic terror, and fled in all directions, the spathar and president of the senate, Prince Brancovano, setting the example. Most of the fugitives proceeded towards the Austrian frontier, and were very generally robbed and ill treated by Vladimiresco's troops. The city was left to the guard of the Bimbashee Sava, a Greek of the Archipelago, who, avowing himself friendly to the Hetœria, maintained a strict police, at the head of a thousand Arnaut horse, and provided for the safety of the Mohammedans resi-

dent there, by escorting them to the Danube. After
a sort of previous negotiation with this personage,
Theodore, on the 27th of March, entered Bukorest in
solemn procession, half military, half religious, followed
by upwards of 2000 Pandours, and 200 Servian
cavalry, under the orders of Hadji Prodan, a captain
of that nation ; the remainder of his forces, amounting
probably to as many more, was cantoned in the neighbourhood. Whatever might have been the real sentiments of this artful adventurer at the beginning of his
career, prosperity inspired him with dreams of ambition on his own account, and with hopes of extorting
from the Porte, by a mixture of force and address, the
dignity of Hospodar. Instead of labouring for the
Greeks, as he had sworn to do, he now proposed to
deceive and thwart them. He employed himself at
Bukorest in circulating addresses, calling on the inhabitants to join with him in petitioning the Sultan to
grant them certain reforms. He likewise recruited Servians and Bulgarians, whose banners were blessed with
much ceremony by the priests ; while his Pandours
sold at a very low price to the Jews, the fruits of their
rapine, the costly furs, shawls, and other spoils they
had gathered on their march. Sava kept aloof, retiring
with his Arnauts into the Metropolitan Palace, a large
ruinous building enclosed, and susceptible of defence,
seated on a height overlooking the city. At the moment that these troubles broke out in Wallachia,
Ypsilanti was making at Kishneff his final dispositions
for passing the Pruth, and rendering himself master of
Moldavia. He had already sent to Yassy, as his confidential agent, George Lassani, in order to arrange,
matters for his reception there ; but in the end of
February, he revoked his powers, and granted them to
Constantine Dukas, who had gone to Kishneff to confer
with him, desiring him to return to Yassy, and prepare

every thing for his own speedy arrival. What appears singular, is, that although Prince Michael Souzzo had engaged in the conspiracy some months before, yet Ypsilanti concealed from him his real design, and sent him word that he intended to set out for the Congress of Laybach. On the night of the 5th March, Dukas assembled at his house all the military chiefs who were privy to the plot, and having administered an oath of secrecy, told them that the generalissimo of the Hetœria would arrive next day ; in consequence a party of 200 horse was despatched to meet him on the Pruth. Ypsilanti crossed that river on the 6th at Skulœni, attended by his brothers George and Nicolas, Prince George Cantacuzene, (a colonel of Russian Hulans,) his treasurer George Manos, a Polish officer named Garnofski, and a few servants, in all about ten persons ; with them and his escort of cavalry, he entered Yassy half an hour after sunset, and had a long interview with Michael Souzzo at the house of the Postelnik Jackovacki Rizo. When he went to his lodgings at four o'clock on the morning of the 7th, he summoned the superior of the Convent of Trierarches, who formed with two other persons the Ephoria, or local committee of Hetœrists, and gave him a manifesto to be printed and published in the city ; a rash paper, containing an assurance, in terms that could not be mistaken, that a great power, evidently Russia, was ready to support the Greeks in asserting their just rights. His first proceedings were marked by a want of sound judgment ; he allowed the principal Boyards of Moldavia, who came to wait upon him, to remain two hours in his antechamber, and then received them in a cold and haughty manner ; and he permitted, if he did not order, the massacre in cold blood of fifty Mussulman prisoners, who had surrendered on condition that their lives should be spared. A tragedy of the same kind

was also enacted at Galatz, where Basil Caravia, an
officer of Arnauts, put to death (March 4) about
thirty Turkish traders, and plundered their barks.
Ypsilanti boasted of this disgraceful exploit in an order
of the day, and rewarded its perpetrator with the rank
of general, a promotion that he had reason to repent.
As notwithstanding the patriotic contributions which
had been flowing in for the last five years, his military
chest was poorly furnished, and the three Hetœrist
ephors of Yassy paid only 10,000 ducats, he forced a
rich banker named Paul Andreas, and his adopted sons,
by threats, to give up the bulk of their property,
amounting to 160,000 ducats. This impolitic action
cooled the zeal of many of his partisans ; and several
wealthy individuals, afraid of spoliation, escaped to
Austria.

To propagate the delusion of approaching aid from
Russia, he put in requisition all the horses of the province, and ordered large magazines to be formed ; but
amidst such useless demonstrations, he neglected more
essential measures, and neither imposed a general contribution of money, nor endeavoured to conciliate the
young nobility, to associate them in his enterprise, and
thus to levy a Moldavian army.

On the 9th, he published an order of the day, fixing
the organization of his troops, and dividing them into
two corps, commanded by his brothers, George and
Nicolas ; to the first were attached three Khiliarchs, or
Colonels, with their regiments, or rather skeletons of
regiments, making up together a few hundred men ;
to the second, the Tagmatarch, or General of Division,
Ducas, the Brigadier Orfanos, and the Khiliarch, Basil Varlaam. A subsequent order of the day appointed Cantacuzene Chief of the Staff, and assigned to him
the separate command of the young Greek volunteers,
who came from different parts of Europe, and were

termed Mavrophorites, from their black uniforms, and
caps impressed with a Death's head, and the words,
" Liberty or Death." On the 11th, the colours of the
Hetœria, bearing a phœnix as their emblem, were con-
secrated with great pomp, in the cathedral church of
Yassy, in presence of all the authorities; at the same
time, an oath was taken of fidelity to the cause of
Greece.

After spending a week in the Moldavian capital,
and distributing 9000 piastres among his soldiers,
Ypsilanti quitted it on the 13th March, and advanced
in the direction of Romano; wishing to keep near the
mountains, and avoid the vicinity of the fortress of
Ibrail, where there was a Turkish garrison. He had
no cannon, very little ammunition, and his whole force
amounted only to 800 horsemen, viz. 600 Arnauts,
and 200 Cossacks, raised by Dukas; 75 of the latter
were real Cossacks, deserters from the Russian border,
and the others Moldavians, armed and equipped in the
same fashion. Had he marched briskly forward, he
might have got to Bukorest before Vladimiresko, and
thus secured the resources that large city was capable
of affording; but his dilatory and vacillating movements betrayed an uncertainty of purpose, and want of
resolution. He employed seven days in reaching Fokshan, on the confines of the two principalities, where
he was joined by Caravia and Anastasius of Argyro-
castro, who brought him from Galatz, two six poun-
ders (ship guns,) and 200 men, Albanians, Wallachians,
Bulgarians, and Greeks. Here he named Caravia General of Division, a step that displeased the other officers, and caused heart-burnings amongst them.

Having passed a week in inaction at Fokshan, the
Generalissimo assembled a council of war to deliberate
on future operations. During the discussion, his two
Tagmatarchs, Caravia and Dukas, quarrelled; the first

proposing to go by the hill road to Tergovisht, the second insisting that they should march straight to Bukorest, without allowing the courage of their troops to cool, and before the enemy had recovered from the astonishment produced by their unexpected appearance. Ypsilanti embraced the opinion of Dukas, who, with the advanced guard, marched in two days by Rimnik to Buzeo, an episcopal town of Wallachia. The Prince arrived, with the main body, on the 28th, in a state of absolute disorder; a herd of cattle, seen at a distance, having been mistaken for a Turkish detachment, the soldiers demanded a supply of ammunition; but as the Khiliarch Colocotroni,* in whose charge it was, had already gained the hills, the others followed his example, and came to Buzeo, by the mountain road of Ployeshti. From hence, by a circuitous route, they reached Bukova and Playeshti;† and on the way were reinforced at Menzili, by George, the Olympian, with 200 good horse.

At Playeshti, Ypsilanti lingered near ten days, alleging that he had received private intelligence from Nicolopoulos, a member of the Ephoria of Bukorest, that Vladimiresko meditated treachery against his person; here, likewise, he reviewed his forces, which now exceeded 1200 men, all cavalry. The project of going to Tergovisht was again discussed, and excited fresh disputes among the principal officers, but at length they determined to move directly to Bukorest.

On the 8th of April, the vanguard, under Dukas, took post at Kolentina, a country-house of the Princess Ghika, within a league of that city, and was met by a multitude of people, who, on beholding the flag of the Hetœria, cried out, " Long live the Freedom of Greece

---

* A Peloponnesian, a relation of the celebrated Colocotroni.

† Ployeshti and Playeshti, are two different places, one distant twelve, the other six hours from Bukorest.

and the Generalissimo !" Next day the prince fixed his head-quarters at Kolentina ; and ordered Dukas to occupy one-half of Bukorest, and assume the military government. All the chiefs of Arnauts, with the Bimbashee Sava, the Archbishop, four Boyards of the first, and three of the second class, who had remained in the city, hastened to pay their respects to Ypsilanti ; but Theodore, neither deigning to recognise nor visit him, observed a sullen silence, and shut himself up in the palace of Brankovanka, with 3,000 Pandours, three pieces of cannon, and abundance of ammunition. His former friend and comrade, Dukas, acted the part of mediator, and at the end of six days, Theodore agreed to wait upon the Generalissimo, on condition that Sava should be delivered to him as a hostage; for he felt, or affected to feel, a fear of being assassinated by the latter. When this was complied with, he went, accompanied by the Bishop of Argish, to Colentina ; and Ypsilanti, to conciliate him, ordered a number of Pandours that had been arrested by his patrols, for committing disorders in the town, to be set at liberty. However, the interview would, in fact, have been fatal to Theodore, if the Prince had not restrained the zeal of one of his generals, who wished, with a select body of men, to attack that adventurer at Colentina. Ypsilanti hoped, by fair treatment, to bring him over to his party, and was unwilling to sacrifice Sava. In the conference which took place, the cunning Wallachian thought he discovered that the Generalissimo was unequal to the situation he held ; to prove it more clearly, he, on the following night, sent him intimation to be on his guard, as 4000 Turks were marching to surprise his quarters ; this false information occasioned, as Theodore expected, a great deal of unnecessary bustle and alarm.

Meanwhile, two deputies came to Bukorest, from

Zemnitza, a small town on the Danube, opposite to
Sistov, announcing that a Bulgarian captain, named
Hadsi Christo Panka, had collected there 76 boats,
and 350 soldiers of his own nation, and that all Bulgaria was ready to rise, as soon as a Greek force should
appear. By that time, however, a communication fell
upon Ypsilanti from a different quarter, which dashed
his hopes to the ground, and cured him of any idea of
crossing the Danube, an enterprise that, considering
the strength of the Turks in Bulgaria, must have terminated in the destruction of his army, and the ruin of
the province. The Emperor Alexander, whose protection he had solicited, on learning at Laybach the
course he had pursued, instantly disavowed his conduct in the most explicit terms, erased his name from
the Russian army list, and commanded his diplomatic
agents in Turkey, and elsewhere, to give the utmost
publicity to his sentiments. In consequence, the Russian Consul-general at Yassy proclaimed his sovereign's
disapprobation, on the 9th of April, and next day the
Moldavian Boyards, headed by the Metropolitan, re-
passed in a body to the residence of Prince Michael
Souzzo, and declared that his reign was ended.

The Hospodar, young and inexperienced, had flattered himself with the chimerical project of retaining,
under the shadow of the Hetœria, a dignity to which
the Sultan's will was his only title—and keeping the
Moldavians in subjection, while he threw off his depend-
ence on the Ottoman empire. He now shed tears,
abdicated the government in a spiritless manner, and
withdrew on the 11th, with his family, into Bessarabia.
The senate of Yassy then resolved to send a deputation,
tendering their submission to the Porte ; and by an
edict, ordered the peasants to treat as enemies any of
Ypsilanti's troops who should be found in the principality after a specified day. At Bukorest, the General-

issimo received, through the medium of the Muscovite embassy at Constantinople, letters from the Counts Nesselrode and Capodistria, bitterly upbraiding him for his rash folly and ingratitude to the Emperor, whose name he had compromised ; desiring him to avoid hostilities with the Turks, to retire into the mountains, and from thence make proposals of accommodation to the Sultan. The knowledge of these letters may serve as a clue to the prince's subsequent measures, which would be otherwise inexplicable. Nothing could be more astounding to the Hetœrists than the Emperor's declaration ; most of those who had taken arms, having done so in a confident expectation of Russian support, were now overwhelmed with consternation and despair. Ypsilanti's principal officers, headed by Captain George, immediately waited upon him, requesting to be informed what private instructions or documents he had from the court of St Petersburgh ; but he absolutely declined any explanation on that subject.

On the 15th of April, the day after his conference with Theodore, the prince left Bukorest, and marched to Tergovisht, where he arrived on the 16th. His army then consisted of near 3000 men, with three guns. Sava remained with his troops, to occupy the Wallachian capital. As for Vladimiresko, he posted himself in the monastery of Cotrocheni, a quarter of a league from the city, and surrounded it with entrenchments ; he began also to negotiate with the Pasha of Silistria, who employed Negris (Callimachi's Kaimakan) to correspond with him from Rudshuk.

Ypsilanti, having established his centre at Tergovisht, threw up fieldworks around that place, and, in order to cover his flanks, detached on his right a corps under George the Olympian, to Piteshti, on the road from Bukorest to Hermanstadt, and the division of

Dukas on his left, to Ployeshti, on that leading from
Bukorest to Cronstad. He thus extended his line in a
very injudicious way, for Piteshti is distant eighteen,
and Ployeshti fourteen leagues from Tergovisht. Caravia was appointed general of the ordnance, and
inspector of fortifications. The Prince had previously
issued orders at Fokshan, that the Mavrophorites, or
young Greek volunteers, should be formed into a battalion of infantry, with the appellation of Hieros Lochos,
or sacred band : this was effected at Tergovisht, and
the enthusiastic youths laboured assiduously to perfect
themselves in discipline ; the greater part of them had
just quitted colleges or counting-houses in Russia,
Germany, and Italy.

To supply the want of lead, it was stripped from
the roof of the cathedral, the most ancient in Wallachia.
Endeavours to obtain ammunition from Austria did
not succeed, but 2000 okes of gunpowder, sent from
Cronstad to Vladimiresko, by some Boyards, his friends,
were intercepted, and taken possession of, and some
stores of saltpetre and sulphur discovered in the hills
by Dukas. The ovens of the army were at Ployeshti,
whence it mostly drew its provisions.

From the commencement of the expedition, the Arnauts had given themselves up to plundering, without
shame or scruple, and the country was terribly harassed
by marauding parties, who drove away all the grain
and cattle they could lay their hands on ; much of the
spoil was sold into Transylvania—for the chiefs seemed
intent on enriching themselves, and Ypsilanti gave a
pernicious example, by sequestrating a quantity of
jewels and valuable dresses deposited in the convent of
Marjeneni. It is true, that he was hard pressed for
money to satisfy his troops, since the ephors of Bukorest, after embezzling most of the sums they collected,
had fled with the remainder into the Austrian states ;

and although the Prince assigned no regular pay to his soldiers, he was nevertheless obliged to make distributions of money from time to time. Notwithstanding the forlorn aspect of his affairs, he indulged in vain pomp and frivolous amusements ; he entertained at his head-quarters a company of players, brought from Bukorest ; and he caused a particular staircase to be added to his house at Tergovisht, by which only his brothers, and those bearing the title of Prince, were suffered to enter. He could not yet entirely divest himself of the idea of one day wearing the crown of Greece ; and he was encouraged in it by many parasites, who found too ready access to his presence, while he rarely admitted other persons.

He had never been master of his army, and the Russian disavowal impaired the little authority he before exercised ; the soldiers were wholly under the influence of their immediate chiefs, and these last, divided by private enmities, frequently disregarded the Generalissimo's commands : Captain George, whose noble character drew universal respect, had no certain rank conferred upon him, and was kept at a distance from head-quarters. Of the two Tagmatarchs, Dukas and Caravia, the first was active and intelligent, but turbulent and intriguing, and greatly provoked Ypsilanti, by repeated opposition, and meddling with matters that did not concern him. The second, Caravia, enjoyed more of the Prince's favour, but was generally detested on account of his pride and insolence, by which he drove into open mutiny the bravest Khiliarch in the army, Anastasius of Argyrocastro ; who, after putting to death two soldiers that refused to follow him, retreated with his regiment of 220 men into a convent, and did not submit until he received a pardon, and permission to leave the division of Caravia, and join that

of Dukas. There is reason to think that the Generalissimo was very jealous of his lieutenants; he first
supected Dukas of a design to supplant him, and sought
pretexts to weaken his corps, the finest and strongest
in the army, composed almost entirely of Servians and
Bulgarians; latterly, however, he became apprehensive
of Caravia, and courted the support of Dukas against
him. What could be expected from an army so constituted and so commanded?

Intercepted correspondence put beyond all doubt the
treacherous machinations of Theodore. On the 23d of
April, two couriers, (one a Turk, the other a Wallachian,) that he interchanged with Negris, were taken
at Falashtoka, betwixt Bukorest and Giurgevo, by a
party sent out on purpose; their despatches being
transmitted to Tergovisht, evidently proved that Vladimiresko was treating with the Pasha of Silistria, to
obtain from the Porte the investiture of Wallachia, as
the price of betraying the Hetœrists. Another of his
agents, a certain Doctor Theodosius, was arrested on
his return from Cronstad in Transylvania, whether he
had gone with letters to the fugitive Boyards, pressing
them to write to Constantinople against the Greeks,
and to solicit Theodore's nomination to the Hospodariat; among the Doctor's papers was found a petition
drawn up and signed to that effect. Vladimiresko
complained loudly of the arrest of this emissary, (who
was soon after set at liberty,) and of the seizure of his
ammunition; at the same time, in his letters to
Ypsilanti, he protested his attachment to the Greek
cause, and his eagerness to fight the common enemy.

While the prospect was so gloomy on this side, the
Hetœrists regained their ascendency in Moldavia.
Pentedekas had been despatched into that province
from the camp of Tergovisht on the 23d of April, to

raise money, and equip and forward the volunteers that were constantly arriving. At Yassy, he found the administration in the hands of the Boyards, but having assembled sixty young Greeks, and by the junction of other adherents, augmented his band to near 200 men, he seized the palace, overturned the Divan, and set up a military government, which the cowardly nobility was fain to recognise.

Nearly two months had now elapsed since Ypsilanti crossed the Pruth, and yet the Turks, ever tardy in their movements, had not hitherto made any hostile demonstration. At length, towards the end of April, they prepared to take the field. On the 27th, the Pasha of Silistria reinforced with 2000 men the post of Kalarash on the northern bank of the Danube, ordering them to push forward to Yalomizza, (half way between Silistria and Bukorest,) and to collect provisions, but without injuring the peasants. The troops of the left wing earnestly desired leave to attack them; however, the Prince made difficulties, and only allowed Dukas to send a reconnoitring party of 700 horse towards Yalomizza, strictly commanding them, if they met the enemy, to lay aside their cockades and standards, that they might not appear to belong to his army. He probably adopted so singular a precaution in compliance with the injunctions contained in Count Nesselrode's letter; it was useless for the present, since this reconnoisance fell in with no Turks. On the 12th of May, Yussuf Pasha of Ibrail opened the campaign, by marching out of his fortress, at the head of a strong body of troops, and approaching the town of Galatz, defended by Athanasius of Agrafa,* with a garrison of 200 Greeks, mostly seamen from the Archipelago, who

---

* A mountainous district comprehending the main chain of Pindus, between Epirus, Etolia, and Thessaly.

had abandoned their vessels in order to serve on shore. On the morning of the 13th, the Pasha's vanguard of 2000 Turks, supported by the fire of eight pieces of cannon, attacked Athanasius, posted, with seventy men and one ship-gun, in an old Russian redoubt in front of the town. The Greeks made a desperate resistance, and the action lasted till night, when, having kindled great fires, they retreated ; while their countrymen in Galatz diverted the enemy's attention by repeated volleys of cannon and musketry. Athanasius fell back to a peninsula at the confluence of the Pruth and the Danube, where he found four merchant-ships, and having embarked nine pieces of ordnance, and a quantity of ammunition and provisions, on board rafts and flat-bottomed boats, remounted the former river, and joined Pentedekas at Yassy. The Turks occupying Galatz on the 14th, put to the sword all the inhabitants that remained there, to the number of three or four hundred.

For a long time Ypsilanti would not believe the news of this disaster ; on the contrary, he gave credit to false and flattering reports of revolts in Bulgaria, Servia, and on the Thracian Bosphorus, and even of a Russian corps having entered Galatz. In spite of the Emperor's fulmination, he was clearly labouring under some delusion with regard to Muscovite policy.

The Ottoman troops now began to show themselves on all sides. Captain George surprised a party of sixty of them on the night of the 18th at Rudshevela, (six leagues from Zemnitza,) and either killed or took the whole ; and the scouts and spies brought intelligence that a column of 8,000 Mussulmans, with eighteen pieces of artillery, had advanced from Silistria to Obileshti, only two marches from Bukorest. Yet Ypsilanti was so infatuated, as at that precise moment, (May 22d,) to detach Cantacuzene with 1000 horse into

Moldavia ; he indeed soon repented, and on the 24th sent a counter-order, but it was too late, for Cantacuzene declined to return.

At noon on the 27th, 4000 men, under the Pasha of Silistria's Kihaya, (lieutenant-general,) took possession of Bukorest, without firing a shot, for the Turks had completely gained over both Sava and Vladimiresko. Sava evacuated the city some hours before the Ottoman troops entered it, and fell back upon Tergovisht ; reporting to the Generalissimo, that his fear of Theodore hindered him from offering opposition to the enemy. Vladimiresko remained during the whole day of the 27th in a posture of defence behind his entrenchments at Cotrocheni, and marched off at night in the direction of Little Wallachia ; his intention was to turn the right flank of the Greeks, and cut off their retreat, while the Turks should attack them in front. The Pasha of Silistria, with a second column of the same force as that led by his Kihaya, arrived in person (May 29th) at Bukorest, where he caused his soldiers to observe very strict discipline. The Metropolitan and the Boyards, who had remained in that city, fled before the Mussulmans, taking the route of Transylvania, and spreading alarm through the country. Dukas arrested them on the night of the 27th at Kimpina, on the road to Cronstad, but released them two days after, much to the displeasure of Ypsilanti, who being incensed against them, because they had sanctioned Theodore's project of obtaining the Hospodariat, ordered them to be pursued. They escaped, however, into Austria, but could not save their baggage, which was conveyed to Tergovisht. On the 28th the Prince commanded Sava to take up a position at Vakareshti, a monastery in the midst of woods, two leagues from head-quarters ; at the same time he wrote to Captain George, to watch Theodore's motions, and if possible find a way of accomplishing his destruction. Here it is necessary to state, that the Hetœrists had organized a conspiracy, against that adventurer, in his own army; his principal officers, Hadji Prodan, Make-donski,* and several captains of Pandours, were privy to it, but hitherto they had been unable to strike a blow; for Vladimiresko was exceeding wary, and put to death in a summary manner any of his followers whose fidelity he suspected.

He was approaching Piteshti with his whole corps, and on the 30th reached Goleshti, whence he sent a message to Captain George, desiring permission to cross a bridge over the river Argish, which runs between those two places. The Olympian, who had been reinforced by 400 men under Prince Nicolas, from Kimpolungi (a town in the Carpathians), answered by requesting him to halt for that day, as he intended to pay him a visit next morning. Accordingly he repaired to his quarters on the 31st, attended by fifty of his bravest Arnauts, and when the first compliments were over, demanded that all the captains should be called together, as he had something of importance to communicate in their presence. As soon as they were assembled, George produced a written agreement betwixt himself and Theodore, drawn up in the Wallachian language, signed on the 27th of December, 1820, and witnessed by the secretary of the Russian Consul-general. This deed stipulated, that Vladimir-esko should be faithful to the Hetœria, that he should raise an insurrection in Little Wallachia, for which purpose George was to furnish him with soldiers, but that to lull the suspicions of the Turks, and obviate their immediate interference, it should appear to be directed, not against the Sultan, but the Greek princes,

---

* Makedonski was a Russian of Macedonian origin, and had served as a captain in the Muscovite troops.

and great Boyards; and that, lastly, he should adopt
no measures without George's concurrence, nor punish
any of his adherents without a regular trial. After
reading the paper, article by article, and laying particular stress on the concluding paragraph, George,
turning to the assembly, said, " Is it then to be borne,
that some of you should be daily immolated to his
tyranny ?" Upon this Hadji Prodan, Makedonski, and
many Captains of Pandours, engaged in the plot, exclaimed, " that they would no longer obey so sanguinary a leader, that they gave him up to be judged by
martial law, and desired to serve under the Olympian."
Theodore endeavoured to excite their sympathy, and
was about to draw his sword, but his voice was drowned in the cries, " Away with the wretch !" and George
causing him to be disarmed, and bound by the Arnauts
of his own escort, carried him to Piteshti, whence
Nicolas Ypsilanti conducted him under a strong guard
to Tergovisht. When brought before Prince Alexander, the latter reproached him for his manifold treason. Vladimiresko defended himself on the plea, that
he had always been at heart a true Hetœrist ; that he
abandoned Bukorest because he was afraid of Sava,
and meant, by corresponding with the Turks, to draw
them into a snare. He was justly put to death, (June
the 4th,) but the Prince, instead of having him regularly condemned and executed, suffered Caravia and
Lassani to butcher him in a barbarous manner with
their sabres.

His army joined the division of the Olympian ; it
consisted of 250 Servian and Bulgarian cavalry, 4000
Wallachians, with four pieces of cannon tolerably well
mounted. George kept a portion at Piteshti, and sent
half the Pandours to occupy Dragashan, and other
posts in Little Wallachia.

There is something singular and striking in the ad-

ventures of this Theodore, who, employed as an instrument by the Hetœrists, turned their artifices against
themselves, and converted into reality what they intended merely as a feint. Had it not been for the
daring and able measures of the Olympian, and the disaffection of his own officers, provoked by his too great
severity, he might perhaps have enjoyed for a short
period the title to which he aspired. His character
was compounded of cruelty and duplicity; he was a
man of small stature, and had not yet attained to the
age of forty years. Vladimiresko's fate alarmed Sava,
who, conscious of his guilt, began to think of securing
himself. He, on specious grounds, asked leave from
the Prince to establish his division in the monastery
of Marjeneni, encircled by strong and lofty walls, and
Ypsilanti granted it, persuaded of his loyalty, although
warned against him.* Towards the left of the Greeks,
Dukas, with a party of 70 horse, surprised, on the
night of the 30th, a Turkish advanced piquet of the
same force, in the large forest of Caldiroshani, killed
52, and took 17 prisoners and 44 horses; then being
too weak to guard the distant position of Ployeshti,
retired to Bakoi, three leagues nearer the hills, and on
the 7th June, by the Prince's command, joined the
head-quarters at Tergovisht. Sava, who had already
admitted secretly into Marjeneni two Turkish agas,
received a similar order, but evaded compliance; he
endeavoured in vain to entrap Dukas at his passage,
by proposing an interview in the monastery, attempted
to seize his baggage, and actually carried off a waggon-
load of biscuit.

The Prince's plan was, to concentrate the troops of

* Letters had been intercepted from Sava to Negris, but they contained nothing of consequence, and the circumstance attracted less
notice, as Sava owed his fortune to Callimachi, who had offered to
make him his Tufinejee Bashee.

his left and centre at Tergovisht, to evacuate that place
which it had cost him so much pains to fortify, and
uniting his own divisions to that of George at Piteshti,
to march against a body of two thousand Turks from
Vidin, who were ravaging Little Wallachia ; then to
turn back upon the Pasha of Silistria. But the Pasha,
so far from being disposed to allow him to execute
these manœuvres at his leisure, was preparing to act
on the offensive.

Remaining himself at Bukorest with 2000 men, he
despatched, on the evening of June the 6th, the rest of
his army under his Kihaya, who bivouacked during
the following night in an extensive wood close to the
Greeks, without their being in the least aware of his
approach.

On the morning of the 8th, just as Ypsilanti's vanguard and baggage were moving off the ground towards Piteshti, an alarm was suddenly given, "that
the white turbans were upon them." In fact, three
hundred Ottoman cavalry had attacked the convent of
Nochetto, defended by sixty men of Colocotroni's regiment ; Captain Shahini, who commanded there, repulsed the Turks ; but having quitted the convent as
soon as he found the outlets clear, they returned and
took possession of it. However, Dukas, Colocotroni,
and Orfanos, coming up with reinforcements, and assailing them in front and flank, they fled, leaving
twenty-seven dead behind them. This retreat of theirs
was a feint, in order to allure the Greeks into the forest,
where their main body was concealed ; but a wounded
Turk having communicated to the Christians the
strength and situation of the hostile army, they did
not pursue. Colocotroni and Orfanos halted at Nochetto, while Dukas took up a position in advance,
with eight hundred men ; two hundred dismounted
troopers, under Anastasius of Argyro-Castro, guarded

in the centre a small hillock, protected on three sides
by woods, and in front by a breastwork ; the others
were drawn up on horseback in the plain, to the right
and left.

Caravia, with the guns and sacred battalion, quietly
continued his march in the direction of Piteshti, and
Ypsilanti remained at the monastery of Vakareshti.
Half an hour before sunset, the same Turks that had
previously been engaged showed themselves again,
and another column of above a thousand of their horse,
issued from the forest of Cornichelli ; a sharp skirmish
ensued, and was maintained with advantage by the
insurgents, until the Ottoman infantry and artillery
beginning to appear at the edge of the wood, and Colocotroni and Orfanos declining to support Dukas, under
pretence that the day was too far spent, the Greek
wings gave way. The enemy then pointed their efforts
against the redoubt of Anastasius, who fought like a
lion, and repulsed four consecutive charges of cavalry ;
at length, three pieces of cannon opening their fire upon
his post, his soldiers, intimidated, abandoned it, and
carried their brave Khiliarch along with them to Tergovisht.

The Greeks assert, that the combat of June the 8th,
chiefly remarkable for the numerous blunders they
committed, did not cost them above fifteen killed, and
thirty wounded. The Ottoman cavalry suffered severely from its rash and headstrong method of attack.

Although the loss of Ypsilanti's troops was small,
this affair had, in regard to them, all the consequences
of a disastrous defeat.   On the same night, as soon as
the fire had ceased, the Prince ordered a general retreat
by the road of Piteshti ; the different corps moving
amidst darkness, with haste and confusion, separated,
and some, mistaking the way, experienced much difficulty in fording the river Dimbovizza, swollen by melt-

ed snow, where they lost part of their baggage, and twelve waggons laden with biscuit.

The generals accused and reproached each other; and the disorder of this nocturnal march, coupled with the check of the preceding day, disheartened the soldiers, and produced a pretty considerable desertion amongst them. The Kihaya-bey, on the 9th, occupied Tergovisht, and was there greeted by the traitor Sava, who, having received forty Mussulman hostages, openly went over to the enemy; he had been seen, with an escort of horse, watching from a distance the event of the previous action, and, to delude the Prince as long as possible, he wrote that he would overtake and join him. A detachment of Turks pushed on to Gayeshti, on the high road from Tergovisht to Piteshti, and, threatening to cut off the divisions of Dukas and Caravia, forced them to make a circuit. Had the pursuit been vigorous, there would have been an end of Ypsilanti's army. On the afternoon of the 11th, the Generalissimo reached Piteshti, and rallied there the troops of his left and centre, except those of Orfanos and Colocotroni—who, through a mistake, had gone to Kimpolunghi—and a rearguard of 200 horse, under the Khiliarch Gripari, posted in front of the last named town.

A violent quarrel now broke out betwixt Ypsilanti and Dukas, and gave rise to a very scandalous scene. Its ostensible cause was, the Tagmatarch's refusal to give up, for the common use of the army, a magazine of biscuit he had brought from Ployeshti; but the true reason proceeded from that factious and intriguing spirit, which is the curse of the Greek character. Dissension was at its height among the officers, and even the two younger brothers of the Prince were plotting to undermine his authority; his secretary, Lassani, lies under the imputation of fomenting these misunder-

standings. For the present they were appeased by the
mediation of Captain George ; but Dukas solicited, and
obtained, a short leave of absence. We have stated
that a body of 2000 Turks from Vidin had passed the
Danube, and invaded Little Wallachia ; their general,
the Ayan of Perkofftcha, did not molest the peaceable
peasants, but used every exertion to carry into captivity the families of the absent Pandours. Distributing
1200 of his troops at Craiova, and other places, he
ordered 800 horse to advance to the large village of
Dragashan.

In the beginning of June, the Olympian despatched
half the Wallachian militia to defend their native district, where, not daring to face the enemy in the plain,
they garrisoned several convents and strong posts in
the hills. He afterwards sent thither Hadji Prodan
and Makedonski, with the remaining Pandours, and a
few Arnauts, keeping only a portion of his cavalry at
Piteshti. The Prince now determined to march in
person into that province, according to his former plan
—stimulated also, perhaps, by a desire to get nearer
the Austrian frontier. On the 12th, he received intelligence that the Pandours had, two nights before, surprised the enemy's horses at pasture near Dragashan,
and taken seventy of them, with two prisoners, and
killed five Mussulmans. Learning, moreover, that the
Kihaya-bey and Sava were coming from Tergovisht
to attack him, he broke up the same evening from
Piteshti, and detaching by the way Captain Farmaki,
with 300 soldiers and three guns, to Corte di Argish,
(an ancient monastery, the seat of a bishop,) arrived
next day at Rimnik, a small town on the right bank
of the Olta ; his troops suffered much from heavy and
incessant rain, especially the battalion of infantry, which
had always been distinguished for obedience and discipline.

All the Pandours being now united, under their four generals, Hadji Prodan, Makedonski, Diamantis, and Mikhal Oglou, and Colocotroni and Orfanos coming up from Kimpolunghi, the Prince saw himself at the head of a considerable force. His cavalry, consisting of the Arnauts, the regiment of Cossacks, and a squadron of Hulans raised at Bukorest by the Pole Garnoffski, amounted to upwards of 2500 men; the infantry was composed of the sacred battalion, near 500 strong, and of from 3000 to 4000 Pandours; his artillery of four pieces of cannon, that had belonged to Theodore, served by some Greek seamen.*

He rested three days at Rimnik, while Yorgaki went forward to reconnoitre the enemy's position.

The village of Dragashan, where were posted 800 Turks, commanded by the son of Kara Feiz,† is distant eight leagues from Rimnik, on the high road to Craiova; in front of it, towards Rimnik, runs a ravine, the bed of winter torrents; the Pandours had lined its hither bank, and from behind trees, kept the Ottoman skirmishers in check by the fire of their carabines, and obliged the Mohammedans to cover that side of the village with abbatis. George, with his own and Dukas' cavalry, stationed himself a league in rear of the Wallachians, and began to take measures for surrounding the enemy.

The Generalissimo, on the 17th, advanced five hours' march, and halting in a village, on account of heavy rain, with the Khiliarchies of Orfanos, of Colocotroni, the Cossacks, and Hulans, sent forwards Caravia, at the head of 500 horse, the artillery, and the sacred battalion. Nicolas Ypsilanti had assumed the command

* All the horsemen, except the Cossacks and Hulans, were clothed, armed, and equipped in the Turkish fashion.

† A celebrated chieftain of mountaineers about Giustendil, famous for his warlike and predatory exploits.

of that corps d'elite, and he and Caravia appeared before Dragashan on the 18th.

The Olympian then ordered a part of the Pandours
to turn the enemy during the night, and intercept the
road to Craiova ; and on the morning of the 19th, he
directed Anastasius, with 300 men, to cross a bridge
over the torrent, and post himself on a little eminence,
in the midst of marshy ground. The Turks, apprehensive of being hemmed in on all sides, made a sally
against this party, with 150 of their best horse, but
were repulsed and driven into the village.

As, however, the troops were fatigued, the ground
soaked by rain, extremely wet and muddy ; and as it
was Tuesday, a day reckoned unlucky in the east,
George resolved to defer a general assault until next
morning, and wrote to the Prince to that effect. The
situation of the Ottomans seemed hopeless, and the
Greeks were resting in confident expectation of an easy
victory, when every thing was ruined by the rashness
of Caravia, who, naturally headstrong, and on this occasion drunk, quitted his station in the afternoon, and
suddenly passing the bridge with his cavalry and the
guns, began to cannonade the enemy. Unhappily the
sacred battalion, hurried on by impatient courage, followed his example. In the first moment of alarm, the
Turks thought of evacuating Dragashan, and endeavouring to escape by the marsh; but perceiving that
none of the other Greeks were moving to support Caravia, and that his artillery did no execution, they rapidly mounted their horses, rode out of the village,
and sabre in hand charged the battalion, which attempted in vain to form a square, while Caravia and
his Arnauts fled in a dastardly manner. The four
guns were taken, and the young volunteers, fighting
bravely, but in disorder, were mostly cut to pieces in
a few minutes. Astonished at so unexpected a catas-

trophe, George galloped to the scene of action, accompanied by Anastasius, Mikhal Oglou, Diamantis, some other officers that happened to be with him, and about 100 troopers, and by a vigorous onset, recovered two pieces of cannon, rescued the sacred standard of the Hetœria, and saved a remnant of the unfortunate Hierolochites.   Nevertheless, having lost in the shock 20 of his horsemen, the Mussulmans returning to the attack, and Caravia making no effort to rally his flying troops, George was forced to retire, and the whole army, seized with a panic terror, continued, throughout the night, a confused and precipitate retreat to Rimnik.   In this fatal engagement, where 800 men routed 5000, on the side of the Greeks 400 were slain, seven-eighths of whom belonged to the sacred battalion, the flower of their nation : the victorious Turks, although they lost very few men, did not pursue, being busy in collecting a trophy of heads.

Ypsilanti, who was at the distance of three hours' march in the rear, joined the stream of fugitives, and with them entered Rimnik, where he halted one day, and on the 21st transferred his head-quarters to the monastery of Kosia, four or five leagues higher up the Olta, and nearer the Austrian confines.   There he spent two days, solely occupied in devising means of escape from the provinces on which he had brought so many calamities.

Having communicated his purpose to Captain George, he desired that officer to get rid of all those whose fidelity appeared doubtful, and especially of the Pandours, whom he suspected of a design to seize his person. George accordingly sent Diamantis to the convent of Bistrizza and Mikhal Oglou to that of Pentekadilikia; Makedonski and Hadji Prodan were likewise ordered to march, but refused to obey. After these dispositions, the Olympian, bidding the Prince a last farewell, went

with his own troops to Argish, joined Captain Farmaki, and determined, in concert with him, to prosecute the war in the best manner that circumstances
would allow.

When he was gone, Ypsilanti still fearing treachery,
or at least a forcible detention in Wallachia, adopted
an extraordinary expedient to deceive his followers.
He forged letters from the general commanding in
Transylvania, announcing that the Emperor Francis
had declared war against the Sultan; and that as the
Austrian troops were on the point of invading the
principality, it was necessary they should have a conference together on the border. These letters he caused
to be translated and read in public, at the same time
commanding a solemn service of thanksgiving in the
church of Kosia, and repeated volleys of musketry, in
token of rejoicing: he then declared his resolution of
going to the frontier, desiring his army to remain and
await further orders. On the 23d, the officers, who
saw through these artifices, waited upon him, protesting that they had no idea of detaining his person, and
requesting to know his real intentions. The Albanian
Anastasius added, " that his Highness would do well
to provide for his own safety; and that the troops, accustomed to irregular warfare, could shift for themselves." Reassured by this frank conduct of theirs,
Ypsilanti gave Anastasius some money, and desired
him to reconnoitre the passes, and guard against any
ambuscade from the Pandours of Hadji Prodan and
Makedonski.

Finding the road clear, he proceeded on the 24th to
Kinin (five leagues from Kosia), accompanied by the
Tagmatarch Caravia, six Khiliarchs, and nearly 2000
men, and encamped at half an hour's march from the
frontier. He was obliged to await for three days an
answer from Hermanstad to his application for leave

to enter the Austrian states. During that time, he despatched several corps towards Kimpolunghi, which he
named as a place of general rendezvous, although it
was then actually in possession of the enemy. At
length, permission having arrived, he passed into Transylvania, taking with him his two brothers, Orfanos,
Colocotroni, Lassani, and Garnoffski, and abandoning
about 1000 soldiers (100 of whom were relicts of the
sacred battalion), with a promise that he would send
Orfanos to bring them to him.

However, after two days of fruitless expectation,
most of them, in despair, took the road of Kimpolunghi, or Yassy. The unfortunate Hierolochites, attempting to follow the Prince, were driven back at
first by the guards on the frontier; but such of them
as could by presents of money, or arms, gratify Austrian cupidity, were finally allowed to enter, though in
a most destitute condition, many of them being without shoes, and almost naked.

It was at Hermanstad that the Prince made his secretary, Lassani, draw up that famous order of the day
(antedated from Rimnik), in which, to excuse his own
want of spirit and ability, he loaded his generals, civil
functionaries, and the bulk of his army, with the bit-
terest invectives, accusing them of treachery, insubordination, and cowardice.* This piece produced for a
time in Europe the effect he expected; but it is now
well understood, that, although the conduct of his followers was, in many respects, highly reprehensible, yet
the weight of disgrace which attended the close of his
expedition, ought mainly to be ascribed to his own incapacity. The insurgent troops in Dacia did not begin

---

* It is asserted, with every appearance of truth, that Lassani made
this instrument a vehicle for pouring out his rancour against his private enemies, especially the rival secretaries, Scouffo and Souzzo.

to give proofs of valour and devotion, until they got
rid of the Generalissimo and his prime favourites.

Ypsilanti escaped the Turkish sabres, only to meet
a worse and more inglorious fate ; being arrested by
the Austrian government, and shut up in the castle of
Mongatz, one of the most unhealthy spots in Hungary.
The place of his imprisonment was afterwards changed,
but he lingered in captivity for six years, until his
frame, wasted by confinement and anxiety, was ripe for
dissolution.

SECTION IV.

After the Prince's flight, the victorious Turks had
only to follow up their success, by destroying, in detail,
the scattered remnants of his army. Already an Ottoman detachment had entered Kimpolunghi, driving
before them the rearguard of the Khiliarch Gripari.
Manos, Skouffo, Souzzo, the Tagmatarch Dukas, and
other Hetœrists, who were in that town, retired to the
Austrian confines, where the three first found shelter,
as well as Gripari ; Dukas, and the Khiliarch Basil
Varlaam, collecting some soldiers, marched along the
frontier, but, being closely pressed by the enemy, were
at length obliged to cross it ; however, the Emperor's
officers, after a few days, compelled Dukas to return
into Wallachia.   The Kihaya-bey and Sava occupied
Piteshti, and from thence endeavoured to cut off the
retreat of Captain George, who was proceeding by
byroads towards Moldavia : they overtook and defeated his rearguard, consisting of Sclavonians of Montenegro, killed fifty, and forced as many more to throw
themselves into Transylvania.   Perceiving himself to
be *accule* to the Carpathians, while Sava posted in
front impeded his further progress, the Olympian took

the bold resolution of entering the Austrian states, with 1500 cavalry, traversed a part of Transylvania, and issuing from it near Cronstad, disappointed the Turks and gained Moldavia.

The Kihaya-bey, after George had slipped through his hands, turned his arms against the Pandours of Little Wallachia, and began by attacking the monastery of Bistrizza. Captain Diamantis defended it bravely for two days, and then, deceived by the insidious offers of Sava, capitulated. The Turks instantly sent off himself and his son, bound hand and foot, to Constantinople, and beheaded on the spot twenty Arnauts of his band, but spared three hundred Pandours.

They next besieged, in the convent of Pentekadilikia, Mikhal Oglou, who repulsed their assaults during three days, and finally escaped over the hills, by night, into Transylvania. Makedonski, Hadji Prodan, and Caravia, after wandering about for some time, obtained, by dint of bribes, a refuge in the same country; and all the Pandours yet in arms dispersed and returned to their homes.

Little Wallachia being cleared, the Kihaya-bey went back to Tergovisht, and his first Bimbashee, with Sava, marched to Kimpolunghi, where they learned that Dukas and a Servian Papas,* renowned for his military qualities, were at the head of six hundred men, in a strong post among the mountains, called Pashari. Hastening thither, they, on the 15th July, attacked

---

* This Servian Papas, or priest, was a man of extraordinary prowess, who had carried arms under Czerni George, as well as in Prussia and Austria, and was decorated with an order from each; one the cross of St George. When brought before the Pasha at Bukorest, he behaved in so noble and dignified a manner, that the Turkish general expressed his admiration, and regretted the necessity he was under of sending him to Constantinople.

those chiefs. A furious engagement ensued, and lasted
for two hours ; the Arnauts, covered by rocks, woods,
and two taverns that they had barricaded, making a
great slaughter of the Turkish horsemen, who charged
their position with blind impetuosity : it was not till
all their ammunition was spent, that the Christians
fled beyond the Austrian border. The Mohammedans
pursued, and twice violated the Emperor's neutrality,
by advancing into his dominions in a hostile manner ;
positively demanding that the Greek leaders should be
given up to them : it is even said, that they massacred
several Austrian subjects. From cowardice, or some
equally base motive, the Transylvanian authorities surrendered the Servian Papas, and two of his companions, to certain death. Dukas escaped in disguise to
Bessarabia, and his soldiers, breaking down the barriers
of the Lazaretto, spread themselves over the country.

Having rendered so many considerable services to
the Moslems, Sava expected a reward from the Sultan ;
he met with one, consonant indeed to his deserts, but
not such as he looked for. Being invited to Bukorest
by the Pasha of Silistria, to receive a pelisse of honour,
his head was struck off at the door of the audience
chamber. He had long served in the Ottoman armies,
and owed his fortune to Prince Callimachi, circumstances almost incompatible with sincere attachment to the
Hetœria : the Russian declaration probably decided his
wavering inclinations.

Hostilities were now at an end in Wallachia, but in
the neighbouring principality they lasted somewhat
longer. As we before mentioned, Cantacuzene left
Tergovisht on the 22d of May, intending to go with a
thousand horse to Yassy, by the road of Fokshan.
When, however, he approached that town, it was discovered that two hundred Turks, belonging to the
Pasha of Ibrail's army, were within it, and had en-

trenched themselves, partly in the house of the Ispravnik (or local magistrate), and partly in the convent of St John the Baptist. The Khiliarchs, Contos and Injè, commanding the vanguard, composed of select troops (Servians and Bulgarians), drafted from the division of Dukas, instantly made an attempt to carry the monastery; their soldiers rolling before them large casks, approached its walls, and were preparing to burn the gate, when Cantacuzene sent them an order to draw off and follow him; for, apprehensive lest he should be overtaken by a fresh summons of recall from Ypsilanti, he changed the direction of his march, and entered Moldavia by Odobeshti. The Ottomans, emboldened by the retreat of the assailants, sallied out, fell on their rear, killed seventeen of the best troopers, and wounded ten.

On arriving at Yassy, Cantacuzene had hot disputes with Pentedekas, who would not acknowledge his superior authority; they threatened to proceed to a civil war, but in the end agreed to compromise the matter, Cantacuzene presiding over the military, and Pentedekas the civil department. Yussuf, Pasha of Ibrail, remained long inactive in the vicinity of Galatz, being afraid to engage himself in the woody defiles that conduct to Yassy. It was not till the latter part of June that he penetrated into the interior of Moldavia, where the people, tired of the Hetœrist yoke, received him with great demonstrations of joy. Informed of his approach, Cantacuzene detached most of his cavalry to Romano, and encamped himself at Stinga, on the Pruth, two leagues from Yassy.

The Turks took possession of that city, without opposition, on the 27th, and Pentedekas joining Cantacuzene, they left Stinga and fell back to Skuleni, where they began hastily to throw up entrenchments: while thus employed, Prince Cantacuzene suddenly passed

the Pruth, and, to the utter astonishment of his troops,
entered the Russian Lazaretto. The other chiefs sent
a deputation to their general to ask the reason of his
strange conduct ; he replied that he was afraid of being
assassinated by Pentedekas. To quiet his suspicions,
the deputies on their return obliged Pentedekas to cross
the river, but still Cantacuzene refused to resume his
command, preferring to remain on the safe side of the
Pruth. In spite of this base desertion, and although
retreat was open, the Russians having consented to
admit them, the Greeks, not exceeding in number four
or five hundred, many of them lads from fifteen to
eighteen years of age, swore to fight to the last extremity : as they were prompted merely by a sense of
honour, their gallant bearing on this occasion reminds
us of one of the brightest pages of Hellenic history.
Among their leaders were Athanasius of Agrafa, who
had so well defended Galatz, the Khiliarchs Injè and
Kontos, and some other officers of known valour ;
three pieces of cannon were placed in battery, and the
Ephoria of Yassy sent them from the Russian bank
bread and cartridges.

On the morning of the 29th of June, six or seven
thousand Turks advanced under the Pasha's Kihaya,
extending themselves on three sides of the position of
Skuleni ; the Greeks, horse and foot, boldly went out
to meet them, and for some time skirmished with success. At length the Kihaya ordered a general attack,
which was repulsed with heavy loss ; he then proposed to batter them with his artillery, but as he
could not do so in front, without a risk of throwing
shot into the Russian territory, he demanded permission of the brave and worthy generals Sabancoff and
Imzoff, who replied, that if a single cannon ball lighted
in Bessarabia, they would commence hostilities against
him. He contrived, however, to plant his guns on the

6

brink of the river, in such a manner, as, without violating the neutrality, to enfilade the Greeks, and do
terrible execution amongst them. The Turks then
made a fresh assault, and, after a severe struggle, carried their slight entrenchments sword in hand.

Above three hundred Christians were killed or
drowned, and little more than one-fourth saved themselves by swimming the Pruth. Athanasius, Injè Contos, and all the officers of note, lay dead on the field of
battle. Hardly was this engagement over, when the
Servian general, Mladen,* made his appearance with a
thousand horse, returning from Romano ; had he come
up two hours sooner, the fate of the day might probably
have been very different. Although, on learning the
result of the action at Skuleni, two-thirds of his troops
abandoned him, yet Mladen, the Tufinejee Bashee Vasily,
the Epirote Captain Ghika, and the Servian Sfetko,
resolved to stand an encounter, and posted themselves
on a tongue of land, washed by the Pruth, where it
was impossible for the enemy to cannonade them,
without firing into Bessarabia ; they had one gun with
them, and blocked up the neck of the peninsula by a
barricade of waggons.

That they might not strengthen themselves farther,
the Kihaya-bey ordered an instant attack, but his soldiers were repeatedly driven back, and suffered greatly,
while the Greeks had not more than ten men killed
and wounded. After the combat had ceased, the Russians at midnight sent boats, and brought them over to
their side of the river ; but Mladen refused to embark,
and making his way across the country, with twenty
chosen horsemen, joined Captain George.

This bloody affair was highly honourable to the

---

* A comrade of Czerni George, and general in the service of
Russia.

Greeks, and cost the Turks a considerable number of
their best troops, reckoned commonly at 1300 hors de
combat; much must still be allowed for exaggeration,
yet it is certain their loss was severe. The Russians,
who, during the whole action, had three regiments
drawn up in order of battle on the opposite bank,
cheered by reiterated shouts the courage of their fel-
low-Christians.

Meanwhile the Olympian, retreating from Wallachia,
arrived at Vrantza, a high mountain of Moldavia, whose
sides are clothed with thick forests, and whose summit
contains several villages, accessible by a single path.
From hence, a few days after the battle of Skuleni, he
sent out a detachment, which surprised and cut to pieces
three hundred Turks at Slatina.

Another party, of ninety Greeks, under the Captains
Leecho and Anastasius of Yannina, retired, fighting,
(July 25th,) before a large body of the enemy, to a
monastery on the confines of the Boukovina. Unable
to force them there, the Turks set fire to the building;
but the Greeks, shutting themselves up in the church,
although now reduced to seventy, and surrounded by
flames, held out for six hours. The Ottoman commander was slain, and his soldiers, discouraged by his
death, and dreading the approach of Captain George,
withdrew to a small distance, when the Greeks, rushing out sword in hand, gained the frontier of Boukovina. The action passed in sight of the whole population of Suczava; and the valour of this handful of
men mollified even the Austrian authorities, who gave
them a kind and cordial reception.

The Olympian had, in fact, set out to relieve them,
but hearing on his march that they were already safe,
he took another direction; and though so weak, from
illness, that it was necessary to carry him from place
to place on a litter, he moved about Moldavia, harass-

ing the Mohammedans, beating up their quarters, and destroying their detached corps, until at length they assembled an army of 6000 men, with four fieldpieces, to attack him. He was informed of their preparations by the imperial commissary of the Boukovina, who, actuated either by generous motives, or a desire to rid the Porte of so troublesome a foe, intimated to him that he might, if he thought fit, retire with his troops into Austria. The Olympian, encouraged by letters from Kishneff, assuring him that war was at hand betwixt Russia and Turkey, and inviting him to stay where he was, answered, " that he would not by flight disgrace his native Mount Olympus ; that, knowing how the Germans had treated the Servian Papas and others, he chose to die like a soldier, and thanked the infidels for sparing him the trouble of seeking them." He then, with Captain Farmaki, and an hundred of his companions, established himself in the monastery of Secka, and made the bulk of his forces occupy the passes in front of it. The Turks, however, led by Moldavian guides, turned the position by a mountain road, and appearing suddenly in rear of the Greeks, the latter dispersed with such precipitation, that they did not even give notice of the enemy's march to their friends in Secka. George, unexpectedly surrounded, declined to attempt escape by a postern gate, defended himself for thirty-six hours, and rejected the fallacious proposals of the Ottoman general, who thrice offered him the liberty of departing unmolested. Aware that his situation was hopeless, he called together his followers, and addressed them in a speech worthy of being recorded, as communicated by his secretary, who survived the general slaughter. " Brothers," said he, " in our present circumstances, a glorious death is all we ought to wish for, and I trust there is no one here base enough to regret his life. Let us imitate those true Greeks,

our comrades, whose dead bodies are stretched on the
fields of Dragashan and Skuleni, and whose blood yet
cries for vengeance.   If we die like them, perhaps on
some future day our countrymen will gather up our
bones, and transport them to the classic land of our
forefathers." Having finished this brief and spirited
harangue, he visited the different posts, and saw, with
deep sorrow, that his exhortations were thrown away,
since Farmaki and most of his soldiers were disposed
to treat with the enemy : hereupon he withdrew to a
chamber, where he had deposited the ammunition, and
perceiving that they had begun to open the great gate
of the convent, put up a short prayer, and then setting
fire to the powder, blew himself into the air, with four
of his attendants.   The Turks immediately broke the
capitulation they had granted, decapitated all the soldiers except two, and sent Farmaki in chains to Constantinople, where he shared the fate of those other
prisoners who were brought thither from the principalities, perishing by a public execution.

George the Olympian seems to have been a real
hero, inspired with sincere devotion, sublime courage,
and an enthusiastic love of his country ; averse to intrigue and double dealing, and quiet, modest, and un-
assuming in his deportment ; having formerly served in
the Russian light troops, he wore on his breast the
decoration of St Vladimir, and when he fell was about
forty-five years of age.   With his death, which happened on the 26th August, all resistance ceased in the
Transdanubian provinces ; they returned entirely under the Sultan's dominion, and gradually began to
breathe again, after their recent misfortunes, having
been wasted for above six months by Pandours, Greeks,
and Turks.   Those last, notwithstanding the moderate
conduct of their generals, committed many cruelties ;
and when hostilities had terminated, they for a consi-

derable period continued to oppress the people, by their presence and exactions. It is said that Wallachia alone lost by the war 50,000,000 of piastres, or upwards of a million and a half sterling. Ypsilanti has been universally censured for the way in which he commenced, managed, and concluded his audacious enterprise, neither has any thing been yet offered in his defence, or in alleviation of his errors. On taking a calm retrospective view of the campaign in Dacia, we must confess that his situation was one of great and uncommon difficulty, requiring not only superior talents, but a profound knowledge of mankind, and especially of the nations that he had to deal with ; nature did not give him the first, and he had no opportunity of obtaining the second. In excuse for the rashness which induced him, with such small resources at his disposal, to enter the lists against the Sultan, we may allege, that he appears evidently to have been the tool and dupe of men far more cunning than himself ; these were the Hetœrists of the Grand Arch, and the Apostles, who persuaded him that the Emperor Alexander would countenance his actions, and that as soon as he gave a signal, every province of European Turkey would revolt. But instead of seeing such hopes realized, he from the first moment experienced only disappointment. Theodore's ambiguous carriage, and selfish ambition, opposed an unlooked for obstacle to his success : Russia disavowed and condemned him ; and the Servians, on whose co-operation he relied, remained, under the pacific guidance of Prince Milosh, neutral and tranquil spectators of the war.

When the Autocrat's sentiments were officially communicated to him, he conceived an idea of applying for that monarch's intervention, to enable himself and his followers to emigrate to America. His friends, indeed, dissuaded him from so preposterous a step, but

henceforth he thought merely of a secure retreat, resigning all prospect of victory, allowing events to go
as they would, and giving himself up to convivial plea-
sures, and the natural carelessness of his disposition.
His correspondence, and orders of the day, vague and
contradictory, attest that he never had any fixed plan,
but obeyed momentary and fleeting impulses. The
quarrels, intrigues, and pretensions of those about him,
of his generals, secretaries, and even his own brothers,
were a source of tormenting inquietude ; and he was
more than once heard to declare, that with such men
nothing could be done ; however, in reposing confidence,
and forming attachments, he showed neither steadiness
nor discrimination, sometimes courting one person,
and sometimes another, and neglecting the honest and
heroic Yorgaki, while he caressed a wretch like Caravia, who knew how to flatter him.

Although the organization of his army was defective,
yet as the troops were chiefly drawn from brave and
hardy tribes, and many of them, both officers and
soldiers, were veterans, trained under Czerni George,
and in the service of Russia, it is likely, that if well
commanded, they would have triumphed over the first
efforts of the Turks, and kept possession for a season
of Moldavia and Wallachia : in these woody countries,
even the Pandours might have been very useful. Their
great fault was a propensity to marauding, which they
indulged to a degree that made the peasantry of the
two principalities decidedly hostile to them, and friendly
to the Ottomans.

After all, Ypsilanti's expedition produced a most
important diversion, by exciting fears of Muscovite encroachment, and, in conjunction with Ali Pasha's rebellion, so perplexing and distracting the Porte, that
it had neither means nor leisure to suppress at once
that more formidable insurrection which burst forth in
the continents and islands of Proper Greece.

APPENDIX

TO

BOOK I.—CHAP. I.

No. I.—*Copy of a Memorial addressed to the Grand Arch, translated from the Greek.*

YASSY, $\frac{Jan.\ 20th,}{Feb.\ 1st,}$ 1821, $\frac{O.\ S.}{N.\ S.}$

AUGUST ARCH,

On the 18th of the present month, I was initiated into the Hetœria, by Basil Varlaam ; my having delayed so long is owing to the Apostles, who, knowing that I was in Ali Pasha's service, took me for a Turkish partisan.   In reply to that charge, I content myself with sending you copies of the attestations I received for my services in Russia ; whence you will perceive, that if I spent my money and shed my blood, it was for the liberty of my dear country.   Although I have no clear idea of the intentions of this Society, (the Apostles having purposely kept me in ignorance,) yet I partly comprehend what is to follow, and that the commencement is to be in Moldavia and Wallachia.   On this subject I remark, that those provinces have indeed a great number of inhabitants, but incapable of carrying arms, if we except the people of the mountains, and the Pandours of Little Wallachia ; the nobility is wavering, inconstant, fond of tyranny, and detests the Greeks, because for more than a century they have obeyed princes of that nation.   However, if the Arch employs persons well acquainted with the countries, I am in hopes that our Society will make progress there, and then we need not fear any change in their sentiments.   The noblesse of Wallachia is better inclined to liberty than that of Moldavia.   Such of our nation as are to be found in the two provinces, are mostly Arendashes, accustomed to handle arms, in order to defend themselves against robbers.   The best soldiers are a few Athenians, Acarnanians, Thessalians, Macedonians, Epirotes, Albanians, Bulgarians, and Servians ; their number hardly amounts to four thousand, and they are infected with many vices.   Let it not escape the August Arch, that Russia, the formidable Russia, having regular troops, cavalry, artillery, and every thing requisite for making

war, remained on the defensive in Wallachia for about two years, and
after sufficient preparation of boats and pontoons, passed the Danube
with difficulty and loss ; for it is well known that the banks of that
river are covered with fortresses, which the Turks understand how to
defend.   The Hetœrists whom we have here, affirm that Bulgaria is
organized, and ready to fly to arms at the first signal.   I answer that
such an assertion is not only improbable but absurd.   It is difficult
to establish the Society on a solid footing in the principalities, where
the government and people are of one religion, where the nobles are
perfectly aware of the meaning of the word " liberty," and where the
youth is taught the Greek tongue, and accustomed to see the deeds
of our forefathers represented on the stage : but the unhappy Bulgaria, and the once glorious Macedonia, have lost all light, and are
leavened by four centuries of tyranny.   Would it were otherwise,
and that I might be mistaken ! for if the Servians and Bulgarians
were to unite with us, it would then be expedient to begin in Moldavia and Wallachia.   Peloponnesus, Epirus, Thessaly, Chios, and
other parts of Greece, are becoming more enlightened every day, and
the Sultan's war against Ali Pasha is very advantageous to our design ;
hence I conclude, that the insurrection ought to commence in the
centre of Greece.   The August Arch should appoint Captain George,
the Olympian, a brave man, a good officer, and a true patriot, to command in the principalities ; as he is well acquainted with the enemy
he has to combat, he is the most capable of defending them, even if
he do not succeed in crossing the Danube.   Besides, the Arch ought
to send a person of the country, expert in military affairs, to the said
Olympian, to arm his soldiers properly, and exercise them in small
bodies ; and when it is time to hoist the banner of freedom, let the
Olympian be advertised, to cause soldiers disguised as merchants to
enter the three fortresses of Ibrail, Giurgevo, and Tourno ; then let
him despatch corps of cavalry and infantry to surprise them, which
may easily be done, from the negligence of the Turks, who have not
at each gate a post of above two men.

The Olympian once master of those forts, the enemy will be panic-
struck, the phlegmatic Bulgarians may probably revolt, and the Arch
will be in a situation to derive great advantage from the diversion in
the principalities.   A man of diplomatic talent should be sent, as soon
as the revolution breaks out, to put an end to the power of the reigning princes, form a popular provisional government, flatter the young
Boyards, and choose the members of government from that class.
When this is done, in the space of twenty days a force of twenty
thousand men may be assembled, commanded by young Moldavians
and Wallachians.   Such is the opinion which my poor judgment takes
the liberty of submitting to the August Arch.

No. II.—*Ypsilanti's First Order of the Day, translated from the Greek original.*

The procurator-general and generalissimo of the Greek army, publishes this present order of the day, at the Greek head-quarters of Galata.* $\frac{Feb.\ 25,\ O.S.}{March\ 9,\ N.S.}$ 1821.

The patriot Constantine Dukas is appointed Tagmatarch in the Greek army, and Stratopedarch (general of the day.)

The patriot T. Lassani is appointed our first Aide-de-camp and Khiliarch in the Greek army.

The patriots Basil Theodore, Contos, Colocotroni, Caravia, and Basil Varlaam, are appointed Khiliarchs in the Greek army.

The patriot Alexander Rizos is appointed Ekatontarch (captain), and our Aide-de-camp.

The Greek army is divided into two corps, the first commanded by our dear brother and Stratege (general), George Ypsilanti; the second by our dear brother and Polemarch (lieutenant-general), Nicolas Ypsilanti.

The Greek army is exhorted to reverence and obey the aforesaid, since the slightest instance of disobedience will be punished according to the rigour and known laws of war.

Here, my brave soldiers! I think it necessary to remind you, that obedience to your chiefs, good order and harmony among yourselves, are the only elements that constitute a regular and victorious army; and that by observing them you will be invincible the orderly and obedient conduct you have hitherto shown, suffice to make you rank with the most regular troops in Europe, and afford to our nation the best guarantee for the future. Only one insolent and unworthy person, Nikoltzios,† has dared to disturb our tranquillity. I, therefore, order the Tagmatarch and Stratopedarch Dukas to assemble a council of war, that the offender may be punished according to his crime, and I am sure that justice will preside over the deliberations of that tribunal : the accusation alone is sufficient to cause his removal from my patriotic army. After our forces are mustered, other promotions will be made. The first corps consists of the troops of the Khiliarchs, Basil Theodore, Kontos, and Colocotroni; the second of those of the Tagmatarch Dukas, the Syntagmatarch Orfanos, and the Khi-

---

* A monastery of Yassy.

† This Nikoltzios, a Servian, was instrumental in slaughtering the Turkish prisoners, for which he declared he had the Prince's order; he afterwards killed one of the guards sent to apprehend him. He was sentenced to be shot, but Ypsilanti granted him a pardon.

liarch Basil Varlaam : all the officers must henceforth strictly obey in every thing the chiefs of the corps to which they belong. Those officers who have soldiers detached to different posts out of Yassy, are hereby directed to recall them by Sunday evening.

(Signed)   ALEXANDER YPSILANTI.

No. III.—*Letter of Ypsilanti, (translated from the Greek original,) dated Tergovisht, April 23d, O. S. (May 5, N. S.) 1821.*

I have received your communication of the 22d, and the bag containing the letters carried by Dr Theodosius. You must give out that all your researches were fruitless, and that the robbers have disappeared : you must proceed in this business with great prudence and policy,* not to disgust certain persons. Set the Doctor at liberty, and write me a despatch, with a report of the affair, that when enquiries are made, I may be able to show it at the proper time. Intelligence transmitted yesterday from the Ispravnik of Soultza, brings the following good news: the Kaimakan, with all his Turks, has retired to Vidin, because the Servians have taken up arms against the enemies of our faith. Other news, which I have to-day, but cannot yet give you as official, state that the Russians are preparing to enter Moldavia.

[Postscript in the Prince's own handwriting.]

At Therapia, Arnautkuy, and other places near Constantinople, there has been fighting, and a great slaughter of Turks and Greeks ; the affair of the Servians appears to be quite true. I know not whether this letter will find you. Let your march be conducted with your usual prudence and tenderness towards the poor people. I send you herewith a proclamation addressed to the Wallachians. I kiss your eyes.

(Signed)   ALEXANDER YPSILANTI.

No. IV.—*Letter of Ypsilanti, in his own handwriting, (translated from the Greek original,) dated Tergovisht, May $\frac{11}{23}$, 1821.*

FRIEND AND BROTHER,

I HAVE received your letter of the 10th. All I can say is, that the movement of Cantacuzene is very necessary to bring us cannon,

---

* Dr Theodosius, (Theodore's emissary,) had been arrested by soldiers disguised as robbers, and Ypsilanti pretended to make search for them.

powder, and the brave men that are at Yassy. You can no longer retain your position with the men you have, whom you must keep together, and, if possible, augment. Always have a strong advanced guard. It was said at Bukorest that the Turks had their head-quarters at Ployeshti; this explains the letter of Theodore, who is behaving very ill. I kiss your eyes.

(Signed)   ALEX. YPSILANTI.

No. V.—*Postscript to a letter of Ypsilanti's, in his own handwriting, (translated from the Greek original,) dated Tergovisht, May* $\frac{15,}{27,}$ 1821.

THEODORE was prevented from flying by Hadji Prodan and others, and he remains as before, at Cotrocheni. Sava is coming here, and that seems to me incomprehensible. Send a speedy order of recall to your troops at Buzeo.

(Signed)   ALEXANDER YPSILANTI.

No. VI.—*Extract from a letter of Ypsilanti, (translated from the Greek original), dated Tergovisht, May* 23 (*June 4th*), 1821.

YOU have probably heard that Theodore Vladimiresko was brought here yesterday, without a drop of blood having been spilt; for the present he is in confinement here. We now intend to march forward, wherefore come hither with your troops as quickly as you can, and bring with you the largest possible quantity of provisions. Do not neglect the powder, of which we are in urgent want.

(Signed)   ALEXANDER YPSILANTI.

No. VII.—*Letter of Captain George, (translated from the Greek original,) dated Piteshti, May* 23, (*O. S.*) *June* 4, (*N. S.*) 1821.

I RECEIVED your fraternal letter, and was glad to hear that you enjoyed good health. I observe what you write to me concerning the Sludjar Theodore. Brother, an oath is a weighty matter, and Divine wrath always punishes the violation of it! The just judgments of God (and not we) have punished Theodore, because that sanguinary man dared to shed the blood of his brethren and children (comrades), killing them secretly during the night, as a butcher selects the best sheep for slaughter.

A few days ago, Theodore intended to hang six of his best captains without trial; only one was executed, the others were saved by the intervention of Hadji Prodan and Makedonski. Is not God a just judge? I pray you what could be expected from a man who dared to lay hands on those most attached to him? This I leave to your discernment. Heaven will likewise punish us if we break our oaths, which God forbid! Brother! you know that we strengthened Theodore, and always favoured and protected him. How was it possible for a man who had received so many good offices to be so ungrateful to his benefactor? Here we see again that Heaven is just, and recompenses men according to their deeds; so his own wickedness hath overwhelmed him, and every thing is come to pass in due course. I inform you, moreover, that the Turks at Bukorest are transporting to Turtukay all the provisions which Theodore amassed with much care and pains, and are retiring, because, as it appears, they have intelligence that the Russians have entered Moldavia. I salute you as a brother.

(Signed)   Yorgakis Olympios.

No. VIII.—*Letter of Theodore Vladimiresko.*

Bukorest, 26*th April, O. S.,* 1821.

Yesterday, on the 25th of the present month, twenty waggons, loaded with various articles, taken unjustly from the country by the late Prince Souzzo, were privately sent away by night (escorted by a corporal and two soldiers of the imperial consulate) to Brashova; accompanied also by four Arnauts, but whose Arnauts I know not. Wherefore I fail not to communicate it to you, that you may send men not only to prevent their further progress, but to turn them back, that the country may not be spoiled. I beg you to inform me immediately. I might have sent had I known it in time, but thought it better to apply to you who are nearer. Your brother and servant,

(Signed)   Th. Vladimiresko.

No. IX.—*Extract of a Letter from Count Nesselrode, received by Alexander Ypsilanti at Bukorest.*

Prince,

My august sovereign has commanded me to intimate to you, that he could never have believed you would have been guilty of so foolish an enterprise—above all, at the very time when his Majesty's ambassador to the Ottoman Porte was protecting the interests of your family, and hoped soon to bring the matter to a favourable conclusion, according to the Emperor's wishes—at a moment, too, when the Greek nation was making rapid progress in civilisation. This imprudence of yours will bring on the Greeks great misfortunes. I therefore command you, in the name of the Emperor, my august master, to proceed no farther, but, on the contrary, to disband, if possible, the unhappy men whom you have misled; and if you have any just claims on the Porte, to make them through the medium of Baron Strogonoff, who is furnished with the necessary instructions on that subject. Do not dare to approach his Imperial Majesty's frontier, where as a deserter you cannot be received. I am commanded to state farther, that if my august sovereign had not been perfectly satisfied with the faithful services of your late father, he would, to enhance your punishment, have expelled all your family from his states.

No. X.—*Official Statement of the Amount of Insurgent Forces in the two Principalities of Moldavia and Wallachia, on the 26th of April* 1821.

General-in-Chief Prince Alexander Ypsilanti.

First Corps, commanded by Nicolas Ypsilanti.

Tagmatarchy of Dukas,	1930	
Khiliarchy of Orfanos,	300	
Company of Ghikas,	50	
Do. of Sclavonian guards of the Generalissimo,	60	
Do. of Manos,	150	
Do. of Costas Valtinos,	60	
Do. of Kaloyani,	100	
Cossacks,	200	
		2850

Second Corps, commanded by George Ypsilanti.

Tagmatarchy of Caravia,	350	
Khiliarchy of Colocotroni,	275	
Khiliarchy of Basil Theodore,	350	
Company of Mikhail,	180	
Hulans of Garnoffski,	70	
Guards of Cantacuzene,	50	
		1275
Carry over,		4125

                                   Brought over,   4125

Corps of George the Olympian.

Arnauts, ...   1500
                                                          ——   1500

Corps of Sava.

Arnauts of Sava, ...   800
    Do.   of Delhi Bashee Mikhali,   .   .   120
    Do.   of Gentch Aga,   .   .   .   100
                                                          ——   1020
Sacred battalion, ...   400
                                                          ——   400
In Moldavia, about   300
                                                          ——   300

Corps of Theodore Vladimiresko.

At Bukorest (supposed)   .   .   .   4000
In Little Wallachia (do)   .   .   .   2000
                                                          ——   6000
                                                          ————
                    Total,   .   13,345

The prince had been obliged to alter his plan of organizing the army in divisions, and to cease making promotions, on account of the jealousy and emulation of his officers.

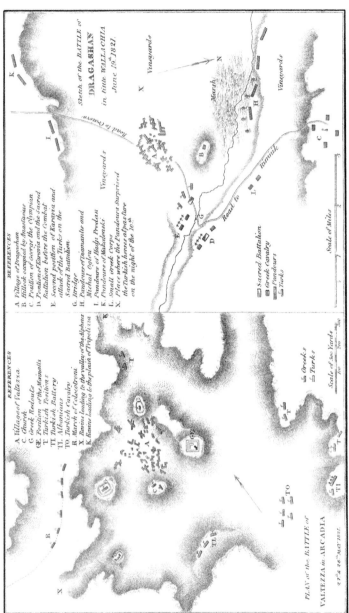

REFERENCES

A. Village of Valtezza
C. Church
G. Greek Redoute
GE. Position of the Manotis
T. Turkish Position s
TI. Turkish Battery
TI. Albanians
TO. Turkish Cavalry
R. March of Colocotroni
X. Ravin leading to the vallies of the Alpheus
K Ravine leading to the plain of Tripolizza

☖ Greek s
☖ Turks

Scale of 300 Yards

PLAN of the BATTLE of
VALTEZZA in ARCADIA
27th & 28th MAY 1821.

Engraved by J. Moffat.

REFERENCES

A. Village of Dragashan
B. Hillock occupied by Anastasius
C. Position of George the Olympian
D. Position of Karavia and the sacred
    Battalion before the Combat
E. Second position of Karavia and
    attack of the Turks on the
    Sacred Battalion
G. bridge
H. Position of Diamante and
    Michal Oglou
I. Pandour of Hadji Prodan
K. Pandours of Makedonski
X. Place where the Pandours surprised
    the Turkish horses at pasture
    on the night of the 16th.

Sketch of the BATTLE of
DRAGASHAN
in little WALLACHIA
JUNE 19. 1821.

Road to Crasow
Road to
Ramnik
Marsh
Vineyards
Vineyards
Vineyards

N

☖ Sacred Battalion
☖ Greek Cavalry
☖ Pandours
☖ Small Greek Corps
☖ Turks

Scale of Miles

CHAPTER II.

Insurrection of Peloponnesus—of the Archipelago—of Northern Greece, and Macedonia.

SECTION I.

WE have, in the foregoing pages, developed the grand causes of the Greek Revolution—religious zeal, patriotism, and national pride, deeply wounded by insult and injury ; on such grounds the Hetœria took its stand.   Two other collateral and subsidiary reasons may be added—the one general, pervading the whole country ; the other peculiar to the Christian notables of Peloponnesus :—1st, The wealth of the Turks, living in luxurious ease amidst their Rayahs, excited the cupidity of the more indigent population, which naturally coveted the lands, treasure, fine houses, arms, and horses of their tyrants ; and, 2d, the Moreote primates, who, under the Ottoman system, derived ample profit from their intermediate station betwixt the government and the people at large, had some private and interested motives for desiring a convulsion.

The principal Mussulmans of that province were split into two factions, headed by Kyamil-bey of Corinth, and Shekh Nejib Effendi, each having in its train a party among the primates ; in the latter class, the families of Londos of Vostizza, and Papayani (now called Delhiyani) of Karitena, made a very conspicuous figure.   Discord lessened the influence formerly enjoyed by these Decurions, and the Turks had begun to exhibit examples of confiscating their fortunes, and even putting them to death—a fate which befell Sotiri Londos and George Delhiyani, the heads of their respective houses.

Had they been prospering, sympathy with their countrymen would hardly have induced them to hazard their lives and goods ; but as, on the contrary, they owed considerable sums to government, a revolution seemed the readiest way of wiping out their accounts, and not only restoring, but strengthening, their ascendency in the districts they inhabited.* A work on the origin of the Hetœria, published about the second year of the war, and written apparently for the purpose of exculpating Count Capodistria from any share in the machinations that brought it on, positively asserts that two Moreote deputies were sent to St Petersburgh and to Kishneff, to ascertain whether the Emperor Alexander was disposed to aid a revolt in Greece ; that one of them, (Kamarina,) having received assurances from the Count that no assistance would be given, was assassinated by the conspirators at Galatz, lest he should divulge the truth ; and that the other (Gousti) produced on his return a supposed ukase, in a different sense, forged by Ypsilanti. The following is the result of enquiries in Peloponnesus touching this subject. The two persons above mentioned did in fact go to Russia to collect information, and were supplied with money at Hydra ; both came back in safety at the beginning of 1821, and were the bearers of a message from the Russian minister, exhorting the Greeks not to stir until the court of St Petersburgh should be embroiled with the Porte. At that period, men's minds were in so feverish a state that moderate advice was thrown away, and there existed a revolutionary spirit not to be allayed by such gentle palliatives.

* Vide Appendix.

In the month of January, Colocotroni, with only three companions, crossed over from Zante to the little port of Koraka, in Elis, and repairing to the mountains of Maina, took up his residence with the Bey, and was there joined by his nephew Nikitas, Anagnostoras, and other outlawed chiefs. While the Peloponnesians were preparing to brave the Sultan, Khourshid Pasha, Vizier of the Morea, a man of reputation and military experience, was ordered to assume the command of the army besieging Yannina : he quitted the peninsula in the first days of January, leading away its best Mohammedan troops, and committing the civil administration to a kaimakan. His departure was immediately followed by troubles, precursors of the coming storm. Although the Moreote Christians had not, like those of Thessaly and Bœotia, suffered from the passage of detachments on their way to Epirus, they yet felt severely the extraordinary taxes that the Ottoman authorities were obliged to impose, in order to meet the expenses of the war waged against Ali Pasha. In the month of February, symptoms of insubordination manifested themselves at Patrass, the most flourishing and populous city of the peninsula of Pelops, the emporium of its trade, and residence of the foreign consuls and merchants ; seated in a delightful plain of the Achaian shore, at the foot of lofty hills, surrounded by a fertile country, and containing 18,000 inhabitants, two-thirds of whom were Greeks.

These, besides putting on an unusual air of assurance, and publicly wearing arms, (a thing forbidden the Rayahs,) began to murmur against the government, and forced the Vayvode, by threats of burning his house, to release one of their citizens arrested for seditious language. Such was the aspect of affairs in Peloponnesus, when Ypsilanti crossed the Pruth ; and thus all circumstances seemed to combine, in order to induce the Greeks to listen more readily to the apostles, who went about the country encouraging them, by passionate discourses and vague promises, to rise against their oppressors. In March, the fermentation was universal among all ranks and descriptions of men, and the first distorted and exaggerated accounts of what was passing beyond the Danube, worked powerfully on the hopes and fears of both Christians and Moslems. Both prepared for hostilities, since the approaching revolution was no longer a secret to any one. The Turks hastily repaired the castle of Patrass, secured their families and effects there, and employed the Greeks (their future besiegers) in dragging up to it heavy ordnance.

The Greeks, on their side, provided arms and ammunition with so much diligence, that by the 25th day of the month there was neither powder nor lead to be purchased in the bazaar of that town. Meanwhile, the principal Ottoman magistrates of the Morea, assembled at Tripolizza, were deliberating what measures it would be proper to take in so alarming a crisis. Turks have but few expedients, and are prone to violence ; accordingly this provincial divan came to a resolution of disarming the Rayahs, and confining as hostages, within the walls of the capital, the leading personages of the Christian persuasion. The kaimakan issued a proclamation, commanding the tributary subjects to deliver up their weapons to the local authorities, ordering the archbishops, bishops, and kojabashees to convene at Tripolizza, and laying on a double capitation tax for the current year. Many of the Greek notables, naturally timid, and trembling at the idea of the perils they were about to undergo, would now fain have retraced their path, had it been still possible ; several of them (including the bishops of Corinth, Arcadia, and Monemvasia) obeyed the summons, and surrendered themselves. On the whole, however, the kaimakan's edict hastened the explosion it was intended to prevent, by compelling the primates to choose between two evils. Germanos, metropolitan of Patrass, after a little apparent hesitation, set out from that city on the night of the 18th of March, accompanied by Andreas Londos, with the avowed purpose of going to Tripolizza. At Kalavryta, (the ancient Cynethus,) a small town of 400 houses, environed by high mountains, and distant fourteen leagues from Patrass, the bishop and primates joined their train, when they proceeded to a place called the Bridge of Katzano, and there turned off from the high road to the capital, pretending to have private information that their lives were in danger ; and, after spending a fortnight in a fallacious correspondence with the Turkish authorities, writing to their friends in other districts, and preparing the minds of the mountaineers, they raised the standard of the cross, and on the second of April (1821) occupied Kalavryta, where the Vayvode, his household, and the Mussulman inhabitants, to the number of 200, capitulated almost without resistance.* Two days afterwards, fighting began at Patrass : the Turks, afraid of being surprised, had spent the previous nights within the fortress ; on the afternoon of the 4th, informed of what had occurred at Kalavryta, by a janissary of the Archbishop's suite, who escaped from thence, they commenced hostilities by setting fire to the house of a primate, named Papadiamandopoulos ; but being attacked by a body of Ionians, that were prepared for the conflict, they fled to the castle, and opened a cannonade against the town. The Greek population immediately rose, and, amidst volleys of musketry, proclaimed with loud shouts the liberty of their country. Fanned by a strong wind,

* This Vayvode was spared, and regained his freedom by an exchange in 1825.

the conflagration spread on all sides ; and, during the horrible confusion of the ensuing night, hundreds of old men, women, and children, sought shelter in the European consulates. On the next day the disorder and the combat continued ; the Greeks having applied fire to the Turkish quarter, a considerable portion of the town fell a prey to the flames ; the castle threw shot and shells at random ; the two parties fought amongst the burning ruins, and massacred each other without mercy : the only prisoners that were spared, owed their lives to fanaticism, some Christian youths being circumcised by the mollahs, and some Turkish boys baptized by the priests. The Mohammedans of Vostizza having already passed over to the northern shore of the gulf, the primates of that place entered Patrass on the sixth, preceded by five Mussulman heads; and soon after the Archbishop Germanos descended into the plain, leading several thousand armed peasants.

A part only of this undisciplined host carried guns ; the rest had slings, clubs, or daggers, attached to the end of long poles : in front marched the clergy and monks, chanting psalms, and promising the crown of martyrdom to those who should fall in battle against the infidels. Germanos bivouacked during the night of the 6th, and on the following morning, conducting his army to the yet burning town, shut up the Turks within the walls of the citadel. The Christian inhabitants welcomed him with great demonstrations of joy ; a crucifix was elevated in the square of St George, the Grecian banners floated from the mosques, and the conflagration that had raged for near three days was at length got under. The archbishop and the other Greek generals, Papadiamandopoulos, Londos, Zaimis, and Sotiri, primates of Patrass, Vostizza, and Kalavryta, set forth a proclamation containing merely these emphatic words,—Peace to the Christians! Respect to the Consuls! Death to the Turks!

They had likewise some communication with the European agents, and engaged to protect the persons and property of foreign subjects. This apparent calm was, however, of short duration; in the evening the fortress, which had ceased firing for a few hours, renewed its cannonade, the flames burst forth afresh, and the Ionian exiles pillaged the warehouses; neither did the Hellenic chiefs possess authority enough to put a stop to such irregular proceedings.

While the commencement of the war was thus signalized by the ruin of a flourishing city, the insurrection gained ground with wonderful rapidity, and from mountain to mountain, and village to village, propagated itself to the furthest corners of Peloponnesus. Every where the peasants flew to arms, and those Turks who resided in the open country, or unfortified towns, were either cut to pieces or forced to fly into strongholds. On the 2d of April the flag of liberty first waved on the confines of Achaia, and on the 9th of that month a Grecian Senate held its sittings at Calamata in Messenia, under the presidency of Petros Mavromichalis, Prince (or Bey) of Maina, who, accompanied by Colocotroni, came down from his rugged domains to place himself at the head of the Revolution. As we shall often have occasion to mention this Laconian chieftain, and his warlike subjects, the present seems a proper opportunity to give an account of them.

Writers of much learned research, but wedded to their own crude opinions, have affirmed that the Mainatts spring from the Sclavonian tribes of the Milengi and Ezerites, who, in the ninth and tenth centuries, dwelt on each side of Mount Taygetus, and, although owning allegiance to the Byzantine Court, were frequently very troublesome to their Greek neigh-

bours. However, the Emperor Constantine Porphy-
rogenete (certainly no incompetent authority) says
expressly in his treatise on the Eastern Empire, that
the people of Maina were of pure Grecian origin, that
they long preserved the rites of paganism, and were
converted to Christianity in the reign of his grand-
father, Basil the Macedonian. In their appearance
there is not the least trace of Sclavonic blood, and their
language is thought to come nearer the ancient Greek
than the dialect of any other canton. We may assert
with confidence that they are lineal descendants of the
Eleuthero Lacones, who, pent up among the crags of
the snowy Taygetus, had little commixture with any
foreign race, while their barren country did not tempt
invasion. No prospect can be more dismal than that
of the Laconian coast about Cape Tænarus (or Matapan ;) stormy waves chafing against huge masses of
rock, bare and pointed mountains separated by deep
chasms, rudely constructed towers surrounded by miserable hamlets, and a squalid and half-naked population—
such are the features of Maina : it is no wonder that
ancient superstition placed there the entrance to Tartarus. Before the revolution it was divided into nine
capitanerias, and three autonomies, ˙or independent
communities, contained above an hundred towns and
villages, and could furnish for its own defence about
eight thousand fighting men, from the age of fifteen to
that of sixty years. Singularly cunning, active, and
hardy—inured to arms, and expert marksmen—ignorant, poor, and rapacious—bigoted to their own church,
but devoid of religious principle, the Mainatts have
for several centuries professed robbery on land and
piracy at ˙sea. The situation of their coast at the
junction of the Egean and Ionian Seas, the extensive
view it commands over the waters, and its numerous
sequestered creeks, adapt it in no common degree to

maritime freebooting, and the poverty and barbarism of the people have in all ages induced them to take advantage of these circumstances.

Sheltered towards the north by Taygetus, their country is almost inaccessible from the land ; and their domestic feuds, which lasted for generations, made every Mainatt a practised warrior. However incredible it may seem, it is nevertheless true, that there were even very lately among the Cacovouliotes, (above Cape Matapan,) individuals who for twenty years had lived immured in their towers, almost deprived of the light of day, and not daring to stir out lest their neighbours should shoot them : their wives brought them bread and cartridges, it being a rule in Maina not to molest a woman. Besides this respect for females, there are two other favourable traits in their character ; they scrupulously observed the rights of hospitality, and in their predatory expeditions rarely committed bloodshed. They paid to the Sultan an annual tribute of 17,000 piastres, and their discord sometimes gave the Pashas of the Morea an opportunity to meddle in their intestine affairs : latterly, they allowed the Porte to nominate from among their captains, a Bash Bogh, or Bey, whose business it was to collect the tribute, and repress piracy. In 1821 that dignity was held by Petros Mavromichalis, (better known both in and out of Greece under the appellation of Petro Bey,) who did not hesitate to declare himself, although one of his sons was a hostage at Constantinople, and another at Tripolizza ; the former, however, effected his escape, and reached Maina in safety. Had the Bey been a man of vigour, endowed with military and political talents, he might have acquired paramount influence in Peloponnesus ; but his disposition was of a softer stamp. The head of a family distinguished for beauty and valour, himself a very handsome man, dignified in

his deportment, mild in his manners, fond of the plea-
sures of the table, lavish in his expenditure, and therefore always pinched for money, Mavromichalis was
fitted by nature rather to indulge in opulent ease than
to take part in a revolutionary tempest. When he
threw off Turkish support, his authority over his own
people became little better than nominal, recognised
merely on account of his inoffensive character and
powerful kindred ; he in appearance indeed commanded
the troops of Maina, but they were generally led into
the field by his brother Kyriakouli, an experienced
soldier, and his eldest son Elias, a high-spirited and
patriotic youth. The present troubles afforded the
Laconian mountaineers a most tempting occasion of
enriching themselves at the expense of friends and
foes : they burst like a torrent into the plains, covered
the roads with flying parties, and plundered both
Christians and Moslems ; however, their aid was so
necessary to the unwarlike Peloponnesians, that they
bore patiently with these depredations, and the primates agreed even to pay the Mainatts at the rate of
fifty piastres a man per month. Amongst the hills,
above the valley of the Eurotas, was settled at Bardounia an Albanian colony, whose establishment in
the peninsula is said to be anterior to the first Turkish
invasion ; they professed the faith of Islam, and were
reckoned even worse robbers than their neighbours of
Maina. The latter directed their first attacks against
them, and, after a short resistance, the Bardouniotes
and the Turks of Mistra abandoned their native seats
and retired to Tripolizza, whose ramparts gave an
asylum to the Mussulman populations scattered
throughout the interior of the Morea.

To the north of the Isthmus, the narrow and rugged territory of Megaris is inhabited by a race of
Christian Albanians, (called in Greece Dervenokho-

riats,) whom the Ottoman government employed to guard the defiles leading into Peloponnesus : this hardy and industrious tribe, possessing five prosperous townships, (Megara, Kondoura, Villia, Pisa, and Pera-khora,) lightly taxed, and subject to the jurisdiction of the commandant of Corinth, was supposed to amount to ten thousand souls, of whom more than two thousand were musketeers. Instigated by an emissary of the Hetœria, they took up arms at Perakhora on the 6th of April, marched to invest the Acrocorinthus, and having in the course of a few days received from Hydra ammunition and ordnance, placed two heavy guns on the peak of Penteskoufia, (to the S. W. of Corinth,) and fired some shots at the impregnable fortress. On the Messenian coast, Gregory, bishop of Modon, assumed the command of the insurgents, and proved himself a bitter enemy to the Moslems. Seized as an hostage, he had address enough to persuade the Vayvode of Modon to send him into the country with twenty soldiers, in order to keep the people quiet. At the first village they came to he escaped, raised the peasants, cut to pieces the janissaries of his escort overcome with wine, and, encamping on the heights above Navarin, blockaded that fort, where, besides the indigenous Turks, those of the town of Arcadia had also shut themselves up with their families.

From Calamata the assembled Greek leaders advanced to the vicinity of Tripolizza, and in a skirmish at Valtezza (April 24th) repulsed a detachment of its garrison ; they then separated, each repairing to his own district, and exerting himself to call out a general levy. Colocotroni, the most popular of the independent chiefs, drew around him a great body of Arcadians, and, after driving the Turks from Leondari and Fanari, entered his native canton of Karitena, and marched to the town of that name, situated in a woody and

romantic country, on the banks of the winding Alpheus,
that washes the base of a rock, round which it is built;
above it was a mouldering Venetian castle, where an
hundred Mussulmans endeavoured to hold out. Destitute
of provisions and water, they must soon have perished,
had not a thousand Ottomans hastened from Tripolizza
to their relief, routed the Greeks by the mere terror of
their approach, and brought off their countrymen. Colocotroni then rallied his followers; and although again
abandoned by them at the sight of danger,* did not
despond, but with what men he could collect, occupied
the defiles betwixt Karitena and Tripolizza, and observed the latter city, whence the Turks made excursions, scoured the plain, and destroyed several Christian villages.

While hostilities were thus prosecuted in every quarter, the insurgents at Patrass met with a severe check,
which in its consequences threatened to be fatal to the
progress of their revolution. We left them blocking up
the citadel, an old fortress in a dilapidated condition,
having been shattered by an earthquake some time before. Want of means, however, and want of skill, rendered it a formidable obstacle to the besiegers, who
opened against it three batteries, mounting six small
iron guns; but this fire made no more impression on
the ramparts than the continual ill-directed discharge
of musketry they kept up, rather from a love of noise
than any prospect of annoying the enemy. The sole
chance they had of reducing the garrison depended on
a scarcity of water, the pipes that conducted it to the
castle having been cut on the first day of the siege.
Incredible confusion prevailed in their tumultuary
army: many, upon reflection, began to repent of the

---

* " I," said Colocotroni, describing these affairs, " having with me
only ten companions, including my horse, sat down in a bush and
wept."

temerity of their enterprise, and the chiefs, to encourage their men, spread the most false and ridiculous reports; such as a Russian declaration of war, Ypsilanti's triumphant march upon Constantinople, and the landing of a corps of Ionians at Gastouni. The Bishop of Kalavryta was detached thither with five hundred followers, under pretence of receiving those auxiliaries, but in reality to oppose the Lalliotes, who from Mount Pholoe carried devastation through Elis, burned Clarenza and a number of villages, and forced the Christian peasantry to evacuate the flat country. Unaccustomed to war, the Turks of Patrass, if left to themselves, could not have held out long; but succour was now at hand. Before these events were known in Epirus, Yussuf Pasha had set out from the Serasker's camp, to take possession of his new government of Negropont. On arriving at Messalonghi, he learned what was passing at Patrass, and immediately went to its relief. Six miles to the east of that town, the entrance of the Corinthian Gulf is formed by the Little Dardanelles, a strait about a mile in width, defended by two castles, crossing their fire, and occupying the promontories formerly termed Rhium and Antirhium. The Greeks might easily have stopped the Pasha, by seizing a pass on the opposite shore, between Messalonghi and the castle of Roumelia; but their leaders, engaged for the first time in military affairs altogether foreign to their previous education and habits of life, managed them as they were wont to do the petty transactions of their communes. While they were disputing who should pay a sum of 500 piastres, requisite for hiring boats to send a party across, Yussuf reached the Little Dardanelles, and transported his troops to the castle of the Morea, whence (so loose was the blockade) he penetrated into the citadel, without difficulty, on the morning of the 15th of April, at the head of three hundred

men, mostly horse. This was Palm Sunday, and the
Christians had prepared to celebrate with pomp a festival ushered in by inauspicious omens; first a smart
shock of an earthquake, then a cannonade announcing
the arrival of Yussuf Pasha, and lastly the appearance
of an Ottoman brig of war, which saluted the fort, and
cast anchor before the town. Consternation fell upon
the insurgents, and the Archbishop and primates, instead of making a stand against an enemy weak in
numbers, retreated with their bands to the hills, thus
abandoning their brethren of Patrass.* The Turks
sallied forth, set fire to the remains of the city, as well
as the suburb of Slatero, and put to the sword or dragged into captivity a multitude of the unfortunate inhabitants, whose flight was not sufficiently rapid. Many
families saved themselves on board forty-two small vessels, (European and Ionian,) which wafted them to the
ports of the Septinsular republic ; and a crowd of helpless and trembling fugitives owed their preservation to
the humanity of the French consul, who sheltered them
in his house, and embarked them during the gloom of
successive nights, in boats sent on purpose from Zante.
The Mussulmans obtained a rich booty, and for several
days the Pasha and his troops amused themselves at
their leisure in impaling or beheading prisoners, and
circumcising Christian children. On the 24th, a corvette and transport brought five hundred soldiers from

* The archbishop and primates attempted to excuse their cowardice, by accusing the English consul of collusion with the Turks, and
publishing a protest against him. That gentleman was hostile to the
Greek cause, and we shall not undertake to be his advocate ; but the
idea of a single pacific individual's introducing a body of troops into
a fortress blockaded by five or six thousand men, is so absurd, that it
needs no refutation. Several of the citizens of Patrass hastily buried
their money just before the sack commenced ; one person was so fortunate as to find again (in 1829) a copper vase, filled with treasure,
that he had hid in a corner of his house.

Prevesa, and these were followed by a body of Albanians, detached by land from the army before Yannina,
under the command of Ahmed Bey, Kihaya of Mehemet, the new titular Pasha of the Morea.

The Ottoman general showed no inclination to push
his success by pursuing the mountaineers, who hardly
lost a man in their retreat ; the Archbishop Germanos
fixed his head-quarters at Nezero, a village distant
four leagues from Kalavryta, and the nightly glare of
watch-fires illumining Mount Panachaicus, warned the
Mohammedans that they would soon have to sustain a
fresh attack.   Nevertheless the Pasha judged it expedient to employ a part of his disposable force in sup-
pressing the revolt in the interior, and therefore dispatched Ahmed Kihaya and an Albanian chief, named
Elmaz Bey, with near three thousand men, ordering them to march along the coast as far as Corinth,
and then make their way by Argos to Tripolizza.
Scarcely were they gone, when the Greeks, descending
from the heights, resumed the offensive, and on the
evening of May the 2d, by a sudden assault, entered
the ruins of Patrass, but did not attempt to maintain
themselves there ; continual skirmishes were fought in
the plain, and the insurgents wasted with fire the farms
belonging to Mussulmans, with which it was studded,
while the latter, to avenge themselves, burned the
Greek houses yet standing in the town, each party labouring to destroy the others' property.   The Greeks
not only intercepted the supplies coming from the castle
of the Morea for the use of the garrison, but frequently
pushed their patrols to the glacis of the citadel, until
Yussuf Pasha, having received reinforcements from
Roumelia, obliged them to retrograde to the hills ; they,
however, soon advanced again, and on the 30th of May,
after a long and desultory engagement, drove the Turks
and Albanians under the protection of their batteries.

Such were the events in Achaia during the months of April and May. The Kihaya-bey, a Tartar by birth, brave and active, vented his fury on Vostizza (the ancient Œgium), which, with its rich and beautiful environs, was peopled by 6,000 Greeks ; the inhabitants had fled, but their dwellings were pillaged and laid in ashes. On the 5th of May he reached Corinth, and found the siege of its citadel already raised, the Megarians having dispersed at his approach, and left behind their artillery, consisting of two battering guns and two brass fieldpieces. Several Greek hostages, (and among them one of the brothers Notaras,) imprisoned in the Acrocorinthus, were, by order of the Turkish general, led forth and beheaded ; their blood tinged the threshold of his residence, and their bones were long allowed to bleach in the court. After storing in the Acrocorinthus the harvests of the surrounding country, and throwing into it a party of Albanians, Ahmed Bey proceeded towards Argos, and sent a message to the primates, requiring a supply of bread, and promising on that condition to abstain from violence. The Argives, reinforced by some islanders under a Spezziote captain, (son to Bobolina,) stood on their defence, and answering that they had only powder and ball at his service, posted themselves behind a wall built to restrain the inundations of the Inachus, while their families, desirous of witnessing the novel spectacle of a battle, covered the adjacent hill of Phoroneus. This overweening confidence was very ill-founded ; for the Kihaya assailing them in three columns, the cavalry on the wings, and his infantry in the centre, they fled after a single discharge. Seven hundred Greeks were killed, fifteen hundred women taken, and Bobolina's son, fighting bravely to the last, was slain by two Ghegs. The Turks, having sacked and burned Argos, sat down before the lofty but ruinous citadel of Larissa, and a solid monastery beneath it, where a portion of the Argives had shut themselves up.

Ahmed Bey brought a cannon from Napoli, and battered the convent, which capitulated : those in Larissa being in want of food and water, escaped in the night-time to the neighbouring mountains. As the Kihaya has been much calumniated, it is due to the memory of a brave soldier to state, that he faithfully executed the capitulation, and behaved with the utmost humanity towards his captives of every class, even setting the females at liberty. Informed that he was at Argos, the Mussulmans of Tripolizza went there to meet him, and having formed a junction with his force (May the 15th), the whole body marched together without further impediment to the capital of the Morea. His arrival in the heart of Peloponnesus with a corps of veteran troops, and his vigorous character, alarmed the insurgents of Arcadia and Laconia, as it was commonly rumoured amongst them, that, including the garrison of Tripolizza, Ahmed Bey had under his orders at least 14,000 armed Turks. The Greek leaders, holding a council of war at Leondari, to consider the best means of resisting him, the majority showed an unwillingness to risk an action ; but Anagnostoras emitting a bolder opinion, and representing that by such timidity they would expose the whole country to devastation, it was finally resolved to take up a position at Valtezza, a village three hours' march from Tripolizza, to the south-west of that city, on a very elevated site, amidst the hills of Mœnalion. Accordingly, the Beyzadè Elias (son to the Prince of Maina), his uncle Kyriakouli, Anagnostoras, and Captain Kefalas, entrenched themselves, with 700 men, on four rocky mamelons overlooking the village, while Colocotroni, Coliopoulo, and other chiefs, remained in the higher mountains, ready to support them. The

Kihaya-bey issued out of Tripolizza, on the morning of May 27th, at the head of about 5000 soldiers, divided his army into three columns, and advancing towards Valtezza, by as many different ravines (himself leading the cavalry), almost surrounded the Greeks, constructed redoubts* below, and opposite to theirs, and placed in battery three pieces of cannon, of large calibre. On the preceding evening his Albanians had executed military dances in the streets of Tripolizza, and he entertained confident hopes of victory, even should he not succeed in storming the position; for the fountains at Valtezza are far from the village, and the Greeks had a stock of water in casks only sufficient for twenty-four hours' consumption. He commenced a canonnade, but his balls passing over the heads of the enemy, fell among his own troops on the other side; and the Albanians were repulsed in three successive assaults upon the village, by a party posted in its church: at the same time Colocotroni suddenly came down, with 1500 men, and attacked the right flank of the Turks. Thus intermingled, on ground where the Ottoman cavalry could not act, both parties kept up their fire till night: each expected that the foe would retire under cover of darkness; but daylight of the 28th found them still in presence. The engagement was then renewed, and lasted five hours, when the Kihaya gave a signal of retreat; induced to that step, as well by the fatigue of his troops, as the unexpected appearance of Nikitas, who, returning by a forced march from Argos,† with 800 followers, was seen

---

* Redoubts, or (as they are called) Tambourias, are indispensable in Oriental warfare, the infantry having neither discipline, nor bayonets; they are constructed of loose stones, or earth, with a shallow ditch, invariably on the inside: the parapet is made thick enough to resist musketry, and the soldiers fire, kneeling, through loop-holes.

† He had gone with 200 men to get lead from the roof of a mosque,

crossing the plain, and threatening to intercept the
road to Tripolizza. As is generally the case in irregular armies, the retreat soon degenerated into a total
rout ; the Kihaya-bey lost his horse, and the Greeks,
vigorously pursuing, took two pieces of cannon, and
raised at Valtezza a trophy of near 400 Mohammedan
heads. The insurgents ridiculously diminished (as, indeed, they never failed to do,) the number of their killed and wounded ; but it does not seem to have really
exceeded 150 men put hors-de-combat.* This affair,
graced by the conquerors with the pompous title of
Battle of Valtezza, was remarkable for the moral effect it produced, exalting the courage of the Greeks, as
much as it depressed that of their enemies : it certainly decided the campaign in Peloponnesus, and, perhaps,
even the fate of the revolution, for, had it been lost,
the consequences might have been as disastrous in the
southern provinces, as those of the defeat of Dragashan
were in the northern. Three days after the victory,
Doliana gave, on the 31st, the complement of Valtezza. Ahmed Bey, anxious to repair his late overthrow, took the field again, with 2000 or 3000 men,
and some artillery. Moving upon the village of Doliana, at the edge of the plain, he there accidentally fell
in with Nikitas, who having about him at the moment
no more than 96 soldiers, and 30 armed peasants of
the hamlet, barricaded them in thirteen houses, and for
eleven hours withstood the reiterated attacks of the
Turks ; at length, Yatrako of Mistra, coming up with
a reinforcement of 700 men, the Kihaya retired, having
lost 200 of his best troops, and left behind him two
small fieldpieces, (the same which he captured at Co-

and on his return was joined by 400 Tzakonians, and other small
bands.

* The single corps of Kanellos Delhiyani had nine slain, and
twenty-three wounded.

rinth,) a part of his baggage, and 16 prisoners. The combat of Doliana laid the foundation of that celebrity which the brave and simple-minded Nikitas continued long to enjoy: son to a captain of freebooters, slain some years before by the Moslems of Monemvasia, he was bred to arms in the service of England. Proud of triumphs more brilliant than they had ventured to hope for, the Peloponnesians marched forwards, and in the beginning of the ensuing month, pitched their camp on the rocky heights of Trikorpha, a branch of the Mœnalian chain, within sight of Tripolizza. The senate of Calamata, now transferred to the monastery of Kaltezzi, promulgated an act, dated the 7th of June, appointing a committee to administer the affairs of the peninsula until the reduction of its capital. Petro Bey was named President and Commander-in-Chief, and the other six members were, Theodoret Bishop of Vresthenes, Sotiri Karalampi of Kalavryta, Athanasius Kanakaris of Patrass, Anagnosti Delhiyani of Karitena, Theokaris Rendi of Corinth, and Nicholas Ponivopoulos of Pyrgos.

SECTION II.

SCARCELY had the Greeks of Peloponnesus burst their fetters, when, ere the lapse of a month, those of the Archipelago followed their example. Here we may pause for an instant, to reflect upon the actual condition of the islands, and the means they possessed of resisting the maritime force of the Turkish empire: three of them particularly deserve this attention, since they gave the impulse to the rest ; for had those three remained quiet, there would have been no movement in the Archipelago. How great would have been the astonishment of an ancient Greek, could some oracle have foretold to him, that the naked and desert rocks of Aperopia, Tiparenus, and Psyra,* would one day assert with their fleets the liberty of Hellas, like Athens and Egina, during the Persian war! They were colonized in the foregoing century by some poor families from Peloponnesus and Ionia, who, at first earning a scanty subsistence as boatmen and fishermen, became by degrees seamen and merchants. Having obtained from the Byzantine admiralty an exemption from the presence of Turkish magistrates, they managed their own internal concerns in as tumultuous a way as that of the old Grecian republics, and, like them, were afflicted by family feuds and civil broils ;† but this tinge of anarchy kept alive the active and bustling spirit of the people, and in the midst of despotism and slavery familiarized them with ideas of independence. They were only constrained to pay a moderate tribute, and to furnish to the Sultan's navy, in common with the other isles, a contingent of sailors, who, being esteemed far the best, had the privilege of serving on board the three-deckers, and those ships that bore an admiral's flag. The Hydriote quota usually amounted to 250 men, and it did not cost the community much less than 20,000 dollars annually. The recent wars in Europe unfolded the finest possible field to their speculative dispositions ; they carried grain to every quarter where the demands were most urgent, and the prices highest, frequently eluding the vigilance of blockading squadrons, and reaping enormous profit : thus a couple of voyages sometimes doubled their capitals, and they often performed seven or eight in the course of a year.

---

* The ancient appellations of Hydra, Spezzia, and Psarra.

† Spezzia was so much disturbed, a short time previous to the revolution, that the Ephors requested the Capitan Pasha to send them a Tchiaush, whose presence might assist them in maintaining order.

Their mariners, inured to the sea from childhood, naturally robust, and extremely agile, were individually excellent; but they possessed little nautical science; and the system of giving to each of the crew a share in the cargo, although it answered well in trade, was a fatal bar to the introduction of discipline or subordination. A momentary glance at their towns sufficiently attested their prosperity. Hydra, built on a sterile rock, which does not offer at any season the least trace of vegetation, is one of the best cities in the Levant, and infinitely superior to any other in Greece: the houses are all constructed of white stone; and those of the primates, erected at an immense expense, floored with costly marbles, and splendidly furnished, might pass for palaces even in the capitals of Italy. Before the revolution poverty was unknown, all classes being comfortably lodged, clothed, and fed. Its port, however, is very deficient, being only a deep and narrow creek, where its shipping was most inconveniently crowded. The island is about five leagues in length, and two in breadth, situated directly opposite to the eastern extremity of Argolis, whence it is separated by a strait three or four miles wide: its position is strong, owing to the difficulty of landing, the asperity of the soil, and a total want of fresh water, except in the cisterns of the town itself. Its inhabitants at that epoch exceeded 20,000, of whom 4000 were able-bodied seamen.

Spezzia, twelve miles to the west of the former, is lower, less stony, and not quite destitute of trees and verdure; its haven also is better, and the narrow channel that divides it from the mainland, forms a commodious roadstead: but, on the other hand, it is incapable of defence, being every where easy of access. The town is an epitome of Hydra, inferior however in its buildings, and containing 8000 people. Psarra, likewise a

barren islet, indebted chiefly for its wealth to the
employment afforded its marine by the merchants of
the industrious and polished Chios, lies at a distance of
five leagues from the north-west point of the latter; its
population, reckoned at 6000 souls when the war began, was afterwards vastly augmented by refugees from
Asia Minor. The Hydriotes and Spezziotes are of
genuine Albanian race, rude, boisterous, unlettered,
addicted to intemperance, and, with few exceptions,
uncivilized: they are bigoted, and have an aversion
to strangers. The Psarrians, Asiatic Greeks, although
eminent among their countrymen for spirit and enterprise, are of a more humane, sprightly, and pliable
temper.

We need not minutely specify the other islands:
some of them boast of fertility, but they are in large
proportion arid rocks, refusing the first necessaries of
life to their indigent natives. Most of them in the
European division were free from any admixture of
Turks, and subjected to a much milder regime than
the provinces on the continent. It may therefore
excite surprise that the islanders so readily engaged in
the insurrection; we can, however, assign several reasons for the line of conduct they pursued. The people
hated the haughty Moslems, and desired to raise their
own church on the ruins of Islamism; the sailors promised themselves a rich harvest of pay and plunder;
and the opulent capitalists saw with disquietude that
the Ottoman Admiralty had begun to squeeze great
sums, by evoking their lawsuits to its own tribunal:
neither was the example likely to be lost on future
Capitan Pashas. Before the end of 1820, the most
influential primates entered into the Hetœria, without
reflecting that a revolt against Turkey would at once
annihilate their trade, and throw on their shoulders the
charge of guiding and feeding a turbulent population,

no light task, especially at Hydra, where there reigned
extremely democratic principles. The maritime strength
of that island, of Spezzia, and of Psarra,* was considerable in number of vessels and seamen, though the
former were not of a kind well calculated for war :
they could without difficulty fit out an hundred sail of
ships, brigs, and schooners, armed with from twelve to
twenty-four guns each, and manned by 7000 stout and
able sailors. Spezzia first hoisted the independent
flag, (April the 9th,) and Psarra immediately afterwards did the same ; but the Primates of Hydra hesitated, and seemed reluctant to take a decisive step :
they even, on the 16th, sent off towards the Dardanelles their contingent of seamen, who, being detained
about Skiathos by contrary winds, were recalled from
thence, when their isle declared itself.   The nautical
mob did not approve the caution of their magistrates,
and a leader suited to their taste quickly presented
himself in the person of Captain Antoni Œconomos ;
actuated by ambition, as well as a private grudge at
the Archons, he stirred up the populace, headed the
malecontents, and for forty days governed Hydra.   As
the suspension of commercial speculations had occasioned distress to the unemployed mariners, he began
by forcing the wealthy citizens to disburse a sum of
1,200,000 piastres, (then about L.40,000 Sterling,)

---

* Pouqueville asserts, that the marine of Hydra counted in 1813
120 vessels of the mean bulk of 375 tons, carrying 2400 pieces
of cannon, and manned by 5400 sailors ; in 1816 they had 40
ships of from 500 to 600 tons burden, built in their own yards.
Spezzia possessed 60 vessels of the mean bulk of 325 tons, and
2700 seamen.   Psarra had also 60 sail of greater burden, their
mean bulk being 425 tons, but with smaller crews and fewer guns ;
their sailors amounted to 1800.   Of these 10,000 mariners, one-third
at least was recruited from other points of the Archipelago.   After
the peace of Paris, their commerce declined and their shipping
decreased.

which was shared out to the lower orders, and he subsequently obliged the municipality to publish a declaration, (on the 28th of April,) announcing its adherence to the cause of liberty.   Having thus, however
unwillingly, plucked off the mask, the Primates exerted
themselves in equipping a squadron, and conferred the
rank of Navarch on Jakomaki Tombazi, one of the
most respectable members of their own body, a man of
information, of known probity, and of a gentle and
conciliatory disposition. He set sail on the 3d of May,
with eleven Hydriote and seven Spezziote vessels,
having affixed to his mainmast an address to the people
of the Egean Sea, inviting them to rally round the
national standard; an address that was received with
enthusiasm in every quarter of the Archipelago, where
the Turks were not numerous enough to restrain popular feeling.   He first touched at Tinos, the richest and
most beautiful of the Cyclades, fourteen leagues in
length, and containing 16,000 inhabitants.   The majority of them belongs to the Greek church ; but there
is also a considerable number of Roman Catholics
descended from the Latins, who usurped the Eastern
Empire ; these last live apart in thirty-two out of the
sixty-five villages existing on the island.   In an interview that he held on the 4th at Port St Nicholas with
the bishop and principal men, Tombazi learned that
they had proclaimed their independence two days before. A proposal was made to the Latins to accede to
the new order of things, but they declined compromising themselves with the Porte ; indeed there subsisted
between the two sects an inveterate animosity.   While
the squadron rode at anchor here, intelligence arrived
of the Patriarch's execution, and the massacres at Constantinople ; news, which inflamed to such a pitch the
passions of the Greek seamen, that they would no
longer hear of giving quarter to the enemy.   It was at

Port St Nicholas that the insurgents had to consider
for the first time the rights of neutrals. A Spezziote
captain having detained an Austrian schooner from
Smyrna with Turkish passengers on board, the vessel
was, upon deliberation, restored, and the freight paid
to the Imperial consul; for in this campaign they
behaved with moderation, and avoided any cause of
offence. On the 6th, Tombazi anchored at Psarra, in
order to concert with the Tetrarchs* of that place measures for revolutionizing Chios, an object specially
prescribed in his secret instructions. This project was
not very agreeable to the Psariotes, who nevertheless
reinforced him with ten sail, and sent to Scio emissaries charged to distribute a proclamation from the
municipality of Hydra. The Turks, however, having
already secured as hostages the Sciote Primates, and
the peasantry appearing lukewarm, the plan was given
up; and Tombazi, after alarming the coast of Asia,
and detaching cruisers in various directions, steered
homewards, and re-entered Hydra on the night of the
21st. The success of the Greek marine in this its first
expedition, was not confined to merely spreading the
insurrection throughout the Archipelago: a swarm of
swift armed ships swept the sea from the Hellespont
to the waters of Crete and Cyprus; captured every
Ottoman trader they met with, and put to the sword,
or flung overboard, the Mohammedan crews and passengers, for the contest already assumed a character of
terrible ferocity. It would be vain to deny that they
were guilty of shocking barbarities: at the little island
of Castel Rosso, on the Karamian shore, they butchered
in cold blood several beautiful Turkish females, and a
great number of defenceless pilgrims, (mostly old men,)

* Psarra was an oligarchy, governed by four Archons, each of whom
had in his custody one quarter of the public seal.

who, returning from Mecka, fell into their power
off Cyprus, were slain without mercy, because they
would not renounce their faith. Some rich prizes
rewarded the vigilance of the cruisers, particularly on
the 10th of May, when two Hydriotes took a vessel
bound to Alexandria, with a large quantity of plate
and jewels. The booty thus acquired heightened the
ardour of the sailors ; but as soon as the existence of
hostilities was known in the distant provinces, the Moslems ceased to navigate. About the same period, two
or three small squadrons, chiefly fitted out from Spezzia,
went to observe the coasts of Peloponnesus : Bobolina,
a wealthy widow of that island, whose husband had
been put to death at Constantinople, and whose eldest
son was killed at the action of Argos, undertook to
blockade the Argolic Gulf at her own expense, and not
only equipped two vessels from her private fortune,
but went on board and commanded them. Five sail of
Spezziotes, learning on their way to Monemvasia that
an Ottoman corvette and brig of war, weakly manned,
and proceeding from Constantinople to Prevesa, were
in the harbour of Milo, hastened thither, and on the
7th of May surprised the corvette, and carried, by
boarding, the brig, which attempted to resist. They
captured on this occasion a field-train of an hundred
brass cannon, and 10,000 quintals of powder, a valuable acquisition had they known how to profit by it ;
but instead of converting it to the public service, they
sold the artillery, divided among themselves the stores
and cordage, and consummated their work of fatuity,
by sinking their prizes in the port of Spezzia, (to its
great detriment,) as nobody would be at the trouble and
expense of fitting them out again. The 23d day of the
same month was marked by a fresh local revolution at
Hydra, which overthrew the influence of Captain Antoni ; that demagogue had rendered himself insupport-

able to the better class of citizens by his insolence and
presumption ; he monopolized all authority, and insisted upon appointing officers of his own faction to
command the Hydriote ships. The Primates, therefore, availing themselves of popular inconstancy, organized a conspiracy against him, and under the direction
of Emanuel Tombazi, brother to the admiral, attacked
him both by land and water, overpowered and took
him prisoner. He was incarcerated in a monastery of
the Morea; but about two months after, having escaped
from thence with a design of creating new troubles in
Hydra, was waylaid, and slain.

SECTION III.

In order fully to comprehend the developement of
the Revolution in Northern Greece, it is necessary to
take a retrospective view of the state of Epirus, where
we left Ali Pasha shut up in his fortress, and the Souliotes waging from their native hills an active partisan
warfare on the flanks and rear of the besieging army.
The wily tyrant evaded as long as possible fulfilling the
terms of the treaty he had concluded with them, by
delivering into their hands the Castle of Kiafa, for he
still flattered himself, that multiplied embarrassments
would induce the Sultan to grant him an accommodation. It is certain, indeed, that if that monarch had been
capable of sacrificing his resentment, Ali would have
been the fittest instrument for crushing the Greeks.
The Serasker Khourshid, arriving at the camp before
Yannina on the 3d day of March, set on foot a double
negotiation ; one with the rebel, and another with the
Souliotes, two of whose captains, Lambros and Zervas,
entered Prevesa, and assisted at conferences opened on
the 15th. However, the pretensions of all parties be-

ing too much at variance, while probably none were sincere, this attempt at pacification came to nothing, and on the 26th the Souliote deputies left the place. By feigning an inclination to treat with the Turks, they derived nevertheless an essential advantage ; since Ali, quickly perceiving, that for him there remained no hopes of an amicable arrangement, and alarmed lest his allies should desert him, executed to the letter his previous compact, and early in April abandoned to the Souliotes, Kiafa, with all the artillery, ammunition, and provisions it contained.   Thus, at a critical moment, just as the revolution was breaking out in Greece, the most warlike Christian tribe in that part of the world was fixed in an impregnable position, amply supplied with every kind of stores.

The military caste of Armatoles settled in the mountains of Acarnania, Etolia, and Thessaly, which might have been expected to stand foremost in this struggle, was, on the contrary, the last to follow the national impulse.   Selfish considerations, and apprehension of losing their lucrative posts, and the pay they claimed for past services, rendered the minds of the captains wavering and doubtful ; and some of them were even, under Ottoman colours, acting against the Souliotes in Epirus ; while, in the eastern provinces of Hellas, (Attica, Bœotia, and Phocis,) the ill-armed peasants showed a readier disposition to rush into hostilities.   In the first week of April, insurrectionary movements in those districts attracted the attention of the Ottoman authorities, and a certain Diakos, formerly Protopallikar, or lieutenant of Odysseus, appeared with a band of 300 men in the vicinity of Livadia, one of the best cities of Northern Greece, built at the foot of Mount Libethrius, and overlooking a fertile and well-watered plain.   Its population amounted to 10,000, mostly Greeks, many of whom were remarked for their opulence and hospi-

tality to strangers. On the 13th, the insurgents took
possession of Thebes without opposition, the Turks of
that place retreating quietly to Negropont.* Diakos,
assembling the Bœotian villagers, marched to the town
of Livadia, and invested its small and ruinous citadel ;
where the Mussulman inhabitants, after standing a
fortnight's blockade, surrendered, and were put to the
sword. Immediately afterwards, Odysseus presenting
himself in the countries where he had once commanded
the troops of Ali Pasha, propagated the revolt in Phocis,
and along the chain of Mount Œta. He came disguised
in a merchant ship from Ithaca to Patrass, about the
1st of April, and was admitted into the house of Constantine Yerakaris, a Zantiote broker ; but finding that
the Turks had private information of his being there,
he passed over to Roumelia, and concealed himself,
until assured of the friendly disposition of Captain
Diakos, who was before at enmity with him.

Agitated by the same spirit, the Albanian peasants
of Attica, collecting in armed bodies among the hills
to the west of Athens, occupied the roads and defiles
leading towards Bœotia and Eubœa, and watched every
opportunity of annoying the Turkish masters of the
city.

Athens, the unfortunate and illustrious Athens, is
seated in the midst of a plain, shaded by olive woods,
and representing the figure of a trapezium ; bounded
on the north, west, and east, by the ridges of Pente-
licus, Parnes, and Hymettus ; on the south by the
Saronic Gulf, whence it is distant five miles.

The modern town was surrounded by a thin stone
wall, ten feet high, inclosing a space of three miles,

---

* Thebes, a mean-looking town, built upon and amongst mounds
of earth formed by the ruins of the old city, was said (in 1810) to
contain 800 Greek and 400 Turkish houses. Nine monasteries and
seventy-two villages belonged to its territory.

and in many places coinciding with the old ramparts, whose circuit was, however, considerably greater. It filled but a moderate portion of the ground covered by ancient Athens, for, besides the difference in circuit, only the parts to the east, north, and north-west of the citadel had latterly been built upon. The inhabitants hardly amounted to 10,000, one-fifth of whom were supposed to be Mahommedans. The Acropolis, crowned by the most splendid monuments of antiquity, is an oblong, isolated, and precipitous rock, about 1000 feet in length, and 150 in height, defended by a lofty wall, (2500 feet in circumference,) raised on the massive remains of its Hellenic fortifications. The Propylœum, facing the west, its only entrance, is approached by a steep and winding path, has four successive gates, and is protected by a quadruple tier of batteries. The principal defect of this fortress, and which has more than once occasioned its surrender, is a scarcity of water, its cisterns not sufficing for a long siege; but to the south, a wall of some thickness encloses and unites to it a considerable area, called by the Turks Serpendje, where there is a well of indifferent water.

Athens, the resort of European travellers, and the residence of two foreign agents, (Messrs Gropius and Fauvel,) distinguished for urbanity, taste, and knowledge, enjoyed a degree of tranquillity and civilisation unusual in the Ottoman states. Even the Mussulmans there, many of them extensive proprietors, were noted for their civil and inoffensive deportment.

The first rumour of troubles in Peloponnesus and Livadia, produced in the city a feeling of intense anxiety, which was enhanced by intelligence, that the people of the large village of Khasha, reinforced by Megarians and Salaminians, had in the end of April formed a camp at Menidi, (the old Acharnæ,) two leagues from Athens. On the night of the 21st, 300 insurgents of

Kondoura and Villia carried off, almost under the cannon of the citadel, 3000 sheep belonging to Moslems. The latter made a show of pursuit next morning with 200 horse, but did not venture far from the walls. The Greeks began to withdraw from the town, and the Primates ceased their functions ; while the Turks, tormented by a sense of danger and weakness, held frequent councils, at which nothing was decided. All their males, from childhood to extreme old age, loaded themselves with weapons; but there were not above 300 really fit for service, and of these, 60 Albanians of the Vayvode's guard alone passed for good soldiers.

A massacre of the Christian inhabitants was twice proposed,and rejected through the humanity of the Khadi, who refused his sanction.* They, however, arrested the Archons, pillaged the houses and shops of absentees, laid up in the Acropolis ammunition and provisions, and thought of taking measures against a surprise. Being too indolent to perform night-duty themselves, they, with unexampled stolidity, employed Greeks to watch the ramparts of the town. These immediately entered into communication with the insurgents without, and agreed upon a signal, to let them know when the garrison should be wrapped in sleep. On the 6th of May, the Ottoman standard was set up before the Vayvode's house, and blessed by an Iman, according to their ordinary method.† On the succeeding night, four hours before day, a quick fire of musketry, and repeated shouts of—" Christ has risen ! Liberty ! Liberty !" announced the capture of Athens. From 1500 to 2000

---

* It is said, that for this conduct he was subsequently decapitated at Constantinople.

† The following is the way in which the Turks consecrate their standards : A sheep being killed, and the belly cut open, an Iman plunges his hand into the entrails, and, saying a prayer, impresses a bloody mark upon the flag.

peasants, mostly armed with clubs, and commanded by the Captains Dimo of Livadia and Meleti of Khasha, scaled the walls, and forced the gates with very little resistance, driving the Turks into the citadel, killing sixty of them, and taking forty prisoners. Among the slain were ten Albanians of the guard, and their banner was captured by the Greeks, who gave an example of humanity in granting quarter, and consigning their captives to the care of the European consuls: the majority consisted of women and children, but there were also some men.

Unhappily the Turks strangled at their birth such sentiments of compassion, by putting to death nine hostages, and throwing several naked and headless bodies over the battlements of the Acropolis. At daybreak of the 7th, three pieces of cannon from the castle began to play upon the town; but the Ottoman artillery, unwieldy, ill mounted, and worse served, did no harm. On the 8th, the insurgents occupied the hill of Philopappus, which is little lower than the Acropolis, and, with the detached and stony heights of the Areopagus and Pnyx, allows an enemy to lodge himself, towards the south and south-west, within a few hundred yards of the fort. The same day they sent in a summons, which the besieged treated with contempt. The Captains Dimo and Meleti, planting their flag on the Vayvode's house, made it their head-quarters. Reinforcements arrived from Salamis and Egina —the accession of armed Athenians increased their force to 3000 men; and they applied to Hydra, in order to obtain from thence a ship of war, with the guns and supplies required for a siege.

Beyond Thermopylæ, the exhortations of Anthimos Ghazi, who, in anticipation of these events, had lived for the last four years in the valleys of Pelion, roused to insurrection his countrymen, the Magnesians of

Thessaly, and, still nearer the Sultan's capital, the
theatre of hostilities embraced the extensive plains of
Macedonia to the east of the Thermaic Gulf. This was
partly owing to the violence of the Turks, and especially of the Pasha of Salonika, who ordered the summary decapitation of the heads of the clergy and principal merchants of that city and of Serres, charged the
peasants to give up their arms, and proceeded to enforce obedience by military execution, thus producing
the very result he wished to avert. Intemperate measures of a like description pushed into revolt even the
peaceful monks of Athos, called by the modern Greeks
the Holy Hill, from the twenty monasteries perched
among its woody cliffs.

According to the most authentic accounts, not less
than 6000 caloyers dwelt in the convents, (where no
female was allowed to set foot,) and in the little town of
Khariess, the only one in the peninsula of Athos; they
were governed by a monastic council and a Mohammedan officer from Constantinople, who had neither
state nor retinue, but was able in a short time to amass
a considerable sum of money. To resist the inroads of
corsairs, always abounding in the Grecian seas, their
monasteries were fortified and furnished with cannon;
and as their numbers were partly recruited from Albanian and Sclavonian tribes, we may readily believe
that in those quiet retreats there existed many whose
early life had been spent amid different scenes, and to
whom the musket was as familiar as the crucifix. The
Pasha insisted that the religious community should admit a garrison of his troops; and on their declining
the proposal, seized the husbandmen who cultivated
their estates in various quarters of the province, and
declared Mount Athos in a state of rebellion. Driven
to extremity, the monks, at the festival of Easter, confined their Turkish superintendent, and prepared to

defend themselves ; while in the course of a few subsequent days all the Christians of Chalcidice, encouraged by the appearance on their coast of some Greek
cruisers, rose in a body, and electing for their general
a merchant of Serres, named Manoli Papas, made incursions to the gates of Salonika. The Moslems and
Jews of that large trading city, where the latter are
very numerous, saw themselves for a brief period
blockaded both by sea and land. But the flat country
of Macedonia, propitious to the Ottoman cavalry, was
unfavourable to the irregular bands of insurgents, and
contained, besides, several Turkuman hordes, descended from the first conquerors, and preserving their original warlike and pastoral habits. Worsted in different
skirmishes, and pressed by the troops of the Pasha of
Salonika and the Bey of Yenijee,* the Greeks quitted
the plains, and concentrating themselves behind the
isthmus of Cassandra, abandoned upwards of seventy
villages, which the enemy destroyed with fire. For
more than a century no woman had entered the precincts
of Athos, but on the present emergency hundreds of
families flocked into the convents, where they quickly
exhausted the granaries, and although safe from the
Ottoman sword, ran some risk of perishing through
starvation, for a body of Turks, encamping at the roots
of the mountain, forced them to exist on scanty and
precarious supplies of corn from the Archipelago. Towards the end of May, the islanders, cruising at the
mouth of the Thermaic Gulf with four or five sail, attacked four Turkish vessels bound to Alexandria, and
captured three ; the fourth, having treasure on board,
with an hundred Mussulman passengers, destined for
Mecka, opposed an obstinate resistance, and was at last
run ashore, and burnt by its own crew.

* A town in Thrace, beyond the river Nestus.

APPENDIX

BOOK I.—CHAP. II.

No. I.—*Detailed Account of the rise and progress of the Hetœria within Peloponnesus.**

THE society of the Hetœria planted itself in Peloponnesus in the year 1818. The first Hetœrist that appeared was Anagnostoras, who came from Russia to Constantinople, and thence to Hydra, where he initiated several persons. As he did not enjoy much consideration in the peninsula, he said nothing to any of the primates, but broke the matter to some captains. About the same time a monk, named Neopbytus, going from Hydra to Tripolizza, sounded the leading men upon the subject. A certain Anagnosti Harvalis, a merchant of Tripolizza, acted with more energy; privately assembling in his house the principal Greek citizens, he, after exacting an oath of secrecy, told them a plan of insurrection was on foot. The primates then resident in that city had a confused idea of the business, but did not dare to communicate with each other respecting it. Soon after, the Archbishop Germanos, who was living at Patrass in constant consultation with the Russian consul Vlassopoulos, sent letters and messages to Zaimis and Londos, desiring an interview. A meeting was held at Vostizza, in the house of Andreas Londos, and they became Hetœrists. On his return home, Zaimis initiated Procopius, Bishop of Kalavryta, and the other notables of that district were made acquainted with the objects of the society by Vlassopoulos.

The next time that a provincial assembly was convened at Tripolizza, they disclosed the project to Papa Alexi of Fanari, who was then at the head of the primates, (and had got some intimation of it from the Archbishop of Derkos,)† and to Kopanizza of Mistra, so

---

* Communicated by some Peloponnesians of distinction, who do not seem to have been aware that Anthimos Gazi had made a progress in 1816, and initiated the Bey of Maina.

† Executed at Constantinople in 1821.

that only two or three Kojabashees remained in ignorance. Kanellos Delhiyani entered with much enthusiasm into the society, and introduced it into Karitena and other districts. At that epoch (1819), the correspondence of the Grand Arch began to circulate in Peloponnesus, and its letters were really curious, since to each man the Arch wrote in the style best suited to please him, whether his ruling passion was power, money, &c. The Arch desired that the contributions of the Morea should be paid in to Kharvalis. Continual deliberations took place among the primates, but they came to no conclusion; however the Archbishop of Patrass, Londos, Zaimis, and Harvalis, pushed the matter on, endeavouring to gain new proselytes, and to render the people diffident of the Turks. Considering that it was not proper that the voluntary donations of Peloponnesus should go out of the peninsula, they resolved to write to the Arch, and send a man on purpose, to demand that the moneys raised in the Morea, the Ionian Islands, and the Archipelago, should be deposited at Patrass, as being the safest place, where there were many individuals under European protection; likewise that the Arch should appoint ephors, to observe the conduct of the Hetœrists, and name Harvalis and Papadiamandopoulos stewards of the sums contributed. Now (1820), began a suspicion of the existence of differences between the Porte and Ali Pasha. It seems that the latter wished to have relations with foreign states, and even to correspond with Count Capodistria, and that previously letters had passed betwixt the Pasha and Vlassopoulos, a fact known to the Archbishop Germanos. Ali hoped that Russia would declare war, and he proposed to join that power, but first he wished to make stipulations with the Emperor. The plan of the Hetœrists was, to embroil the Pasha with the Porte. As he determined to send Paparigopoulos with letters to the Emperor, the Hetœrists of Peloponnesus took the same opportunity of writing to the Arch; they also thought this would be an occasion of finding out, whether the Autocrat felt any interest towards the society. Paparigopoulos went by way of Constantinople to St Petersburgh, and brought back the reply of the Arch. Being questioned whether the conspiracy was known at St Petersburgh? He answered, " It was." " Will military aid be given?" He stated that Count Capodistria said, " Possibly it might, but such things could not be spoken of beforehand." " Where did he receive the answer of the Arch?" " At Constantinople." " Where does the Arch reside?" " I know not:" nevertheless he gave assurances that it was an important body. The reply of the Arch announced that the moment of action approached. It granted the request of the Peloponnesians touching its funds, and appointed Harvalis and Papadiamandopoulos stewards, and the Bishops of Monemvasia and Christianopolis ephors of the Hetœria.

Ali Pasha, through the channel of his son Veli, sent a priest to Zaimis and Londos, promising them two millions of piastres to raise the Morea against the Porte, offering to leave the fortresses in the hands of the Christians, and assuring them his family was ready to co-operate.   They answered, that they would not sell themselves, and had no cause to mistrust the Porte; but that if he was persecuted, and prepared to resist, he must begin by altering his conduct, and then perhaps he might find many auxiliaries.   From Naupactus Veli Pasha sent a message to Odysseus at Livadia, desiring him to work upon the exiles of the families of Pettimeza and Komaniotis, and persuade them to excite troubles; and when the latter went to visit him at Lepanto, he (Veli) told them, "he would throw off his turban and put on a Russian hat."   Deceived by such speeches, they revealed to him the existence of the Hetœria. " Go," said he, " to Livadia, attack the Turks, and I am your comrade." From Lepanto they crossed over to Vostizza, and conferred at midnight with Andreas Londos, who advised them to undertake nothing, because Ali Pasha only wanted to make a display of the Greeks, in order that the Porte might give him a commission to suppress them. Londos engaged them, moreover, to write to Veli Pasha that the Greeks were ready, if he would send one of his sons to head their insurrection.   They hearkened to this advice; and learning on their return to Livadia, that a Tartar was coming from Constantinople, they lay in wait for and slew him, that they might discover from his despatches whether the Porte had any information of the Hetœria. However, the papers contained nothing of the sort.

Soon after, Papa Flessa arrived at Spezzja from Constantinople, bringing ammunition and 50,000 piastres ; and having intimated his advent to the primates assembled at Tripolizza, they wrote to him to pass by Corinth to Kalavryta and Patrass.   It was proposed to hold a meeting to hear his report, and Vostizza was fixed upon as a proper place.   To obviate suspicion on the part of the Turks, the Kojabashees of the other provinces gave to those of Patrass and Kalavryta full powers to act for them ; and it was asserted that Papa Flessa had a mission from the Patriarch relating to the monastery of Megaspileon, and that the Metropolitan of Patrass and the Bishops of Christianopolis and Kalavryta were directed to consult with him, and to invite the neighbouring primates to assist at their deliberations.   Thus, in November 1820, was brought about the congress of Vostizza, attended by the three above-mentioned prelates, the two Zaimis (father and son), Andreas Londos, Sotiri Karalambi, and Asimaki Fotillas. Papa Flessa declared " that Alexander Ypsilanti, being in the Russian service, had undertaken the revolution with the consent of the Emperor Alexander ; that the Servians and Montenegrins had entered into the conspiracy ; that at Constantinople thousands had embraced the Hetœria, and were disposed to burn the fleet, and seize the arsenal ; that Prince Constantine Morousi would command there ; and that men were ready to assassinate the Sultan when he went out disguised or in his boat." The primates knowing that Ignatius (Ex-metropolitan of Bukorest) belonged to the Hetœria, resolved, after much hesitation, to write to him, and point out their wants, and they dispatched Tomaropoulos with the letter. Meanwhile they agreed, that if the Ottoman authorities summoned them to Tripolizza, they should obey, and await there Ignatius's reply and a confirmation of Papa Flessa's reports ; but that if the prelates were likewise called to that city, then no one should go, since such an order would indicate danger, and be a proof that the Turks apprehended either foreign or internal war. Under the circumstances so contemplated, they decided that it would be expedient to go in a body to Hydra, consult with the primates there, and expect the result of Alexander Ypsilanti's movement. If the Hydriotes showed an inclination to co-operate, they might then return to Peloponnesus, and take up arms ; but that if they found those islanders backward, they should proceed to Constantinople, and petition the Sultan for a change of system and a renovation of obsolete privileges ; they relied a good deal on Khalet Effendi, who had always protected them. In any case they determined not to take arms yet, but cover their disobedience with the pretext of its being impossible to pay the imposts. The assembly broke up after a session of seven days, and Papa Flessa went into Laconia ; however, the militia and peasants began to have an insight into the affair. When the Turks did actually summon the prelates and kojabashees, the Bishop of Christianopolis (Arcadia), and those who deputed him, overstepped the bounds of their common agreement, and repaired to Tripolizza, whither Petro Bey, after taking counsel with them, sent his son. The Archbishop of Patrass and the primates of Kalavryta remaining out, the Ottomans wrote to them to come, but they put off in order to gain time, resolving to defend themselves if violence was offered. They had always some armed men about them, pretending that they kept them in pay to prevent their enlisting in Ali Pasha's service. Just at that period the Turks intercepted at Mistra letters written in the cipher of the Hetœria, and forwarded them to Tripolizza ; the Lalliotes likewise arrested a man of Kalavryta, who knew the whole affair, and got from him a confession of the plan of the primates. They gave information to the principal authorities, but the latter judged it better to keep the thing secret until all the kojabashees should be in their power. As the Turks of Patrass also became uneasy, and began to utter threats, the Archbishop Germanos took fright, hurried out of Patrass, pretending a design of going to Tripolizza, and proceeded to Kalavryta, followed by Andreas Londos. Fresh deliberations ensued. Sotiri and the Bishop of Kalavryta seemed inclined to go to Tripolizza, but were opposed by Zaimis, Londos, and Fotillas. The Archbishop was for some time doubtful, but finally adopted the bolder sentiment, and preparations were then made for hostilities. Nevertheless they left Kalavryta, and took the road to Tripolizza, accompanied by an hundred armed Greeks and thirty Turks; but when they reached the bridge of Katzano, they met there, according to appointment, a courier with a letter they had forged, purporting to come from a Mohammedan, who warned them not to appear in the capital. They read it with an air of earnestness to the Turks, and advised them to move on, since they (the primates) would proceed no farther. Then they wrote to the chief Turks of Tripolizza, enclosing a copy of the forged epistle, and excusing their own non-appearance, on the plea that it would be but folly to expose their lives, and declaring they would go to Constantinople. They, moreover, beseeched the authorities not to break the peace of the Sultan, whose wrath was inevitable, and not to listen to base men, since all the world knew that the Morea was the quietest province in the empire. They turned back to the convent of St Laura, and staid there six or eight days, collecting men, and preparing their minds for any crisis. At the same time they wrote to the Vayvode of Kalavryta, explaining the cause of their return, and to the Boulukbashee,* who being bound to Zaimis by oaths, escorted to Kerpeni the families of Sotiri and Fotillas. The Vayvode was credulous enough to believe their letter, and even bastinadoed two or three Turks who expressed a different opinion. At Tripolizza the Ottomans disputed with each other, some insisting that Kyamil Bey was author of the warning letter, others affirming it was Mustafa Bey. They despatched Kalamogdarti to reassure the refractory primates, who replied their suspicion could not be allayed by words. These last then separated, Sotiri and Theokaropoulos going towards Corinth to organize an insurrection, and, if possible, discover where Kyamil Bey's treasures were hid, that they might distribute a part of them among the Dervenokhoriats, and thus induce them to seize the passes. The Archbishop and Andreas Zaimis proposed to surprise Patrass, and old Zaimis and Fotillas to organize the province of Kalavryta. They sent to Langadia a monk of Megaspileon to acquaint the Delhiyaneis, and wrote to Papa Flessa. He and they answered that they were ready. A month before, Colocotroni had arrived in Maina, and was in correspondence with the Delhiyanei. However, Vlassopoulos prevented the capture of Patrass, engaging to bring the garrison to terms, while the Delhi-

---

* Commander of the police guard.

yanei sent word that the Turks were coming to attack them, and the Mussulmans of Patrass deliberated about making the Christian inhabitants captive. These delays being irksome, the associated primates determined to plunge at once into hostilities ; and old Zaimis and Fotillas raising the peasants, took Kalavryta.

No. II.—*Manifesto addressed to Europe by Petros Mavromikhalis, Commander-in-Chief of the Spartan Troops, and the Messenian Senate, sitting at Calamata.*

THE insupportable yoke of Ottoman tyranny hath weighed down for above a century the unhappy Greeks of Peloponnesus. So excessive had its rigour become, that its fainting victims had scarcely strength enough left to utter groans. In this state, deprived of all our rights, we have unanimously resolved to take up arms against our tyrants. All our intestine discord is plunged into oblivion as a fruit of oppression, and we breathe the air of liberty. Our hands having burst their fetters, already signalize themselves against the barbarians. We no longer run about day and night to execute corveés imposed by a merciless taskmaster. Our mouths are opened ; heretofore silent, or employed only in addressing useless supplications to our tormentors, they now celebrate a deliverance which we have sworn to accomplish, or else to perish. We invoke therefore the aid of all the civilized nations of Europe, that we may the more promptly attain to the goal of a just and sacred enterprise, reconquer our rights, and regenerate our unfortunate people. Greece, our mother, was the lamp that illuminated you ; on this ground she reckons on your active philanthropy. Arms, money, and counsel, are what she expects from you. We promise you her lively gratitude, which she will prove by deeds in more prosperous times.

(Signed)   PETROS MAVROMIKHALIS.

Given at the head-quarters of Calamata, $\dfrac{\text{March } 28,}{\text{April } 9,}$ 1821.

CHAPTER III.

Effect that the Revolution produced on the minds of the Turks—
Executions and massacres at Constantinople, and elsewhere—Negotiation betwixt Russia and the Porte.

SECTION I.

HAVING thus traced the progress of revolution from
the banks of the Pruth to the southern extremity of
Peloponnesus, it is time to turn our eyes towards Constantinople, and observe the effect it produced on the
Ottoman Court and people. After carefully weighing
facts and probabilities, we are of opinion that the
Turks had no clear insight into the conspiracy of the
Hetœria, before Ypsilanti appeared in Moldavia : at
least the only signs of suspicion they manifested were
pointed at the Servian nation. The Pasha of Vidin
having perused the papers found upon Aristides, endeavoured, by the lure of a conference, to seize the person of Prince Milosh ; but the wary Servian eluded the
snare, and maintaining an armed neutrality, restrained
the ardour of his subjects, while he avoided any just
cause of offence to the Sultan, who, nevertheless, caused
his agents at Constantinople to be thrown into prison.
In other respects, the Porte did not depart from its
usual phlegmatic demeanour, until seriously alarmed
by intelligence of the occurrences at Yassy and Galatz.
As it was thought impossible that Ypsilanti should
have engaged in so gigantic an enterprise, without
hopes of powerful support, the Turks naturally concluded that Russia was at the bottom of the whole af-

fair; and this persuasion, confirmed by the tenor of his proclamations, was not much impaired by the positive disavowal of him, which the Court of St Petersburgh made haste to promulgate. The irritation thus excited in their minds, was greatly heightened by the discovery of a plot hatched in the capital itself, for the total overthrow of Ottoman power ; a plot, which (however small the chance of its final success) might have crippled the resources of the Empire, and would certainly, if not checked in time, have brought on incalculable bloodshed. At the head of it was the Hydriote Captain Juisti, who commanded the naval contingents of the Archipelago, and he depended chiefly on the co-operation of 100 of his countrymen working in the dockyard : their project was to fire the arsenal, assassinate the Sultan on his way to a mosque, seize the park of artillery at Top Hanè, and arm the Greek population of the city. These things they would actually have attempted, if private mercantile reasons had not induced one of the conspirators to delay the execution: in the interval, a discovery took place, and Juisti, with his accomplices, was arrested and imprisoned in the Bagnio. Circumstances of such a description might have provoked the mildest government and people to overleap the limits of moderation ; and it is not, therefore, surprising that they should have filled the Turks with sensations of rage and terror, which were wrought up to a pitch of frenzy, by the reported insurrection of most of their European provinces. Supposing themselves surrounded on every side, by open or concealed enemies, ready to extirpate their religion and nation, they saw no security, except in the utter destruction of the Greek Rayahs. Under the influence of this feeling, the Janissaries and the populace, both at Constantinople and in the villages on the Bosphorus, began to commit murders, and to break into houses ; and as the

Porte seemed not simply to tolerate, but rather to countenance such excesses, universal dismay passed into
the breasts of the Christians.   At the same time, the
Sultan, by an imperial rescript, called upon his Mohammedan subjects to gird on their weapons, and stand
prepared to defend their faith and monarchy menaced
by infidels : by his orders, too, the Patriarch of the
Eastern church fulminated an excommunication against
Ypsilanti and his adherents.   In the month of March,
and the commencement of April, the torrent of wrath
being kept within certain bounds, a multitude of Greeks
escaped by sea, some directing their course to the Archipelago, but the greater part towards Odessa, which was
encumbered with fugitives.   When, however, advices
arrived of the rebellion of the Morea and the islands,
the Sultan's indignation fell with terrible weight upon
the nobility, clergy, and merchants.   Many, doubtless,
in the two latter classes, were privy to the schemes of
the Hetœrists ; as the ecclesiastics, out of religious
zeal, and commercial men from a love of liberty, had
long sighed for emancipation : but the Fanariotes, constantly opposed to the hierarchy, and wedded by the
ties of self-interest to Ottoman despotism, were certainly guiltless of the imputations laid to their charge.
It happened unfortunately for them that the Sultan's
favourite and confidential minister, Khalet Effendi, had
strong personal motives for persuading his master into
a belief of their complicity.   His sole partiality having, against the wishes of the divan, elevated Michael
Souzzo to the Principality of Moldavia, it became him
to show, that among the Greeks of rank, his protected
client was not a single instance of disloyalty, and he
therefore involved all the leading families in the same
accusation.   We may add, moreover, upon no slight authority, that Ypsilanti contributed to their ruin by a
very culpable manœuvre, having written and despatch-

ed letters to several Fanariotes, the former adversaries
of his house, for the express purpose of compromising
them.   On the 16th of April, Prince Constantine Morousi, Dragoman to the Porte, was apprehended, without any previous warning, conducted to a summer-
house of the Seraglio, called the Alœikiosk, and there
beheaded.   Immediately afterwards, ten conspicuous
personages of the Fanar (including a brother of Prince
Hanjerli, a Mavrocordato, a Scanavi, and Theodore
Rizo) were executed, and a similar fate overtook many
rich merchants and bankers.   The interest that waited upon their deaths, and the simultaneous detruc-
tion of a crowd of obscurer victims, was soon absorbed by a deeper sympathy for a more illustrious suf-
ferer.   Gregory the Byzantine Patriarch, a Peloponnesian by birth, was an aged prelate, of blameless life
and manners, whose piety and virtues commanded general esteem ; indeed the high opinion entertained of
him, had, during the course of a long life, caused his
repeated promotion to the metropolitan throne of the
east.   As he was leaving his chapel, after the celebration of divine service, on the evening of Easter Sunday
(April 22d), he was arrested by some Turkish officers,
stripped of his pontifical robes, and hanged at the gate
of his own palace : his body left suspended for three
days, was then cut down, delivered to a squad of Jews,
selected from the lowest rabble, dragged through the
streets, and thrown into the sea.   Next night, a few
zealous Christians fished up the mortal remains of the
martyr, and conveyed them to Odessa, where, on the
1st of July, they were interred with solemn pomp.   At
the instant of the Patriarch's execution, three Archbishops (those of Ephesus, Derkos, and Anchialus), and
eight priests of a superior order, were put to death in
different quarters of the city, and their bodies treated
with equal indignity.   Gregory's deplorable fate ex-

cited throughout Europe a profound feeling of horror and pity, and exasperated tenfold the animosity of the Greeks, insomuch as to render their reconciliation with the Porte impossible. The Sultan's conduct, in thus cutting off, in the gross, the highest ecclesiastical dignitaries, the objects of the people's veneration, was both cruel and impolitic; yet we dare not affirm that the Patriarch and the members of the Synod were entirely innocent of plotting against the state: we have, on the contrary, reason to believe that Gregory knew the Hetœria's existence, and that some of the other prelates were deeply engaged in its machinations.

While the government was taking such rigorous measures, the soldiery and the armed mob spread slaughter and conflagration through the city and suburbs, massacred thousands of Greeks, rifled the churches where they expected to find military depots, and insulted the hotels of the Christian legations: several Europeans were assassinated, and the insolence of the populace went so far, that the foreign ambassadors made energetic representations to the divan, and extorted a promise that the disorder should cease. In fact, comparative tranquillity was partially restored, and continued above a month. But although, after the end of April, Constantinople was less disturbed by the outrageous scenes of violence previously enacted there, yet hardly a day passed without public executions; in June the Sultan's severity seemed to grow more intense, and on the 15th of that month, five archbishops, three bishops, and a great number of laymen, were hanged on the streets, and 450 tradesmen and mechanics sent off to work in the mines on the Assyrian border. It was thought, that in the first days of July, more than seventy Greeks died by the executioner's hands. Those who had been enjoying marked favour, or whose characters were deemed the most inoffensive

and unenterprising, were condemned to exile : the two
Princes Callimachi, banished to Boli in Bithynia,
perished there by the sword, or by poison ; others were
allowed to return to the capital, after spending five or
six years in remote and inhospitable towns of Anatolia.   Amidst this butchery, Sultan Mahmoud did
not neglect his warlike preparations : by land and by
the Black Sea, troops hastened towards the Danube,
levies were ordered in all parts of the Empire, and
every nerve was strained to fit out a fleet for reducing
the Archipelago.   These preparations were not, however, solely intended against the Greek rebels ; apprehension of a war with Russia gained ground daily,
since the headstrong conduct of Turkey had led her
into an angry discussion with that power, which she
dreaded and hated ; it was therefore judged necessary
to assemble the largest possible force on the northern
frontier. The Sultan wished the Janissaries to march,
but that refractory and turbulent corps refused to quit
Constantinople, alleging that their presence was indispensable to keep down the disaffected Rayahs, and
defend their families. They expressed so much discontent, that the government found it expedient to negotiate with them, and on the 5th of May, in a full council of state, they obtained an extraordinary concession,
namely, that for the future, their corps should be
represented in the divan by three deputies of their
own choice. Many provinces in Europe and Asia witnessed tragedies in all respects similar to those of the
capital : every where the Greeks were looked upon as
public enemies, and even countries far from the seat of
revolution, where nothing of the sort had ever been
whispered, had no exemption from Mussulman vengeance.   At Salonika, the battlements were garnished
with heads, and yet the Janissaries of that city threatened to rise against the Pasha, because he would not

allow them to exterminate the Christian inhabitants. At Adrianople, the ex-patriarch Cyril, his protopapas, eight other ecclesiastics, and twenty merchants, were hanged in one day, (May the 3d,) before the Metropolitan church.

But it was on the coasts of Asia Minor that the most sanguinary reactions prevailed, and the city of Smyrna was remarkable for the atrocity and duration of its troubles, and the torrents of blood shed there. That great emporium of the Levant trade, situated at the bottom of a spacious gulf, into which the Hermus pours its waters, was supposed to contain 180,000 people, among whom might be reckoned natives of every part of the world. Here, as at Constantinople, reports of Ypsilanti's entering Moldavia produced a fermentation, which gradually augmented, as rumours of a vast conspiracy formed by the Rayahs were transmitted from the capital. A body of recruits arriving from the interior, and quartered round the town, indulged in unbridled license, assassinating the Greek peasants, and threatening to kill all the infidels. For a time, the Janissaries of Smyrna, taking upon themselves the police of the city, and Hassan Pasha of Cesarea, who came to govern it, maintained a degree of order, interrupted occasionally by single murders, tumults, and panic terrors, sometimes proceeding from trivial causes; thus, on the 11th of April, the discharge of a pistol excited so much alarm, that multitudes rushed to the harbour, and several persons were drowned in their hurry to escape. Two months elapsed in this state of painful suspense, and day by day fresh levies from the inland parts of Anatolia reinforced the troops encamped without, and destined to effect a landing in the Morea.

As the islanders cruising before the gulf hindered them from putting to sea, and no means had been

adopted for their subsistence, the soldiers, abandoned to
want and inactivity, infringed the regulation prohibiting them from going into the town, where they signalized their presence by robberies and excesses; the
shops were closed, the market-places deserted, and
Christians did not dare to move through the streets.
Meanwhile the Greeks fled from the city by thousands,
and took refuge in the islands; little or no opposition
being made to their departure, it is said that 15,000 of
them emigrated from Smyrna.   At length the news of
a defeat sustained by the Ottoman marine off Lesbos,
brought popular fury to a crisis on the 15th of June;
on that and the following day, 3000 ruffians assailed
the Greek quarter, plundered the houses, and slaughtered the people; Smyrna resembled a place taken by
assault, neither age nor sex being respected.   The
Mollah and Ayan magistrates presiding over the religious and civil tribunals were cut to pieces by the
mob, because they would not give a written sentence
sanctioning an indiscriminate carnage of the Rayahs.
Seeing themselves exposed to danger in spite of the attachment they professed to Turkish tyranny, the Frank
merchants, with their families, embarked on board the
ships of war and trading vessels in the harbour.   In
these melancholy circumstances, the conduct of the
French Consul (Monsieur David) did him high honour;
his house and garden being crowded with Greek fugitives, the rabble of assassins was on the point of breaking in, and his Janissaries did not venture to resist;
when the Consul, placing himself at the gate with one
companion, overawed the incensed Mohammedans by
his dignified carriage, until the boats of a French corvette coming to his assistance, forced the villainous
throng to seek some easier prey.

After the horrors of June 16th, Smyrna became
more calm; in a few days the Franks returned to their

dwellings, and in August even the surviving Greeks began to resume their customary avocations. It was long, however, ere confidence and perfect security were re-established, for a company of Candiot Moslems, prowling about, committed with impunity the worst crimes; and in addition to this cause of inquietude, the plague broke out, and swept away numbers of citizens. In the delightful island of Cos, now called Stanchio, some hundred Rayahs were slain; and at Rhodes, the Turks fell upon the Greeks, and, according to report, (apparently exaggerated,) massacred 3000 of them; there and every where else, their resentment was chiefly directed against the priests, who were sure to suffer first.

Did we write for the purpose of rendering exclusively odious one nation or party, it would be easy to prolong this catalogue of slaughters, sometimes springing from the systematic cruelty of a barbarous government, but oftener from the blind rage of an infuriated populace: enough, however, has been said on the subject, and we shall therefore end the list by a narrative of the calamities of Cyprus. That celebrated island (140 miles in length and sixty-three in breadth) is intersected by a range of mountains, called Olympus by the ancients, terminating towards the east in a long promontory. The soil is fruitful, and although but a small part of the land was under cultivation, the merchants of Larnaka nevertheless exported annually, during the late wars, many cargoes of excellent wheat to Spain and Portugal. Its population, (thought in 1814 not to exceed 70,000,) was daily diminishing; half were Greeks under their Metrópolitan, and the remainder Turks, with the exception of a few Franks at Larnaka. A Mutesellim, appointed by the Cápitan Pasha, ruled the isle, and next in authority to him were the Archbishop and Dragoman, (the latter a

I

Greek nominated by the Porte,) charged with the affairs of the Rayahs, and responsible for their contributions. As those functionaries played into each other's hands, no division of the Empire was more heavily taxed; and the peasants, reduced to total indigence, embraced opportunities of expatriating themselves. The most fertile and agreeable region is near the old Paphos, where flourish fine forests of oak, beech, and pine, with groves of olive and mulberry trees. Cyprus is renowned for the quality of its fruit, wine, oil, and silk; it abounds in oxen, sheep, fowls, and game; and the natives boast, that the produce of every soil and climate will not only flourish there, but attain to the highest perfection. Its trade is carried on at Larnaka, a town of 5000 souls, built on the site of Citium, at the bottom of a deep bay, making an excellent roadstead. Nicosia, the capital, is an inland and more populous city : Famagosta, on the east coast, once a strong place, is now dismantled and ruinous. The military force consisted of 300 guards of the Mutesellim, and 4000 Janissaries, badly armed, and without discipline or courage. The character of the people is mild ; and it is said that few instances of cruelty occurred, and that the Mussulmans lived on a very amicable footing with their Rayahs. Separated from European Greece by a wide expanse of sea, the Cypriotes beheld with a sort of indifference the commencement of the revolution, vainly flattering themselves that it would not disturb their tranquillity. But towards the end of May, certain Turks, gratifying private malice under political pretexts, assassinated some individuals, and the principal Greek merchants then fled. This transient gloom might perhaps have passed away, had not the Porte resolved to secure its dominion of the island, by introducing a body of forces from the neighbouring provinces ; a resolution that ruined Cy-

prus, but which was notwithstanding reasonable in
itself.   The insurgents in their vessels hovered round
its shores : the native Mohammedans were unwarlike,
and a plan to revolutionize it was already hatching by
the Archbishop's nephews then in France.   In obedience to firmans of the Sultan, the Pashas of Aleppo
and St John d'Acre assembled 10,000 Syrian troops,
the scum of that barbarous country, and shipped them
off from Acre and Tripoli, whence their navigation
was short and prosperous, the hostile cruisers having
withdrawn, to co-operate in defending the Archipelago.
Hardly had those vagabonds disembarked at Larnaka,
(in June,) when they gave themselves up to every species of villainy ; the remonstrances of the French Consul having obliged the Mutesellim to provide for the
safety of Europeans, he ordered the Syrians to march
to Famagosta, but this measure only tended to spread
their ravages more extensively, Seduced by their
example, the militia of the Isle joined the strangers in
their career of crime ; the Metropolitan, five bishops,
and thirty-six other ecclesiastics were executed. Nicosia
was sacked, as well as Famagosta, and the whole of
Cyprus converted into a theatre of rapine and bloodshed.

SECTION II.

FROM the recital of so many horrors, we now proceed to a subject of a different nature, that long fixed
public attention—the protracted negotiation betwixt
Russia and the Porte, growing out of the events just
related.   Did we possess a much more intimate knowledge of diplomatic secrets than we lay any claim to,
it would still be an irksome task to follow the wind-
ings of this lengthened discussion, since the disputants

seemed chiefly bent on reciprocal insult and defiance.
What human patience could wade through so many
prolix notes and useless conferences, where the ministers of the mediating powers wearied themselves in
efforts to keep asunder antagonists who showed little
real inclination to come to blows ?   If any dishonour
is to be inferred from such a position, it must rather
attach to the Emperor Alexander, the first to bully,
to menace, and demand a reparation which he never
obtained.   The firmer deportment of the Sultan not
unfrequently appeared to verge upon scorn.   It cannot
be doubted, that the Autocrat saw himself placed in a
false and embarrassing situation : on one side, a fair
opportunity offered for realizing ideas so long cherished
by the cabinet of St Petersburgh, and familiar to him
from his cradle ; the glory of his crown, the prayers of
his clergy, the earnest wishes of his army, nobility,
and vassals of every degree, called upon him not to
abandon the Greeks, holding the same form of Christianity with himself, and clinging to him as their pro-
tector.   On the other hand, he felt a dread of revolution, and was occupied at Laybach, when the troubles
of the East broke out, in proclaiming, by the declaration of May 12, his adherence to the purest doctrines
of legitimacy.   As that term, in the acceptation then
assigned to it, comprehended all monarchical govern-
ments, however acquired, or however exercised, provided they bore the stamp of a generation or two, and
scouted popular rights, it would have been unjust to
exclude from its pale either the Grand Turk, or any
other potentate, down even to the King of Ashantee.
Besides, in fairness to Alexander's character, we may
believe, that a love of peace, and reluctance to embroil
Europe anew, after he had done so much for its pacification, contributed to inspire that amiable prince with

moderation and forbearance towards the haughty and
obstinate Ottomans.   Whatever might have been the
Emperor's personal sentiments, his ambassador at Constantinople, Baron Strogonoff, showed no indications of
a patient and complying disposition, but caught with
avidity those grounds of quarrel which the Porte, in
its actual temper, was not slow in affording him.   The
Russian minister could not behold with indifference the
ignominious death of the head of a church to which
his master belonged.   His strong remonstrances were
answered by an assurance that Gregory had been executed, not as a Patriarch, but as a rebel ; that, to avoid
scandal, he had been previously deposed ; that there
existed, in writing, proofs of his guilt ; but these proofs
the divan refused to produce, when summoned to do
so.   The deposition of the Grand Vizier, Benderli Ali,
although owing to reasons altogether different, was
also held out as a sort of atonement.   New causes of
dispute sprung up daily, and it might almost be believed, that the Turks, inwardly convinced that the insurrection was fomented by Russian intrigue, desired to
bring matters to a decisive issue.   We have seen above,
that, in the first moment of dismay, numbers of Greeks
escaped by sea from Constantinople and Smyrna ; after
a short time, however, the Porte, resolved to prevent
the evasion of these objects of its wrath, assumed
a right it had never before claimed, of searching foreign vessels previous to their departure.   The other
ministers tamely submitted, and even carried their com-
plaisance so far, as to send to the consuls circular letters,
strictly prohibiting the shipmasters of their respective
nations from receiving on board fugitive Greeks, and
denouncing the penalty of confiscation against such of
them as should be guilty of the crime of humanity, in
saving innocent victims from the knives of their but-

chers.*   Mr Strogonoff alone resisted this assumption of authority, and directed Russian subjects to enter a formal protest whenever they were visited by the Turkish police. The Ottoman government then made another regulation, which drew fresh remonstrances from the ambassador. Apprehending that the disturbances of Wallachia and the Archipelago would deprive the capital of its usual supply of food, and wishing likewise to straiten the revolted islanders, it laid an embargo upon vessels laden with grain from the Russian ports in the Black Sea; nevertheless proffering to buy the cargoes at a price fixed by itself, but sufficient to remunerate the owners. This ordinance gave great dissatisfaction to the Baron, who insisted it was an infraction of the treaty of Bukorest, as indeed it clearly was. The state of the Transdanubian principalities, and their future settlement, also came under discussion. The court of St Petersburgh had readily consented to the Turks marching troops into them, in order to suppress the Hetœrists; but Ypsilanti being expelled, it now demanded that the forces should be withdrawn, Hospodars appointed, and all things put upon the old footing.

A circumstance, considered, not without reason, by Mr Strogonoff as a grievous affront, still remains to be told. There prevailed formerly in Turkey, a custom of allowing the representatives of foreign powers to grant to the Porte's tributary subjects diplomas, called Baratts, by which they were exempted from the capitation tax, and became amenable solely to the jurisdic-

---

* In consequence of this ill-judged facility, the master and crew of a Sardinian vessel, with a whole ship-load of Greeks, were cruelly put to death at Smyrna. The captain of the French frigate La Jeanne d'Arc, was disposed to protect them; but he yielded to the requisition of the consul, who was deceived through the fair promises of Hassan Pasha, himself intimidated by the clamours of the mob.

tion of the legation, whose protection they acquired through favour or purchase. The Turks, it is true, had lately abolished this privilege, dangerous and humiliating to any government, but Russia never acquiesced in its abolition.

At this period the banker of the Muscovite embassy was a Greek, named Danesi, a clever man, who seems to have possessed a good deal of Mr Strogonoff's confidence. On the 29th of April, that individual was placed in custody, because, as was then alleged, he refused to cash a bill of exchange for 300,000 piastres, drawn by Callimachi, whom the Porte had nominated Prince of Wallachia. Having quickly obtained his release through the intervention of the Russian minister, he concealed himself; nevertheless, the Reis Effendi sending for him on the 2d of May, he went to the Porte, accompanied by a Russian Dragoman, and was immediately arrested. The ambassador caused him to be claimed next day as his banker, but was told, in reply, " that Danesi being a Rayah, Baron Strogonoff had no right to interfere." Upon this, Mr Dashkoff, a gentleman attached to the embassy, went in state to the Porte, and demanded his liberation. After waiting five hours, he was dismissed with a contemptuous refusal. The Baron going there in person, was not more successful in a conference with the Grand Vizier; neither his entreaties, threats, nor expostulations, produced the least effect—on the contrary, Danesi was committed a close prisoner to the Seven Towers. Mr Joseph Fonton, first counsellor of legation, and a veteran diplomatist, made a fresh attempt on the 4th, desiring that the ambassador's memorial might be handed to the Sultan. His request being denied, he stood in the street through which that monarch passed, returning on Friday from the mosque, exclaiming that he had a memorial to present from the minister of Russia. These words he

repeated thrice before the Sultan deigned to notice
him.   At length the paper was taken by an officer, but
no answer ever given.*

Incensed at such supercilious treatment, the ambassador secluded himself at Buyukdere, broke off all
communication with the Porte, and laid before his
sovereign the whole matter.   In consequence of instructions transmitted to him, he sent in to the Ottoman ministry a note, dated July the 18th, and containing the Russian cabinet's ultimatum.   This state paper,
interlarded as usual with professions of amity and moderation, after insisting on the right Russia derived
from the treaty of Kainardji, to interfere in affairs
touching the security and honour of the Eastern
church, as well as in those relating to Moldavia and
Wallachia, proceeded to demand, that the Sultan should
exhibit a proof of his desire to put an end to the persecution then raging against Christians, by stopping
the excesses which the Turks were committing throughout his dominions ; that a distinction should be drawn
between unoffending Greeks and those engaged in open
rebellion ; that the churches which had suffered demo-
lition or damage should be rebuilt and repaired, and
full protection extended to the Greek worship.   If
within the term of eight days the Porte did not listen
to these proposals, the ambassador was directed to quit
Constantinople, and to take measures for removing the
Russian subjects established in Turkey.   No reply
having been made ere the lapse of the prescribed
period, Baron Strogonoff embarked in a brig awaiting
his orders in the Bosphorus, but contrary winds long
prevented him from setting sail.   Meanwhile the Porte,

* From the esteem and consideration enjoyed by Danesi, the Porte
imagined he must be a leading conspirator, and an instrument of the
designs of Russia. However, his friends positively assert, that, having
no confidence in Ypsilanti, he had declined becoming a Hetœrist.

swayed probably by the representations of other diplo-
matists, prepared an answer to the ultimatum, which
he would not receive; it was therefore forwarded by
a courier to St Petersburgh.   In its note, which was
drawn up in a clear and forcible style, betraying no
want of argumentative skill, the divan asserted, that
the Greek nation, for many generations subject and
tributary to the Sultans, had been governed with singular mildness; that the church, in particular, had always
enjoyed a special degree of favour and respect; * that,
notwithstanding the ingratitude of that people, in re-
volting against their clement sovereign and benefactor,
means of conciliation had been tried to bring them
back to their duty through the medium of the Patriarch; but that sufficient evidence having been obtained
that he was himself the prime mover of the rebellion,
which first broke out at his native town, Kalavryta,†
he had been executed after previous deposition, and a
successor appointed; that, however, no disrespect was
thereby intended to the Christian faith.   The note
then went on to state, that it was true protection was
stipulated for that religion in the treaty of Kainardji,
but that religion had nothing in common with rebellion; that innocent Greeks were not molested, and if
outrages against them had happened on certain points,
efficacious steps were already adopted to prevent their
recurrence; and that, moreover, the Porte was not
ignorant that a Russian Patriarch had been put to
death, and the dignity suppressed by the Czar Peter.
After censuring the harsh expressions used by Baron
Strogonoff, and protesting, that with regard to the provinces beyond the Danube, Turkey had no other object
in view than to restore tranquillity by driving out the

---

* An assertion as true as the preceding one was false.

† A mistake of the Turks—the Patriarch was born at Dimir-
zana.

robbers that infested them, the paper concluded with
a demand, that Michael Souzzo, and the insurgents
who had found an asylum in the Russian territory,
should be delivered up to the Sultan's justice.

Having thus officially explained its sentiments, the
divan showed some indirect signs of a desire to avoid
coming to open extremities with the Emperor, by
removing (August the 8th) the embargo laid upon shipping from the Black Sea, and commanding the new
Patriarch Eugenius to publish an encyclic epistle, inviting the Greeks to submit, on promise of an amnesty.
To this invitation they of course paid no attention;
indeed, they never acknowledged either Eugenius (who
died soon after) or his successor; and it was a current report amongst them, that a disguised Jew occupied the metropolitan chair of the martyr Gregory.

Neither did these tardy concessions, if such they may
be deemed, alter the ambassador's resolution. Availing
himself of a shift of wind, he sailed from the Bosphorus
on the 10th, and on the 13th of August arrived at
Odessa, whence he hastened to communicate with the
Emperor, whom he met at Veliki Louki. His abrupt
departure caused not only in the East, but all over
Europe, an expectation of immediate hostilities, and
every circumstance appeared to confirm the idea. The
Muscovite agents retreated from the Sultan's dominions as from an enemy's country, and bodies of troops
were continually traversing the southern division of
the vast Russian empire, to reinforce the army cantoned on the banks of the Pruth, and impatiently waiting for a signal to advance. The Greeks especially
were full of exultation. The Patriarch's funeral had
been celebrated at Odessa with extraordinary solemnity,
and the Emperor Alexander had generously bestowed
pecuniary aid upon some noble fugitives from Constan-

tinople. They did not reflect, that the objects of such
honour and bounty were supposed not to be implicated
in the revolution ; and that, at the same time, Dukas,
and several officers of Ypsilanti's army, were confined
as state prisoners in the fortress of Bender.

The representatives, at Constantinople, of England,
France, and Austria, anxious to avert war, endeavoured
to persuade the divan to lower its tone ; but they made
no impression ; and the replies to two notes written in
that sense by the Austrian internuncio and the French
charge d'affaires, were couched in terms exactly similar
to those used in answering the ultimatum of July the
18th. Preparing for the worst, the Turks did all in
their power to strengthen the force which, under the
Serasker, Yussuff Pasha of Ibrail, guarded the Trans-
danubian principalities—a force neither calculated from
its numbers nor quality to stand the first shock of the
Russian armies, had the latter gone farther than demonstrations. However, after a long period of alternate hopes and fears, the storm was hushed, to the joy
of some, the disappointment of others, and the surprise
of all. Count Capodistria withdrew from the Russian
councils ; Baron Strogonoff appeared to have fallen into
disgrace ; and the sword, which for twelve months
hung suspended over the East, was quietly returned to
its scabbard. Not that a perfect reconciliation followed, abundant points being still left open to discussion, as embers, which Russia might, when she thought
fit, blow into a flame ; neither were diplomatic relations betwixt the two courts re-established according
to the usual forms, until the end of the year 1826,
when a totally new scene began to unfold itself.

Laying aside all considerations of wounded pride,
dignity, or affection, and contemplating the business
merely in a political point of view, we are bound to

confess, that the cabinet of St Petersburgh acted with most consummate and statesmanlike prudence, perfectly judging the Ottoman character, the nature of the struggle in Greece, and the events likely to ensue. Had Alexander declared war in 1821, besides placing himself in contradiction to his avowed principles, by upholding the cause of revolution, he could hardly have failed to see arrayed against him a league of the greater European powers, all at that moment more or less actuated by the same dislike to freedom and innovation, which he had been ostentatiously proclaiming at Laybach. A stronger motive, jealousy of his ambition, would have induced them to step in, to interpose between him and his destined prey, and to set limits to his success. Greece might, indeed, have the sooner attained to a precarious and anarchical independence, but Russia must have been content with an additional slice of Moldavia. One of two conditions is requisite to enable that empire to carry into complete effect her design of subverting the crescent, and permanently planting her eagle on the shore of the Propontis; either that her Western rivals should be fighting with each other, or that they should make common cause with her. The first hypothesis offered itself to Catherine in 1792, but she had just then signed the peace of Yassy, and was engaged in the partition of Poland. Paul was guided in his alliances and enmities by passion instead of policy; and Bonaparte's aggression, ravishing from Alexander the fruits of an expensive contest, had no doubt convinced him, that it was useless to exhaust his finances in attacking Turkey without a fair prospect of reaping the profit of his labour. By temporizing, by spinning out the negotiation, often threatening to strike, and still deferring the blow, Russia disquieted the Sultan, and drawing his attention to the Danube, efficaciously served the Greeks; while, under the mask of moderate and pacific sentiments, she never ceased to hold fast a plausible reason for going to war, whenever a favourable opportunity should arise.

CHAPTER IV.

Operations of the Greek and Turkish Fleets during the Summer and Autumn of the year 1820—Transactions in Peloponnesus till the middle of October.

SECTION I.

AFTER long and strenuous preparation, a Turkish squadron, intended to bring to subjection the revolted Isles of the Egean, sailed from Constantinople on the 19th of May, and having loitered a fortnight in the Propontis and Hellespont, issued out of the Straits, and advancing as far as Lesbos, anchored near the little Islands of Mosconisi, on the coast of Asia ; it consisted of one line-of-battle ship, three frigates, a corvette, and two brigs.　The Greek fleet, of twenty-two Hydriote, seven Spezziote, and nine Psarrian vessels, put to sea on the 30th of the same month, to watch the enemy's movements, and prevent him from attacking Samos, against which this expedition was supposed to be directed.　They encountered (June the 5th) an Otto-man ship of seventy-four guns coming to reinforce the hostile squadron, and apparently steering towards Scio : on seeing the Greeks, however, she tacked, and endea-voured, under a press of sail, to gain the port of Sigri, on the western side of Mitylene.　Perceiving, that be-fore he could accomplish this, his pursuers would come up with him, the Turkish captain, deprived by fear of all presence of mind, cast anchor in the neighbouring roadstead of Erisso (or Negropont), where he received on board a party of troops.　The islanders, after firing

some distant and ineffectual broadsides, deliberated
whether they should attempt to carry the ship by a
combined attack, when one of the captains proposed to
employ a fire-ship against her. His idea meeting with
general approbation, an old vessel was forthwith converted into a brulot, and a gratification of an hundred
dollars promised to each mariner who would volunteer
on that service. Their first attempt failed, the train
having been fired too soon; on the next two days, contrary winds and calms hindered them from making a
fresh essay, but on the 8th they succeeded completely.
In spite of the Turkish artillery and musketry, two
fireships, linked together, fell athwart the bows of the
two-decker, and instantly wrapped her in flames; the
captain having cut his cables to allow her to drift on
shore, she struck on a sand-bank, and burnt to the
water's edge. The crew took to their boats, or jumped
into the sea, in order to save their lives by swimming.
but being pursued with deadly animosity, five or six
hundred of them perished. This victory, which they
owed to the extreme stupidity and cowardice of the
enemy, produced the same favourable impression on
the minds of the Greek sailors, that the battle of Valtezza did on the Peloponnesians. The rest of the
Ottoman fleet, informed of the catastrophe by a despatch
from the Pasha of Mitylene, returned precipitately to
the Dardanelles.

Being now, for a time at least, undisputed masters
of the Egean, the islanders began to consider to what
point they should turn their attention; the deliverance
of Lesbos seemed within their reach, and it is even asserted that, in concert with the Samians, they had conceived a design of attacking Smyrna; but neither of
these projects was executed, and the hope of an easier
acquisition led them towards the Eolian shore. On
that shore, on the ruins of a petty village, was founded

about forty years before the city of Kydonia, or Aivali,* which, under the auspices of a priest named Œconomos, became in a short period very flourishing. Its founder, a man of singular ability and perseverance, obtained from the Porte the government of his native place, with a grant of such privileges as had never been conceded to any town in Anatolia. It was included in the pashalik of Broussa, and the Sultan kept there an officer of the customs, a khadi, and a military commandant; but all this was merely a form, the whole and sole authority being vested in the primates, who were chosen annually. The population of thirty thousand souls was entirely Greek, unmixed with any other sect, and the city was embellished with several handsome churches and an episcopal palace, where resided a prelate, suffragan to the Archbishop of Ephesus. The port, although spacious and deep enough within for large vessels, admitted only small barks, on account of shoals which block up its entrance. This obstacle the inhabitants might easily have removed, had they not feared to attract thither Turkish ships of war; nevertheless they carried on an extensive trade, and the advantages of Aivali drew every year numbers of new settlers from the Archipelago and the mainland. It contained in 1820 upwards of 3000 stone houses, forty oil-mills, thirty soap-works, various other establishments of industry, and two magnificent hospitals, built at the community's expense, and well supplied with medical attendance. But what chiefly distinguished Aivali was its beautiful college, erected in 1813, celebrated for the excellence of its professors, and affording education to more than three hundred students. The Kydonians, feeling no inclination to share in the

---

* These two appellations, the first Greek, the second Turkish, signify the same thing, and are derived from the abundance of quince-trees.

present struggle, were, notwithstanding, sucked into
the vortex by the passions of the contending parties.
The Pasha of Broussa, thinking it proper to send troops
thither, as well to secure the fidelity of the inhabitants,
as to guard against the enterprises of the insurgent
marine, his Kihaya entered on the 13th of June, at the
head of six hundred men; and on the same day the
Greek fleet appeared in the offing. Many of the richest citizens had already deemed it prudent to emigrate,
and numerous families were following their example,
and passing over to the opposite group of islets called
Mosconisi, on one of which stood formerly a famous
temple of Diana. Unaccustomed to the sight of Turks,
the people beheld their arrival with pain, and speedily
quarrels occurred betwixt the natives and the Kihaya's
soldiers, who behaved with that arrogance which Moslems are wont to display in their dealings with Rayahs.
Obliged by popular indignation to evacuate the town,
and post his troops on an eminence, the Kihaya craved
reinforcements, and receiving them on the 14th, was
thus enabled to occupy the principal quarters of the
city. As is usual in the East, he demanded a large
sum of money from the primates; but the latter found
it impossible to comply, for there did not remain above
one half of the inhabitants, and these, appertaining to
the poorer classes, refused to contribute. The Kydonians treated coldly the first overtures made them by
the navy, and the islanders were preparing to sail away,
when intelligence reached them that the temper of the
people was changed, and that the refugees on Mosconisi begged to be taken on board. Exclusive of the
duty of saving their countrymen, a knowledge that
Aivali possessed much wealth stimulated the zeal of
the seamen; accordingly, two hundred men landed on
the island to drive away the Turks and facilitate the
embarkation of the fugitives, and it was resolved to

I

assail the town on the next morning. Two hours before noon of the 15th, a great number of launches belonging to the squadron, furnished with artillery, and
bearing armed sailors and a company of eighty Roumeliote soldiers, embarked at Psarra, approached the
harbour, and cannonaded the Ottomans, whose infantry
was entrenched in the houses near the sea, while their
cavalry, marching out, stationed itself on an adjacent
height; their force amounted perhaps to two thousand men. In the beginning of the action, the inhabitants were afraid to interfere, until about noon the
Kihaya's troops having set fire to several houses, they
saw that their town was doomed to destruction, and
therefore opened upon the garrison a discharge of musketry from their windows and terraced roofs. The
islanders then landed under the protection of their ordnance, and the fight was maintained with vigour till
five o'clock in the evening, when the Turks were entirely driven out. In their retreat, however, they
spread the conflagration, and the once flourishing
Aivali was reduced to a heap of ashes. During the
engagement, that part of the population which was incapable of fighting, hurried down to the quays and into
boats prepared to receive them; but the majority saved
only the clothes they wore, every thing of value that
escaped the flames being pillaged by friends or foes; at
eight o'clock the evacuation of the burning city was
completed. According to a very vague reckoning, five
hundred Turks perished, and two hundred Greeks,
mostly Kydonians, who lost their lives by fire, water,
or the sword. The fleet spent the night in the channel
of Aivali; and having on the morning of the 16th
embarked four hundred persons concealed in the vicinity, sailed for Psarra, the nearest friendly port. The
vessels were excessively crowded with so many thousand unhappy fugitives of every age and sex, some of

them expiring from wounds or disease, and others, women, in the pains of labour.   No less than seven hundred were cooped up in Tombazi's corvette, the The-
mistocles ; and it would have been scarcely possible to
transport them all, if four fresh ships from Hydra had
not joined the squadron. At Psarra they were landed,
and afterwards distributed over the islands of the
Egean, accompanied by circular letters from the naval
commander, recommending to the fervent charity of
Christians the unfortunate Aivaliotes, who, by encouraging education, had conferred such obligations on
Greece.* Having proceeded a second time towards the
Dardanelles without meeting a hostile flag, the three
squadrons separated before the month was out, for
which their crews had been paid in advance, and the
25th of June Tombazi returned home with the Hydriotes. Since the expulsion of Captain Antoni, Hydra
had become more quiet, and precautions were taken to
resist an attack by erecting batteries facing the sea,
and forming a national guard, headed by the principal
citizens, who commanded in rotation the service of the
place.

   While Tombazi was acting on the Asiatic coast, another division of the Greek marine steered towards the
western shores of Peloponnesus, and was reinforced
there by two Ionian vessels, which, in defiance of the
neutrality, combated the Turks, without even changing their colours. On the last day of May twenty-
three sail passed Zante, and appeared (June 1st) within
sight of Patrass.   Yussuf Pasha, expecting to be besieged both by sea and land, resolved in that case utterly to destroy the remains of the town, and shut himself up in the castle. In consequence of his expressing
this determination, the foreign consuls departed. Five

* Vide Appendix.

Turkish ships of war, (the largest a corvette of twenty-
six guns,) on perceiving the van of the Greeks, retired
for protection under the batteries of Lepanto. On the
2d, the islanders, regardless of a cross fire from the
forts on each side of the Little Dardanelles, forced the
passage, and entered, without loss, the Gulf of Corinth.
The two castles contained an hundred pieces of cannon, but in miserable plight, destitute of carriages, and
so unskilfully served that only a single ball struck
one vessel. After this exploit, they attempted in vain
to burn with a brulot the Ottoman ships; they then
established on shore a battery of three guns, in a position sheltered from the artillery of Lepanto, and played with considerable effect, both on the town and the
shipping; but at length the garrison, provoked at the
annoyance, sallied out and stormed their battery. Patrass had been hitherto open to Albanian reinforcements, whose successive arrival enabled Yussuf Pasha
to repel the insurgents as often as they ventured to
approach it, and to preserve his communication with
Lepanto. Now, however, there was an end to all hopes
of succour from Epirus, for the appearance of the Grecian navy having decided the revolt of Messalonghi and
Anatoliko on the 7th and 8th of June, the total defection of Etolia and Acarnania immediately followed. If
the islanders had persevered in their maritime blockade, they might have famished a stronghold, whose
possession was essential to the success of their cause;
but satisfied with riding triumphant for three weeks in
the waters of Achaia, they went home, in obedience to
a most pernicious custom of not remaining out beyond
a month, and on the 27th and 28th proceeded in two
divisions towards the Archipelago, leaving a free navigation to the Turks, who instantly poured supplies
into Patrass. Meanwhile, Yussuf Pasha was so little
afraid of his enemies, that he undertook an expedition

to relieve the Lalliotes.* That warlike Albanian tribe, the scourge of the surrounding country, had prosecuted hostilities for the last three months, ravaging the districts of Gastouni and Pyrgos. The Greeks on their side occupied the defiles near Lalla, and harassed its people by every means in their power, but they could not do much until a body of Ionians came to their assistance, under the Count Andreas Metaxa of Cefalonia. Partaking largely of the enthusiasm which the events of Greece infused into the natives of the Septinsular Republic, Metaxa eluded the vigilance of the English authorities, and with two or three hundred of his countrymen landed in Elis, where he was joined by about four hundred Zantiotes, who likewise quitted their own island in a clandestine manner. This corps, well armed, and not devoid of courage, was, however, altogether averse to subordination, and fully as much disposed to wage war upon the herds of cattle that pastured the plains as upon the Turks. With his Ionians, and a greater body of Peloponnesians, commanded by Sisinni, Primate of Gastouni, Metaxa advanced to Lalla, which, although unfortified, was strong from its situation, and the way in which the houses were built. Although approving the motives that induced the Count and his principal associates to fight for Hellenic liberty, we must censure an ill-advised step they took in sending into the place a summons in their own names, as generals of the Zantiote and Cefalonian army; a gross mistake in point of judgment, as well as propriety,

---

* Monsieur Pouqueville, who visited Lalla in 1816, describes it as a large straggling place, presenting vast palaces and detached groups of houses, pierced with loopholes for musketry. Like all Albanian towns, it was divided into Pharès or factions, ruled by elders or beys, whose influence was in proportion to their wealth and the number of soldiers they could maintain. It was celebrated for producing a great quantity of cherries; the air and water are excellent, and the Lalliotes were a haughty, robust, handsome, and courageous race of barbarians.

and an insult to their government, which had till then winked at their conduct. Surprised at the reception of such a paper, the Lalliotes forwarded it to Yussuf Pasha, and by him it was immediately transmitted to Corfu. Two emissaries, who carried it to Patrass, and traversed by night the hostile posts, were likewise bearers of a letter from the chiefs of Lalla to the Pasha, informing him that being straitened for want of provisions, and hemmed in by foes, they had determined to abandon their town, and therefore implored his aid to clear the passes and secure their retreat. Anxious to save this colony of soldiers, Yussuf marched on the 21st of June, at the head of twelve hundred men, and arriving at Lalla, found the Greeks encamped before it, on the banks of a little river of the same name. They had already encountered the Lalliotes in two skirmishes, which, although without any decisive result, somewhat cooled the ardour of the Ionian volunteers, most of whom dispersed up and down the country, going wherever caprice or prospect of booty led them. Strengthened by the accession of fifteen hundred Lalliotes, the Pasha caused his cavalry to turn Metaxa's position during the night, and prepared to attack him at break of day. On becoming aware of their perilous situation, the insurgents would fain have effected their escape; and had the Turks left any passage open, they might have fallen upon them, and cut them to pieces as they were marching off; but being enclosed on every quarter, they had no option but to resist to the last extremity. Their force amounted to about 1500, (including 150 Cefalonians and Zantiotes, 700 Christian Albanians of Soulima, a canton in Messenia, 300 men of Gastouni, and a detachment of Colliopoulos' troops,) with two nine-pounder guns.

An engagement ensued on the 24th, long, obstinate, and bloody, the Mussulmans making furious but fruit-

less assaults upon the Greek entrenchments, which were
defended with the courage of despair. Darkness and
lassitude put an end to the contest, the Turks retiring
into Lalla, and thus allowing the insurgents to gain
the mountains; the former returned next morning to
the field of battle, carried away the two guns, which
they found abandoned, and impaled twenty prisoners.

In this combat the Greeks lost 280 men, and Metaxa
was severely wounded in the hand by a negro, who
climbing a tree, from thence shot seven Ionians, and
was at length killed by a cannon-ball. Among the
Turks also the slaughter was considerable, and the
Pasha's sword-bearer fell at his side. The Ottoman
general, however, accomplished his purpose of bringing
off the Lalliotes in safety; after burning their town,
and destroying all the property they could not transport, they set out under his escort on the 30th of
June, and entered Patrass on the 6th of July, with
their women, children, and cattle.

The disgrace that attended the Porte's late naval
enterprise in the Egean irritated rather than discouraged the Sultan and his ministers: preparations
were pushed for equipping a more formidable armament, and orders despatched to the Pasha of Egypt,
and the Barbary regencies, enjoining them to furnish
auxiliary squadrons. The Capitana Bey, Kara Ali,
hoisting his flag in a three-decker, left the Hellespont
on the 14th of July, with four line-of-battle ships, five
frigates, and so many corvettes, brigs, and gun-boats,
that the whole fleet exceeded thirty sail. Navigating
in two divisions, and passing to the east and west of
Mitylene, they rendezvoused on the 17th at Scalanova,
and anchored there with the avowed intention of attacking Samos. That island, one of the largest and
finest in the Egean Sea, is twenty-four miles long,
twelve broad, and seventy in circuit, containing forty

thousand inhabitants, seven thousand of whom were able to bear arms : two ridges of lofty hills run through it, enclosing several valleys fertile in oil and wine, and a strait, not half a league in width, separates it from the continent of Asia. The Samians, a brave and hardy race, addicted to agriculture, and little accustomed to maritime pursuits, had not shared in the prosperity so remarkable on some barren rocks of the Archipelago ; with the exception of a few rich landowners, they were in a state bordering on indigence. Nevertheless, the dawn of freedom was nowhere hailed with greater joy ; the Khadi, and a few Janissaries kept there by the governor of Scalanova, were massacred in an instant, and .the Samians began to make descents on the coast of Anatolia, killing the Turks, plundering their habitations, and driving away their herds and flocks : they persevered in the same system throughout the war, although the vengeance of the Porte was repeatedly pointed at them, until at last the Mohammedans did not venture to travel along the shore unless in numerous and well armed parties. For these reasons the Capitana Bey had precise instructions to commence his operations by reducing the island ; and in order to provide him with a land force, a strong body of Asiatic troops was directed to assemble at Scalanova, a thriving commercial town, with a large Christian and Mohammedan population. Elez Aga, one of the great military vassals of the crown, and head of a distinguished family, which for generations had ruled Scalanova and the adjacent territory, was charged with the command of the army, composed of twelve or thirteen thousand men, and comprehending those vagabonds who had perpetrated so many enormities at Smyrna. Notwithstanding the strict police observed in his states, and the constant protection he extended to Rayahs, it was impossible for him to restrain

this disorderly multitude awaiting in idleness the
coming of the Ottoman fleet; they pillaged the neighbouring country, and threatened the town itself, which
Elez Aga, at the head of his household troops, with
much trouble and personal risk, endeavoured to preserve from their rage. A Greek, mortally wounded
by a Turk, having in a fit of despair slain the assassin
with his own weapon, that circumstance caused a general mutiny of the soldiers; those who had hitherto
remained faithful to their Aga joined the unruly portion; several hundred Greeks were immolated, their
wives and children enslaved, their shops and houses
ransacked, and the town having been set on fire, was
saved from total conflagration only through the exertions of its Mussulman inhabitants: the irregular
army then disbanded, bearing away the spoils of the
province. The Capitana Bey arriving after this tu-
mult was over, although deprived of the co-operation
he expected, did not give up his design, but endeavoured to reassemble the land forces, and summoned
the people of Samos to submit, assuring them that
Hydra, Spezzia, and Psarra had surrendered at discretion. Wishing to gain time, the Islanders demanded three days to consider his proposal; provided with some cannon and gunpowder from Psarra,
they had formed batteries to defend Vathi, their
chief town and port, but they trusted more to the
strength of their rocks, which defy artillery. On the
18th Kara Ali approached, and sent a thousand men
in boats to effect a landing; scarcely however had
they touched the beach, when the Samians surrounded,
attacked, and defeated them with such carnage, that
two hundred dead bodies were subsequently washed
ashore by the waves. Their repulse discouraged those
who were following, and induced them to return to
the ships, while Kara Ali tried to take his revenge by

an useless discharge of cannon balls against the mountains. He was preparing to make a fresh effort, as soon as he should have collected a sufficient corps of troops, when the apparition of the Greek fleet suddenly altered his plans. Never did the insurgents, at any period of the contest, put to sea with such numerous squadrons ; informed of the danger of Samos, they united their marine at Psarra, and on the 19th of July passed before Scio with 90 sail, to the astonishment and dismay of the Turks of that island. Afraid of their brulots, the Ottoman admiral weighed anchor, and, standing to the southward, by his pusillanimity threw a notable advantage into the hands of his adversaries. On the 21st the Greeks descried ten hostile transports, full of troops, coming out of Janakli, and going to join the Capitana Bey : they instantly gave chase, upon which the Turks, after attempting in vain to regain the harbour, ran their vessels aground, and posting themselves behind a wood, opened a musketry fire ; but the insurgents soon dislodged them by a shower of grapeshot, and then de patching their boats, burnt the transports. The Samians were thus delivered from immediate apprehension, for the Asiatic soldiers positively refused to embark again. Entering the channel that separates the isle from Cape Mycale, the Hellenic fleet anchored in the roads of Colones, where the captains held a council of war, to deliberate how they might best assail the Sultan's powerful armament, that was so ingloriously retiring before them. Early in the morning of the 23d they sailed in quest of the Turks, and finding them on the 24th at the island of Cos, sent four fireships to attack them, but in consequence of the wind failing, met with no success. Kara Ali having manned his launches, the Greeks on board the fireships were obliged to leave them precipitately ; three were

consumed without doing any damage, and the fourth
fell into the enemy's hands.   The Capitana Bey was
very proud of this affair, which, in his despatches to
Constantinople, he represented as equivalent to a victory.   The Greeks, returning to Colones, landed there
a quantity of ammunition for the use of the Samians,
and the Capitana Bey proceeded to Rhodes, where he
was reinforced by a flotilla belonging to the Pasha of
Egypt, consisting of one frigate and thirteen smaller
vessels, and having on board several hundred Albanian
troops: lest it should be intercepted on the way, Mehemet Ali kept its departure secret, and laid an embargo on the port of Alexandria from the 15th of June
to the 14th of July.   While the Mussulmans lay at
Rhodes, the principal officers of the Hellenic fleet were
considering what measures they ought to pursue, and
on the 7th of August, (off the Isle of Nisyra,) Emanuel
Tombazi sketched a disposition, which he submitted
to their judgment; proposing, that when they gave
battle, their force should be drawn up in two columns,
one of Hydriotes and half the contingent of Psarra,
the other of Spezziotes, with the residue of the Psarrians; that the fireships, of which they had seven,
should be placed in the centre, and that each column
should act against one extremity of the hostile line.
His plan was adopted, but, when put to the proof, the
Greeks discovered that it required too much obedience
and discipline for them to execute.   After the junction
of the Egyptian squadron under Ismael Gibraltar, the
Turkish admiral quitted Rhodes, and encountered
(August the 10th) the insurgents in the waters of Patmos.   They engaged him without any favourable result, only a small portion of their fleet went into action,
and was saved from imminent peril by its skilful manœuvres: a fireship was uselessly burnt, and the confusion was so great, that had the Turks bore down

with spirit they might have entirely defeated them. Fortunately a dread of the brulots paralysed the movements of the Mohammedans. During some days the armaments continued to observe each other, that of the Capitana Bey sailing always in a dense mass; the Greeks had now remained out for upwards of a month, and the sailors, as usual, insisting upon going home to revisit their families, their commanders were compelled before the end of August to return into the ports of their respective islands. Indeed for several past weeks the defection of single ships had been gradually weakening their squadrons; from 90 sail, they were, on the 25th of July, reduced to 53, and each morning discovered new desertions. Emanuel Tombazi being sent out again in a fast sailing schooner to watch the Turks, came back to Hydrā on the 3d of September, with intelligence that they were steering for Candia; however we shall presently see, that Kara Ali, as soon as his motions were free, sailed to the Morea.

SECTION II.

THE arrival in Greece of Prince Demetrius Ypsilanti, second brother to the Generalissimo of the Hetœria, forms a sort of epoch in the history of the first year of the Revolution. Appointed by Prince Alexander to conduct the war in the southern provinces, he set out from Kishneff, traversed in disguise the Austrian states, and embarking at Trieste, reached Hydra on the 19th of June, 1821.* He was received with the firing of cannon, ringing of bells, and other demonstrations of joy, and the Hydriotes made no difficulty about acknowledging the validity of the commission he held. Prince Gregory Cantacuzene accompanied him, and several persons of his suite, that were

* The very day on which his brother was routed at Dragashan.

in another vessel, having been driven by contrary winds
into Cefalonia, rejoined him shortly after in the Morea.
He spent a week in the islands, and sailing from Spezzia
on the 27th, landed next day at Astros, on the shore
of Cynouria, and was there welcomed by a deputation
of Peloponnesian senators and generals; among the
latter was Colocotroni, who drew up some hundred
soldiers on the beach, and saluted him with three volleys of musketry.   Their progress from thence to Vervena (a village near Tripolizza, where the seat of government was provisionally established,) resembled a
triumphal procession : the peasants, headed by the
priests, showered on them as they passed along, bene-
dictions, and the appellation of liberators ; and when
Ypsilanti alighted from his horse at the church of Vervena, Mavromikhalis Bey of Maina embraced him, saying, " Prince, I and my family are ready to shed our
blood for our country and your Highness !"   So brilliant a reception seemed to promise the happiest results,
but unfortunately this fair prospect was soon clouded.

    Here it is necessary to enter into some minute
details respecting the characters and private views of
those persons who enacted the most prominent parts
in the scenes that are about to flit before our eyes.
Demetrius Ypsilanti (lately a captain in the Russian
service) was 25 years old, had received a liberal education, and been accustomed to the best society: nature had favoured him more in mind than in his cor-
poreal frame, for his diminutive stature, bald head,
awkward carriage, and indistinct utterance, were ill
calculated to win the opinions of those who beheld him.
On the other hand, it was difficult to know without
esteeming him, for even his enemies were forced to
confess, that to ardent patriotism he united courage,
integrity, and humanity, disregarded the allurements
of pleasure, and had much goodness of heart, with a

steadiness of purpose which at times bordered upon obstinacy. His constitutional apathy and love of sleep made him appear almost torpid ; he conceived too high an idea of the validity of his title to govern Greece, and had too little sharpness and energy: but what hurt him more than all the rest, was his suffering himself to be guided by men of indifferent character, altogether unworthy of his confidence. Cantacuzene, as short in stature as Ypsilanti, was however of a more agreeable figure and engaging manners, acute and lively in his disposition.

Of the Hetœrists in Ypsilanti's suite, the principal were, the Chevalier Affendouli, a knight of Malta, Candiotti (previously valet-de-chambre and political emissary of Count Capodistria), who laboured under the imputation of having purloined 8000 florins, subscribed by a commercial house in Vienna towards defraying the expenses of the war, and Vambas, formerly Rector of the college of Scio, an ecclesiastic of unfeigned piety and learning, but fitter to preside over an academy than a turbulent nation : nevertheless, Ypsilanti named him secretary of state.   Besides these, the Prince was followed by Count Mercati of Zante, by Sala, a Bessarabian, who acted as his aide-de-camp, Anagnostopoulos, a member of the Grand Arch, Antinopoulos, his treasurer, and a few young Greeks recruited in Russia. The majority of his companions seemed to suppose that they had come to administer every thing at their pleasure, and had only to select such employments as suited them best ; they found, however, men quite as ambitious as themselves, more skilled in intrigue, and possessing the immense advantage of long established influence in the country.   In the first rank of the Peloponnesians stood forth Theodore Colocotroni, whose origin and adventures merit special notice.   Sprung from a lineage that never acknowledged the sway of

the Turks, nor deigned to pay them tribute, Colocotroni was inured from his cradle to danger, fatigue,
and the stratagems of mountain warfare.   His father,
after signalizing himself for many years, was put to a
cruel death ; his brothers shared a similar fate, and
Theodore, heir to the reputation of his house, fully
sustained it by his own predatory exploits, until obliged
to emigrate, when he served with his sword the Russians, and then the English, in the Ionian Isles.   On
his return, in 1821, the family of Delhiyani seconded
him with all their might, and procured him the command of the troops of Karitena, next to the Mainatts
the most numerous and warlike in Peloponnesus.   He
was a valuable acquisition to the insurgents from his
tact, experience, nay, we may say genius, for the kind
of operations which they had to carry on,* since his
military talents as a partisan were unparalleled in
Greece ; at the same time, it cannot be denied, that his
sordid avarice, and mean ambition, which was merely
a handmaid to the former passion, severely scourged
his country.   It would be impossible for a painter or a
novelist to trace a more romantic delineation of a robber chieftain, than the figure of Colocotroni presented ;
tall and athletic, with a profusion of black hair and
expressive features, alternately lighted up with boisterous gaiety, or darkened by bursts of passion : among
his soldiers, he seemed born to command, having just
the manners and bearing calculated to gain their confidence.   Besides his ancient fame, renovated by the

* The following anecdote, illustrative of the Kleftic character,
reminds us of the age of Homer.   The family of Colocotroni having
been bound in close intimacy with that of Ali Bey of Lalla, when the
latter was besieged in his tower by Veli Pasha, he craved aid of the
former, then an exile in Zante ; Colocotroni instantly set out, and
with seventeen companions threw himself into the tower, which the Bey
and he defended, till the Pasha granted a capitulation, securing life
and fortune to the Lalliote rebels, and a safe retreat to their Greek allies.

laurels of Valtezza, and the friendship of the Delhiya-neis, he derived considerable support from his brother-in-law Colliopoulo, his nephew Niketas, and two brave sons of a military age. Anagnostoras, an aged and renowned Kleftic leader, had next to Colocotroni the greatest weight in the councils of the insurgent captains : his adventurous career had been of the same description, for after long braving the Turks, he commanded a company in the corps raised by Major Church. They were linked in the bonds of strict amity, although differing in character : years and corpulence had impaired the vigour of Anagnostoras, but his calmness and prudence obtained for him, among his colleagues, the name of Nestor.

It now remains for us to speak of the Primates and the Hierarchy, two classes that were equally conspicuous throughout the revolution. The former, called also Archons and Kojabashees, and subsequently Ephors, were municipal magistrates invested with a vague and ill-defined jurisdiction in the civil and fiscal affairs of their communes, collecting and apportioning the imposts : the bishops had a voice in their deliberations, and, in addition to their spiritual authority, exercised judicial functions, deciding, according to the Byzantine law, those causes, which the Christians were unwilling to submit to Mohammedan tribunals. Being thus rendered a medium of communication between the government and the Rayahs, the Primates necessarily acquired power in their provinces, and too often abused it in a way most discreditable to themselves, and injurious to the people. It is true, that their post was irksome and dangerous, and that as the Turks made them responsible for the taxes, while in cases of public distress they were frequently obliged to borrow money on their own security, at a high rate of interest, for the benefit of their districts, they could hardly be satisfied with the stipulated retribution of a thousand piastres per annum. With few exceptions, the Kojabashees showed themselves as base as so vicious a system might reasonably be expected to render them ; nursed in effeminacy amidst the adulation of their dependents—cringing to the Turks, who, unable to dispense with their acuteness and information, looked upon them as necessary evils—having just education enough to enable them to deceive the masters, and tyrannize over the slaves—living in constant fear, though puffed up with puerile vanity, they were ready instruments of oppression, and seldom failed to share the spoil. The views of the higher clergy coincided pretty nearly with those of the Primates, as they had always acted in concert, and the latter in point of dignity yielded precedence to the Hierarchy. Both hoped, in promoting the insurrection, that having once got rid of the Turks, they should engross all power and profit, and establish an Oligarchy ; trusting to intrigue and political sagacity, for acquiring a complete ascendency over the captains, whose swords were necessary to the success of their plans, but whose capacity they despised. The arrival of Demetrius Ypsilanti was agreeable to this numerous and aspiring body, because they stood in need of a show of Russian protection, to encourage the lower orders ; but his pretensions to little less than absolute sovereignty, alarmed their jealousy, and greatly displeased them. The Archons of Hydra and Spezzia promptly acknowledged his claim to command, thinking they would, through his means, obtain from the Morea some compensation for the charges they had been put to ; for, in those democratical republics, it was altogether impossible to draw money from the people ; and the magistracy, although alluring to the ambition of the principal citizens, proved a perpetual source of trouble and expense ; but in Peloponnesus, the peasants were submissive, and authority brought lucre as well as honour. Hardly had the Prince set his foot at Vervena, before the Senate manifested its strenuous opposition to his projects ; an opposition confirmed by the news of his brother's defeat, and the certainty that he had with him very slender resources, consisting only in 150 stand of arms, and about 200,000 piastres in money, most of which he imprudently lent to the Bey of Maina.   The bearing, too, of several persons of his retinue, and their airs of superiority, were offensive to the pride of the Moreotes ; afraid lest, by concession, they should place a master over their heads, the leading men of the Peninsula immediately conspired together to weaken the Prince's influence, thwart his views, diminish his popularity, and even disgust him with the country.   They began by furnishing his table with a scanty supply of provisions, under the false pretext of a scarcity, left part of his suite two days without bread, and positively drove away, through hunger, a number of islanders, who had volunteered to serve him : an Ephor of Mistra actually countermanded a convoy of fifteen mules laden with bread, that were on their way to Vervena.   Shortly after coming there, Ypsilanti proposed to the Senate a draft of a constitution, in twenty-four articles, the two most essential of which were, that a national assembly should be convoked from all Greece, and that he, as his brother's vicegerent, should be invested with the entire command of the army ; this being a degree of power they never intended to give him, the primates instantly rejected his constitution. The Prince, who had already begun to confer offices, and send commissioners to different provinces, renewed his proposals through the medium of Candiotti, when the latter was so rash as to threaten the Senate with the vengeance of Russia and Alexander Ypsilanti ; a ridiculous bravado, that only tended to irritate their

refractory spirits. As the eloquent Vambas in vain
employed his rhetoric to persuade them to comply, and
the breach was widening every day, the Prince resolved
to quit Peloponnesus, and put himself at the head of
the Epirote insurgents : on the 10th of July, he departed abruptly from Vervena, and proceeded towards Calamata, in order to embark there. This step produced
the consequences his advisers had anticipated ; a violent
commotion broke out in the camp of Trikorpha, the
soldiers declaring they would disband if Ypsilanti was
not brought back : and at Vervena, they surrounded
Petro Bey's house, where the Senate was assembled, and
demanded an account of the conduct of that body. Terrified by the ebullition of popular feeling, the primates
sent Anagnostoras in pursuit of the Prince, whom he
overtook beyond Leondari, and engaged to return ; not,
however, to Vervena, but to the camp before Tripolizza,
where, on the 15th, he assumed the command, amidst
such tokens of affection and gladness, that had he in
the first moment availed himself of the good-will of the
troops, he might probably have crushed the adverse faction. He undoubtedly committed a grievous error in not
obliging the Senate to sign the constitution he had offered, or, at least, to grant him some definite powers by a
formal instrument ; on the other side, the Kojabashees,
supposing that in going away he was instigated by a
desire to get them assassinated, never forgave him the
fright they had endured.

Let us now consider the state of the Morea, at the
period when Demetrius Ypsilanti entered upon his
functions as general in chief. After the evacuation of
Lalla, the Turks had no longer any footing in the
open country, but were forced to confine themselves to
the possession of nine fortresses, viz., in Achaia, Patrass, and the Morea castle, forming one system of
defence with the opposite castle of Roumelia, and with

Lepanto ; Navarin, Coron, and Modon, in Messenia ; Napoli di Romania, and the Acrocorinthus, in Argolis ; Monemvasia, in Laconia ; and Tripolizza in the central plain of Arcadia. As the Greeks, without artillery, engineers, working tools, or pioneers, could not undertake a regular siege, they contented themselves with observing those fortresses, and blockading them more or less strictly, according to local circumstances, and the strength of their garrisons. None of them (except Corinth and Napoli) contained magazines sufficient for a long resistance, since the insurrection had been so sudden and universal, that it afforded the Turks little time to collect supplies. Patrass, indeed, drew provisions from the Ionian Islands, and the troops within it were so numerous, that the insurgents, posted at the bottom of the hills skirting its plain, could only watch their movements, and endeavour to prevent their making excursions to any considerable distance from the walls. The Acrocorinthus, situated farther from the sea, and weakly garrisoned, was easily blockaded by the peasants of the adjacent cantons. Napoli di Romania, the most important stronghold in Peloponnesus, was observed by fifteen hundred Argives under Captain Nicholas, brother to Nikitas, while Bobolina, with two vessels of her own, cruised in the gulf. Monemvasia, Coron, Modon, and Navarin, closely blockaded by Mainatts, Messenians, and Spezziote vessels, that hovered on the coast, were already reduced to the deepest distress. The two parties, on all these points, carried on their operations according to a method as old as the siege of Troy. The Greeks, encamping on the strongest ground they could find, just out of cannon shot of the forts, pushed forward every day detachments of volunteers, who stealing on, and sheltering themselves behind stones, engaged with the enemy an interchange of musket balls, and opprobrious epithets, sometimes interrupted by a temporary truce, during which, soldiers of both nations might be seen sitting in groups, smoking and conversing on the chances of the war, their private affairs, and the health of their acquaintances; these truces were very seldom violated. The Turks frequently made sorties, not so much with a hope of driving back their opponents, as to breathe a freer air, and divert their ennui; on such occasions, the main body of the Greeks advanced to support their outposts, and actions ensued remarkable rather for noise and waste of powder, than for the loss sustained; until the Moslems thinking they had taken sufficient exercise, and pressed by superior numbers, retired behind their ramparts. Such affairs generally occurred early in the morning, or just before sunset; during the noontide heat, besiegers and besieged slept and took their meals, and the nights were passed in so perfect a repose, that had either chosen to be on the alert, they might have surprised the enemy. The Turks, however, like other Orientals, are averse to fighting in the dark, and the Greeks resigned themselves to slumber, in as profound security, as though no foeman had been near.

Monemvasia (called by the Italians Napoli di Malvasia) was the first to open its gates. That extraordinary fortress stands on a little islet, communicating with the mainland of Laconia by a bridge or causeway; the town is on the south-east side, surrounded by a rampart, and behind it rises the citadel on a high and steep rock, accessible by a single pathway, every inch of which is exposed to the fire of the garrison. Nature has rendered it so completely impregnable, that no works have been erected, save where batteries are placed; but on account of its defective roadstead, and the parched and rugged mountains that isolate it from the rest of the peninsula, it is of minor consequence as a military post. Its Turkish inhabitants, shut up since the 14th day of April, were so sorely afflicted by famine, that after eating a quantity of cotton seeds, which caused a deadly sickness amongst them, they subsisted for some time on human flesh. The Mainatts were entrenched at the head of the causeway, and two Spezziote vessels lay before the town; while the governor, occupying the citadel with a select party of men, prepared to hold out to the last extremity, and refused to share his provisions with the people below, who, having no alternative between submission and death, began to treat with Prince Cantacuzene, sent by Ypsilanti from Vervena to conduct the siege. The negotiation being protracted, the Prince made one or two fruitless assaults upon the bridge; hunger, however, was doing his work more surely, for the Agas of the lower town, seeing that the commandant would listen to no terms, seized the gate of the citadel by stratagem, disarmed his troops, and on the 3d of August surrendered to the Greeks on the following conditions:—1st, that their lives and honour should be safe: 2d, that private property should be respected. 3d, that the garrison and inhabitants should be transported by sea to the coast of Asia. It was impossible, with an army of Mainatts, to fulfil the second of these stipulations; but through the spirit and firmness of Cantacuzene, the first and third were generally executed. A few Turks, indeed, fell a sacrifice to the vengeance of persons who had lost relations during the siege, but the bulk of the captives (500 in number) were shipped on board three Spezziotes, and landed on an island off the Asiatic shore, whence they passed to Scalanova. The Agas most instrumental in delivering up the place, not daring to return to Turkey, received permission to remain where they were. In this business Cantacuzene behaved in a manner that gave a favourable idea of his character, doing his duty with resolution, and paying no regard to the seditious clamours of his troops, who, as was usual in Greece, raised tumults about the division of spoil ; at one time he was compelled to barricade his house, and order his body-guard of Roumeliotes to fire from the windows on a party of mutineers.   Nevertheless, when he arrived at the camp of Trikorpha, Ypsilanti treated him coldly, and no cordiality henceforth reigned betwixt them.

The capture of Monemvasia was followed by that of Navarin, a more valuable conquest, as it possesses the largest haven in Europe : the town, small and ill fortified, had before the revolution a trifling population, but at the period in question, contained from 2000 to 3000 Mohammedans, most of whom had flocked thither from Arkadia (the ancient Cyparissia), and from villages in the neighbourhood. Invested by 2000 Messenian peasants, and 200 Ionians, under the Bishop of Modon and Count Mercati, the besieged made a vigorous resistance, and several sorties, until worn out by disease, hunger, and thirst, the Greeks having cut the aqueduct that supplied them with water ; they even mined their houses, determined rather to perish than submit to the enemy.   Having at length consumed every article of food, and even the leather of their slippers, and hoping to obtain their lives from Ypsilanti's clemency, they proposed to capitulate on the same terms as those of Monemvasia, if the Prince would guarantee their safety.   Ypsilanti, accordingly, sent there as his commissioners a French officer named Balesto, and Tipaldo, a Cefalonian physician, who had accompanied him from Bessarabia. They, clearly perceiving that no capitulation would be kept, wisely refused to compromise the Prince's honour by making him a party to the negotiation.   It was evident that the Moslems could only spin out their defence for a

very few days, but the Greeks were extremely anxious
to abridge the term ; for besides their apprehensions of
the Ottoman fleet, their soldiers, as well as the crews
of two Spezziote vessels that blockaded the place by
sea, were suffering from a scarcity approaching to famine. Two deputies, Photius, an Albanian, and Poniropoulos of Pyrgos, less scrupulous than Tipaldo and
Balesto, signed therefore a convention, promising to
the unhappy Turks what they neither could, nor, indeed, ever intended to grant, namely, a secure passage
to Africa. On this assurance, the besieged threw open
their gates about the middle of August, when the insurgents, giving a loose to the worst passions, perpetrated a dismal tragedy : all the prisoners, except 160,
were either massacred, or left to perish on a barren
rock in the harbour. Unhappily the Greeks, like the
Eastern nations in every age, rarely paid any attention
to their oaths or faith plighted to an enemy ; a species of treachery which, although profitable to worthless individuals, was highly prejudicial to their cause.
In the present instance, if ever so well disposed, they
could not have fulfilled the terms of the capitulation,
since they had no means either to feed or embark the
captives.*

On the very same day that the Hellenic banner was
planted on the walls of Monemvasia, there occurred a
circumstance different in its nature, but more important in its effects ; this was the arrival in Greece of
Alexander Mavrocordato. Descended from the oldest
of the noble Fanariote families, which had often reigned in Dacia ; distinguished in early youth by his ability,

---

* So weak was the moral perception in Greece, that one of the ne-
gotiators above mentioned boasted to the author, of his address in
purloining and destroying a copy of the capitulation given to the
Turks, that no proof might remain of any such transaction having
been concluded.

polished manners, and extensive learning ; comely in
person, and speaking with the utmost fluency many
languages of the East and West, Mavrocordato held,
in 1818, an eminent post at the court of Karadja, Hospodar of Wallachia, (whom he attended on his flight
into Austria,) and was living at Pisa when the revolution broke out. Ambitious, aspiring, and aware of
his superiority over his most enlightened countrymen,
he lost no time in hastening to a field where he might
fairly hope to leave all competitors behind, and expended his small fortune, and what sums he could draw
from Karadja, in the way he thought most beneficial.
Having freighted a Hydriote brig under Russian colours, he proceeded from Leghorn to Marseilles, and
taking on board some young Greeks, some French and
Italian officers, and 2500 stand of arms, sailed for
Greece on the 10th of July, and landed at Messalonghi
on the 3d of the following month.   There he spent a
week consulting with the primates and captains, and
then crossed the gulf, and visited the camp before Patrass. The necessity of dislodging the Lalliotes having
during June absorbed the attention of the insurgents
of Achaia and Elis, Yussuf Pasha enjoyed a respite
from their attacks, and was able to go to the assistance
of the Albanians of Lalla; however, as soon as the
Greeks had got rid of that nest of hornets, they again
advanced towards Patrass.   Mavrocordato found near
5000 men assembled there, full of enthusiasm, but very
badly armed, and in a state of complete disorder : the
Archbishop Germanos had gone to join the Senate in
its deliberations ; and the army was commanded by an
infinity of petty captains, acting independently, and
disagreeing with each other. The monastery of Om-
bloz, where resided the Primates Zaimis and Kanakaris,
contained their magazine and ovens, and served as a
depot for the wounded, who were without any surgical

aid : two small fieldpieces composed their park of artillery. Including the Lalliotes, the armed Turks at
Patrass amounted to 4000, encumbered with families
and cattle ; as the town was in ruins, and the castle
not spacious enough to hold them all, many were
forced to pass the nights round the exterior foot of the
ramparts. Mavrocordato came just in time to witness
a general engagement, for on the 14th of August the
Mussulmans executed a brisk sortie, covered by the
fire of three heavy battering guns, which they dragged
forth the evening before to a burial-ground without
the castle. After a smart action of two hours, they
were repulsed towards the cemetery ; Yussuf Pasha
then marched out in person, with a body of fresh troops,
restored the battle, and was on the point of taking the
Greek camp, when the European officers played the
two fieldpieces upon the Turks with so much effect,
that they were again driven back, chased from the positions where they attempted to rally, and finally compelled to retreat under the protection of the citadel.
Their cannon, left slightly guarded in the burial-
ground, might have been captured, had the insurgents
ventured on a night attack. About 100 Turks were
slain, and 15 taken and beheaded : the Greeks had
20 killed, and twice as many wounded, several of whom
subsequently bled to death for want of instruments and
bandages. Having remained a few days in the vicinity of Patrass, Mavrocordato proceeded to Tripolizza,
whose reduction was an object of paramount interest
to the Peloponnesians.

That city, the seat of provincial government, and
ordinary residence of the Pashas of the Morea, lies in
the heart of Arcadia, on an extensive and elevated
table land, enclosed by the peaks of Mounts Mænalion,
Parthenius, and Artemision, and is at nearly an equal

distance from the ruins of Mantinea and Tegea.* It
was defended by a wall of stone, two miles in circuit,
and 14 feet high, with a number of small towers, and
at considerable intervals some demi-bastions, on which
cannon were mounted : the lower part of the rampart
was six feet thick, the upper not above three, thus
leaving, at a height of nine feet from the ground, a narrow and inconvenient banquette, with a double row of
loopholes for musketry.   At its western extremity,
within the wall, stood a citadel of more modern date,
provided with bomb-proof casemates ; being commanded, however, by a knoll at the distance of 200
yards, and of very confined dimensions, it was incapable of resisting a regular attack.   Thirty pieces of
cannon, mostly of small calibre, and out of repair, were
planted on the ramparts of the town and citadel, and
served by a company of Topjees (or gunners) from
Constantinople.   Although Tripolizza boasted of one
or two vast palaces, it was an ugly and a dirty place,
with a population computed, previously to the war, at
15,000, of whom 7000 were Greeks, and 1000 Jews :
the Christians had chiefly fled, but this void was much
more than filled up by the Mohammedans of Mistra,
Bardounia, Leondari, and Fanari, to whom must be
added the Kihaya-bey's troops.   The lowest statement
that has yet been published, rates the whole number
of persons shut up there at 30,000, but we are inclined
to believe it never exceeded 25,000, of whom, perhaps,
9000 carried arms.†   After the battle of Valtezza, the
insurgents took post among the crags of Trikorpha,
whence they gradually descended to lower ground, as
the strength and spirit of the besieged appeared to

---

* The cold and naked plain of Tripolizza is at an altitude of
2600 feet above the Argolic Gulf ; one of the tops of Mænalion rises
4000, and Malliovo, a peak of Artemision, 3000 feet higher.

† Such was the estimate of a Turkish prisoner of rank.

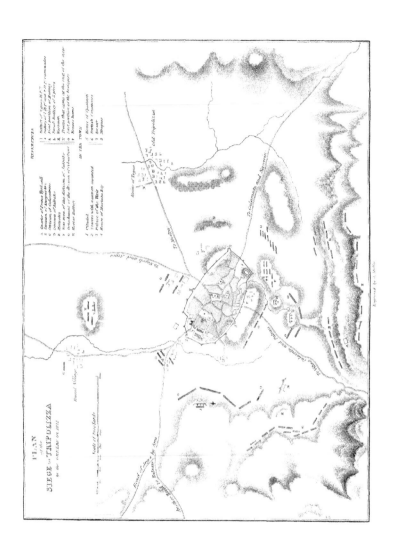

PLAN
of the
SIEGE OF TRIPOLIZZA
by the Greeks in 1821

REFERENCES

1 Battery of Tipus N.ᵒˢ
2 Battery of the Front of C.ᵗ commander
3 First position of Battery
4 Small Battery of 2 pieces
R Barracan
K Troops that came in the rout of the siege
S Last position of the Barrigan
P Roman Ruins

In the Town

A Quarter of Prince Ypsilanti
B Castain of Anagnostaras
C Castain of Colocotroni
D Cottana of Kliftaki
E Mavrodas
F Ten siege of the division of Zaiteri
G Detachment of the division of Colocotroni
H Massa Ruthei

1 Citadel
2 Tower with eastern mounted
3 Palace of the Three
4 House of Mustaba Bey

5 Houses of Ypsilanti
6 Turkish Cemeteries
7 Bazaar
8 Mosque

evaporate : they cut off the aqueduct, and established a battery of three guns (one 24-pounder, and two 12 lb. carronades), at a distance of 1400 yards from the town.

For a long time, their cavalry rendered the Ottomans masters of the plain, until fodder growing scarce, that species of force dwindled away; provisions also became rare, and an epidemic fever made terrible ravages among them. Nevertheless, they rejected with disdain an offer of capitulation proposed to them by Ypsilanti; yet they did not undertake any vigorous attempt to disperse the besiegers, which would not have been very difficult, since, till the close of September, the garrison was certainly superior in number to the blockading army. Turkish courage, though sometimes flashing out in a short-lived access of fury, is in general mere impassibility ; and, besides this national inertness, the Moreote Moslems were strangers to war, and discord divided the principal Beys. Daily skirmishes were fought, without any other result than the loss of a few lives: on the approach of horse, the Greeks fell back to the root of the mountain, behind rocks, and walls of loose stones, where the enemy durst not assail them. The main body of the Peloponnesians was hutted on the slope of Trikorpha, at somewhat more than a cannon-shot from Tripolizza; Colocotroni's corps, reckoned at 2500 men, formed the left wing; Anagnostoras commanded 1000 in the centre, where Ypsilanti pitched his tent; Yatrako of Mistra, who from a quack doctor had been converted into a general, was posted on the right, with 1200 Laconians ; lastly, the Bey of Maina, with a reserve of 700 or 800 Mainatts, occupied the steepest summit, behind the centre and right. Under direction of the primates, provisions were sent into the camp from the different districts, each furnishing rations equivalent to the

computed amount of its soldiers. As many of them
were always absent from their colours, on journeys to
their native villages, the surplus rations were allotted
to the Prince's suite and the Mainatts ; but the former
often wanted bread, while the latter frequently plundered, without ceremony, convoys on their way to the
army. Some detachments guarded various defiles, on
the skirts of the plain : Nikitas, with 300 men, held
the strong pass of Steno, leading to Argos, and another party of 150 watched the road to Leondari.

In the end of August the Greeks obtained a marked
advantage over the Kihaya-bey, who issued out of the
city with a body of cavalry and many sumpter-mules,
in order to carry off maize from a village called Grana,
on the side of Mantinea, and a league and a half from
Tripolizza. Encountered with valour and judgment
by Captain Manolaki of Prasto, who commanded there,
the Turks were beginning to retreat with the grain
they had reaped, when Colocotroni came up and fell
upon them at the head of 500 men, while Anagnostoras
threw himself on their line of retreat ; thus encircled,
they were entirely defeated, and would hardly have
been able to re-enter Tripolizza, if a reinforcement had
not sallied out to support them. Colocotroni returned
to the camp in triumph, having an hundred Mussulman heads borne before him, and all the mules with
their loads remained in the hands of the insurgents.
Immediately after this affair, Mavrocordato reached
Trikorpha on the 26th of August ; his presence did
not give satisfaction to Ypsilanti, who saw in him a
rival as much superior to himself in tact and address,
as inferior in political honesty. For the same reason
the aristocratical faction received him with pleasure,
and his conciliatory manners soon procured him numerous adherents ; among others, Cantacuzene, who,
already disgusted with the Morea, attached himself to

Mavrocordato, and resolved, in concert with the latter, to attempt organizing Northern Greece : on the 9th of September they departed together for Messalonghi. The assembly of Vervena was now broken up ; but the Peloponnesian Senate, or rather a provisional junto of Kojabashees, sat at Sarrakova (a village near the camp), and derived weight and popularity from the appearance and co-operation of the Archbishop of Patrass. That prelate was far from wanting capacity ; and his power of language, his high dignity in the church, and energetic behaviour at the commencement of the revolution, made him be looked up to by the people ; their admiration, however, slackened, when it was too plainly seen, that unbounded pride, ambition, and love of pleasure lurked under the mask of religious zeal. Germanos soon threw aside his assumed sanctity, and showed himself in camp and council, dressed in gaudy apparel, with the airs of a sovereign. Another prelate (the Bishop of Helos) offered a strong contrast to the secular pomp of the Metropolitan ; with every external sign of humility, he was a real enthusiast, always ready either to preach or to fight, and consequently had an extraordinary ascendency over the soldiers.* Germanos's influence was then at its zenith, and he used it to oppose and cry down Ypsilanti. Next to him in consideration at Sarrakovo, and not behind him in factious intrigue, were Anagnosti Delhiyani of Karitena, and Sotiri Karalambi of Kalavryta, both great primates ; the matters in dispute were still the same as before the Prince's secession from Vervena, to wit, the degree of actual authority to be granted him in his qua-

---

* One day the Bishop of Helos delivered in camp a discourse on the duty of sparing women, children, and unarmed persons, and denounced an anathema against those who should injure any such ; few of the Greek clergy professed similar sentiments of humanity.

lity of Generalissimo, the title being no longer denied. Ypsilanti demanded very extended powers, subject only to the control of an assembly to be hereafter called together from all parts of free Greece: the Ephors insisted that he should be strictly dependant upon, and accountable to, not an Hellenic, but a Peloponnesian Senate, that he should do nothing without consulting them, should neither reward nor punish officers without their concurrence, nor retain in his service any foreigner. The truth is, the Prince aimed at absolute sway, and the primates wished to set up an oligarchical tyranny, and maintain every thing on its old footing, with the single exception of abolishing the Turks. Although Ypsilanti had assisted them to pay the Mainatts, they refused to furnish him with the smallest supply, and even charged him an exorbitant price for the subsistence of a corps of regulars he was endeavouring to form at Calamata. Provoked at their obstinacy, he proposed to make use of the military chiefs as a counterpoise; but he could not succeed in gaining Colocotroni, who was influenced by the Delhiyaneis, and although treating Ypsilanti with outward respect, did not conceal from others his contempt of him. To add to this perplexed state of affairs, the islanders brought forward a claim for compensation on account of the expense they had incurred in guarding the coasts of Peloponnesus, threatening, if it was not allowed, to withdraw their ships. Amidst these dissensions, the siege of Tripolizza proceeded, with a sure prospect of final success, as the enemy's distress was fast augmenting. On the 3d of September several hundred Greeks lodged themselves in the ruins of some burned houses on the northern side of the wall, and for two hours braved the fire of the place; however, a party of horse issuing from an opposite quarter, and turning their position, obliged them to retire with loss.

A few days after, Colocotroni adopted a measure that effectually ruined the cavalry of the besieged. They were accustomed to send out their horses every morning to pasture, covered by a detachment, posted in a village 1200 yards from the town, within whose walls both the horses and their guard passed the night : Colocotroni having established himself before daybreak in the village, with an hundred men, the Turks, when they came out as usual, finding it occupied, quietly turned back without a thought of retaking it, and henceforth their horses, restricted to the withered herbage at the bottom of the rampart, either died or became unserviceable : the Greeks, not at all afraid of their enemies on foot, then closely invested the city. Meanwhile, their minds were alternately agitated with fear and hope by reports from various directions : on the 9th intelligence arrived that the Ottoman fleet had appeared off the southern coast of the Morea, relieved Modon and Coron, and menaced Calamata. It soon indeed sailed away; but as Patrass was its certain destination, apprehensions prevailed lest it should take troops on board in Albania, and land them in the peninsula, while it was no secret that a Turkish army was on its march from Macedonia to join the corps which had already recovered Thebes and Athens, and attempt the relief of Tripolizza. In the course of a day or two, these anxieties were dispelled by official news, that the Roumeliote Greeks had gained a complete victory near Thermopylæ, and accounts from Epirus, that Khourshid Pasha was too deeply engaged in hostilities with the Christians and Mohammedans of that country, to be able to despatch any succours to the Morea. As the insurgents were eager to accelerate the surrender of Tripolizza, they prepared to besiege it in form ; brought cannon from the islands, and three heavy mortars, (two of thirteen and one of ten inches,)

with a quantity of bombs and bullets from Monemvasia. An Italian saddler from Smyrna, who gave himself out for an engineer, having burst, at his first essay,[*]
the only mortar which was in good condition, the
Prince confided the business to a young French officer
named Raybaud, who, aided by all the Western Europeans in the army, acquitted himself extremely well,
and showed much ingenuity and perseverance in contending against obstacles that seemed insurmountable.
However, from the defective state of the ordnance, the
want of workmen and stores, the attack was but a vain
shadow. The artillery consisted of two mortars, (both
spiked and dismounted,) a brass 24-pounder burst at
the muzzle, two iron 18-pounders, two 12-pound carronades, and three little mountain-guns : there were in
the camp but one smith and one carpenter, and the
stock of balls did not suffice for firing above an 100
rounds from the heavy pieces, which were managed by
a company of thirty Italians, Dalmatians, and islanders.

A chain of little heights runs from the base of Trikorpha to within 200 yards of the citadel, and at their
extremity is a natural breastwork of rocks ; behind
these were stationed 800 of Yatrako's troops, who from
thence fired musketry into the Turkish embrasures.
On the same crest of the eminence were placed two batteries, one of two 18-pounders, to batter the wall, and
another of three fieldpieces to oppose sorties. At the
centre of the ridge Raybaud excavated a sort of square
redoubt, where he planted the two mortars, which
after infinite pains he had unspiked, and mounted on
beds formed of enormous trunks of trees linked with
bands of iron. At length, every thing being ready, the
bombardment commenced in the middle of September,

---

* He would have paid dear for his impudence, if Ypsilanti had not
screened him from Colocotroni's resentment.

and a few shells were thrown daily.   If those projectiles did little harm to the enemy, they at least amused
and delighted the soldiers, tired of a protracted blockade, and exposed to the autumnal storms of that lofty
region.   The Turks scarcely returned the fire of the
Hellenic artillery : their ammunition was scanty, and
famine and disease made such havoc amongst them, that
numbers came out to the Greeks, preferring the chance
of immediate death to a lingering agony.   Their Beys
quarrelled more bitterly than ever ; and the Albanians,
declining to take any farther share in the defence, and
monopolizing the remaining provisions, began to treat
with the besiegers, proposing to rejoin the banners of
their old master, Ali Pasha.   At this critical moment,
when it was evident that the capital of the Morea was
about to fall, Ypsilanti announced the singular determination of quitting the camp and marching towards
Patrass ; thus abandoning to others the honour of finish-
ing the siege ; and, in spite of the remonstrances of his
friends, he persisted in so impolitic and intempestive a
design.   On the afternoon of September the 23d, there
happened a sharp encounter, superinduced casually by
the interruption of a scandalous traffic betwixt the
Mainatts and their ancient neighbours of Bardounia.
It had been found impossible to prevent the former
from holding markets under the walls, where they sold
the Turks bread and fruit.   Their general, Kyriacouli,
brother to Petro Bey, perceiving on that evening a
great concourse assembled and trading together, went
down and fired his musket at them ; upon which the
Mohammedans snatched up their arms, and charged
the Greeks, while a body of their countrymen sallied
out of the town.   The insurgents ran to meet them,
and the action was maintained in the plain for two
hours, amidst a brisk fire from the Christian batteries.
Pressed by a cloud of skirmishers, turned by Coloco-

troni, who made a circuit round the place, and attacked
in front with drawn swords by a party of Ionians, the
Moslems were finally routed, and driven into the town
with some slaughter. Next day, 400 troops of Karitena set out on their march to Patrass, commanded by
two sons and a nephew of Colocotroni. Ypsilanti followed on the 25th with his staff, three companies of
regular infantry, and one mountain gun. These regulars, who had been embodied at Calamata by Balesto,
and amounted to about 200, were paid out of the
Prince's private funds, clothed in black uniforms, and
armed with European muskets and bayonets. The
Bey of Maina assumed the command of the army before
Tripolizza ; and Ypsilanti's secretary, Anagnostopoulos, remained in camp to watch the negotiation that
was on the point of being opened with the besieged, who
had at last demanded an armistice, in order to treat
about a capitulation. A tent having been set up in the
plain, and declared neutral, several of the principal
Turks of the Morea came out on the 27th, and conferred with the Greek leaders. All that they could obtain from the latter, was a promise of having their
lives spared, and being embarked for the coast of Asia,
on condition of disbursing 40,000,000 of piastres (then
worth L.1,500,000 sterling) in specie, and delivering
their arms and half their moveable property. The
deputies returned to communicate these proposals,
engaging to give an answer in two days. However
hard the terms, there was no chance of their being
observed ; for putting aside the natural perfidy of the
Greeks, how were they to feed, much less transport,
such a multitude, since their own camp was already
pinched for want of provisions, owing to the crowds
that flocked in to share the wealth of Tripolizza, so
that the army was swelled to near 10,000 men ? Sensible of this difficulty, the Turks wasted their time in

useless disputes, and instead of embracing the opinion
of the Kihaya-bey, who exhorted them to force a passage to Napoli di Romania sword in hand, preferred
treating individually, or by communities, with such
Greeks as they thought would, from old intimacy, hope
of ransom, or any other motive, be willing and able to
protect them.

Elmaz Bey, general of the Albanians, separating his
cause from that of the Ottomans, after repeated inter-
views, came to an understanding with the insurgents,
that his troops should be permitted to go with their
arms and baggage to Epirus, there to uphold the interests of Ali Pasha. At the expiration of two days, the
Greeks hearing nothing from the deputies of the garrison, pronounced the armistice at an end, and recommenced hostilities ; which they nevertheless prosecuted
very faintly, their chiefs being more profitably employed
in concluding particular conventions with rich Turks
and Jews, and receiving their treasures under cover of
night. The Spezziote heroine, Bobolina, who came to
Trikorpha, allured by thirst of gold, trusting to the
safeguard of her sex, entered the city, and returned
loaded with costly gifts, bestowed upon her by Mohammedan ladies of rank. The Bardouniotes surrendered themselves *en masse* to the Mainatts ; and hundreds of famished wretches, wandering in search of the
vilest aliments, and braving every danger with desperate apathy, passed the lines of the besiegers, and were
allowed to herd behind the camp. The Greek soldiers
saw with indignation the conduct of their generals,
and rightly conjecturing that it would defraud them of
the best part of the booty, only awaited the departure
of the Albanians to make an attempt upon the place,
with or without their officers' consent. Such was the
posture of things on the morning of the 5th of October, when, just as a fresh negotiation was begun, and

a truce verbally agreed upon, a fortuitous incident precipitated the inevitable catastrophe of Tripolizza. Some Turkish sentinels having, for the sake of buying grapes, imprudently suffered a few Greeks to approach the wall, the latter suddenly climbed up, and were followed by Captain Kefalas and his company, who seized a tower near the gate of Argos, and erected a flag there. As soon as the cross in their standard was seen from the camp, a general movement took place ; every one rushed to the assault, the ramparts were scaled, the sole gate that the Turks had not walled up burst open, and the whole army poured in, amidst a heavy discharge of musketry, and a fire from the cannon of the citadel, which the gunners pointed against the town. A scene ensued of the most horrible description : The conquerors, mad with vindictive rage, spared neither age nor sex—the streets and houses were inundated with blood, and obstructed with heaps of dead bodies. Some Mohammedans fought bravely, and sold their lives dear, but the far larger proportion was slaughtered without resistance. In this confusion, El-maz Bey, at the head of his Albanians, retired into the court of the Pasha's palace, and claimed performance of the stipulations he had entered into with the assailants. Unwilling to reduce to despair so strong a body of good troops, the latter permitted them to march forth, and establish their quarters in that part of the camp previously occupied by Colocotroni. The Turks of distinction, assembled at the residence of the Kihaya-bey, were taken prisoners, and put under a guard. Colocotroni, and the other Peloponnesian generals, arriving on horseback after the city was already forced, in vain endeavoured to restore order. Flames blazing out from the palace and many houses, lighted up a night spent in rapine and carnage, and the return of day brought with it no remission. Inflamed as the

insurgents were, by the remembrance of a long bondage, as well as by recent injuries, it was too natural
for them, in the first moments of victory, to wreak
their vengeance on the Moslems ; but their insatiable
cruelty knew no bounds, and seemed to inspire them
with a superhuman energy for evil, which set lassitude
at defiance.   Every corner was ransacked to discover
new victims, and the unhappy Jewish population (even
more than the Turks, objects of fanatical hatred) expired amidst torments which we dare not describe.*   During the sack of the city, the air was close, dull, and
oppressively hot, and the whole terrible picture afforded
a lively image of Tartarus.

On the 7th, the Albanians, whose presence and menacing countenance began to cause disquietude, received
orders from Petro Bey to depart instantly.   They
marched to the number of 1500, and, being furnished
with provisions on the road, and escorted by 500
Greeks, traversed the Morea, and crossed over from
Vostizza into Roumelia.   On the same day, a sanguinary band, not yet glutted with blood, vented their
fury on the families that had come out of Tripolizza
before its capture ; near 2000 persons, mostly women
and children, were massacred in a defile of Mount
Mænalion.   The flower of the Turkish garrison, shut
up in the citadel, without food or water, surrendered
on the 8th, with the single condition of their lives
being spared.   Colocotroni took possession of it, and
is said to have found there considerable treasure.   The
Bey of Maina did not enter the town, but sent off to
his own domains two camels and twenty mules laden
with spoil.   It is impossible to say with precision, how

---

* A bitter religious animosity, from the period of the Eastern
empire, perhaps even earlier, divides the Greeks and Jews, and it
derived fresh virulence from the treatment of the Patriarch's body.

many of the vanquished perished in the assault and
subsequent butchery; famine and disease had much
thinned the population, yet we can scarce reckon the
amount of slain so low as 8000. After all, there remained a great number of prisoners, of whom not a
few (especially young women) were carried into Maina.
The most eminent captives, who owed their preservation, and the comparative respect with which they were
treated, to the prospect of a large ransom, were the
Kihaya-bey, the Kaimakan, Kyamil Bey of Corinth,
Mustafa Bey of Patrass, Shekh Nejib Effendi, and the
ladies of Khourshid Pasha's harem.

About forty Turks, clinging to the only reasonable
hope of safety, cut their way through the assailants,
and reached Napoli di Romania, as none thought of
pursuing them. Of the Christian hostages confined in
the place since the month of March, only three permanently survived their liberation : these were, the Bishop of Androusa, Sotiri Notaras, and the Bey of Maina's son, whose attendants had been put to death by the
Kaimakan ; the others soon died through a too sudden
change of diet, and transition from want and fear to
joy and plenty. The loss of the insurgents in storming the city did not probably exceed 300 men killed
and wounded ; no one, however, took the least account
of it, all being fully occupied in the scramble for plunder. It is to the sack of Tripolizza that more than
one family of the Morea is indebted for its present
opulence : the booty was immense, consisting of money,
jewels, fine shawls, dresses, and furniture, besides several thousand muskets, pistols, and sabres, (many of
them inlaid with gold and silver,) which proved an
useful acquisition to the insurgents, before very ill provided with arms. The division of the spoils gave rise
to quarrels and heartburnings, the powerful frequently
stripping the weak, and Colocotroni being the first to

exhibit so scandalous an example. The Mainatts, accomplished marauders, secured the best share, and conveyed it to Laconia on the shoulders of their wives, who descended in troops for that purpose. Nothing was rejected by those mountaineers; they tore the lead from the roofs of mosques, and extracted old nails from the buildings. The bulk of the soldiery immediately took the road to their villages, with such prizes as fortune had allotted them, and many days after, when nothing of the slightest value was left, peasants might be seen driving away asses loaded with doors and window-shutters, insomuch that the town presented only ruins, blackened carcasses, and naked shells of houses.

SECTION III.

WHILE the capital of the Morea was thus wasted with fire and sword, and the arrogant tyranny of its former masters avenged by deeds of which even they would hardly have been guilty, Ypsilanti was executing an useless military promenade in the northern parts of Peloponnesus. It must be owned, notwithstanding, that the Prince's movement was well adapted to counteract danger from the enterprises of the Turkish fleet, which was now on the coast. When, by the spontaneous retreat of the Greek squadrons, at the end of August, the Capitana Bey saw himself clear of molestation, he shaped his course for the Morea, appeared off Cerigo on the 3d of September, and on the 7th touched at Coron, which place, as well as Modon, he relieved and revictualled; had it not been for this seasonable succour, both must soon have submitted. The Janissaries of Coron, always noted for their perverse disposition, celebrated the admiral's arrival by hanging the

bishop, and several priests and Christian inhabitants
of the suburb. The sight of the Ottoman fleet terrified
the unwarlike Messenians, and twelve sail having, on
the afternoon of the 7th, entered the Gulf of Calamata
with a favourable breeze, the people instantly fled ;
the military commandant hastened to the mountains,
and the enemy might have landed unopposed, but for
the resolute behaviour of a stranger. Balesto, son to a
French merchant of Marseilles, long settled at Canea,
had served in the armies of Napoleon, and risen to the
rank of lieutenant of grenadiers at the conclusion of
peace in 1814 ; he then lived six years with his father
in Crete, and happening to be at Trieste, on commercial business, when Ypsilanti and Cantacuzene passed
through it, he agreed to follow them, and to undertake
the organization of a regular corps, a task for which
his knowledge of the language qualified him. Calamata
was chosen as a proper station, and Balesto receiving
from the Prince a small sum of money, recruited Aivaliote refugees, and had made some progress in forming
a battalion when the Capitana Bey appeared. Not
intimidated by the immense disproportion of force, he
marched down to the beach with his handful of regulars, two fieldpieces, and an hundred Mainatts, under
Captain Myrzinos, and ranging his party behind sand
hills, with wide intervals, so as to cause it to seem more
numerous than it really was, spent the night in that
position. On the morning of the 8th, an Egyptian
frigate, a schooner, and eight corvettes and brigs, again
approached within half cannon-shot, but finding Balesto
ready to oppose a disembarkation, tacked, and stood
away. Neither were the Turks more successful in
attacking a Spezziote corvette, on her return from
Navarin, which they blockaded for three days in the
little port of Khytries ; in three days' cannonading they
did not strike her once, and she finally escaped without

damage. The enemy repeatedly showed an inclination
to land, but never attempted it, the sound of Balesto's
drums and bugles sufficing to keep their ships at a
respectful distance. It happened that the day on which
they were first seen was a market-day at Calamata, and
a crowd of Mainatts, collected for the purpose of trade,
wished, in conjunction with the vagabonds of the town,
to assassinate sixty Turkish prisoners detained there
since its surrender. Balesto prevented that atrocity
by threatening to charge them with the bayonet ; as
he was, however, obliged to repair to the strand, a
base and cowardly Greek, named Paraskevi, whom
Ypsilanti had appointed governor of the place in his
absence, encouraged the populace to murder the Mohammedans ; but Balesto, informed of these proceedings, hurried back in time to save the Vayvode, and
some others. After a week's delay in the waters of
Messenia, the Capitana Bey sailed to Zante, where he
experienced a most friendly reception, and obtained
refreshment for his crews ; then despatching his rear-
admiral to bring from the roadstead of Gomenizza the
squadron that had been acting against Ali Pasha, he
steered for Patrass. Yussuf Pasha was by this time
greatly straitened, the insurgents being encamped close
to the fortress, the garrison in a state of mutiny, and
the Greek cruisers having, at the end of August, resumed their station before it. The first vessel they
arrested was an Austrian brig from Trieste, with a
cargo of flour, rice, and biscuit ; but a frigate of the
same nation released and convoyed her into Patrass :
had other naval powers copied the infamous example
of the cabinet of Vienna, no Ottoman stronghold on
the sea-coast could ever have been reduced by blockade.
On the 18th of September, Kara Ali anchored in the
roads, to the utter dismay of the Peloponnesians ; the
ships of war and the castle cannonaded the advanced

posts ; and the Turkish troops, making a sally on the
21st, routed them after a slight combat, and captured
their feeble artillery.   Such was the intelligence communicated to Ypsilanti at Vitina by a person present
at the action, while a Christian sailor, escaped from
forced service on board the Sultan's fleet, assured him
that it was in bad condition, in want of supplies, and
infected with the plague.   The Prince arrived on the
28th at Kalavryta, an important position, at the point
of junction of those difficult passes which lead from
Achaia into the heart of the peninsula.   Learning that
the enemy did not follow up his success, and that 700
mountaineers had reassembled in the defiles of Pana-
chaicos, and were rapidly increasing in number, he
abandoned his previous intention of going directly to
Patrass, proposing rather to keep an eye on the Isthmus of Corinth.   Alarmed on the night of the 29th,
by a report that the Ottomans had landed at Vostizza,
and were on their march to Kalavryta, he advanced to
meet them at the head of 1000 men, with one mountain gun ; but on approaching the sea, he found they
had reimbarked after burning the custom-house, and
carrying away a flock of sheep.   From the summit of
the hills, above the ground on which the city of Bura
once stood, he descried in the Corinthian Gulf a hostile
flotilla of one frigate and thirty brigs, almost all Egyp-
tians and Algerines, the latter having joined the Capitana Bey at Patrass.   On the 1st of October, the Prince
descended into the plain of Vostizza, and the enemy's
squadron stood up the gulf towards Galaxidi, a commercial town of 800 houses, situated at the entrance of
the Crissœan bay. Its inhabitants had, by industry and
parsimony, acquired wealth, and possessed, besides
numerous small barks, near sixty merchant vessels ;
their marine was, indeed, since the commencement of
the war, confined within the castles of the little Darda-

nelles, but it had never ceased to annoy the Mussulmans of Lepanto. Expecting an attack, the Galaxidiotes
embossed their ships across the mouth of the harbour,
and placed a battery on a neighbouring islet. The
Egyptian commodore, Ismail Gibraltar, who was accompanied in this expedition by Yussuf Pasha and several
hundred Albanian soldiers, on the evening of the 1st
cannonaded the place for two hours, when night closing
in, the engagement terminated for that day; it was
renewed next morning, and for three hours the firing
was very heavy. Completely overmatched, the Galaxidiotes sustained a total defeat, and their battery being
silenced, and their shipping taken, fled to the mountains
of Salona; the Algerines were the first to land, the
other Mohammedans followed, and the town was involved in a general conflagration; the victors returned in
triumph to Patrass, dragging their prizes after them.*
Having witnessed from the opposite shore the sad
spectacle of the destruction of Galaxidi, Ypsilanti
moved by long marches towards the Isthmus, and reaching Vassilika on the 4th, halted for some days amidst
the ruins of Sicyon, and there received information of
the fall of Tripolizza, a piece of news which induced
the Colocotronis, with their irregular bands, to hurry
to that city, in order to glean a remnant of plunder.

Convinced at length of the impolicy of prolonging
his absence from the centre of operations, the Prince,
after visiting Cenchræa, and conferring with the officers
who commanded in Megaris, began to retrace his steps,
and proceeding by Argos, entered the capital of Peloponnesus on the 14th of October. Supposing that its
fate might have intimidated the garrison of the Acro-

* Among these prizes were the two Ionians which had so glaringly
violated their neutrality. The Greeks asserted that an English vessel,
the Zenobia, (hired as a transport by Yussuf Pasha,) committed as
open a breach of it, by firing upon Galaxidi.

corinthus, he, in passing, caused it to be summoned, but
the Turks replied with cannon-shot. Meanwhile the
Capitana Bey was celebrating at Patrass the victory
gained by his lieutenants at Galaxidi, whence they
brought in thirty-four prizes, besides burning many
others of little value. Satisfied with the eclat of this
success, with having rallied the division so long detained on the coast of Epirus by fear of the Greeks,
and with having driven the insurgents from the vicinity of Patrass, he resolved to return to the Dardanelles. That season was now approaching, beyond
which the Ottomans have ever been reluctant to continue military, and far less naval operations—his stock
of provisions was at a low ebb, and pestilence thinning
his crews. In consequence of the quarrel between the
Hydriote and Spezziote Primates, and those of the Morea, the islanders had for more than a month lain inactive in their harbours; roused, however, by Ypsilanti's
remonstrances, they again launched thirty ships, and
met the Capitana Bey in the Ionian Sea. On the 6th,
7th, and 8th of October, the Turkish fleet touched at
Zante, and after a short stay prosecuted its voyage;
but a contrary wind, and still more the enemy's appearance, soon forced it to run back to the same friendly
port. On the 12th, an Algerine brig of war, separated
from her consorts, and assailed by eighteen Greek brigs,
after a most spirited resistance was driven ashore a
total wreck in the Bay of Chieri, to the south of the
isle, and the surviving mariners conducted to the Lazaretto. This incident excited troubles in Zante, leading to executions and the proclamation of martial law.
The Ottoman admiral, who had under his command
above fourscore sail, sixty-six of which were men-of-war,
might easily have destroyed five Greek vessels embayed
under the point of Klarenza; but he merely fired distant broadsides from his ships of the line, and running

up the channel, cast anchor in the roads of Zante. His small craft essayed an attack, and were repulsed, after an action of five hours. Subsequently, however, the Algerines took one Spezziote vessel near the mouth of the Alpheus, but her crew got safely to the shore. The expectations of those persons who looked for a general engagement were disappointed, as nothing of importance happened; the Christians being afraid of the enemy's superior strength, and the Mohammedans, sensible of their deficient seamanship, desiring to avoid collision. The Greeks having cruised off Cefalonia until the 20th, went back to their islands, and the Capitana Bey, quitting Zante on the evening of the 15th, quietly sailed to the Hellespont, only stopping for an instant on his way to devastate the unoffending Isle of Samothrace. On the 24th of November, the bulk of the Ottoman fleet entering the haven of Constantinople, displayed to the city thirty Greeks hanging from the yard-arms of the Galaxidiote prizes. It was commonly believed that those poor wretches were not prisoners, but sailors who had been serving throughout the campaign. To recompense the very moderate exploits of Kara Ali, whose conduct was a tissue of folly and cowardice, the Sultan, as capricious in rewarding as in punishing, promoted him to the dignity of Capitan Pasha.

APPENDIX

TO

BOOK I.—CHAP. IV.

No. I.—*Account of the destruction of a Turkish line-of-battle ship at Erisso in Lesbos, from the MS. journal of Admiral Tombazi.*

Tuesday, May 24th, O.S.

June 5th, 1821.

In the morning we discovered in the waters of Mitylene two sail, one of which appeared to be Turkish, and we conjectured that it was either a line-of-battle ship or a frigate; the other was a brig under the Russian flag. We all stood towards the Turk, who altered his course, and steered for Mitylene under a press of sail. The wind being light, all our captains assembled on board the brig of Anastasius Ty-amado. In the afternoon we neared the Turk, and made her out to be a ship of the line. Being unable to get away from us, she was forced to anchor at Erisso (or Negropont.) Our foremost vessels approaching, fired upon the enemy without effect, only proving to the Turks the small calibre of our guns. Nevertheless, the sailors clamouring for a general attack, a signal was made for all our vessels to close, and prepare for action. When the line of battle was formed, the Spezziote commodore, Androuzzo, desired to speak with me; I therefore neared him, and he and all the captains coming on my quarter-deck, we resolved to get a fire-ship ready to burn the enemy. We sought out the smallest and most unserviceable barks, and pitched upon two, but the captain of one would not give her up, and the other, wishing to be paid half the value of his, demanded 20,000 piastres. Then the Captain Lazzaros Antonio Papa Manoli, and his brother-in-law, Lazzaros, mentioned the vessel of John Theodosius, and her captain agreed, on condition of receiving a written obligation on our three islands, signed by all the captains of the fleet, for 40,000 piastres. We promised to each sailor who would volunteer to man her, a certificate of good conduct, and an hundred dollars in money. Two hours past midnight we despatched the fire-ship; when she was near the enemy, the men kindled the train and left her: it seems that she changed her direction, for she passed outside, and was consumed without harming the Turk.

Wednesday, May 25th, O. S.
June 6th.

IN the morning we neared the two-decker, and fired upon her; one man was killed, and two wounded on board Zakka's vessel. Several captains came on my quarter-deck, and we consulted about preparing another brulot: the Psarriote commodore, Nicholas Apostoli, sent to Psarra for the fire-ships that were ready there. Saw a sail, which we took for a frigate, and resolved to engage her; made a signal to our ships to close, but in the meantime she hoisted English colours. At noon Captain Nicholas Triandafilo gave up his vessel for a fire-ship; we fixed her value at 20,000 piastres, and got her ready for the evening, but the wind freshened so much from the south-east that she could not go in.

Thursday, May 26th, O. S.
June 7th.

IN the morning we were at a distance of two or three miles from the coast of Mitylene. At $7\frac{1}{2}$ hours A.M., a fire-ship arrived from Psarra: at eight, a strong gale with showers, which lasted three hours: at noon the wind fell, saw a sail, and made a signal to the schooner Terpsichore to speak her. In the evening the two fire-ships were ready, but it was so calm that they could not act. The Terpsichore reported that the sail she visited was a Russian schooner, bound from Smyrna to Constantinople; her captain reported, that at Smyrna the Turks were killing the Christians in their houses, and that they had news of Prince Ypsilanti having entered Adrianople.

Friday, May 27th, O. S.
June 8th.

IN the morning the captains assembled on board Nicholas Apostoli, and it was resolved that all our vessels, with the fire-ships, should attack the enemy; made a signal to form the line. At nine, A.M., the cannonade began, and the fire-ships fell aboard the two-decker; in half an hour she was in flames, which first burst out from her fore-castle: two launches full of Turks, pulled away from her. At eleven, A.M., her magazine took fire. At noon, all the captains assembled in the vessel of John Bulgari, and questioned some Greeks, who had been serving on board the enemy, and were picked up by our boats. They stated that the Turks were at first panic-struck, but took courage on being reinforced by troops from Mitylene under four Beys, and that with these the crew amounted to 700 persons, all of whom perished, except 150 who escaped in the launches. We wrote letters

to Hydra, Spezzia, and Psarra, announcing the success of the two
fire-ships.

No. II.—*Copy of a Circular Letter addressed by the Greek Fleet to
the Islands of the Egean, in favour of the Kydonians.*

Brothers and countrymen! You have for some time past been informed of the expedition of our Grecian fleet, as well as of the phi
lanthropic motives which induced it to put to sea: you know likewise that it is composed of Hydriote, Spezziote, and Psarriote vessels. Its exploits hitherto are matter of notoriety, particularly in
what regards the destruction of a Turkish line-of-battle ship, the consternation of the rest of their armament, and the extermination of
private craft that might have annoyed the islands. We hope, moreover, to vanquish the squadrons of Prevesa and Patrass. After sweeping our Turkish tyrants from the sea, we thought it incumbent upon
us to deliver, as far as we could, those who are still under their abominable yoke. When off Mitylene, the people of Mosconisi and
Kydonia called upon us to rescue them from the worst evils, nay, from
death itself. We accordingly liberated them, but as the city of Kydonia was surrounded by 3000 Turks, who plundered and set it on
fire, we could not save their effects, and they were obliged to leave
behind every article except the clothes they wore. Philanthropy,
patriotism, religion, and humanity, enjoin us to liberate from Turkish
tyranny as many individuals as possible : therefore, all our fleet requests and commands you to receive these persons we send you, and
to supply their necessities until they can repatriate, or otherwise establish themselves, which we assure you will not be a long period. You
must reflect that the citizens of Kydonia have a claim on our bene-
volence, because they were the first to found good schools, and maintain learned masters to teach our youth sciences and theology, whence
our nation has been enlightened, and we have at least been taught to
estimate ourselves. Finally, our whole fleet, trusting in Christ alone,
begs you to comply with our request; if you misunderstand the rights
of nature and humanity, you will be responsible to them, to us, and
to the nation, and will have to dread the vengeance of heaven. As
you are freed from the terror of the Turkish armaments, and other
pirates, we hope you are in no need of our aid : if, however, you
desire any thing of us, apply to our islands, and we will content you
as far as we can.

Given from the Hellenic fleet at Psarra, this $\frac{6th}{18th}$ of June, 1821.

(Signed)   JACHOMO M. TOMBAZI.

2

No. III.—*Official Return of Ordnance captured by the Greeks at Tripolizza.*

BRASS ORDNANCE.

Number of guns.	Calibre.	Remarks.
8	6 lb.	Seven in battery, one dismounted; two only in good repair.
2	9 lb.	Out of repair.
1	12 lb.	Mounted, but unserviceable.
1	24 lb.	Do. do.
1	8 inch mortar.	In good condition, but dismounted.
—13		

IRON ORDNANCE.

1	4 lb.	Dismounted, but in good repair.
2	9 lb.	Mounted, and in a good state.
9	12 lb.	Mounted, but out of repair.
4	18 lb.	Do. do.
1	9 lb. carronade.	In good order.
—17		

Total, 30 pieces of ordnance.

There were found 855 cannon balls, and 10 packets of case shot; the powder magazines were empty.

CHAP. V.

Progress of the war in Epirus, Macedonia, and Northern Greece,
till the conclusion of the year 1821.

SECTION I.

THE Serasker Khourshid Pasha, commanding the
imperial army before Yannina, although placed in
very embarrassing circumstances, justified by his prudence and firmness the confidence that the Sultan reposed in him, and the high reputation he enjoyed in
Turkey. Surrounded as he was on every side by enemies, he never suffered himself to be diverted from his
main object, the reduction of Ali Pasha, which he pressed with one hand, while with the other he kept in
check the bands of mountaineers that harassed his
rear, and endeavoured to starve his camp. He had to
secure two principal lines of communication, one with
Thessaly, whence he drew his chief supplies, the other
with the Ionian Sea. The first he maintained by means
of garrisons stationed in the Wallachian towns of Pindus, Mezzovo, Kalarites, and Syrako; the second by
occupying Arta and Prevesa. A third, with Upper
Albania, gave him less trouble, as it was only occasionally interrupted by tribes of Mohammedan Arnauts,
who still faintly adhered to the interests of Ali Pasha;
but their irregular efforts, prompted by caprice, were
neither vigorous nor persevering, and it was easy, by
a judicious distribution of money, either to bring them
over, or to set them against each other. The strength

of his army (including numerous detachments) is said
to have fluctuated betwixt 40,000 and 25,000 men;
that of his foes was much smaller, for the most formidable of them, the Souliotes, although augmented
by the accession of Epirote Christians, did not exceed
4000, and the Greek force on the whole line, from the
Adriatic to the Malian Gulf, fell short of 12,000 soldiers. Besides this superiority, the Serasker possessed
other advantages : he was amply provided with cavalry, and field artillery, he had money and ammunition
in abundance, and unity of command reigned in his
camp ; while in all those respects the Christians were
either utterly destitute, or extremely deficient. Nevertheless, the activity and bravery of the Souliotes,
and especially of the gallant Mark Bozzaris, for some
time rendered doubtful the issue of the contest in Epirus : in the months of May and June, they twice defeated an Albanian Bey named Tahir Papoulis, and
on the second occasion, at Kandja, took him prisoner;
and Mark Bozzaris carrying the fortified tower of
Regniassa, on the coast of Cassiopia, propagated revolt through the neighbouring districts, particularly
that of Lakka, whose inhabitants are considered singularly warlike. Exposed to perpetual ambuscades
among the mountains, the Turkish troops were frequently surprised and routed, and the Souliotes more
than once appeared on the edge of the hills above the
Serasker's camp ; but they could advance no farther,
and the array of horsemen and cannon hindered them
from descending into the plain of Yannina. In the
mean time, Ali Pasha's resources were gradually
dwindling away, and his forces so much diminished,
that he could not undertake sorties with any chance
of success : yet he still hoped to weary out the Porte
in this struggle of money and patience, and refused, by
admitting a body of Souliotes, to put himself into

the power of his Christian allies; being perfectly
aware, that only the pressure of danger induced them
to associate their cause with his, and that as soon as
the danger ceased to exist, they would become his bit-
terest enemies. Of the three posts which he held, viz.
the Castle of the Lake, Litharizza, and the Island, the
latter was, towards the end of May, taken, through
treachery, by Khourshid: that general then battered
Litharizza with great fury, and having effected a practicable breach in the fort, assaulted in June, and failed
completely.

It was impossible for the Armatoles to remain any
longer neutral, in spite of the pacific disposition of
some eminent captains, and the cautious policy that
the Ottoman authorities observed with regard to them.
Already meetings of the chiefs had taken place, and
parties of their soldiers, assuming the character of robbers, and assassinating the Turks, who attempted to
travel betwixt Arta and Vrakhori, the governors of
those two towns (Hassan Pasha, and Nourka Bey),
apprehensive of a conspiracy, seized as hostages the
Bishops and Primates. In the first days of June,
Messalonghi and Anatoliko, having, at sight of a Hydriote squadron, hoisted the independent flag, immediately became the head-quarters of revolution in the
western provinces, and several of the Armatolic leaders
assembled there. One of the most powerful of them,
George Varnakiottis, captain of Xeromeros, showed
the greatest reluctance to commence hostilities, but he
was obliged to yield to the opinions of his colleagues,
and of his own brother, Yiottis, and to unite with them
in a scheme for raising simultaneously all Etolia and
Acarnania, and surprising the city of Vrakhori, the
seat of a Mohammedan and Jewish population, where
some rich Beys and Agas had palaces built with the
strength and solidity of castles. On Monday the 11th

of June, it was assailed on one side by the Captains
Makrys and Valtinos (who marched the day before
from Messalonghi and Anatoliko), and on the other by
the troops of the Canton of Vlokhos, under Alexakis
Vlakhopoulos, formerly a captain in the first regiment
of Greek light infantry in British pay. The Armatoles first carried the Greek quarter, and then penetrating into the bazaar, drove the Turks from house
to house, and finally shut them up in the palace of
Alay Bey: they displayed great courage in attacking
so many massive buildings, defended by 1000 Mussulmans, one half of whom were Albanian soldiers of
Nourka. On the 12th, the brother of Varnakiottis came
up, and on the 13th Varnakiottis himself, with their
followers, increasing to 3000 the besieging numbers,
and at the same time, the Sclavonian master of a merchant ship brought them from Messalonghi a piece of
cannon, with men to serve it. After a siege of seven
days, the Turks surrendered: Nourka, with his cavalry, had previously escaped by night, through the
connivance of Varnakiottis, who, however, intercepted
and plundered them of their money and arms at Karpenizza. Ismael Pliassa Pasha advanced from Arta,
with a body of troops, in order to relieve Vrakhori,
but the Captain Andreas Iskos, posting himself, with
only 40 men, in a tower at the defiles of Makrynoros, obstructed his passage, and compelled him to turn back.
The main body of the Greeks having taken and burnt
Vrakhori, proceeded against another Mohammedan
town in its vicinity, named Zapandi, where 600 Turks
had been allowed leisure to fortify themselves, owing
to the negligence of Varnakiottis, who, marching towards it, at the head of 700 soldiers, halted on a verbal assurance that the enemy would submit; instead,
however, of doing so, they made a vigorous resistance
for above a month, and on the 27th repelled an as-

sault, killing 16 Greeks, and wounding many more. Varnakiottis was detached with 700 men, to occupy Makrynoros, which he omitted to do, preferring to go and secure his booty in the Isle of Kalamos.

Vlakhopoulos, Makrys, and Valtinos were pushing the siege of Zapandi, never doubting that the passes were properly guarded, when to their astonishment a letter arrived from Iskos, announcing that a Turkish army was encamped at Combotti, and that the few Greeks under his command, disgusted at not receiving succours, had dispersed. In this emergency, Valtinos hastened to Makrynoros, and by his entreaties persuaded Iskos, and another captain of reputation, named Gogos Bakoulas, to station themselves in the defiles, where they were joined by a small band of Albanian Moslems, under Suleyman Meta, a chief sent by Ismael Poda, and Hagos Bessiaris, two of Ali Pasha's partisans, to confer with the insurgent leaders at Zapandi.

On the morning of the 30th, this envoy set out to continue his journey, when Pliassa Pasha suddenly appearing, he, actuated by a noble sense of honour, turned back to assist the Greeks entrenched at Langada: their force amounted only to 207 soldiers, viz. 185 Armatoles of Gogos, Iskos, and Valtinos, and 22 Albanians of Suleyman Meta. The Ottoman troops, 1800 strong, but including the shopkeepers and populace of Arta, made repeated attacks upon them without success; their horsemen could not act among thick woods; the irregular infantry of the East is as little capable of storming positions, as it is obstinate and dangerous in their defence, and the insurgents having blocked up the paths with large stones and trunks of trees, poured on them a heavy fire of musketry. Entirely baffled, the Turks retired with a loss of near 150 killed, partly to Combotti and partly to Arta; neither did they for the fifteen subsequent months make any farther attempt upon Makrynoros.* Deprived of every hope of relief by the issue of this combat, the people of Zapandi surrendered at discretion, and were put to the sword. On the same day that the insurrection broke out in Etolia, the Acarnanians took up arms under Captain Tzongas, and reduced without difficulty the small forts of Playa and Teke, opposite to Santa Maura. Passano, a Corsican adventurer, in the service of Ali Pasha, fitted out two gun-boats in the Ambracian Gulf, and arming them with two twelve-pounder guns taken at Playa, went against Vonizza, and landed his cannon ; but being surprised by a flotilla commanded by Bekir Jocador, Vayvode of Prevesa, he was forced to save himself by flight, and lost his boats and guns. Towards the centre of Northern Greece, Panourias, an aged captain of robbers, invested the Castle of Salona,† and became master of it in twelve days, thus opening a communication betwixt the Ionian Sea and the Channel of Euboea ; while from the high mountains which separate Epirus and Thessaly, a considerable emigration came down to increase the resources of the revolted provinces. In the upper valleys of Pindus, have long been settled some Wallachian tribes, amounting it is said to 70,000 persons, and perhaps a remnant of the colonies which the Emperor Aurelian transplanted from Dacia into Dardania. By virtue of a favourable capitulation with the early Sultans, they were lightly taxed ; and although Ali Pasha augmented their burdens, they still lived comparatively

* A palikar of the district of Valtos, named Kateva, slew three Turks with his own hand, and rescued one of his comrades, whom they were dragging away.

† Salona, the ancient Amphissa, capital of Ozolian Locris, contained before the revolution 1000 houses, of which 400 were Turkish ; its citadel appears to have been built by the Catalans on the basement of the Hellenic Acropolis, and its territory produces excellent olives.

unmolested and protected from Turkish intrusion by
their snowy peaks and rigorous climate. Many of
them are nomadic shepherds, wandering about with
their flocks and herds; and those who dwelt in towns
such as Mezzovo, Kalarites, and Syrako, were a quiet
and frugal race engaged in woollen manufactures,
which latterly they carried to such a pitch, as to undertake distant journeys, and trade with foreign countries.
The war of 1820 between the Sultan and the Satrap
of Yannina, affected their prosperity, by exposing them
to the passage of troops, and the expense of garrisons,
maintained at their cost. This they bore with a certain degree of patience, until the revolt of their neighbours, the Etolian Armatoles, rendered it impracticable for them to remain indifferent spectators of the
contest. Detachments of the latter approaching their
towns, they rose upon the garrisons, but as the Roumeli Valesi immediately sent powerful reinforcements,
after some days fighting, the people of Mezzovo, Kalarites, and Syrako, as well as those of many Wallachian villages, emigrated in mass, and at Messalonghi
and in the forests of Etolia, found an asylum for themselves and 80,000 head of cattle, which they brought
along with them. Encouraged by the co-operation of
the Armatoles, the Christians of Epirus gathered fresh
laurels during the month of July, defeated the forces
of Khourshid in various actions, and compelled a Pasha
and his corps to lay down their arms at Variades, on
the road from Yannina to Souli. Mark Bozzaris proposed, in concert with the Greeks of Pindus and the
Mussulmans of Middle Albania, to hem in the Serasker on every side, but a wound that he received in a
skirmish obliged him to suspend his operations for
some time. Nevertheless, the Beys attached to Ali's
party collected their followers; and an Albanian army,
recruited from different tribes, advanced from Tepeleni

to within a few miles of Yannina, but quickly dispersed again, leaving the Souliotes to stand the brunt of
the enemy's efforts. In the dispute betwixt those brave
mountaineers and the Roumeli Valesi, the point that
attracted the attention and exertions of both, was the
road leading from Yannina to the sea-coast, where the
Turks possessed the maritime place of Prevesa, built
on a low promontory at the mouth of the Ambracian
Gulf, opposite to Actium, and near the ruins of Nicopolis. Struck with its convenient position, as well as
the beauty of its environs, Ali Pasha often resided
there, and besides throwing up around it a rampart
faced with stone, erected a palace, a citadel, and a mole,
protected by a half-moon battery. The communication
from thence to Yannina is by the gulf as far as Sala-
ghora, distant four leagues from the city of Arta, one of
the most considerable in Epirus, although depopulated
in 1815 by a dreadful pestilence. Before that calamity
it had 2000 houses, chiefly inhabited by Greeks and
Jews, with a dilapidated castle, evidently constructed
on the site of an older fortress. A rapid river (the
Aracthus) flows past the town, and the extensive plain
that surrounds it is extremely fertile, but marshy, and
therefore traversed by a causeway. It lies thirty miles
directly south from Yannina, to which latter city Ali
Pasha made a highway running across the hills, and
fortified two posts commanding the most difficult
passes ; the Han of the five wells, (seven hours' march
from Yannina), and that of Koumkhades, five or six
miles to the south of the former, and at about the same
distance from Arta. Alternately taken and retaken,
these two posts were generally in the hands of the
Souliotes, who thereby exceedingly harassed the Serasker. After the insurrection of the Armatoles, parties
of them descending from the high mountains to the
east, contributed to straiten Arta, where the enemy

constantly kept a strong division of troops. Gogos
Bakoulas having ventured to encamp at the village of
Petta, two leagues from it, with only 250 Greeks, the
Turks determined to dislodge him on the 27th of July;
but although infinitely superior in number, they were
beaten still more disgracefully than at Langada. All
their assaults upon his entrenchments (on an eminence
in front of the village) were repulsed, and Gogos,
sallying out sword in hand, drove them back to Arta:
their loss in killed was heavy, while his was very
trifling. The victories of Langada and Petta, of which
the Armatoles are justly proud, were owing as well to
the heroism of the veteran Gogos, as to the stupidity of
the Moslems, and the enormous disadvantage which
irregular infantry labours under in attacking men
covered by a breastwork, and expert in the use of their
muskets. In the war with their revolted subjects, the
dominant idea of the Turks was to carry every thing
before them by a violent onset, whereas a little patience
would in most instances have surely caused them to
succeed, and at least saved them much dishonour, and
thousands of lives thrown away in mere wantonness.
Hassan Pasha, relieved at Arta, September 12th, by
the *cidevant* Serasker, Ismael Pasho, immediately endeavoured to make his way to Yannina, but in the
defile of Koumkhades, Mark Bozzaris charged, defeated, and forced him to retrograde to the place he set
out from. Notwithstanding these repeated checks,
Kourshid's perseverance, backed by vast means, finally
turned the chances in his favour: tired of a protracted
campaign, the Souliotes withdrew to their fastnesses,
and he re-established his communication with Arta,
Prevesa, and the sea. The siege of Yannina was proceeding slowly, but advantageously for him; his shells
having produced a conflagration in the castle of the
lake, which consumed a considerable proportion of

Ali's magazines. During the summer some of the unfortunate Parguinotes, invited by their brethren of Souli, undertook a clandestine expedition from Corfu, with a view of recovering their country; being, however, intercepted by the Ottoman ships of war, they were obliged to run their barks ashore at Paxos, and were, as a punishment, expelled from the Ionian states. Such was the condition of the western provinces, when in the middle of September Mavrocordato returned from Peloponnesus to Etolia. Besides Cantacuzene, the Bishop of Talanta, and other Roumeliote deputies, who had been sent to consult with the primates of the Morea, he was accompanied by Constantine Caradja and Theodore Negris, whom he met at Vitina. The first, son to the fugitive Hospodar of Wallachia, was in all respects an insignificant personage ; he had sailed from Italy after Mavrocordato's departure, touched at Navarin and Patrass, and seemed to be roaming about Greece without any fixed purpose. We cannot say as much for Negris, who, in a dwarfish body, concealed a mind of fire, and was one of the most acute, cunning, and unprincipled politicians that the fanar of Constantinople ever gave birth to. Appointed Ottoman chargé d'affaires at Paris just as the revolution began, he learned its first events on his passage to Marseilles, threw his credentials into the sea, and repairing to Spezzia, joined the insurgents. As Ypsilanti, knowing his character, treated him coldly, he vowed vengeance against the Prince, and adhered to his rival for as long a period as suited his own interest. Vexed by military oppression, and anxious to enjoy a regular system of administration, and to see an equal repartition of public burdens, the Etolians gladly hailed the presence of Mavrocordato, the only man who had talent enough to accomplish so salutary a work. Yielding to their solicitations, and those of the Roumeliote

deputies, he wrote from Salona circular letters signed
by himself, Caradja, and Negris, convening at that
town, for the 28th of September, an assembly of notables from all the cantons of Northern Greece. Whilst
they were awaiting there with the Bishop of Talanta,
Drossos Mansolas of Thessaly, Alexander Axiottis,
John Scandalides, &c. the expected arrival of numerous
representatives, a division of the Turkish fleet destroyed Galaxidi in their immediate neighbourhood.
The consternation which this blow occasioned instantly
dissolved the nascent congress ; the deputies, who had
already met, hurrying away, some towards Messalonghi, others to Arakhova. The peasants of Delphi,
indignant at their pusillanimity, apostrophized, in no
courteous terms, the flying prelates and ephors, summoning them to face about and provide for the national
welfare. Cantacuzene, entirely disheartened, and despairing of the cause, went on board a ship bound for
Leghorn, and abandoned Greece altogether. When the
danger was past, and the Capitana Bey gone, a convention was at length held at Salona, in November,
under the presidency of Theodore Negris, a court of
Areopagus installed, and certain dispositions laid down
for the government of Eastern Greece, comprehending
Attica, Bœotia, Phocis, and Locris. Mavrocordato,
meanwhile, exclusively turned his attention to the
affairs of Epirus, Etolia, and Acarnania, countries extremely difficult to manage, on account of the feuds and
pretensions of the Armatolic captains, who, after re-
pulsing the enemy, were disposed to fight with one another. By patience and address he overcame many
obstacles, and not only persuaded those intractable
chiefs to adjourn their private animosities and go to
the assistance of the Souliotes, but likewise brought
about an alliance between the Christian insurgents and
the Mohammedan supporters of Ali Pasha, whose an-

cient minister of police, Tahir Abbas, came to Messalonghi, in company with Alexis Nouzza and Hagos Bessiaris. It would have been better policy to have conducted the negotiation on the frontiers rather than in the heart of the country, since two bad consequences resulted from Tahir Abbas's visit; in the first place, the sight of the ruined mosques of Vrakhori offended his religious prejudices, and secondly, his sagacity detected the real weakness and poverty of the insurgents, who, instead of large sums of money, which he and his associates expected, could only give him 100 barrels of powder from Mavrocordato's stores. However, he dissembled for the moment, and a treaty was concluded. The Albanians, indifferent to what was passing in Hellas, desired to expel out of Epirus the Ottoman Turks, and the Greeks could not disguise from their own minds the peril they would be exposed to if the Porte was enabled to crush Ali's rebellion. His situation was now become more critical than ever, for the garrison of the castle of Litharizza delivered it up, in the end of October, to Khourshid Pasha, and the Serasker then confidently promised the Sultan that he would soon send him the traitor's head, the whole force of the latter being reduced to 600 men. The Souliotes, who had resumed active hostilities, and were actually blockading Prevesa on the land side, again proposed to introduce into his stronghold a detachment of their warriors ; but as they might thus have disposed at their will of the Satrap's life and treasure, he declined aid of that description, and advised them rather to march against Arta, where his abhorred foe, Ismael Pasha, was stationed. His suggestion being adopted, Greeks and Albanians agreed to unite their arms in an attempt upon that city. Mavrocordato did not attend the expedition, being called to Peloponnesus by the prospect of more efficaciously employing his talents in

the national congress about to assemble at Argos.
Petta and Combotti having been fixed upon as points
of reunion, the Souliotes formed a junction there with
the Armatoles of Epirus, Etolia, and Acarnania, and
with a body of Mohammedan Albanians, commanded
by Hagos Bessiaris, Elmaz Bey (the same who capitulated at Tripolizza), and the son of Mourta Zalik,
Ali's former governor of Souli.   The combined army,
amounting to about 3000 men, of whom one-third were
Mussulmans, moved towards Arta, preceded by two
detachments, one of 300 soldiers, under Mark Bozzaris,
Karaiskaki, Koutelidas, and Zalik, the other of 100,
led by Natches Fotomarra and Makriyani. There were
in Arta four Pashas, Ismael Pasho, Hassan, Ismael
Pliassa, and Kars Ali, Kourshids Khasnadar, or treasurer.   On the approach of the confederates, Ismael
Pasho sallied out with 800 cavalry and infantry, supported by artillery, and fell upon their vanguard in the
gardens of the village of Marat.   He was, however,
vigorously repulsed, ran some risk of being taken prisoner, and only saved his cannon by hastily withdrawing them.   On the following night the main body of
the insurgents, animated by this success, assaulted the
strong position of Phaneromeni, defended by a chosen
body of Ghegs, and carried the outer enceinte, Gogos
being the first to enter it, sword in hand ; but it was
subsequently abandoned, owing to a change of plan, and
to reinforcements coming to the enemy's support. Next
day, (November the 25th,) they forced the bridge of
twelve arches, and stormed half the city; when Mark
Bozzaris, having set fire to the houses, to prevent his
soldiers dispersing in quest of plunder, the flames stopped their progress, and covered the retreat of the Turks.
Hassan Pasha shut himself up in the Archiepiscopal
palace, Ismael Pasho in a mosque; Ismael Pliassa in some
houses below the castle, and the Khasnadar occupied

that citadel. Here they were blocked by the confederates. Alarmed at the idea of losing the important
place of Arta, Khourshid resolved to use every effort
for its relief, and, besides despatching troops, skilfully
availed himself of Albanian inconstancy and perfidy.
As the Ottomans were gathering at the villages of
Plakka and Lamari, Mark Bozzaris, Gogos, and Tzongas went to oppose them; unluckily at that very time
Tahir Abbas returned from Messalonghi, and communicating to his countrymen his own conviction that the
Greeks were not struggling for the interests of Ali
Pasha, but to overthrow the Mussulman faith, induced
them to listen to the Serasker's offers, and to harbour a
scheme for betraying their Christian allies. The latter
receiving intimation of this project, had no alternative
but to retire without noise during the night to Petta
and Combotti, after having for a fortnight maintained
possession of half of Arta; they probably would not
have got off so easily, if Mark Bozzaris had not taken
the wise precaution of securing as pledges the sons of
Tahir Abbas and Hagos Bessiaris. One of the Albanian chiefs (Zalik) stands cleared of the charge of
treachery, for he had been mortally wounded fighting
against the Turks by the side of Bozzaris. Such proved
the issue of the last diversion essayed in behalf of the
tyrant of Yannina, who was henceforth left to his fate,
all the Mohammedan tribes of Albania ranging themselves under the Sultan's banners. The rest of winter
slipped away quietly on the frontier of Epirus, the
Turks keeping close in Arta, and the Greeks watching
them from the positions of Petta and Combotti.

SECTION II.

THE first triumphs of the insurgents in Phocis and Bœotia were speedily chequered by reverses, Khourshid having ordered two of his lieutenants, Omer Vriones, Pasha of Berat, and Mehemet, titular Pasha of the Morea, to march thither with 3000 or 4000 troops. After the capture of Livadia, Captain Diakos and the Bishop of Salona advanced, at the head of 700 Greeks, to the Straits of Thermopylæ, where they encountered (May the 5th) the Pashas, who, passing the Sperchius at the bridge of Alamanna, overpowered, and entirely defeated them. The brave Diakos, who fought on foot to encourage his men, was severely wounded and made prisoner; the prelate shared the same fate, and both were immediately executed. There is a story current in Greece that Diakos, whose memory is venerated by his countrymen, offered Omar Pasha a sum of money if he would keep him in a dungeon till he could learn the result of the revolution, and that Omar caused him to be roasted. Another version states that he was beheaded, and his fellow-prisoner, the bishop, impaled. The Pashas then crossed Mount Oeta, and descending into the upper valley of the Cephisus, at the Han of Gravia, on the confines of Phocis and Doris, met with Odysseus hastening too late to reinforce Diakos. As this Han is a post of great consequence on the road to Salona, Odysseus and his satellite Ghouras occupied it with 180 soldiers, some other captains promising to remain on the adjacent heights and support them, a promise, however, which they broke. An obstinate engagement ensued, the Albanians assaulting with such fury, that they frequently grasped the muzzles of the Greek muskets protruding through loopholes, and several Beys were slain, with numbers of private men. The defence of Gravia vastly enhanced the reputation of Odysseus, who evacuated the Han at night, marched to Arakhova, and, collecting some troops, took up a fresh position on the road from Thermopylæ to Livadia. Instead of advancing to Salona, the Pashas encamped near Mendenizza,* and lay there till the middle of June, when their army proceeded towards Livadia. Odysseus retiring on their approach from his entrenchments at Kastrani, the Turks appeared before the city about the summer solstice, carried it by storm upon the first attack, and laid it in ashes ; most of the inhabitants fled to the castle, and held out for a day or two. The Ottoman generals summoned them, and employed in the negotiation a Souliote, named Palaskas, who was then in Mehemet Pasha's service. Through a collusion with him, the greater part of the besieged escaped by night, and the rest, with their primates,† submitted, and were mildly treated. Masters of Livadia, the Turks once more gave battle to Odysseus, posted, at the head of 1000 men, at Scripu (the ancient Orchomenus), and beat him completely, partly owing to surprise, and partly to the insubordination of his followers, who, contrary to their general's orders, suffered themselves to be drawn into a plain by the enemy's skirmishers, and being charged by the Ottoman cavalry, were routed with much slaughter. Odysseus lost fifty of his officers, and hardly saved himself from the pursuit of some horsemen. Although there was no Greek force in Attica and Bœotia able to cope with the Pashas, they acted in

* Mendenizza, or Bodonizza, a small town on the borders of Phocis and Epiknemidian Locris, with an old castle and a splendid convent of dervishes.

† When the primate John Logotheti laid his arms at the feet of Omer Vriones, the Pasha said with a smile, " Keep your pistols, I fear them not !" The primates subsequently were either exchanged or effected their escape.

a slow and cautious manner, and allowed a month to
elapse before they attempted to relieve Athens, spending the intermediate period about Thebes and Negropont, and assisting the Eubœan Moslems against the
Christians of that island. Meanwhile, Odysseus rallied
his bands at Arakhova, blocked up the garrison they
had left in the castle of Livadia, and concluding a convention with the Albanian portion of it, sent them safely
to their own country; but remembering too well old
grounds of offence that ought to have been forgotten,
he was far from showing the same lenity to the unhappy
Livadiote fugitives who came to his camp.

We shall now carry back our narration to the siege
of the citadel of Cecrops, where we left the Athenians
waiting for supplies that might put them in a condition
to undertake something like regular operations. In
fact a schooner, sent by the brothers Condouriotti,
having arrived from Hydra, (May the 14th,) with 11
pieces of cannon on board, they immediately began to
work at a battery, in spite of the fire of the Acropolis.
Next day they established two guns on the Museum
(or hill of Philopappus), while at the same time a company of 40 men came to their aid from the island of
Ceos or Zèa. As these auxiliaries all wore hats, were
furnished with a drum and trumpet, and commanded
by a certain Pangalo, dressed in the uniform of a Russian major, their appearance alarmed the Turks, who
wrote a letter to the European consuls, enquiring whether the Christian Kings had declared war against the
Sultan. On the 16th, the besiegers began to exchange
cannon-shots with the castle, and likewise formed another battery near the theatre of Bacchus. On that
day they learned the dismal tidings of the defeat and
death of Diakos; but this discouraging news was coun-
terbalanced by the sight of a vessel loaded with men
and guns from Cefalonia, which entered Piræus on the

17th. The Cefalonians raised a battery near the temple of Jupiter Olympius, while the Zèans placed theirs between the theatres of Bacchus and Herodes Atticus ; powder and provisions came from Hydra on the 21st, and the Greeks having before the end of the month brought six pieces of cannon to bear on the Acropolis, not only battered it, but prepared to sink a mine under its walls. It is true that their artillery, inferior even to that of the garrison, was perfectly harmless ; but the insurgents had too little experience of military matters to judge the insufficiency of their means, and cherished sanguine hopes of soon reducing the fortress. Almost equally unwarlike, the Turks amused themselves by letting off every day four or five bombs or cannon-balls, and engaging with their foes in a continual musketry fire, which occasioned a few casualties on each side. In order thoroughly to intimidate their opponents, the Athenians once made an absurd procession round the castle, some on foot, some on horseback, and others mounted on asses ; but a cannon-ball, discharged *apropos,* having slain a Hydriote, put the whole to flight. The British Minister, Mr Frere, being at Athens, on his way from Constantinople, witnessed this farce.

At the commencement of June, the ordnance of the besiegers was augmented by a 24-pounder, and their miners laboured with spirit, although several of them were wounded by shots from the citadel. On the 8th the Moslems set at liberty thirty Greek women they had in the fort, saying, " it was their custom to release their slaves at the festival of Ramazan." On the night of the 12th they attempted a sortie, but were repulsed. After thirteen days' labour at their mine, the Greeks sprung it an hour before daybreak on the 21st, hoping to overturn the castle ; great, however, was their dissappointment, for the mine being neither carried far enough, nor charged with a proper quantity of

powder, produced not the least effect. During the
night of the 22d twelve Turks got out of the fort,
reached the sea-side, and finding a boat, arrived safely
at Negropont, and by their representations prevailed
upon the dilatory Pashas to take steps for succouring
the garrison, which was threatened with a scarcity of
provisions, and especially of water, no fewer than
1662 persons having been cooped up in the Acropolis ;
to insure a regular distribution, and obviate waste,
the Vayvodes Albanians constantly guarded the well in
the Serpendjè. Party spirit and mutual jealousies now
came to a head among the besiegers, who were an
undisciplined crowd made up of Athenian citizens,
Albanian villagers, and volunteers from various islands.
Wishing to counteract the exorbitant pretensions of
Captain Meleti, they raised to the chief command the
archbishop and the primate Zaccharias ; but this did
not cure the evil, for a violent sedition breaking out on
the 28th, they threatened to kill Meleti, (who concealed himself in the Dutch consulate,) and pillaged
the house of Zaccharias.   Intelligence that the Turks
had stormed Livadia, and occupied Thebes, spread
universal dismay, and at the close of June many families retired with their effects to the harbour.   On the
11th of July, a Hetœrist, named Liberius, arrived from
the Morea, with a commission signed by Ypsilanti,
empowering him to assume the command before
Athens; and apparent harmony being restored, Captain
Meleti marched next day in the direction of Thebes,
with the Salaminians and Khashiotes, to oppose the
enemy's advance.   On the 14th the garrison made a
sally an hour after nightfall, routed the troops of Zèa,
and took their standard ; they then attacked the Eginetans, defeated them likewise, forced their battery,
and seized their banner, which was, however, recovered through the courage of one Eginetan : they

finally assailed Philopappus, but the Hydriotes who were
posted there, repulsed and drove them back to the citadel. It was after this sortie, that, to avenge the deaths
of some of their friends, they executed nine hostages,
an act which the Greeks proposed to retaliate, by
slaughtering the Turkish prisoners confined in the consulates. The consuls, by their firmness, saved the intended victims, but found themselves placed in a painful situation, as the insurgents menaced violence to
their houses, and Liberius had not authority enough to
protect them. Amidst this anarchy, the news from the
frontiers of Attica became more and more alarming;
the militia sent to watch the passes, mistaking a herd
of cattle for Ottoman horsemen, fled, and no doubt
remained that Omer Pasha was preparing to advance
from Negropont. The Hydriotes reimbarked their
large cannon on the 23d, and sailed away next day.
Early on the morning of the 26th, the Turks again
made a sortie towards the Ilissus, and finding the posts
evacuated, burnt a church and some houses, and took
thirty or forty kiloes of grain from a thrashing-floor:
the Greeks at length assembling, charged, and after an
action of an hour, chased them into the citadel with the
loss of thirty killed and wounded; bringing in as trophies nine heads, four of which were those of female
black slaves. Seven of the insurgents were slain, and
the Captain Dimo of Livadia had his leg fractured by
a pistol ball fired at him by a Turk whom he had
wounded, and died of gangrene shortly afterwards.
On the 28th the Eginetans transported from their
island a heavy piece of ordnance, but learning next day
that the enemy was only six leagues distant, shipped
it off again. In the evening the besieged perceiving the
Ottoman banners in the olive grove, set up shouts of
joy, while the Greeks, seized with consternation, hurried to Salamis; and many Athenians, quitting the

Piræus in small boats, spent three days on a desert
islet without water. During the night of the 29th,
the besiegers entirely disappeared ; and at six o'clock
on the morning of the 30th, the Acropolis was relieved
after a blockade of eighty-three days ; Omer Pasha
Vriones, and Omer Bey of Carysto, entering the city at
the head of from 1500 to 1800 troops, almost all Albanians and Ghegs. It is said, that by pressing their march
they might have cut off a number of Christians, but
that the Pasha avoided the effusion of blood, supposing
the revolt would be easily quelled ; only a few feeble
old persons, too weak to fly, were discovered and slain
by the soldiers.

From this period to the month of October very little
worth notice occurred in Attica ; some villages in the
southern parts of that country submitted, but the bulk
of the population resided at Salamis and Egina, waiting
for a change of fortune. The barbarous Illyrians of
Omer Vriones plundered without distinction houses
and consulates, and they, as well as the indigenous
Turks, made forays (called by them Greek hunts) in
quest of Christian prisoners, whom they might have
the satisfaction of torturing : in a skirmish thus casually brought on, the Pasha had a narrow escape, an
aged peasant having snapped his musket within a yard
of his body. On the 15th of August, Omer Bey set out
on his return to Eubœa, and was attacked, while
marching along the coast, by a body of insurgents,
whom the Bishop of Carysto had assembled to intercept him; these he routed without difficulty, upon which
the prelate, who was a spectator of the combat from the
deck of a Hydriote vessel, quitted his diocese, and
withdrew to the Morea. In the mean time, Mehemet
Pasha, with a corps of 3000 men, fixed his head-quarters at Thebes, expecting the arrival of an Ottoman
army from Macedonia, destined to act in concert with

him, to enter Peloponnesus, and raise the siege of Tripolizza ; however, his soldiers, as well as those of his colleague Omer Vriones, gorged with spoil, looked with a feeling of apprehension to the coming of these auxiliaries, lest it should oblige them to take the field again before they had secured their booty. The Greeks, deriving courage from the inactivity of their enemies, selected their measures with judgment ; the mountains on the borders of Attica and Megaris were guarded by a party of Mainatts, and the whole force of the Dervenokhoriatts, under the Beyzadè Elias and the Archimandrite Dikaios Papa Flessa ; a detachment held the post of Dobrena on the Gulf of Livadostro, Odysseus stationed himself in the neighbourhood of Parnassus, and several brave Roumeliote captains prepared to dispute the passage of Mount Oeta. Towards the end of August, four Pashas advanced from Larissa, with an army of 5000 men (mostly Asiatics) to Zeituni, where one of them (Hadji Bekir) suddenly expired ; the other three, Bayram, Memish, and Shahin Ali, encamping on the bank of the Sperchius, sent a party of two or three hundred Delhi horse* to reconnoitre the Straits of Thermopylæ, defended by about 2000 Greeks. This vanguard was repulsed, and lost a few men and a standard. Next day, September the 4th, the Pashas moved forward, and attacked the insurgents, strongly posted at Fontana, or Vasilika, on the high road to Livadia. The latter allowed them to advance until completely engaged in a long defile of Oeta, and then poured a heavy fire upon the flanks of their column, embarrassed with cavalry, baggage, and a train of artillery : the victory was nevertheless doubtful, until a captain named Lapas, appearing with a

---

* Delhi in Turkish signifies mad ; the cavalry bearing that appellation was distinguished by a high black cap.

small reinforcement, a cry rose among the Greeks that
Odysseus was come; whereupon they drew their
sabres, and rushing upon the Turks, routed them with
immense slaughter, considering the numbers in action.
Not less than 800 Moslems lay dead on the field.*
Memish Pasha was killed, Shahin Ali dangerously
wounded; and besides standards, horses, camels, tents,
and booty of every description, the Christians captured
seven pieces of cannon: they owed their victory in a
great degree to the example set them by the brave Captain Ghouras, who is said to have slain Memish Pasha
with his own hand.   The Turks were so panic-struck,
that in their flight to Zeituni they broke down the
bridge of Alamanna to hinder pursuit.   Thus was
Thermopylæ once more the theatre of a battle most
important to Greece, inasmuch as it ruined the enemy's
plan of campaign.   Deprived by its result of the co-
operation they expected, the Ottoman generals in
Bœotia and Attica had no solid motive for protracting
their stay in an exhausted country; they were only
masters of the plains, and some affairs of outposts about
Dobrena and Eleusis by no means turned to their advantage.   On the 10th of October, Omer Vriones,
informed of the fall of Tripolizza, marched with half
his corps to Thebes, and the other half followed on the
22d, leaving Athens to the guard of its native Mussulmans, and the Acropolis well stored with provisions.
Perhaps with a view of concealing their real intentions,
the Pashas forced, after a smart skirmish, an advanced
position on the frontier of Megaris; they then hastened
towards Epirus, picking up by the way the garrison of
the castle of Livadia.   Crossing the mountains amidst
rain and snow, and abandoning their sick and baggage,

* Odysseus, in his official report to Ypsilanti, stated the number of
slain at 1200.

they reached Thessaly by the route of Talanta, (or Opus,) the only one that was left open; for Odysseus had occupied the pass of Petra, betwixt Livadia and Salona, and the conquerors of Vassilika held the main road over Oeta. Immediately after the enemy's departure, the Athenians began to agitate schemes for the recovery of their city: however zealously bent upon that object, they did not agree about a plan for effecting it, some wishing to trust to their own exertions, and others proposing to solicit aid from the Morea and Hydra. Councils were summoned, and the matter warmly debated at Salamis and Egina; they at length resolved to apply to the Peloponnesians for troops, but in the interval a few bolder spirits assembled a party of volunteers, and entering Attica, approached Marathon.

The Turks, instructed by the events of the past siege, entertained no thoughts of defending the town of Athens; they retired every night into the citadel, but during the day scoured the neighbourhood, where armed Greeks occasionally showed themselves. On the 15th of November they surprised and dispersed some of the latter in the olive grove, took eight women, and beheaded three male prisoners. Next day they sallied out with an hundred picked men, and went in search of those Athenians who were keeping the field on the side of Marathon: finding them, to the number of two hundred, at Khalandri, the Turks, attacked, were defeated, and pursued to the gates of Athens, with a loss of twenty-two killed; two Greeks fell, one of them a captain named Leckas. Emboldened by this victory, which in their simplicity they compared to that gained by Miltiades, the Athenian refugees quitted their hiding-places, and their general, Liberius, with the Ephors, hiring a martigo* as a

* A sort of square-rigged sloop common in the Levant.

store-ship, prepared to sail from Egina.   On the night
between the 16th and 17th, a body of insurgents silently
introduced themselves into Athens, and sought con-
cealment in the empty houses, hoping to surprise the
Mohammedans, when they should, as usual, descend
to the town, and penetrate along with them into the
Acropolis.   It is possible that they might have accomplished this, if the barking of dogs, and some shots
imprudently fired, had not alarmed the Turks, who
did not unlock the castle gates.   In the course of a
few days the blockade of that fortress was regularly
established, upon the arrival of Liberius and the Ephors,
who brought a small quantity of ammunition ; as it
was by no means sufficient for their wants, each Athenian citizen contributed one oke of gunpowder.   Their
agents having returned from the Morea, with no succours except letters and promises, they determined to
abridge the siege by a coup-de-main.   At three o'clock
on the morning of the 24th, they scaled the wall of the
Serpendjè, stormed a Tekè (or chapel of Dervishes),
and a coffee-house, that served the enemy as advanced
works, and possessed themselves of the two outer barriers of the Propylæum, together with an external
battery on which five guns were mounted ; this they
however abandoned again, but carried away a 12-
pounder placed near the Tekè, and which the Greeks
had left behind on the termination of the former siege :
they narrowly missed taking the inner gate, the garrison having just time enough to barricade it.   It is
said that this bold exploit cost the Athenians forty
killed and wounded, and that fifteen of the besieged
were slain ; the rest of the Turkish guard, amounting
to about thirty, lay hid all next day in the ditch of the
Acropolis, and were at length drawn up by their friends
in a musket-proof box, or rather cradle.   The principal, and indeed a very important result of the enter-

prise, was to deprive the enemy of the use of the well in the Serpendjè, and oblige them to trust to their cisterns for a supply of water. Sensible of the advantage they were likely to derive from this circumstance, the Greeks laboured strenuously to strengthen themselves in the posts they had conquered, while the Turks did their best to dislodge them, and for that end dropped down live shells on the vaulted roof of the Tekè, but without avail, the besiegers propping it up from within with stout beams and stanchions. On the 1st of December the Athenians placed in battery, at the Areopagus, the piece of cannon they had captured, and on the 15th of the same month they again endeavoured to make their way into the citadel, by a subterraneous passage to the left of the Propylæum : they imagined it would conduct them into the place, but finding it blocked up with stones, were forced to retire. Not yet discouraged, they attempted to storm at four o'clock on the morning of the 17th, and set fire to the inner gate; the Turks, however, heaping up behind it a quantity of earth, repulsed the assailants, with a loss of four killed and five wounded. The garrison succeeded no better in an effort they made on the 28th, to retake the exterior barriers ; two Greeks lost their lives, but the enemy was driven back. Having thus done every thing that it was in their power to achieve, the besiegers desisted from their useless exertions to reduce the Acropolis by force of arms, and for two months limited their attention to a rigorous blockade.

SECTION III.

WE have more than once had occasion to allude to
the tranquil happiness enjoyed by certain sequestered
and mountainous districts in Greece, where the Ottomans had not thought it worth while to settle Mohammedan colonies, and the Rayahs possessing the soil,
and rarely afflicted by the presence of their overbear-
ing lords, had only to pay the ordinary taxes.   Not
the least prosperous of these favoured regions, was
Magnesia in Thessaly, a pleasant country, diversified
with hill and dale, bordering on the sea, shaded by fine
forests, and containing thirty-five populous villages,
the most considerable of which, Makrinizza, might
rather be termed a town, since it boasted of a thousand
houses.   It was not difficult for Anthimos Gazi to
excite the people to revolt, but, that point accomplished,
he was altogether unable to guide their movements.
After exterminating the Turkish inhabitants of the
canton of Lekhena, they quarrelled about the division
of their property (always a primary object with the
insurgents), and busied themselves solely with that
miserable question, instead of listening to Gazi's advice, and instantly marching against the city of Volo.
Mahmoud, Pasha of Drama, who happened to be at
Larissa, with 4000 troops, came down upon them in the
midst of the discussion, ravaged Magnesia with great
fury, burned Makrinizza, and most of the other villages, and sent into Thrace a multitude of female captives.*   In their distress, many of the Magnesians fled
to the forests of Pelion, while others, (and among these
last was Anthimos Gazi himself,) escaped in boats to

* A numerous bevy of Thessalian beauties on their way to Drama
was liberated by the Macedonian Captain, Kara Tasso.

the neighbouring islands of Skiathos and Skopelos. A third portion took shelter in the maritime town of Trikeri, cut the isthmus on which it stands, and having been lucky enough to capture an Ottoman vessel laden with ammunition, defended themselves there. In Macedonia the cause of independence had declined almost since the commencement of the war, the Mussulmans in that province being numerous and brave, and the Olympians, the most powerful body of Armatoles, wasting their time in vain deliberations. In the month of May, Captain Manoli Papas marched close up to the walls of Salonika, at the head of 1500 armed Caloyers of Mount Athos, expecting that the islanders would second him by attacking it from the sea: in this hope he was disappointed, and the Yuruks (or nomadic Turks) charging him in the immense plains around that city, defeated the warriors of the cloister, and killed his lieutenant-general, a monk named Basil. The Sultan's troops then quickly cleared Chalcidicè of rebels, carried fire and sword through its rich territory, and prepared to force the Christians in their last positions. Beyond the Thermaic Gulf, and betwixt the noble rivers Axius and Strymon, the coast of Macedonia is broken into three large promontories ; Athos on the east, Sithonia in the centre, and Pallene to the west. The first is the more spacious, being twenty-seven geographical miles in length, eight at its greatest breadth, and swelling into rugged mountains. The other two are less hilly, and Sithonia (or Toronè) is wide at its entrance, and easy of access, but Athos and Pallene are joined to the continent by narrow necks. The latter peninsula is eighteen miles long, from north-west to south-east, and in one part ten miles wide; the isthmus in front of Pinaka, (the ancient Potidæa, or Cassandra,) comprises, from sea to sea, a space of 1400 yards, across which the insurgents of Chalcidicè dug a deep trench, or rather perhaps, more properly speaking, cleared out a fossé, the work of former ages. They erected batteries, armed with ship guns received from Psarra, and confided to the direction of Russian monks, (who in martial qualities surpassed their southern brethren,) and from hence they maintained a communication with Athos and Toronè. Some Greek vessels supported them, and a reinforcement of 400 Olympians arriving under Captain Diamantis, the number of fighting men at Cassandra amounted to 4000, while their families resided securely in the interior of the peninsula. At the end of June, Yussuf Pasha of Salonika encamped at St Mamas, on the site of Olynthus, and endeavouring to pass the isthmus, (July the 4th,) was repulsed with loss. A subsequent attempt during the summer was not more fortunate : he brought up heavy artillery to batter their lines, but the Greeks, by a vigorous sortie, seized at once nine cannon and mortars. Nevertheless they suffered considerably from a scarcity of bread, and an epidemic malady, which weakened them much, and in the ennui and ill humour necessarily engendered by their uncomfortable circumstances and gloomy anticipations, there was little harmony among the chiefs. After sustaining a fresh defeat on the 31st of October, Yussuf Pasha resigned the command to his successor, Mehemet Aboulaboud, the new Vizier of Salonika, a man of great courage and activity, as well as craft and dissimulation, qualities which he had learned at the courts of the notorious Jezzar, and the Viceroy of Egypt. This general made formidable preparations, and, on his arrival at the camp of St Mamas, summoned the insurgents to lay down their arms, promising them generous treatment. His offers being rejected, he attacked them on the night of the 11th of November, when his cavalry, filling up a part of the ditch with fascines, penetrated into the peninsula, and the Cassandrian gates were forced : the Greeks perceiving that their musketry did not arrest the enemy's progress, betook themselves to flight, and were pursued with great slaughter. Diamantis * and many of his companions got on board ship, but vast numbers of the vanquished were made prisoners, and experienced mild usage from the Pasha, who desired to gain a reputation of clemency. It was said, notwithstanding, that 4000 Greek women were sold soon afterwards by his soldiers in the slave-market of Salonika ; and it hath been asserted, with an appearance of probability, that 10,000 Christians of every age and sex were killed or taken. The conquest of Pallene was immediately followed by the submission of Toronè, the people there surrendering their cannon and weapons. Such signal successes were the more important at that critical moment, as the Olympians had at length resolved to take an active part in the war. Aboulaboud, after indulging his pride by a triumphal entry into Salonika, turned his views towards Mount Athos, reserving Olympus for another campaign. The religious community, posted in fortified monasteries, well provided with artillery and ammunition, and having at its orders 3000 combatants, might have opposed a long and obstinate resistance ; but the superior monks, divided in opinion, had never heartily imbibed the spirit of the Revolution ; they regretted their former indolent and peaceful life, and, seduced by the Pasha's affected lenity, agreed to capitulate, and accept an amnesty, on condition of delivering up their arms and ordnance, paying a contribution of 2,500,000 piastres, and admitting into their convents Turkish garrisons. However, about one-half of the Caloyers disapproving

---

* Pouqueville calls him the Bœotarch Diamantis ; for what reason we know not, since he was a Macedonian, and the title of Bœotarch has slept for twenty centuries !

of this arrangement, and preferring freedom to repose, emigrated to the Archipelago before their convents were occupied, and carried with them part of the church plate, as well as the most revered relics. Captain Manoli Papas, who withdrew at the same period, died at Cape Sunium, and was interred in the Isle of Hydra. On the 27th of December, Mehemet Aboulaboud took possession of the Holy Mountain, and thus terminated unfortunately the insurrection of Macedonia beyond the Axius, where the catastrophe of Cassandra, one of the great calamities of this sanguinary war, left a long and profound impression of terror.

CHAP. VI.

Affairs of Peloponnesus, from the capture of Tripolizza to the end of the year 1821—Insurrection of Crete—Some general considerations on the state of Turkey and Greece, and on the feelings with which the revolution was regarded in Europe.

SECTION I.

WHEN, in the middle of October, Demetrius Ypsilanti, returning from his useless excursion to the north of the Morea, drew near Tripolizza, he was saluted by discharges of cannon and small arms ; and Colocotroni, and most of the other chiefs, mounted on fine steeds, and decked out in gaudy apparel, which had lately belonged to the Turks, met and conducted him into the town : it was, however, remarked, that the Mainatts stood aloof, and paid him no mark of respect. The streets presented a deplorable spectacle of half-burnt houses, and dead bodies in a state of putrefaction, and as Ypsilanti rode slowly along, he encountered a striking example of the instability of worldly grandeur in the person of Kyamil Bey of Corinth, who, before the revolution one of the richest grandees of the empire, and distinguished by a noble and imposing form, now bowed before the Prince, a miserable captive, and implored his protection. The other Moslems of rank waited upon him next day, and were courteously received ; the Kihaya Bey conversing with him fluently in the Russian language, which he had learned when a prisoner in Muscovy. The ladies of Khourshid

Pasha's harem likewise requested an interview, but
this he declined, although he took care to shield them
from insult: indeed, the Greeks, aware that a large
ransom might be expected, not only abstained from
molesting them, but were complaisant enough to send
a courier to Mehemet Pasha at Thebes, assuring him
of their safety. Ypsilanti endeavoured to restore order at Tripolizza, where confusion was at its height,
every individual acting as he thought fit, without regard to primates or captains : fires occurred continually,
and he was himself burnt out of his quarters two days
after his arrival. He threatened rigorous proceedings,
and established a military police ; but what mainly
contributed to put a stop to disorder, was the rapid
melting away of the army, for the soldiers finding nothing to plunder dispersed to their homes, and left
only the chiefs, and their domestic retainers, a force,
which, united to the weak battalion of Balesto, was
barely sufficient to do duty at the gates, and guard the
Turkish prisoners. As the latter inspired apprehension, the captains (without Ypsilanti's knowledge or
consent) took measures for thinning them, by conducting out of the place, and shooting on successive nights,
detachments of the stoutest among them.* A part of
the surviving Mohammedans was employed in removing
and interring the bodies of the slain ; but the infection
of so many thousand putrid carcasses, aggravated by
the autumnal rains, which set in with violence, had
already tainted the air, and the same epidemic disease
that afflicted the garrison, communicated itself to the
conquerors, and, spreading over Peloponnesus, swept
away a multitude of people. One hope which the
Greeks had conceived from the reduction of Tripolizza,

* In answer to Ypsilanti's reproaches, they excused themselves on
the plea, that they could neither maintain, exchange, nor guard so
many prisoners.

namely, that the government would find there sufficient treasure to prosecute the war, and organize an
internal administration, vanished completely, for not a
particle of the booty was assigned to the public chest.
The Prince's daily conferences with the primates ended in strife and mutual disgust, a faction, headed by
the Archbishop Germanos, pertinaciously opposing all
his plans; his finances were exhausted, and his regulars, pinched by want, mutinied against their officers.
To get rid of a powerful rival, he tried to persuade
Colocotroni to march beyond the isthmus; but the old
general, too wary to fall into the snare, peremptorily
refused to quit Peloponnesus, while he offered to undertake the siege of Patrass.   Thwarted in every
thing, and weary of constant bickerings, Ypsilanti resolved to throw himself on the people, and despatched
to the different provinces confidential agents, bearers
of a circular address, whose tenor attested the extreme irritation he felt towards the Kojabashees (Vide
Appendix), calling together a general assembly ; a step
that gratified the nation at large, for besides a pre-
valent wish to establish the government on a solid
basis, each man hoped that the approaching congress
would promote the triumph of his own interest, opinion, or party.   As the infectious malady was becoming more and more fatal at Tripolizza, twenty or
thirty persons dying daily, the Prince selected Argos
as a place of meeting, that town being nearer the
islands, and enjoying a better winter climate : he accordingly proceeded thither on the 14th of November.
Missions poured in at this period from various quarters, either to petition for aid, or simply present their
homage to Ypsilanti, his name having more weight
attached to it out of the Morea : the most remarkable
was a deputation of Olympians, who came to request
assistance, which was readily granted.   Although the

Hellenic representatives had been invited to assemble
on the 11th of November, yet as a long delay elapsed
ere they came together, the Prince, in his quality of
Generalissimo, took the command of the troops blockading Napoli di Romania, and caused its environs to
be carefully reconnoitred by European officers.   The
Greeks were very anxious to gain a stronghold that
has been looked upon as the key of the Morea, and
they knew that next summer the Turkish fleet would
certainly endeavour to relieve it ; except, however, by
a tedious blockade, there seemed no reasonable prospect of accomplishing their object.

Napoli, although defective in some respects, (especially in the want of outworks,) is really a place of
great strength ; and its siege must always be a matter
of fatigue, difficulty, and doubtful issue.   It stands on
a bluff promontory, running out nearly from east to
west, into the smooth and deep Argolic Gulf, (which
forms an excellent roadstead,) and at the edge of one
of the finest and richest plains in Greece ; the town,
facing the north, is built on a slip of low land confined
betwixt the sea and the fort of Itch Kalè, occupying the
table top of the promontory, whose sides, to the south
and west, are rocky and precipitous.   The frequent
recurrence of pernicious fevers must be ascribed to the
nature of its position hindering a free circulation of
air, and to the vicinity of unwholesome marshes.   Itch
Kalè, comprising the ground on which old Nauplia was
erected, is defended by four tiers of batteries rising
above each other ; the two interior enceintes are in a
state of total decay, and its powder magazines not even
bomb-proof ; the ramparts show the workmanship of
successive ages, from the Hellenic walls of Nauplia,
destroyed by the Argives before the Persian invasion,
to the labours of Venetian and Turkish engineers.   The
two faces that the town presents, are covered by a cur-

tain, with bastions of irregular shape and dimensions, except towards the port, where there is only a *chemise* of masonry ; but a debarkation is rendered difficult by rocks, and the ruins of a Venetian mole, and only small craft can penetrate to the bottom of the harbour.   Its mouth is guarded by a stone castle called the Burj, (on an islet level with the water,) consisting of an upper and lower battery, mounting a score of guns, crossing their fire at the distance of half musket shot with the sea batteries of the town.   To the east of, and immediately above Napoli, the frowning citadel of Palamide rises to a height of near 750 feet, covering the spacious summit of a round and steep rock, whose base is washed by the sea towards the south-west ; it includes three closed forts, and four detached batteries, laid out with great judgment by the Venetians, and carefully defiladed.   As this citadel commands all the rest of the place, an assailant ought to begin with its siege, which offers serious obstacles ; precipices protect it on three sides, and towards the east, whence it may be approached, the naked soil affords no earth.   Palamide is supplied with several beautiful cisterns cut out of the rock, and there are fourteen in Itch Kalè.   Napoli has two gates, one to the land, the other to the sea, and a small water port under the battery of the Five Brothers, so called from five very long brass guns of the calibre of 36 and 48 lbs. ; its land front is exceedingly narrow, and accessible by an isthmus of low swampy ground between the shore and the foot of Palamide, somewhat resembling, on a small scale, the approach to Gibraltar ; along this neck runs a causeway exposed to a plunging fire from above, a flanking fire from the Burj, and a direct fire from the curtain, and a bastion betwixt the gate and the sea.   Palamide has two outer gates, and communicates with the town by a long, steep, and zig-

zag flight of steps, covered by a wall pierced with loopholes ; its exterior enceinte is defended by a stone rampart, twenty feet high, without any fossé ; the inner
forts have revetements thirty feet in height, and the
loftiest castle, commanding the whole, is bomb-proof.
On all these works the Turks had mounted nearly four
hundred pieces of cannon, of every variety of calibre,
but, as is usual in their fortresses, in most miserable
condition. The garrison, reckoned at 1500 combatants,
was embarrassed with a multitude of useless mouths,
and, apprehending the inroads of famine, had turned
out of the town a considerable number of Christian
women ; however, at the end of October, an English
or Maltese vessel, with a cargo of grain and rice, was
suffered to enter the port, through the culpable negligence of the Greek cruisers, and was unloading there
when Ypsilanti arrived at Argos. Captain Nicholas
(brother to Nikitas) headed the militia blockading Napoli, and established in three divisions, on the hill of
St Elias, among the Cyclopian ruins of Tyrins, and at
a village on the road to Kranidi ; his soldiers were in
point of force equal to the garrison, and their chief,
brought up in the English service, and a zealous partisan of European discipline, had introduced a species of
order into his irregular bands. Among the foreign
officers who came to Greece, was a certain Dania, a
Genoese by birth, and a *chef d'escadron* in Napoleon's
army ; a man of intrepid courage, but endowed, it
would seem, with more temerity than sound judgment.
Having passed some weeks at the quarters of Captain
Nicholas, he imagined a plan for surprising Napoli,
and submitted it to Ypsilanti ; the latter consulted
Europeans in whom he had confidence, and they with
one voice pronounced it to be impracticable. Nevertheless, by importunity, by availing himself of the en-

thusiasm which the storming of Tripolizza had excited in the minds of the Greeks, Dania persuaded the Prince and the other generals to adopt his project. The Archons of Hydra and Spezzia received directions to equip a squadron of twelve ships of war, and a flotilla of forty launches, manned by 2000 seamen, while the districts of Peloponnesus were ordered to furnish contingents of troops, and the company of artillery prepared scaling-ladders in the adjacent villages. A report, purposely spread, that Napoli was about to surrender, attracted so many volunteers eager to assist in sacking it, that 7000 were thought to have traversed Argos in the course of a few days. During the time spent in preparation, a French officer, named Voutier, who commanded Ypsilanti's artillery, planned an enterprise for getting hold of the Burj, close to which the Maltese brig lay at anchor ; observing that the Turks withdrew every morning the detachment that guarded it at night, and only left a post of eight or ten men, he proposed to board the vessel in the dark, and disguising his companions as English sailors, to seize the Burj at daybreak, as soon as the Moslems crossed over to the town. He set out from Lerna with two large boats containing a dozen European volunteers, and sixty Greek soldiers and seamen, preceded by a two-oared skiff, in which was a person who perfectly understood the English language, and who was to tell the master that no harm would be done him, and that his brig would be soon restored. They drew near undiscovered, but the sailors in the launches, fancying they perceived a port-fire burning on the vessel's deck, were struck with fear, and rowed back to Lerna in spite of their officers. Two days after, the Maltese set sail, and was captured at the mouth of the gulf by the Greeks, who ought to have hindered her from entering, and subsequently released through the interference of an English frigate.* On the 8th of December twenty Hydriote and Spezziote vessels appeared with a number of armed launches, and repeatedly engaged with the Burj a distant cannonade : the troops being collected by the 12th, and the scaling-ladders ready, orders were issued on the 15th to assault at two hours after midnight, and the following dispositions prescribed. General Nikitas, with six hundred men, was to escalade the wall and take possession of the land gate and adjoining bastion, and Colonel Balesto was to support this storming party with one company of European Philhellenes, two companies of Greek regulars, the company of artillery, and a company of Cretans ; General Colocotroni, with a thousand irregulars, and one regular company under Captain Justin, was to make an attack on the Palamide, while the flotilla should effect a disembarkation in the harbour, covered by the fire of the ships of war, which were directed to approach within half cannonshot ; Yatrako commanded the reserve, and Prince Ypsilanti stationed himself on a rocky eminence in the plain. So excessive was the negligence of the besieged, that with somewhat more resolution, the assailants might perhaps have got into the place. At two o'clock on the morning of the 16th, the different columns were put in motion, but Balesto, on reaching the foot of the rocks of Palamide, found the scaling-ladders abandoned, and to his astonishment saw nothing of either Nikitas or his troops ; he soon learned from Dania, the projector of the assault, that Nikitas had only been able to assemble fifty of his soldiers, the courage of the

---

* Although the Greek blockades were not yet formally acknowledged, there existed an understanding with the commander of the British naval force in the Archipelago, that they might prevent merchantmen from revictualling Turkish fortresses ; however, the islanders chose rather to allow them to pass, that when they went out they might take them with the price of their cargoes on board.

others having failed. Balesto posting his party in ruined huts, within pistol-shot of the gate, went forward to reconnoitre, and perceived that perfect stillness reigned within ; at that moment, just as the moon was setting, Ypsilanti gave the signal of attack, and Colocotroni discharged against the Palamide a volley of musketry, which the Turks answered with a cannonade ; while those at the land front likewise taking the alarm, began to ply with round, grape, and small arms the corps of Balesto. The Greek irregulars then fled, but the Philhellenes and regular companies stood their ground for three hours, hoping that the morning breeze would allow the flotilla to co-operate ; they at length retired in obedience to Ypsilanti's orders, carrying off their wounded, although pursued by the enemy, and exposed to the fire of seven pieces of cannon, which fortunately were ill-directed. The flotilla did not act at all, only a few ships advancing and interchanging with the Burj some ineffectual cannon balls ; the rest and the armed launches kept aloof ; the Turks seized the scaling-ladders and transported them into the town. The loss sustained in this mad attempt, falling entirely upon the Philhellenes and regulars of Balesto's column, did not exceed 16 killed, and 31 wounded ; in the former list were included the Wirtemberg Captain Liching (who had both legs shot away), and the standard-bearer Dorat ; in the latter, the Captains Gubernati and Persat.

On the western side of Peloponnesus the insurgents met with a still more disgraceful discomfiture, in their efforts to reduce the castle of Patrass. When about the 20th of October the Ottoman garrison heard of the fate of Tripolizza, their consternation became so great, that had it not been for the Lalliotes Patrass would have been evacuated. The Albanian mercenaries (about 1000 strong) first insisted on departing, and, as little

reliance was reposed in their fidelity, were allowed to
cross the gulf, and quarter themselves at Lepanto:
the native Mohammedan population had already sought
shelter in the castle of Roumelia, the Lalliotes having
expelled them from the citadel, and Yussuf Pasha, unable to control these last, resided with his household
troops at that of the Morea: 3000 Lalliotes, one-third
of whom were able to fight, occupied the citadel, and
were provisioned for three months. Deeming the opportunity favourable, the primates of Pyrgos, Gastouni, Kalavryta, and Vostizza, made levies in their
districts, and on the 3d of November, an hour before
day, 5000 Peloponnesians by a sudden assault gained
possession of the ruins of Patrass: they were commanded by Thanos Kanakaris, Zaimis, Londos, and
Sisinni, and the Princes Mavrocordato and Karadja
came over from Messalonghi to join them, bringing
some pieces of cannon, and 1500 European muskets.
The Greeks, entrenched in houses and minarets close
to the castle, annoyed its garrison by a continual fire,
while the Lalliotes endeavoured to dislodge them with
their heavy artillery, and executed frequent sorties,
which gave rise to smart fighting in the streets. In
order more effectually to gall the enemy, Mavrocordato
caused a small gun to be placed on the roof of a mosque,
formerly the church of St Sophia, and now again a
Christian temple. As had ever been the case at Patrass, utter disorder reigned in the army, rations were
irregularly distributed, and nothing was done to obviate a surprise, nor any guard kept without the camp.
In this way the siege went on for a month, until the
insurgents tasted the bitter fruits of their negligence
and contempt of discipline. On the 4th of December
Yussuf Pasha, repeating the manœuvre that had succeeded so well in April, marched from the Morea castle
with 400 men (chiefly cavalry) and entered Patrass at

noon, before the besiegers had the least intimation of his approach ; at the same instant the Lalliotes sallied, and the Greeks, who had been two days without bread, were routed and dispersed. As they opposed a slight resistance, and fled swiftly to the hills, their loss in killed was not heavy ; Mavrocordato and Karadja escaped with difficulty, and their artillery, baggage, and magazine of arms, fell into the hands of the Turks. The insurgents rallied at Kalavryta, and when their terror was dissipated, parties of them again approached Patrass, where the Pasha laboured to make the destruction of the town as complete as possible, that it might not afford cover to his enemies. Mavrocordato, Karadja, and Theodore Negris, proceeded to Argos, and arriving there while the National Congress was assembling, found that place a focus of political intrigue, to which their presence gave fresh fuel. Ypsilanti's authority, which had been long declining, was become almost null after his repulse at Napoli ; the Peloponnesian primates scarcely showed him outward marks of respect, and the islanders, disappointed in their hope of obtaining an indemnity from the treasures of Tripolizza, loudly exclaimed against his conduct in quitting the siege. Before transferring his residence to Argos, he had experienced a severe humiliation ; having appointed to the government of Tripolizza, Sekkeris, a native of that city, but educated in the west, Colocotroni objected, and obliged the Prince to compromise the matter, the general's eldest son, Panos, being named military commandant, and Sekkeris civil governor. The talents and insinuating address of Mavrocordato, seconded by the intriguing Negris, and by the influence of the Archbishop of Patrass, immediately formed a powerful party. Germanos incessantly represented to the Peloponnesians, that they ought to avail themselves of Mavrocordato's services

without dreading his ambition, which could never be
so dangerous as that of Ypsilanti, since he did not, like
the latter, assert pretensions to command the army,
had no *appui* out of Greece, and might at any moment
be laid aside. The two rivals met in public society,
and behaved to each other with the forms of civility;
but Negris openly manifested his animosity to Prince
Demetrius, who, perceiving that he was altogether
supplanted, resigned the struggle, and quitting the
arena of political strife, thought only of prosecuting the
war. He remembered the effect of his secession at
Vervena, which brought his opponents to composition,
and on every disgust he was ready to reiterate the ex-
periment, as he had done previously to the fall of Tripolizza, although the result was no longer the same:
Understanding that the garrison of the Acrocorinthus
desired to treat with him, he left Argos on the 24th
of December, and moved to Corinth, accompanied by
his staff, the battalion of Balesto, the Generals Colocotroni and Yatrako, and Kyamil Bey, who promised to
put the fortress into their hands, The Hellenic deputies continued their deliberations under the guidance
of his adversaries and rivals: hardly however was he
gone, when the Turks of Napoli began to be so troublesome, that it was judged expedient to choose another
place of meeting. Informed, through the evasion of a
prisoner who saved himself on one of Germanos's horses,
that Ypsilanti had departed with most of the troops,
600 Janissaries marched out on the 26th with two
fieldpieces, drove the hostile posts before them, and
would have taken Argos, if Nikitas, rallying round
him a few brave volunteers (Greeks and Philhellenes),
had not, after a long combat, forced them to retrograde.
The fugitive population then returned to the town,
and, with a degree of cruelty equal to their cowardice,
shed the blood of the unfortunate Mohammedan cap-

tives confined there: many survivors of the Tripolizza massacre perished on that day. Alarmed and shocked at this occurrence, Mavrocordato proposed that the Congress should remove to a more tranquil situation, and at an assembly held in the house of the Archbishop of Patrass, it was resolved to adjourn its sittings to the little town of Piada on the Saronic Gulf, about six miles to the N. W. of the ancient Epidaurus.

SECTION II.

WE have now concluded our narration of the principal military and political events that happened on the continent of Greece, and in the Archipelago, during the year 1821; one important point, however, (the Isle of Candia,) still remains unnoticed: we shall, therefore, in this section, offer some account of that country, and describe the first features of its revolution. The island of Crete, lying under the 35th degree of north latitude, and between the 23d and 27th of east longitude, is upwards of forty-seven geographical leagues in length, and ten at its greatest breadth: the celebrated Ida, (the cradle of Jupiter,) now called the White Mountains, rising from the western coast, traverses most of it, and even down to the sea its surface is hilly. Numerous rivers descending from those mountains, whose tops are half the year enveloped in snow, form, in winter and spring, impetuous torrents, mostly dried up by the summer heats. The climate is delightful, and the beauty and fertility of the country excite the admiration of all strangers who visit it: Crete is indeed the garden of Greece, and were it thoroughly civilized and cultivated, would produce in vast abundance corn, wine, oil, silk, wool, honey, and wax. In the state, however, to which this superb

island was reduced, grain, silk, and cotton were im-
ported from other provinces, and its exports consisted
only in a large quantity of oil, (the staple commodity,)
wine of fair quality, excellent soap, and cheese of
Sfakia, much esteemed in the Levant. The land is
stocked with game, the sea with fine fish; fruit is plentiful, and of delicious flavour; its valleys are adorned
with a variety of flowers and aromatic shrubs, and
with groves of myrtle, orange, lemon, pomegranate,
and almond trees, as well as interminable forests of
olives. The southern coast is destitute of ports, and has
scarcely any safe roadsteads; but on the northern side
are several excellent and capacious harbours. There
is something peculiar in the appearance and disposition
of its inhabitants: they are taller than the other natives of Greece, strong, active, and especially remarkable for agility and swiftness; daring, vindictive,
venal, rapacious, and unwilling to submit to the re-
straints of law and order: they retain, in short, those
distinctive characteristics of the old Cretans, which
caused their mercenary troops to be so much esteemed,
and their name to be so deeply detested throughout
Greece and Asia. They likewise differ from their
neighbours in respect of dress and arms; instead of
the shaggy mantle, camise, and classic buskin of Roumelia, or the cumbrous garments of the Ottomans,
they wear short jerkins and drawers of light texture,
thin white cloaks, and boots (generally red) reaching
to the knee, but extremely pliable; and in place of the
ill-poised Albanian musket, which has hardly any
stock, or the ponderous Turkish carabines, they use
long and light guns mounted like European fowling-
pieces. In handling these weapons they display as
much skill as their ancestors did in shooting with the
bow: they are reckoned the best marksmen in the East,
but their warfare is entirely one of ambuscade and

bush-fighting, resembling that of the North American
Indians, where it is considered the chief excellence of a
soldier to take aim at the foe without suffering himself
to be seen. A very high authority (General Mathieu
Dumas) rated the whole population at 250,000 souls,
of whom above one-half professed the religion of Mohammed ; latterly, since many foreigners have had an
opportunity of examining the interior of the isle, an
opinion has gained ground that the number of Christians was more considerable than he imagined. Even
the Candiots, attached to the faith of Islam, must be
looked upon as Mussulman Greeks rather than Turks,
their origin being mainly derived from apostasy, and
the custom of intermarrying with Greek women. So
much alike are the Christians and Moslems in speech
and semblance, that in action they found it difficult to
discriminate friends from enemies, and the Greeks
adopted a practice of fighting bareheaded, in order that
their own party might recognise them by their flowing
locks. It would be natural to suppose that this similarity, relationship, and continual intercourse, ought to
have modified the rigour of the Ottoman yoke : on the
contrary, however, no Rayahs were so harshly treated
as those of Candia, and nowhere did the ruling caste
exercise so inhuman a degree of tyranny.

It was this abominable system that pushed so many
Christians to apostasy ; but many, although outwardly
Mohammedans, retained in secret, from generation to
generation, the religion of their forefathers, and had
their children privately baptized. Such were the two
brothers Kormouli, who not only resumed, at the outset of the revolution, an undisguised profession of
Christianity, but, after spending an ample fortune in
its defence, died before Athens, for the cause of Grecian liberty, in the campaign of 1827. There is one
district on the south-western coast which has always

enjoyed a certain share of independence, though tributary to the Porte—a circumstance for which it was
indebted to its asperity and poverty : it is called Sfakia, and is neither extensive nor populous, the number
of its shepherd-warriors not exceeding 800, or 1000 at
most. According to general opinion, confirmed by
their manly and truly Grecian beauty, they are Cretan
aborigines. Some, indeed, have started an idea, that
they are colonists from Sfax, in Africa, who came over
with the Saracens ; but this error seems to have arisen
from their name, and from confounding them with
another tribe, (the Abadiotes,) evidently of Arabic race.
The latter does not now exist, having been swept from
the face of the earth during the progress of the war.
Inhabiting a narrow and mountainous territory, the
Sfakiots were brave, hardy, and laborious, but greedy
and arrogant. It may be a question, whether their
pride and avidity did not do more to retard, than their
valour to advance, the emancipation of Crete. Their
town, built on the flanks of two opposite hills, and containing 1200 people, carried on a little trade in cheese
and honey, although its port, called Loutro, is so much
exposed to the south winds, that they were obliged to
haul up their barks on the beach. The fertile islets of
Gozo, in the Lybian Sea, composed a valuable part of
their possessions.

The Turks had thrown the ten ecclesiastical divisions of Crete, established by the Byzantine Emperors,
into three Pashaliks—Candia to the east, Rhetymo
in the centre, and Canea on the west. The first was
the largest, and its governor had the title of Beylerbey,
or viceroy. The others were Pashas of two tails, sub-
ordinate to his authority. Candia, the metropolis,
(called also the great fortress,) is a strong city seated
in a rich plain near the ruins of Gnossus, with a population of 12,000 or 15,000 souls ; so at least it was

stated before the insurrection. Its harbour having
been neglected, is half choked with sand, and only
capable of admitting merchant vessels. Rhetymo, the
old Rhetymna, eighteen leagues to the west of the
former, is a small town, environed by gardens and
villas, with a port fit for shipping of moderate burden. It is protected by a wall from fifteen or eighteen
feet high, with towers on which artillery is mounted,
and has a regular bastioned citadel facing the sea.
Canea, (formerly Cydonia,) twelve leagues west of Rhetymo, is the most flourishing and commercial place in
the island. Its works are in pretty good repair, consisting of a strong rampart, a broad and deep ditch
hewn out of the rock, four bastions on the land side,
surmounted by cavalier batteries armed with heavy
ordnance, and a raveline at the north-east corner. As
the Turks have allowed the harbour to be filled up
with rubbish, large ships can hardly approach within
half cannon-shot, and the magnificent arsenal and dockyard built by the Venetians are totally gone to decay.
This Pashalik includes some of the finest cantons, such
as Suda, Selino, Kissamos, and Apocorona. At the distance of five leagues from Canea, on the other side of a
long promontory named Cape Malek, stands on an islet
the fortress of Suda, surrounded by a triple line of
ramparts covered with a formidable artillery. It is a
military point of the utmost importance, on account of
its excellent roadstead, where fleets can ride in perfect
safety. The impregnable castle of Karabusa, famous
in the modern annals of piracy, is perched on a detached rock, washed on every side by the sea, at the western extremity of the island. Besides the above, there
are in Crete about a dozen fortified posts, which we
need not here particularly specify.*

* Spina Longa, on the north-east of the isle, is said to be as strong
a place as Karabusa, with a much better haven.

Considering the character of the Candiote Mussulmans, and their habitual cruelty in peaceable times, we can easily conceive that the Greek Rayahs were exposed to imminent danger when the revolt of the Morea was announced, and numerous cruisers, sailing under the Hellenic flag, blockaded the coast of Crete. The Turks were dismayed at first; but fear sharpening their ferocity, they began in the towns to butcher the Christians. They then proposed to disarm the Sfakiotes, and experiencing on the part of the latter a positive refusal to deliver up their weapons, prepared to use force as soon as the feast of Bayram should be over. While, however, they were waiting for a junction of the troops of the different Pashaliks, the Sfakiotes, whom the people of the lower country invited to their assistance, suddenly descended, at the end of June, to the plains of Canea with a force of 800 muskets, (which the accession of other Cretans soon increased to 1300,) and took post at Therison, under the command of Captain George Tchelepi. The Turks, going out to meet them, were beaten (July the 2d) in a sharp action, fought at Loulo, within a league of Canea, and left thirty-seven dead on the field. In a few days the insurgents captured the towers of Prosuero and Armyros, in the province of Apocorona; and on the side of St Basil, the brothers Kormouli defeated a party of 200 Turks from Rhetymo, killing seventeen, among whom was their leader, Ismael Koumdouris, and a valiant Aga named Ali Mustafa. Enraged at these checks, the Moslems avenged themselves by massacring the Rayahs still in their power. It is said that 400 were slaughtered in the city of Candia, 200 at Canea, 150 at Rhetymo, and 300 in the canton of Sitia: all the bishops perished. During the months of July and August, many engagements happened on various points, generally to the advantage of the Christians, who repulsed the enemy's attempts to recover Therison, and routed them with great loss on the 18th of July, at Askouphi, near Rhetymo, taking their baggage, standards, and ammunition.   But the Sfakiotes, to whose courage these successes were chiefly due, having effectually plundered the flat country, returned to their own territory, and occupied themselves there in dividing the booty.   Meanwhile the Ottomans collected their strength from every quarter, and being supported by artillery, and headed by the Beylerbey in person, stormed Therison on the 30th of August, after an obstinate combat.*   In September, an army, reported to amount to 10,000 Janissaries, and guided by a treacherous priest of Kissamos, turned the passes, penetrated into Sfakia, burned the town and villages, and compelled the people, with thousands of refugees from other districts, to seek shelter, either on inaccessible peaks, or on board some barks at Loutro.   Had the invaders protracted their stay, these fugitives must have been starved; but, fortunately for them, the Turks, afraid of wanting provisions, and supposing they had quenched the insurrection, began to retreat on the 17th, separated their troops, and shut themselves up for the winter in their respective fortresses, where they extirpated the few remaining Rayahs.

The revolt then spreading anew through the western and central divisions of the island, the Sfakiotes again appeared in the vicinity of Canea, and established a sort of blockade.   Its Mussulman inhabitants, cooped

---

* At the outset, the enthusiasm of the Cretans rose very high. During a fruitless attack made upon Therison by the Turks, the Greek women of that village animated the men, and supplied them with water and fruit.   One of these heroines had a jar on her shoulder broken by a ball, but, notwithstanding this accident, she went gaily on through the fire with a basket of grapes.

up within their walls, were afflicted with disease, and
the misery of thirst; for the insurgents having cut the
pipes that conveyed water into the city, drove them
to the necessity of digging wells, whence they drew a
brackish and unwholesome fluid.   The use of this
water aggravated the malady, insomuch that, during
October, thirty persons frequently died in one day.
The Pasha having ventured to send 80 head of oxen
and 200 sheep (his own private property) to graze outside of the ramparts, the Greeks, by a sudden inroad,
carried them off; and the Agas of the town were tantalized by the sight of a fine crop of olives growing on
their lands, which they dared not attempt to gather.
It would seem, however, that on the setting in of the
rainy season, the corps observing Canea fell back to
the high grounds, and that the Turks were then able
to repair their aqueduct.   The industrious natives of
Cassos, a small commercial island to the N.E. of Crete,
whose existence was hardly known to geographers,
armed fifteen merchant vessels, and cruising along the
shore, intercepted the maritime communication betwixt
the enemy's fortresses; while from different parts of
the Archipelago, Cretan emigrants hastened to join the
insurgent bands; thus, by the close of the year, they
had several thousand men in the field, and held most
of the inland cantons.   As they were in great want of
ammunition, Antonio Melidori, and Nicholas Zervas,
had been despatched as deputies to the Morea, in September, to crave assistance, and procure, if possible, a
leader of repute, and skilful officers to direct their operations.   From Ypsilanti (himself destitute of resources)
they could only obtain a small quantity of gunpowder,
an article of the utmost value to them, since, in 1821,
it sold in Candia at the price of 22 piastres an oke;
Cantacuzene declined putting himself at their head, but

the Chevalier Affendouli accepted the command, and sailing from Calamata, arrived at Loutro in the beginning of November.

SECTION III.

WHILE in the southern parts of European Turkey, the Sultan's dominion was daily fading, Constantinople and the Ottoman Empire offered a melancholy picture ; disquieted by apprehensions of a Russian war, harassed by the seditious clamours of the Janissaries, and vexed at the little success of its efforts to put down the Greek insurrection, the Porte consoled itself with the spectacle of public executions.   In order to gratify its taste for blood, prisoners taken in Moldavia and Wallachia, were transported from a distance of some hundred miles to suffer decapitation in the streets of the capital ; such was the fate of the Servian Papas, and the Captains Farmaki and Diamantis.* In passing the Isle of Samothrace, on its voyage from Zante to the Dardanelles, the Turkish fleet made an unprovoked descent, and seized near fourscore of its peaceable inhabitants ; most of them perished from the effects of ill treatment on board the ships of war, but twelve were executed at Constantinople.   Amidst the Sultan's embarrassments, the King of Persia suddenly declared war against him ; the hostilities, however, of this new enemy, prosecuted in a desultory manner, and on a remote frontier, little affected the Porte, deeply engaged as it was in the affairs of Greece, and its discussion with Russia.   The negotiation was still spun out through

---

* Many Europeans at Constantinople, and even some of the legations, with their usual ignorance of Turkish matters, mistook Farmaki for George the Olympian, and published that the latter had been beheaded.

the medium of the English and Austrian ministers, with a very doubtful prospect of amicable adjustment. In February, 1822, intelligence of Ali Pasha's death occasioned a fever of exultation among all classes at Constantinople, and the Divan assuming a higher tone, a grand council was held at the Porte on the 25th, and the probability of a speedy rupture with Russia announced to the principal officers of Janissaries, and the heads of the thirty-two trading corporations of the capital. The people seemed disposed to support the government, but the excitement thus infused into their minds, vented itself in a fresh series of murders, robberies, and excesses ; insomuch, that the Turkish tradesmen, complaining loudly, sent a deputation (March 10th) to the Kihaya Bey, or minister of the interior, offering the keys of their warehouses, and threatening to leave the city ; it was not till the middle of summer that tranquillity could be fully restored.   In Asia Minor, the persecution against the Greeks, which had relaxed for two or three months, broke out again with new virulence in autumn, partly owing to accounts of the sack of Tripolizza, and partly to the increasing boldness of the Samians, who made frequent descents on the opposite shore, and fought battles with the Turks, in which they were generally victorious.   That island yielded to no other portion of the Hellenic confederacy in spirit and love of liberty ; its proximity to danger exalted the courage of its youth, and a more than usual share of method and prudence appeared in the measures of its leading men.   The population having been augmented to fifty thousand by refugees from Ionia, all those able to bear arms were formed into regiments, the accessible points defended by intrenchments and batteries, and an impregnable convent in the interior designed as an asylum for the women and children.   In order to oppose the Samians, the Turks persisted in filling with troops

the unfortunate town of Scalanova; as soon as one
corps disbanded, another supplying its place. Hence
it followed, that one mutiny trode on the heels of
another, and as each produced a massacre of Greeks,
that description of citizens, the most useful and industrious, and reckoned previously at ten thousand, was
entirely exterminated. Troubles recommenced at Smyrna in October, and the rage of the populace no longer
respected the subjects of foreign powers in amity with
the Porte. On the 20th and 21st of November, the
Frank quarter was menaced, and some lives were lost
in partial rencounters; the Turks, however, meeting
with resistance, and overawed by the demonstrations of
the European ships of war in the harbour, turned their
fury against the Greeks, and slew numbers of them.
Similar scenes occurred throughout Anatolia, each community of Rayahs, belonging to the Byzantine church,
suffering in its turn. If any were exempt from bloodshed, yet the measure of their affliction was doubled by
a more intense pressure of Mussulman hate. In truth,
the condition of the Asiatic Greeks was deplorable;
those detected in an attempt to emigrate were punished
with death, and if they remained at home, the fear of
assassination was for ever before their eyes.

During that same winter, European Greece was far
from presenting a satisfactory aspect to her most enlightened patriots, and the warmest friends of her cause.
Revolutions, like the one of which we are treating,
although bright and dazzling when contemplated from
a distance, discover to a close and scrutinizing regard
many dark spots, especially in a nation contaminated
by long misrule and pernicious example; united in
detestation of the Turks, and a resolution to combat
them, the Hellenes were, in every other respect, divided
by a thousand petty passions and jealousies. They had
rushed into a perilous contest without counting chances,

and had within themselves few elements of success;
there was neither public treasure, regular force, nor
system of government deserving that name. Slaves
broke loose are always reluctant to return under a
moderate degree of restraint, and the volatile temper of
the Greeks is rather averse to subordination ; the established authorities were removed, and in most of the
provinces there was nothing fixed or stable to replace
them. The Roumeliote captains in their Armatoliks,
the Primates in the Isles, the Peloponnesian Kojabashees in their districts, and the Bishops universally, had
indeed enjoyed a certain jurisdiction, based, however,
on the Sultan's supremacy, and the delegated powers of
his Pashas and Vayvodes ; now that the new order of
things rested simply on popular will, none of this dis-
cordant multitude of notables was sufficiently elevated
above the surface to make his ascendency felt beyond
very circumscribed limits. Commands were little better than requests, and could seldom be enforced until
they had undergone public canvassing and approbation.
Add to this, that not a few of the chiefs were, in point
of education, and still more of principle, on a level with
the populace. Law no longer existed ; men trusted
for protection to their own strength, or that of their
friends ; and every crime, except treasonable correspondence with the enemy, passed unpunished. Acts
of brigandage were comparatively rare in Peloponnesus, where the character of the peasantry is tame and
quiet ; they were more frequent in the islands, and at
the end of the year a swarm of piratical boats infested the Archipelago. Psarra was distinguished by its
enthusiasm, the activity of its cruisers, steadiness in
its administration, and obedience in the people. Hydra
and Spezzia were not so easily managed, and the Primates of the former lived as it were on a volcano, in
constant dread of seditions. When the Ottoman fleet

withdrew to the Hellespont, and winter, suspending the march of the Sultan's forces, removed all immediate cause of apprehension, local disturbances manifested themselves in various cantons of the Morea, and several aristocrats were assassinated, either through the envy of their rivals, or the indignation of their fellow citizens whom they oppressed. The dissension of two captains splitting into factions the garrison of Navarin, brought on a skirmish in which one of them was slain; and at Pyrgos a Primate was shot at noontide in his own house, by a party of his townsmen weary of his insolence and tyranny. Whatever national or individual wrong the Greeks may have endured, it is impossible to justify the ferocity of their vengeance, or to deny that a comparison instituted between them and the Ottoman Generals, Mehemet Aboulaboud, Omer Vriones, and the Kihaya Bey, would give to the latter the palm of humanity. Humanity, however, is a word quite out of place when applied either to them or their opponents; at the same time, we must own, that in contests of a like nature, every civilized nation has, in its turn, committed equal barbarities; the difference is, that the Greeks and Turks openly avowed, from the beginning of the war, their murderous intentions towards each other!

Another moral feature, peculiarly Hellenic, merits observation; it is the narrow and selfish complexion of their patriotism, which seldom glanced farther than to the limits of their own province, island, or canton. Thus, when a deputation of ecclesiastics from Mount Athos represented to the Senate of Hydra, that upwards of 30,000 Christians were pent up on the holy mountain, and at Cassandra, a prey to the horrors of famine, the Hydriotes, although assured of payment, would not send a single ship-load of corn to their relief, until they received the money in advance. In

Western Europe, the struggle excited a degree of attention disproportioned to the dimensions of the combatants, and of the arena in which they fought. The existing generation had been sufficiently accustomed to battles and revolutions, but there was something that piqued men's curiosity, and refreshed their historical recollections, in the spectacle of Grecian fleets and armies facing those of the Barbarians of Asia, at Thermopylæ, Athens, and Mycale. The most sanguine of the Greeks did not expect that any power, except Russia, would draw a sword in their behalf; but they reasonably hoped that their gallant efforts would be viewed with sympathy, that applause would wait on their successes, and compassion attend their misfortunes. The moment, however, was unpropitious; the rulers of the earth, terrified by the phantom of revolution, had bound themselves in a solemn compact to uphold arbitrary power, and instead of experiencing favour, Hellas had good ground to congratulate herself, that, as in the cases of Spain and Naples, a foreign force was not employed to restore the domination of a sovereign, whose legitimacy was declared unquestionable. It was, perhaps, her weakness, the little apparent chance of her resistance being prolonged, and the pride of the Porte, that obviated such interference. Nothing more astounded the insurgents, than the expressed reprobation of Russia, since they had confidently reckoned on her support;* but their minds were partly set at rest on that subject, by private assurances, communicated through the medium of a distinguished statesman, that the Autocrat's temporizing policy was the result of circumstances, and would ultimately change. Austria, in proclaiming her bitter

---

* When the Greek squadrons put to sea in 1821, it was in the full persuasion that, before two months elapsed, a Russian fleet would join them.

enmity, followed the usual system of that dull, oppres-
sive, and inglorious monarchy, the sworn foe of liberty
and knowledge: a decree. (published in autumn at
Trieste), forbidding the admission of any Greek into
the imperial states, was simply an ebullition of mean
and cowardly spite ; but a real injury was inflicted by
Austrian men-of-war conveying into Patrass transports laden with grain.   Among the European govern-
ments, England was probably, next to Austria, the one
most hostile to Greece at that period, when her foreign
policy was guided by a spirit akin to that of Metternich ; the hired organs of ministry were loud in defence of Islam, and gall dropped from their pens on the
Christian cause.   France (although there is no reason
to think that the sentiments of her cabinet were a whit
more favourable) maintained a decent neutrality, and
her naval commanders and consular agents extended
an active protection to the victims of war, whatever
their religion or party.   In the few countries where
opinion connected with political events could be freely
emitted, the Greek cause was at first feebly taken up
by public feeling, and attracted curiosity rather than
affection : besides royal and aristocratic frowns, two
other incidents were adverse to it.   The most eminent liberals, disgusted by the extravagance of the
Spaniards, and the ignominious failure of the Italian
Carbonari, feared to compromise the credit of their
sect, by patronising a movement whose prospects seemed so desperate, and many of them saw in it only a
scheme of Russian ambition.   The second reason of its
cool reception, is to be charged directly to the Greeks
themselves, who did nothing calculated to win a friendly disposition, and much that tended to throw obloquy
on their exertions.   Had they moderated their revenge,
observed the capitulations granted, and behaved with
magnanimity to the vanquished Turks, such generous

conduct, contrasted with .Mussulman immanity, must
have gained them universal good-will.   But when
every report coming from the east recited some instance of Grecian cruelty and baseness, it is not surprising that. the zeal of their partisans, and especially
of the religious world, waxed cold.   The slender aid
the insurgents received in money and stores, came almost wholly from a few of their wealthy countrymen
settled in Italy, Holland, and Russia.   A good many
officers, stimulated rather by the irksomeness of inaction, than any particular regard for Greece, joined her
banners, and generally found abundant cause to regret
the step they had taken.   Their military experience in
regular service was of no use among undisciplined
bands, whose language they did not understand, and
whose rude manners, spare diet, avidity for plunder,
and ignorance of the laws of honour, greatly displeased
them.   On the other hand, the Greeks, although they
never ceased to invite strangers, treated with cordiality those alone, who, by living on their own means,
proved that their assistance was disinterested, and were
inclined to ridicule tactics altogether, as inappropriate
to their desultory method of making war.   It is too
true, that many needy or improvident Philhellenes
suffered severe privations, and, therefore, on their return to the west, gave a gloomy description of the
country and people they had just quitted, and where
there was, indeed, a taint of slavery not soon to be ef-
faced.

In the great European capitals, the Greek insurrection occasionally fixed the attention of statesmen, heated
the minds of a few enthusiasts, and offered a wide field
of disputation to the professors of jarring political
creeds ; but the Ionian republic, patched up out of some
broken fragments of Hellas, was more seriously shaken
by the tempest which almost touched its shores.   The

natives of Corcyra, and still more those of Ithaca, Leucadia, Cefalonia, and Zacynthus, although torn away
by the force of events from their brethren on the main
land, were yet, in religion, language, and affection, as
closely identified with them as before the dismember-
ment of the Byzantine empire. Totally demoralized
through the corrupt government of Venice, whose Pro-
veditors encouraged assassination by selling impunity,
and consequently divided by ten thousand family feuds,
they passed successively into the hands of the Russians,
French, and English, and at the Congress of Vienna
were mocked with the title of an independent republic,
under the protection of the King of Great Britain, who
appointed as his delegate an officer of the highest talents, but of manners so coarse and rough, and a temper so violent and despotic, that instead of respect and
love, his subjects felt towards him fear and aversion.
So far from the match being a happy one, this union
of supercilious strength and peevish weakness gave a
public scandal to Europe, and, as often happens in similar cases, the mutual reproaches and recriminations
of the ill assorted pair accurately pointed to each others
defects. The English taxed the Ionians with duplicity,
insubordination, ingratitude, adulation, and a vindictive and treacherous disposition ; they boasted with
some reason of the benefits they had conferred upon
them, in rendering the administration of justice pure,
introducing order into the finances, improving the
cities and harbours, constructing roads, promoting navigation and commerce, and releasing the peasantry
from the insupportable yoke of the nobles. The Ionians
replied with equal truth, that although these ameliorations might be real, yet that little gratitude was
due for favours so ungraciously bestowed ; that they
did not choose to be dragooned into happiness ; that
many of the expensive projects of the English autho-

rities were in fact useless, and entailed a heavy burden on the country ; that, with other blessings, they
had to thank the English for that of taxation, before
unknown ; that under the semblance of a free constitution they were treated like Rayahs, and exposed to
insult and humiliation from their military protectors ;
and lastly (neither was this the lightest nor worst
founded of their complaints,) that superfluous places,
paid out of their money, were created by the ministry
at home, to feed impoverished branches of the British
aristocracy.   In summing up the heads of the controversy, we shall venture to add, that a military government can never be a good one, and that the Ionian regime, being in reality a perfect despotism, the prosperity and repose of each individual isle depended too
much on the personal qualities of its resident or commandant ; so that while some were administered with
wisdom and mildness, another that we could name,
groaned for years under the iron rod of a wretch, whose
odious tyranny would have disgraced a Turkish Pasha.*
Exclusive of open grounds of quarrel, there were two
deeper sources of animosity rather felt than uttered :
the Lord High Commissioner perceived with pain, that
his Ionians were zealous adherents of Russia ; while
they saw in England a power interested in upholding
Turkey, and therefore hostile to the triumph of their
faith and nation.   The cession of Parga came just
apropos to wind up the anti-Anglican prejudices of the
Greeks. Amidst this reciprocity of hate and scorn,
the revolution of 1821, removing the thin veil that
covered the schism between the Ionians and their

* Sundry attempts were made to bring before Parliament the
grievances of the Ionians ; but Ministers always met them with a system of absolute denegation, and the legislature with indifference :
nothing more was required to establish the credit of their most frivolous complaints.

rulers, the former instantly gave way to extravagant transports of religious and patriotic fanaticism, and the latter, having in vain endeavoured to calm the popular effervescence, and urged by reiterated provocation, sullenly espoused the opposite side. A proclamation, issued April the 9th, denounced the forfeiture of British protection towards any native of the Septinsular republic who should join either of the belligerents; and a second, dated June the 7th, prescribed the strictest neutrality. At first, nevertheless, the line followed by government was one of temper and conciliation, since it bore with patience continual infringements of the sanitary and police regulations, and permitted 7000 Moreotes to take shelter in Zante. But at that moment of fervour, the Ionians, insensible to tolerant measures, gave no slight indications of a desire to get up a revolution of their own. Two of their merchant vessels joined the Greek fleet, without deigning to change their flags, and Count Metaxa, Captain Pannas, Kaliva, and others, organized in Elis a soi-disant Zantiote and Cefalonian army, and (if they are not belied) even wore the English uniform in presence of the Turks. As the authorities had acted with the utmost moderation in winking at their departure, which, however, was sufficiently public, such conduct implied a want of gratitude as well as prudence. Then, at last, the Lord High Commissioner put his previous threats in execution, by confiscating the property of Metaxa and his associates, and declaring that the two shipmasters should be treated as pirates. All this was necessary, and perfectly justified by international law; but unfortunately the government of Corfu henceforth set at nought th neutrality it professed, and manifested a bias in favour of the Turks, by receiving into its ports, and furnishing with supplies, the Capitana Bey's fleet, and transmitting through its health offices the corre-

spondence of the Ottoman generals and admirals, while
all Greek letters were broken open at the police;
and the Navarch Tombazi, whose presence the Zantiotes hailed with transports of joy, was insulted by the
authorities. Sir Thomas Maitland was suspected of
fomenting intrigues in Epirus to disunite the enemies
of the Porte; and he certainly let slip no opportunity
of affronting and mortifying the Greeks. The exas-
peration of the people meanwhile assumed a deeper
hue, and some sort of commotion appeared inevitable,
when a sea fight, which occurred off Zante, on the
12th of October, brought things to a crisis. An Algerine brig being driven on shore, the peasants not
only fired upon her, but also attacked a party of troops
sent to the spot to maintain the quarantine laws.
About the same period, the inhabitants of Karavass,
a village in Cerigo, inhumanly slaughtered 40 Turks
(only five of whom were men), that, having been spared
by the insurgents, sought hospitality on their shore.
The two islands were immediately subjected to martial
law, the principal Zantiotes arrested as hostages, and
a general disarming ordered, which being soon extended to the whole republic, relieved the government from
a disquietude not altogether without foundation. Four
persons were executed for rebellion at Zante, five for
murder at Cerigo, and partial writers, sworn foes to
England, taking their text from thence, falsely painted
the Ionian coasts as lined with gibbets and dead bodies
of martyrs.

Thus, beyond the sea and the mountains, all was
adverse, dark, and unpromising to Greece, and within
her girdle the prospect was not cheering: but the
light-hearted Hellenes, strong in the justice of their
cause, and trusting to Heaven, little heeded the heavy
clouds that hung around them. They began to rebuild
Tripolizza, which quickly became again a considerable

town, and the peasants profited by the repose of winter to set cheerfully about the labours of agriculture. Order and a constitution was the universal cry, and they expected a panacea for all their ills from the meeting of the National Congress. So great was the enthusiasm which then prevailed, that notwithstanding the fatal termination of the campaign in Macedonia, and their late reverses in Peloponnesus, many of them hoped, ere the conclusion of another year, to plant their standards on the walls of Constantinople.

APPENDIX

TO

BOOK I.—CHAP. VI.

Proclamation of Ypsilanti *convoking a National Assembly.*

Citizens of Peloponnesus! ecclesiastics and laymen, young and old, inhabitants of every rank and age! the time is come for you to assemble here at Tripolizza, to give your opinion on the rights and wants of your country. I, Demetrius Ypsilanti, am come hither to fight for your liberty; I am come to defend your rights, honour, lives, and goods; I am come to give you just laws, and equitable tribunals, to the end that no person may injure your interests, or play with your existence. It is time that tyranny should at length cease, not only that of the Turks, but also the tyranny of those individuals,* who, sharing the sentiments of the Turks, wish to oppress the people. Unite, Peloponnesians, if you desire to abate the evils that have hitherto afflicted you. I am your father who heard your groans even in the heart of Russia, and have come to protect you, to render you happy, to labour for your deliverance, to insure the felicity of your families, to release you from the abject state to which you were reduced by impious tyrants, and the friends and companions of those tyrants. Assemble then! hasten from your towns and villages to assert in my presence your rights as free citizens, to point out to me the persons you judge most capable, that I may give them to you as ephors and guardians of your interests. Lose no time; be not the dupes of perverse men attached to tyranny; show that you understand what liberty is, and recognise your general and defender; thus you will give to the rest of Greece the example of a wise and lawful government.

On the 30th day of this present month, I desire to see you assembled round me, to discuss freely your rights under the eye of your chief and father; I, therefore, send good patriots, charged to read to you this paper, and to represent to you by word of mouth the necessity of your meeting.

Tripolizza, $\frac{6}{18}$ *of October* 1821.

(Signed)   Demetrius Ypsilanti.
                    Lieutenant of the Generalissimo.

---

* Invectives applied to the Kojabashees.

BOOK SECOND.

CHAP. I.

Constitution of Epidaurus, and establishment of a Central Government in Greece—State of Turkey, and remarks on her political relations—Transactions in Peloponnesus during the first six months of the year 1822.

SECTION I.

THE commencement of the year 1822, the second of the war, was marked in Greece by the acts of the National Assembly of Piada, which promulgated a declaration of independence, and sanctioned the outlines of a constitution, entitled the Organic Law of Epidaurus. Anxious to overthrow Ypsilanti and the Russian party, the Peloponnesian primates lent all their weight to Mavrocordato, elected him president of the Congress, and readily accepted the new constitution, presented under his auspices by Theodore Negris, and chiefly drawn up by an Italian named Gallina. It was enacted with singular unanimity, published on the 1st of January (O. S.), and subscribed by 59 deputies, including Mavrocordato himself, the Prince of Maina, the Archbishop of Patrass, the Bishops of Talanta and Agrafa, Anthimos Gazi, and many opulent and respectable citizens of the islands and the mainland. Divided into seven sections, ten chapters, and 107 paragraphs, and treating of religion, civil rights, the administration of justice and form of government, the organic act was framed on the most enlarged and liberal principles, of tolerance in matters of faith, equality before the law, and freedom of the press; the latter being restricted only from licentious attacks against Christianity, public morals, and private character. Every Greek, without distinction of birth or fortune, was declared eligible to all employments, slavery abolished, and its existence proscribed on the Hellenic soil; and it was moreover decreed, that no citizen should remain in prison above twenty-four hours without being informed of the causes of his arrest, nor more than three days without being brought to trial. While the Byzantine form of worship was pronounced the national established church, the constitution held forth full toleration to every sect; however, Mohammedans and Jews, debarred from political, could only enjoy civil rights. The scheme of government, purely republican, recognised two powers, executive and legislative; the first composed of five members presiding over the general administration, naming the ministry, and having a voice in passing laws; the second consisting of seventy national representatives, subject like the former to an annual election, enjoying equal authority in proposing and rejecting laws, and invested besides with the sole right of laying on taxes, which it could impose for twelve months, the legal period of its own existence. To this second body (or Senate) was committed likewise the delicate task of impeaching and degrading delinquent members of either council. Each had a president and vice-president; and the executive was provided with one, the legislative with two secretaries. Some preliminary dispositions were laid down for instituting courts of justice, and drawing up a new code of laws; for the present those of the Emperor Basil were declared to be in force, except in commercial disputes, which were to be decided according to the French code. Another measure, indifferent in itself, manifested, however, on the part of the assembly, an inclination to depreciate the Hetœrists, and seems to have been aimed at Ypsilanti and his adherents; instead of black, which they had introduced, light blue and white were fixed upon as national colours, and the emblem of the Phœnix replaced by the Athenian owl.

Such is a slight sketch of this constitution, excellent in theory, but totally unfit for the people to whom it was addressed; hardly did it see the light, when some of its best provisions were openly trampled upon, and others forgotten; indeed the organic law of Epidaurus soon became a dead letter, used only in the following years as a watchword for faction. It may appear surprising, that its authors should have given institutions so thoroughly democratical to a nation, which, after groaning for centuries under despotism, was fast verging towards the worst kind of oligarchy, and that such a charter should have been accepted by the aristocrats, who made up a large portion of the assembly. No one in fact thought this mode of government practicable in Greece; but the ambition of so many individuals, (each afraid of seeing a rival invested with solid and permanent power), rendered it necessary to generalize, and ostensibly to refer every thing at short intervals to the mass of the people. Each man looked upon the constitution as a stepping-stone to the highest offices, and its framers were not the least aspiring Having no natural hold on the country from long residence or family connexions, their business was to oppose legal barriers to the great captains and primates; thinking themselves sure of success in a career where victory depended upon political finesse. On the other side, the Peloponnesian Kojabashees had already taken

precautions to hinder any extraneous authority from
rooting itself in the Peninsula, and to keep to themselves the management of its affairs. For this end, before the organic law was sanctioned, the Moreote deputies, in a particular assembly held at Piada, January
the 8th, selected a committee of twenty to represent
their province in the Congress, and to compose a Peloponnesian Senate, destined hereafter to sit at the
city of Tripolizza. They likewise emitted a provincial
constitution, so contrived as to leave the central government little room to interfere in any of their transactions, since, with many professions of deference to the
former, it virtually secured to their own Senate the
military, financial, and municipal regulations of the
Morea. (Vide Appendix.) It was conceived indeed in
the same spirit that animated their previous discussions with Ypsilanti ; yet by a strange anomaly they
chose that Prince for their president. Twenty-four
deputies of Peloponnesus signed this act, and the Generals Colocotroni, Yatrako, and Anagnostoras sent in
their adhesion to it.

Having ratified the law of Epidaurus, the assembly
proceeded to choose magistrates for the current year, and
appointed Mavrocordato president, Athanasius Kanakaris of Patrass, vice-president ; John Logotheti of Livadia, Anagnosti Delhiyani of Karitena, John Orlando
of Hydra, members ; and Theodore Negris, secretary of
the executive council. Demetrius Ypsilanti was named,
in his absence, president of the legislative body, a post
nowise equal to his pretensions. The ministry was
arranged as follows :* Negris assumed the portfolio of
foreign affairs ; Panouzzas Notaras, that of finance ;
Boulgari, of the marine ; Dr Coletti, of war ; the
Bishop of Androussa, of public worship ; Count Me-

---

* There were some fluctuations in the ministry, which it is not worth
while to notice.

taxa, of the interior and police, and Count Theotoki, (a Corfiote,) of justice. On the 28th of January, the President Mavrocordato closed the session of 1822, and the executive, after passing a decree for the then hopeless purpose of raising a loan of 5,000,000 of piastres, repaired to Corinth, which, having just surrendered, was ordained to be the capital of Greece until the reduction of Athens.

An event of very great importance signalized in the East the beginning of this year, the ruin and death of the tyrant of Yannina ; a circumstance that aggravated the dangerous position of the Christian insurgents, and relieved the Sultan from a part of his embarrassments. Open or menaced hostilities, making the very existence of the empire precarious, had, during 1821, beset the Porte from four different quarters. That source of disquietude, whence the others appeared to spring, (Ali Pasha's rebellion,) was now removed by his downfall ; of the three remaining subjects of alarm, the misunderstanding with Russia, the revolt of the Greeks, and the Persian war, the first was the more formidable, and the last comparatively of trifling moment. So little did Sultan Mahmoud regard the enmity of a kingdom long the rival of Turkey, that he rejected an accommodation concluded by the Pasha of Bagdat with the Persian Prince of Kermanshah. Russia, although her demands were met with a show of resolution, instilled serious terror ; but the cabinet of St Petersburgh having betrayed signs of hesitation, having avowedly separated her quarrel from that of the Greeks, and intrusted the negotiation to mediators, the Turks saw a prospect of averting a rupture at the price of exceedingly moderate concessions. They gradually withdrew most of their troops from Moldavia and Wallachia, re-establishing there the miserable system of administration that prevailed before the revolution. In spring, two deputations, (each of seven Boyards, the most considerable in point of rank and fortune,) were called to Constantinople from their respective principalities, and after the festival of Bayram, the wonted epoch for conferring offices, Dacia received two new Hospodars in the persons of Gregory Ghika for Wallachia, and John Stourdza for Moldavia. Both were natives of the countries they were about to reign over, and so far at least the arrangement was an advantage to their vassals delivered from Fanariote intrigue and cupidity, These princes began their journey from the capital, August the 23d, loaded with honours; nearly at the same period, the decease of the Greek Patriarch afforded the Porte an opportunity of marking its respect towards the Eastern church, and consequently towards the Autocrat who followed its ritual, by celebrating his obsequies with unusual magnificence, 2000 Bostandjis, (or foot-guards of the Sultan), escorting the funeral procession. By the middle of summer the crisis was over, and although regular diplomatic intercourse between the two courts was not restored, they yet held communication through the medium of the English Ambassador, and the Austrian Internuncio. As the Ottomans persisted, however, in keeping a small corps of troops beyond the Danube, Russia thus found a pretext for prolonging a discussion she by no means wished to terminate.

That feverish excitement which in 1821 distracted the Mussulmans of Turkey, and produced so many bloody scenes, subsided by degrees in the subsequent year : during the first six months of 1822 it was still intense, and the fluctuating chances of war frequently rekindled its violence. We have already stated, that at Constantinople the excesses of a band of ruffians, whose object was plunder, had so harassed the industrious classes of Mohammedans, that they threatened to cease

from their habitual avocations. In vain the Divan
summoned the Janissary Aga to repress such misdeeds,
in vain severe examples were made ; until this anarchy
becoming intolerable to the Sultan himself, he crushed
it with characteristic vigour. At the season of Bayram, a crowd of notorious malefactors was on several
successive days publicly executed in the streets ; and
these rigorous proceedings, the disarming a part of the
populace, and an energetic declaration of the Grand
Signor, that he would rather change his residence than
be a spectator of further disorders, at once pacified the
capital.

As the political horizon of Turkey cleared, its court
and people, as well as the venal or slavish abettors of
arbitrary power throughout Europe, entertained sanguine hopes that the rebellion of Greece would quickly
be stifled. Ascribing the continued struggling of the
insurgents to the multiplied difficulties the Porte had
laboured under, and the necessity of disseminating her
forces, the Austrian Observer, and the Oriental Spectator, (one the speaking trumpet of Metternich, the other
of the Frank merchants of Smyrna,) confidently predicted their speedy annihilation, by the tremendous
fleets and armies that were ready to issue forth against
them, now that the almost undivided strength of the
empire would be turned into a single channel. The
Ottoman preparations, both by sea and land, though
really on a great scale, and such as it seemed impossible
for the Greeks to resist, did not intimidate the latter,
who judged and even exaggerated the incapacity of
their enemies. Ali Pasha's destruction was indeed a
discouraging blow, as it let loose upon them the army
of the Roumeli Valehsi, and the fierce tribes of Albania;
but in the capture of the Acrocorinthus they had a
compensation for that misfortune, and a happy presage
of the result of the campaign. There Kyamil Bey had

deposited his treasures; and as it was known that he
had for years been hoarding foreign specie, obtained, in
exchange for Turkish coin, from the traders who visited the Gulf of Lepanto, the Peloponnesians cherished
extravagant expectations of the immense sums which
would accrue from its fall, and enable the government
to provide a national fund. When Ypsilanti perceived
that the tide of politics was running strong against him
at Argos, and that his opponents were sure to triumph
in a congress of his own convocation, he proposed to
acquire some credit by conquering this fortress, and
disposing of so rich a prize. At Tripolizza, two months
earlier, he had opened a negotiation with Kyamil Bey,
who, being a man of address, and confiding in the
friendship of several of the first Moreote families, demanded favourable terms, and sought to amuse the
Greeks, hoping perhaps that an alteration of fortune
would oblige them to crave his intercession with the
Porte. On the 25th of December 1821, Ypsilanti
appeared before Corinth, and took the command of the
blockading corps; he carried the captive Bey along
with him, and was attended by Colocotroni and Yatrako, whose presence was not likely to hasten the
citadel's surrender, but they would not be absent where
spoil was to be shared. The Acrocorinthus crowns the
rough and flat summit of a rock, rising to an elevation
of 1900 feet above the level of the sea, which is half a
league distant; it is of an oval shape, 1200 yards long,
and 5000 in circumference. The sides of the rock are
every where perpendicular, or very nearly so, and a
single winding path leads up to the gate facing the
west, and defended by a triple line of ramparts and
batteries; in other quarters there is merely a simple
wall, generally of moderate height and strength. Within the castle are several cisterns, and the copious fountain of Pirene, so that, when provisioned, its garrison

has nothing to fear except a sudden surprise or escalade. A few shot and shells might indeed have been thrown into it from the sharp peak of Penteskouphia, (to the south-west,) where the Greeks subsequently raised a detached work.

Although the Acrocorinthus does not, strictly speaking, command the entrance into Peloponnesus, since troops can pass on either side of it, yet it must always, from its situation at the extremity of the Isthmus, and the head of the Corinthian and Saronic Gulfs, be a place of vast importance to Greece. The Ottoman garrison amounted to 600 men, one-fourth of whom were Albanians, left there by the Kihaya Bey; and it was supposed that their magazines would suffice till the month of March. Kyamil Bey's authority was the engine the insurgents intended to use, in order to obtain its speedy rendition, and they spared neither promises nor threats to induce him to comply with their wishes. He reluctantly assented, and began a correspondence with his wife and mother, who were in the place; but the treaty went on slowly, and the besiegers suspected the sincerity of their prisoner, especially when they observed that he received and transmitted letters unknown to them. They remarked, that after one of his servants was permitted to go into the fort, the Turks directed shells with such good aim against Ypsilanti's quarters, as to force him to remove : this they attributed to the man's being a disguised gunner, though we may more easily account for the circumstance, by conjecturing that he pointed out the Prince's residence. Meanwhile the Albanians, always disposed to extricate themselves at the cost of their comrades, indicated a desire to treat separately. Captain Panourias, of Salona, who was acquainted with many of them, arriving at the camp, they came to an understanding with him, and stipulating for a free

passage by sea to the vicinity of Lepanto, and the faculty of retaining their arms, and 1000 piastres each,
marched forth on the 22d of January, (176 in number,) and were embarked in four Greek boats, where,
as we have too much reason to believe, one-half of
them perished through treachery. Their defection
engaged the Ottomans to capitulate on the following
conditions :—That they should be transported to Asia
Minor in a neutral vessel, keeping the clothes they
wore, and a small sum of money, not exceeding 600
piastres, for the first of three classes into which they
were divided; 400 for the second ; and 200 for the
third. On the 26th, the Grecian standard was hoisted
on the Acrocorinthus. According to Ypsilanti's preconcerted dispositions, the battalion of Balesto alone
occupied the fortress, and no other troops were suffered to enter it : this regulation, however, could not be
long enforced, and by degrees the irregulars got in.
Individual vengeance and rapacity then had full sway,
and instead of being sent away with a fraction of
their property, the Turks were stripped of every
thing, even to their skull-caps. When nothing more
could be snatched from them, the soldiers, on the 15th
of February, butchered most of the prisoners, reserving, however, Kyamil Bey, his family and attendants. Some women and children escaped death, and
were sold for slaves, in spite of the recent law of Epidaurus. With regard to the booty they so greedily
coveted, the captors were utterly disappointed, Kyamil
Bey pertinaciously refusing to say where his treasures
were hidden ; and besides the arms and clothes of the
Moslems, the Greeks found only about 100,000 piastres in specie, and a small value in jewels. The Bey's
obstinacy was unconquerable, although his old political foes, of the houses of Notaras and Delhiyani, actually employed tortures to make him confess ; a fact

of which the Greeks are now ashamed, and which they would fain bury in oblivion. Having been at the head of one of the great Moreote factions, Kyamil was almost adored by some of the primates, and bitterly hated by others, who at that moment were the most powerful. He had always persecuted the family of Notaras, and brought about the execution of the father of the Delhiyani. In his misfortunes, the rancour of his enemies was more active than the zeal of his friends. The infamous breach of faith committed at Corinth, grievously vexed the upright mind of Ypsilanti, who saw that his tottering influence struggled in vain against lawless violence; he fell dangerously ill, and on his recovery determined to quit Peloponnesus. Being without money to pay his regulars, the soldiers deserted; and his best officer, Balesto, accepted an invitation to go and serve in Crete, while other Europeans, who had hitherto been assiduous in their attentions to him, embraced the party of Mavrocordato, from a propensity to worship the rising sun. Prince Demetrius demanded an authorization to put himself at the head of a body of Peloponnesian troops, then under orders to reinforce Odysseus, at Thermopylæ, and his request was cheerfully granted by rivals who wished to be rid of him. Disdaining the title of President of the Senate, and choosing the humbler appellation of patriot, he, early in March, moved towards Roumelia, marking his entrance into Northern Greece by an act which left no doubt as to the extent and nature of his pretensions. On passing the Isthmus, he displayed his brother's flag, (proscribed by the constitution,) and designated himself Lieutenant of the Generalissimo, an imprudent measure, that ruined the little popularity remaining to him. Colocotroni, understanding his own interests better, proceeded, as soon as Corinth surrendered, to assume the command of the army in Achaia;

the recent marriage of his eldest son, Pano, to a daughter of Bobolina, had strengthened his party, and the glory of subduing Patrass seemed alone wanting to raise him above all competitors.

SECTION II.

SENSIBLE of the necessity of operating by sea, the Porte accelerated her maritime preparations, and, breaking through ancient usage, resolved to send out a division of light vessels in the depth of winter, while the Capitan Pasha hastened the equipment of the grand fleet that was to follow early in spring. Seven Egyptian, five Tunisian, and seven Tripolitan ships of war, arriving in the Dardanelles at the beginning of the year, and uniting with the Algerines, some Ottoman vessels, and those of Mehemet Ali, which had lain there since October, the Capitana Bey set sail with three frigates, fourteen corvettes, and eighteen brigs and schooners, as well as a number of transports, having on board from 3 to 4000 troops, commanded by Kara Mehemet Pasha, formerly Topji Bashi, or Master of the Ordnance. The Vice-Admiral steered for Hydra, in the bootless expectation that a perfidious intrigue would deliver into his hands that bulwark of Greece. We now tread upon an obscure point, whose details were carefully hushed up. It is certain, however, that there existed a plot to betray Hydra to the enemy, fomented by the wife and brother-in-law of that Constantine Juisti, who being, in 1821, captain of the Christian seamen serving at Constantinople, was arrested on the discovery of a plan for firing the arsenal. His life had hitherto been spared, and the Sultan did not order his death until convinced that no use could be made of him. Seven hundred persons were, it is said, engaged in the conspiracy, but the vigilance of the primates overawed them, and prevented any internal commotion.   After laying-to for half a day in sight of the island, the Capitana Bey, perceiving that his signals were not answered, continued his course to Modon; there he projected an enterprise calculated in some degree to console his court for the disappointment experienced at Hydra, and which, but for a casual circumstance, would probably have succeeded.   Learning that the fort of Navarin had a weak garrison, he concerted, with the governor of Modon, a combined and sudden attack by sea and land, hoping to carry it by a coup-de-main.   On the 11th of February, a frigate bearing the flag of the Egyptian admiral, Ismael Gibraltar, a corvette, and a brig, tried to enter the harbour, and kept up a long cannonade, damaging a few houses, while the Modon Turks advanced on the land side. Their appearance was enough to daunt the Peloponnesians, who evacuated the town and fled; fortunately a band of forty-two Philhellenes, natives of different countries, had arrived just before, in a vessel from Marseilles.   Under the direction of one of their number, General Normann, they prepared to defend the place, and being joined by a score of Greeks, captains and their servants, manned the batteries, and returned the enemy's fire.   Meeting with a firmer resistance than they had reckoned upon, the Turks gave up the attempt, which did not cost them more than ten men. The Christians had three or four wounded.

Prosecuting his voyage to the northward, the Ottoman admiral anchored, on the 14th, in the roads of Zante, where contrary winds detained him till the 25th;* he then sailed to Patrass, and landed there the

---

* No Greek vessel would have been allowed to drop her anchor for a moment.

troops of Mehemet Pasha, and a complete train of
twenty fieldpieces, with carriages, caissons, horses and
harness. In the mean time, the three naval islands of
Hydra, Spezzia, and Psarra, fitted out their armaments
with great expedition, and a Greek fleet of near 60
sail, passing in sight of Zante at the end of the month,
doubled the promontory of Araxus; it was under the
orders of Andreas Miaulis Vokhos, (who, on Tombazi's resignation, was appointed Navarch of Hydra,) and
the ancient Patriarch of Alexandria, Anthemius, had
embarked with him to encourage the seamen, and prevent their enthusiasm from flagging.

On the 4th of March, a distant and trifling action
occurred off Cape Papas. Its importance was singularly magnified by the friends of both parties ; but, in
fact, it had no result, a gale of wind separating the
combatants. On the same evening, after dark, the Ottomans poured into the roadstead of Zante, in so disorderly a manner, that two of their vessels grounded
near the lazzaretto ; and the batteries, as well as the
English and Austrian ships of war, apprehensive of
being run down, fired at the squadron, and did some
execution. The Capitana Bey threatened, in return,
to open his broadsides on the town, declaring that the
Greeks were behind him, and he could not keep the
sea. The Ionian policy being then all conciliation towards the Turks, and harshness to the insurgents, he
was suffered to remain until the 6th, and his stranded
vessels were floated off. Desirous of fighting him, the
Greeks hovered about the isle, but he deceived them,
by pretending to steer for Patrass, altered his course in
the night, and sailed directly to Alexandria, where a
fresh tempest assailed his fleet, and totally wrecked one
of the Sultan's frigates. The islanders, having lost all
trace of him, proceeded again to the waters of Patrass,
intending to attack the transports which the Turks had

left there. Seeing the Hellenic flag on the 9th, the latter cut their cables, and ran into the Gulf of Lepanto, but two of them, unable to get away in time, and obliged to anchor under Patrass, were exposed to a heavy cannonade from the whole insurgent fleet, and yet sustained very little injury ; for the Greeks, like their opponents, invariably gave their guns too much elevation. The Christian squadrons then went back to the Archipelago, with the exception of five sail of Hydriotes, which remained with Miaulis in the Ionian Sea. His object was to capture or destroy an Ottoman flotilla, consisting of one frigate, weakly manned, a corvette, and four brigs, moored at the port of Mourto, opposite to the southern extremity of Corcyra. He took on board at Phanari a detachment of Souliotes, who were to seize a height, whence their musketry could plunge on the Turkish decks ; and he would certainly have succeeded, if the Ionian government had not been guilty of gross partiality, in sending a brig of war to forbid his approach to the channel of Corfu, where the Mohammedans navigated at pleasure. Treaties concluded with the Venetians, precluded the Turks from introducing armed ships into the strait betwixt Corfu and the mainland, or erecting forts on the shore ; but these stipulations, if not forgotten, had fallen into desuetude, and were now only acted upon to the prejudice of the insurgents. If the latter had no right to approach the Isles of Syvota, what business had the Turks there?

Miaulis having immediately despatched a schooner to Corfu, to seek explanations regarding Ionian neutrality, no answer was vouchsafed, and the authorities there seized the vessel, alleging that the Greeks had carried off sheep from Leucadia. It is true that they had done so, and also taken unwarrantable liberties with Ionian boats ; but such offences could not justify the Lord High Commissioner in extending the shield of English protection to an Ottoman squadron on the Sultan's coast, especially since the Turks had recently committed several outrages of the same description.* The schooner Terpsichore was at length restored, on the Hydriotes promising to give satisfaction for their violation of the Leucadian territory; when, however, George Spagnolaki went, in April, from Corinth to Corfu, on a mission touching these affairs, he was contemptuously dismissed by an official letter from the Lord High Commissioner, which is sufficiently known, and must ever be looked upon as a perfect specimen of passionate arrogance.†

The Turkish land forces, disembarked at Patrass, were chefly composed of Asiatics, unacquainted with, and unfit for, mountain warfare. Hence, although not deficient in spirit, they fared very ill in their skirmishes with the Peloponnesians under Colocotroni. On the 19th of March, Mehemet Pasha sallied out with his whole garrison, (Anatolians and Lalliotes,) by the impetuosity of his onset routed the advanced posts of the insurgents, and took two standards. Yani Colocotroni, (second son to the Stratarch,) was surrounded in a tower, and the contingent of Kalavryta shut up in the monastery of Hierocomion, which the enemy battered with two pieces of cannon. Old Colocotroni, on this occasion, showed abundance of courage and conduct; rallying his scattered troops, he led them back to the charge, and, after a desultory action of seven hours,

---

* The seizure of the family of Perrouka of Patrass, and its subsequent release through Captain Hamilton's intervention, is a matter that all the world has heard of. The Turkish cruisers frequently obliged Ionian barks to enter Modon, and exhibit their papers; and one of their schooners pursued for several hours, and cannonaded a boat, carrying to Cerigo a new resident, who wore his uniform.

† Dated April 28th, 1822, and signed by the government secretary, Sir Frederic Hankey.

defeated the Turks, and chased them to the foot of their ramparts. The Greeks brought in three hundred heads, and three bayraks, or flags. They likewise captured the Pasha's Tufinegee-Bashee, and immediately put him to death ; but they repented of their precipitation next day, when his general sent to offer a large ransom for him. Deterred by this check from undertaking sorties, and pent up between the hostile position and the walls of the citadel, which the Lalliotes did not allow them to enter, the Asiatic levies mostly perished in a short time, through the effects of pestilence, whose contagion they brought with them from Constantinople. For the next three months, nothing of any moment happened within the Morea. The people of that peninsula reposed in a false security, and only a faint sound of war was heard around the blockaded fortresses.   At its south-western point, 400 Turks (50 of whom were horsemen) defended Modon, and amused themselves by skirmishing with 500 Greeks, posted about Navarin, under Anagnostoras. Coron, seated on an eminence, and garrisoned by 300 men, was observed by parties of Mainatts, and similar combats passed in the plain before it. Those two towns were amply provisioned ; but Napoli di Romania began to suffer severe distress. Invested for almost a twelvemonth, on the land side by Captain Nicholas, and at sea by the masculine Bobolina, the Turks there were compelled to sacrifice some lives daily, in order to gather wild herbs from the vicinity of its works.

On the 30th of April, the insurgents sent the Senator Poniropoulos to propose a capitulation, which the besieged rejected, still flattering themselves with hopes of relief.

During this interval of comparative quiet, the Hellenic government was busied with a negotiation set on foot at the close of the foregoing year, through the me-

diation of Sir Thomas Maitland, for liberating Khourshid Pasha's harem, and the Kihaya Bey and Kaimakan,
taken at Tripolizza. The sorest disgrace that can befall a
Mohammedan, is to see his women in the power of strangers, particularly of infidels ; and therefore Khourshid
made it a point of honour to procure their release at
any price. Managed on one side by Theodore Negris,
on the other by Dr Stephano, a merchant and proprietor of Zante, the treaty was spun out to a period of
five months, a delay that induced many persons to
think that the Lord High Commissioner did not limit
his views to one object. The principal difficulty rested
on a clause, which the Greeks wisely insisted on as a
sine qua non; namely, that the Souliote hostages previously delivered to Ali Pasha, and then in Khourshid's
hands, should be included in the exchange. Amongst
them was the brother of Mark Bozzaris, who came
from Epirus to Corinth, to watch the progress of this
affair.

From the mediator's undisguised partiality, there
was ground to suspect that he would throw obstacles
in the way, and thus weaken the attachment of the Souliotes to the Greek confederacy ; but his agent was forced to yield, and the freedom of Constantine Bozzaris
was secured, as well as that of the Primates of Livadia. The minister of finance, Notaras, received a sum
of 80,000 Spanish dollars ; and, in the last days of
April, the ladies of Khourshid's harem, with their suite,
(in all 150 individuals,) sailed from Corinth to Prevesa, in a transport, convoyed by an English brig of war.
Soon after, a British frigate carried away the Kihaya
Bey and the Kaimakan. While the last-mentioned personage, a Georgian, detested in the Morea for his cruelty, was permitted to depart in safety, Mustafa Bey, of
Patrass, whose mild character had deserved and obtained the good-will of the Rayahs, was barbarously

murdered at Tripolizza, by Panos Colocotroni, instigated (we fear) to that deed by the Archbishop Germanos ;
for the prelate was anxious to take off the unhappy
Bey, to whom he had sold a delusive promise of life
and liberty ! The influx of so much money might, at
another epoch, have caused bickerings among the needy
and covetous Greeks, but the prudence of Mavrocordato, whose integrity in pecuniary matters hath always
stood clear, obviated the evil. Ypsilanti received an indemnity for what he had advanced to the state the year
before ; a like favour was granted to others, probably
less worthy of it, and one-fourth of the whole sum was
paid into the public chests of the naval islands.

This ransom and exchange was the most important
affair transacted by the provisional government during
its residence at Corinth. It published, indeed, (as if to
constate its existence,) a number of laws, edicts, and
proclamations, which were not much attended to beyond its own horizon. The members of the Executive,
and the ministers puffed up with their dignities, indulged too lavishly in pomp and pleasure, and even
the President was not exempt from such reproach. We
shall here cite a few of their official acts, before repeated
disasters altogether overthrew the credit of government. On the 25th of March, the minister of foreign
affairs transmitted to the consular agents settled within
the Hellenic bounds a declaration of blockade, comprehending all the coasts of European Turkey, from Salonika to Durazzo, and likewise those of the island of
Crete. A law enacted May the 7th, fixed the rate
of territorial imposts : the national lands, or those
formerly belonging to Turks, were subjected to a tax
nearly equal to one-third of their annual value, while
those originally appertaining to Christians had only to
pay a tenth. On the 9th of the same month, the Executive proclaimed its resolution to send special com-

missioners to administer the Isles of the Egean, and
collect their tributes : of course that measure did not
affect Hydra, Spezzia, and Psarra, independent communities, which allowed no interference with their
internal polity. The national assembly had erected
Northern Greece into two provinces, denominated
Eastern and Western Hellas, and subdivided into districts, or Eparchies, and had confirmed the institution
of the court of Areopagus, appointed in the preceding
November, at the provincial congress of Salona.   The
duty assigned to this ambulant tribunal, was to organize the eastern departments of Roumelia, choose municipal officers, and correct abuses.   Its president was
the virtuous Bishop of Talanta, (an Athenian by
birth,) and Anthimos Gazi, Drossos Mansolas, (both
Thessalians, and men of letters,) the patriotic merchants,
Thassican and Axiotis, and Euxenosa, a professor
of Athens, were its first assessors, with power to re-
cruit their numbers : Athens was intended for its ulti-
mate seat.

   A Sciote, named Homerides, was despatched to Crete,
to sap the authority of Affendouli, and bring that large
island into the pale of the general government. A more
delicate and dangerous task was confided to the Epirotes, Alexis Nouzza and Palaskas ; nothing less than
to deprive of his command, and perhaps of his life, the
Roumeliote General, Odysseus, who heeded neither
constitution nor executive council ; this mission had a
very tragical result.

   It was evidently Mavrocordato's aim to abolish all
local influence, and strengthen the hands of the central
governing commission ; but the oligarchal spirit of the
Greeks, and their propensity to federal republicanism,
vastly overbore him.   Nevertheless, the fearful example of Chios, at that moment before their eyes, might
have impressed upon them the necessity of close and

indissoluble union. Summer was now wearing on, and it was time to prepare for resisting a serious invasion. The success of the Serasker Khourshid, at Yannina, and the Capitan Pasha's easy triumph over the unwarlike Sciotes, enabling the Porte to dispose of her fleet and army, the sole doubt was, against what part of Greece the most formidable attack would be directed. As the Roumeli Valehsi marched towards Souli, this uncertainty seemed to be cleared away, and Mavrocordato, having by dint of money and persuasion induced the islanders to put to sea again, and watch the Turkish navy, determined to go in person and oppose Khourshid. He had attained to the highest civil office, but he felt, that in the state in which his country was, he could not long maintain himself at its head without gaining military reputation.   On taking the field sundry considerations engaged him to select as his theatre Western Greece.   There he had first touched the Hellenic soil, and there, during the previous campaign, his wise conduct had acquired him an ascendency which he could not expect in Peloponnesus, and still less in Eastern Greece, where Odysseus was his declared enemy.   On public grounds, specious reasons were not wanting to justify his resolve : on the frontier of Thermopylæ, the Mussulmans had hitherto been acting on the defensive, and the Morea appeared for a season to be beyond their reach.   It was urgent to relieve the Souliotes, and it would be no small advantage to occupy the Sultan's main army amidst the mountains of Epirus, on the outskirts of Greece, and far from her vital regions. On the 23d of May, the legislative assembly passed a decree, (confirmed immediately by the executive,) appointing Prince Alexander Mavrocordato director-in-chief of military and political affairs in Western Greece, for the term of two months.   He neglected no step that

cautious foresight could dictate, for collecting around
himself a respectable force. The regular corps (levied
by Ypsilanti,) was reorganized, divided into two battalions, and augmented by recruits from the Archipelago,
to an effective strength of six hundred men. Besides
this regiment, the President wished to be accompanied
by the foreign officers who had flocked from Europe
to assist the Hellenes, and whose courage and talents
had been hitherto almost useless. Nearly an hundred
of those gallant volunteers answered his call, and waving the claims of rank, agreed to carry the musket and
knapsack. They formed two companies of Philhellenes, (Frenchmen, Germans, Poles, Italians, Swiss,
&c.,) officered from their own body, enrolled for the
space of six months, and paid according to the grade
they held, not in the corps, but the Greek army. Their
nominal pay was the same as that in the French service, but francs were represented by piastres of half
their real value, and they drew only one-third in specie,
and the rest in worthless government paper. To do
honour to this band of veterans, precedence was given
it over every other corps, the President ranked as its
colonel, and Count Normann as chef-de-battailon; the
latter, however, being charged with the functions of
chief of the staff, the Genoese Dania, captain of the
first company, led the Philhellenes, with the brevet
rank of colonel. Some young Greeks of good family
enlisted as privates, in order to learn military discipline,
and every Philhellene, who had not been previously an
officer, was rated as a sub-lieutenant from the moment
of his enrolment. On the 26th of May, the Philhellenes, and the regular regiment under the Piedmontese
colonel Tarella, sailed from Corinth for Vostizza, and
next day Mavrocordato moved towards the same place
by land, with a detachment of Souliotes commanded

by Mark Bozzaris, a company of Ionians, and several hundred Moreotes. Believing, inconsiderately, that Colocotroni would obey an order from the executive to attend him at the head of 2,000 men, he trusted, by the accession of all the Armatoles of Western Greece, to raise the amount of his force to 8000 muskets. Having halted twenty-four hours at Vostizza, and reviewed his troops, the President arrived (June the 1st) at the camp before Patrass, where he had an interview with Colocotroni, who, as he might easily have foreseen, positively refused to quit Peloponnesus, although he consented to send his son Yani with 300 soldiers ; and to these were added 250 Mainatts under the brave Kyriakouli. On the 2d, Mavrocordato embarked his little army on board eight brigs that were waiting for him, and next morning landed at Messalonghi.

After his departure from the Peninsula, the executive and legislative bodies, regardless of reports stating the assemblage in Thessaly of a great mass of Ottoman troops, thought of nothing but the approaching submission of Napoli di Romania. Famine and misery having at length tamed the pertinacity of its defenders, tired of looking for succour, they demanded a capitulation, and their overtures being transmitted to Corinth, the government went from thence to Argos about the middle of June. Recollecting the instances of Trippolizza and the Acrocorinthus, it determined, this time at least, to prevent a general pillage. As they suspected that Colocotroni would come spontaneously to participate in the spoil, the primates attached to government had simultaneous letters recalling their soldiers, written privately by the heads of villages, and forwarded to his camp. This extraordinary stratagem fully succeeded, for his army of 5000 or 6000 men immediately dwindled away to a few hundred soldiers

of his own province of Karitena. Stung to the quick
by such an insult, he raised the blockade of Patrass, and
the Turks issuing out, burned and wasted the neighbouring country. The members of the ruling party
were not yet at their ease : Colocotroni advanced to
Tripolizza, breathing vengeance, and his nephew Nicholas Stamatelopoulos claimed the command of Nauplia,
when it should be surrendered. He seemed to merit
that reward for his perseverance in blocking it, and
800 soldiers, absolutely devoted to him, seconded his
pretensions. Nor was this all : from every corner of
Peloponnesus and from Maina, a multitude of armed
men hastened to Argos, insomuch that 8000 troops
were cantoned in and around the town. On the 30th of
June a capitulation was signed, stipulating, that if not
relieved within twenty-five days, the Turks should give
up the fortress, and be shipped off for Asia, with their
families, and one-third of their effects ; that the Greeks
should forthwith occupy the insular castle of the
Burj, and for the intervening period, until the final
evacuation of Nauplia, should supply the garrison with
daily rations : forty hostages were mutually exchanged,
and a party of Kranidiotes,* on whose fidelity the government relied, took possession of the Burj. Had the
vessels been ready, and some indulgence offered on the
score of their property, the Moslems would willingly
have anticipated the term of surrender : but the Greeks,
afraid lest any article should escape their vigilance,
were wrapped up in the ideal contemplation of booty.
Many scribes were introduced into the fortress, charged

---

* Kranidi is a town of Argolis, on the eastern shore of the Gulf,
between Napoli and Spezzia, built on a height an hour's walk from
the sea : it has a good port for small craft, and its inhabitants, who all
speak the Albanian language, and are reckoned the best boatmen in
Greece, boast that they can muster 1000 muskets.

to take an exact inventory of every thing it contained, while the executive, senators, and ministers, waited at Argos, whither Ypsilanti, disgusted with his campaign in Roumelia, likewise repaired, as well as the Bey of Maina. Such was the situation of Peloponnesus in the beginning of July 1822.

APPENDIX

BOOK II.—CHAP. I.

———

*Extracts from the Provincial Constitution of Peloponnesus.**

THE Peloponnesian Senate is composed of provincial deputies, each province sending one; the Senate names, from amongst its members, a president and vice-president.

It appoints to public employments, watches over the internal administration of the Peloponnesus, and verifies every month the accounts of the public revenue presented by the provincial Ephors.

It delivers the necessary instructions to the generals and Ephors.

A committee of four Peloponnesian generals will attend the residence of the Senate, and be consulted on military matters.

The Senate, at certain fixed epochs, submits its acts to the National Congress. It recognises every legal measure decreed by that Congress; but when the taxes are excessive, the Senate may remonstrate, and assign reasons for refusing to pay them.

All acts regarding a public loan must be signed with the Senate's seal.

The Senate judges state criminals by appointing a supreme court of twelve senators; it also dismisses and replaces public functionaries.

Until ulterior dispositions are made, Peloponnesus will have six or eight generals elected by the Senate, and each province will choose one or more captains to command its militia; the choice must be confirmed by the Senate, which ratifies also the nomination of all inferior officers.

The generals and captains must obey the orders of the Senate.

This long paper has been already published by Colonel Raybaud; we have thought it best to cull a few striking passages, to give an idea of the spirit in which it was framed.

CHAP. II.

Affairs of the Archipelago—Insurrection of Scio—Naval operations on the Asiatic coast.

ALTHOUGH none of the revolted islands (except Samos) had been as yet attacked, or even threatened, their security was extremely precarious, and most of them, conscious of their own weakness, looked with dismay to the opening of the naval campaign. The Capitana Bey, in traversing the Archipelago, committed no hostility ; but the more formidable fleet of the Capitan Pasha was about to follow, and there was reason to apprehend that it might sweep away some of the feeble and isolated populations of the Cyclades. Amongst the latter, fear struggled with enthusiasm, and preparations for defence, the influx of fugitives from Asia, and expeditions for Crete and Eubœa, kept the islanders in a continual bustle, not unattended with disorder ; for the Cretans, as well as volunteer corps, proceeding to Carysto, laid their countrymen under contribution.

Psarra and Samos, on account of their geographical position, and the incessant provocation they gave the Turks, seemed likely to sustain the first onset, and were ready to meet it ; the Samians being elated with the stand they had already made, and the Psarriotes animated by a dauntless spirit, that might be called sublime. Informed that the brass guns of two Turkish ships of war, wrecked many years before, were to be found on an islet of the Strymonic Gulf, the Psarrians sailed thither in January, brought away the artillery, and mounted it on their batteries; they, moreover, took into pay a considerable body of Olympians.

With inferior resources, Tinos and Naxos showed as fixed a resolution to brave the enemy; the congregating of strangers swelled the strength of Tinos to several thousand combatants; and the Naxians, equally determined, invited the people of Paros and Myconè to join and make common cause with them, as soon as the Sultan's navy should approach. Both there and at Tinos, the Latins were exposed to danger from the violence of the Greek populace, arising out of the enmity which reigned betwixt the two sects. The Catholics imprudently professed their attachment to Turkey, pretended to live independent of the Hellenic authorities, and objected to disbursing their quota of taxes; hence, European vessels of war were obliged more than once to interpose in behalf of the weaker party. The government of Greece did what it could to promote harmony, by strictly enjoining that the Latins should be respected, and requesting their spiritual head, the Bishop of Tinos, to come to Corinth, and assist in concerting measures for the maintenance of future tranquillity; but the furious bigotry of the Catholics was not to be soothed.

A good deal of distress was felt throughout the Egean sea, owing to the stagnation of trade, the interruption of men's ordinary pursuits, a scarcity of provisions, and epidemic diseases produced by an excessive augmentation of inhabitants. It is not improbable that the Mussulmans would have ravaged the smaller isles, had not their wrath been concentrated on one point, and spent itself on the unhappy Sciotes.

Of all the Ottoman provinces, that, sheltered by special privileges, prospered under and in spite of Oriental despotism, the most flourishing and beautiful was Chios. That island, 30 miles in length, 12 in breadth, and

separated from the shore of Ionia by a strait of seven
miles, contained a large and well built city, 68 villages, 300 convents, 700 churches, and a population of
100,000 Greeks, 6000 Turks, and a small number of
Catholics and Jews. Its capital, situated on the eastern
side, and at an equal distance from the northern and
southern extremities, was remarkable for the beauty
and solidity of its edifices ; 30,000 people resided there,
including all the Mohammedans and Israelites. Celebrated for its fertility, and the enchanting aspect of its
gardens, Chios carried on a brisk trade in silk and
fruit ; from thence Constantinople was supplied with
oranges, lemons, and citrons ; but the most valuable
production of the country is gum mastic, expressed from
the seed of a species of lentiscus, a substance highly
prized by the Eastern ladies, who amuse their indolence
by chewing it, deriving from that practice as much
gratification as their male relations enjoy by inhaling
the fumes of tobacco. As it is peculiar to one district,
the 22 villages furnishing mastic were an appanage
of the Imperial Harem, while the remaining 46 belonged to the metropolitan church of Constantinople.
The character of the Chians partook of the softness of
their climate, and the delicacy of the products of their
soil. Mild, gay, lively, acute, industrious, and prover-
bially timid, they succeeded alike in commerce and literature ; the females were noted for their charms and
grace, and the whole people, busy and contented, neither
sought nor wished for a change in their political condition.* At Constantinople and Smyrna, thousands of
Sciotes found employment as boatmen, gardeners, and
handicraftsmen ; and there, as in the west, they had
established the wealthiest and most considerable Greek

---

* This of course refers to the mass living at home ; the Sciote
merchants settled abroad were generally zealous in the cause of liberty.

commercial houses. Ardent promoters of education,
and passionately fond of their native land, the rich
citizens, sparing no expense to embellish it, had founded
in their town a splendid college, library, museum, print-
ing-presses, and hospitals. As soon as the revolution
broke out, the Greek fleet, commanded by Tombazi,
appeared before Scio, and disseminated an incendiary
proclamation. It is said they might then have seized
the castle, the Turks as well as their Motesellim (governor) being completely panic-struck. Very different,
however, from their Samian neighbours, the effeminate
Chians trembled at the idea of danger ; the Primates
besought Tombazi not to compromise their safety, and
this step of the Hydriotes served only to alarm the
Porte, which despatched there a body of Asiatic and
Candiote troops. From that moment there was an end
to the peace and happiness of Scio ; the soldiers robbed,
and even murdered the peasants ; and the Archbishop
and Primates, who had vainly flattered themselves that
their isle might rest in neutrality, were imprisoned in
the castle as pledges of the people's submission. The
number of hostages, not exceeding four at first, was
gradually increased to 80, selected from the most opulent and respectable class, and chiefly fathers of families. They were so closely confined, that some of them
died without being allowed to bid adieu to their friends,
and one was assassinated in sport by his Moslem guards.
Terror, meanwhile, hung over the city and villages,
and amidst present suffering from the outrages of their
garrison, the Sciotes contemplated the future with shud-
dering, lest it should heap on them worse misfortunes.
The Turks attributed their passive resignation not to
fidelity but cowardice ; and the revolted Greeks inveighed bitterly against their craven temper and lukewarm patriotism : their coasts were continually disturbed by the visits of insurgent corsairs, and the incur-

sions of the Samians, which gave the Ottoman officers and troops a pretext for renewing their barbarous acts. In the month of January 1822, Vehib Pasha assumed the command of the island, and to a certain degree restored order ; the hostages hitherto detained were exchanged for others, and the Primates, willing at any sacrifice to purchase partial repose, agreed to pay a monthly stipend of 34,000 piastres for the charges of the garrison and the Pasha's household, without reckoning the sums squeezed from the community by indirect methods. It is probable, that, like the adjacent provinces of Anatolia, Scio would have been at length tranquillized, that the Turks would have sunk into their wonted lethargy, and the Christians betaken themselves to their peaceful occupations, had not the restless genius of two men plunged into an abyss of blood and wretchedness the fairest country in the Archipelago.

In the foregoing November, a certain Bournia, a Sciote by birth, and formerly captain in the regiment of Chasseurs d'Orient raised by France, presented himself at Ypsilanti's head-quarters with a revolutionary project. The Prince heard him coldly, and did not encourage schemes tending to the destruction of an industrious and unwarlike population. Thus repulsed in Peloponnesus, Bournia went to Samos, where he found another adventurer disposed to second his views. Lycurgus Logotheti, formerly a physician at Smyrna, although enjoying a questionable reputation, had, by dint of family connexion, intrigue, and energy, acquired a complete ascendency over his Samian countrymen, and become a dictator among them. Vain and ambitious, he readily espoused the rash plans of the Chian exiles, at whose head was Bournia, and resolved, in union with them, to risk an invasion of Chios. Their design having transpired, the Turks redoubled their precautions, and sent four primates as hostages to Constantinople ; while the principal citizens despatched, with the Pasha's permission, messengers to Samos, begging the leaders there to lay aside their fatal projects. In fact, the moment was most unpropitious, as the grand Ottoman fleet was on the point of sailing from the Hellespont, and the approach of spring allowed the Sultan to act with vigour by sea and land. The commencement of winter would have been a more proper season ; but two motives may be assigned for the Samians having chosen the month of March to execute their enterprise ; first, a hope of averting impending danger from their own shores, and, secondly, a desire to get hold of the mastic crop, which is gathered in at that period of the year. On the night of the 22d of March, Logotheti and Bournia, arriving with a flotilla of eight brigs, and thirty launches, or sakolevas,* effected a disembarkation to the south of Scio. Versions differ with regard to the force that accompanied them. It was then stated, in Smyrna, at 5000 ; later accounts diminished it to 2500 ; and the most moderate reports make it amount only to 500 Samians and 150 Chian exiles, with two pieces of cannon ; but this last estimate seems altogether inadequate to the number of transports. A corps of several hundred Turks detached against them fled precipitately, supposing itself attacked by 30,000 men ; and all the exterior positions being abandoned with equal cowardice, the insurgents, reinforced by a body of peasants, entered the city. The citizens, overwhelmed with consternation, shut themselves up in their houses. However, when, at three hours after noon, the Christian

---

* A sakoleva is a bark, low and sharp at the prow, with one mast and an enormous spritsail aft. They are very much used on the coast of Anatolia, and are perhaps the same with those vessels which, having been (according to Plutarch) invented by the Samians, thence took their name.

standards were borne through the streets in procession amidst shouts of " Liberty! Liberty !"' they from their windows greeted the strangers with a faint and insincere welcome. The villagers, less timid, and provoked at the ill treatment they had experienced, cordially joined the invaders, with such weapons as they had concealed, or could at the instant procure ; their rulers having long before prescribed a general disarming.

On taking possession of the town, the troops of Lycurgus pillaged and burnt two mosques, ransacked the Turkish houses, and even some of those belonging to Catholics ; but Logotheti, by a proclamation, invited the Latins to reclaim their effects. A few Mohammedans were slain ; but the number must have been very small, from the haste with which they retired to the citadel. The Oriental Spectator, afterwards seeking pretexts to excuse Turkish cruelty, asserted that thirty Mussulmans were killed when the Samians entered ; and that Lycurgus having commanded his troops to give quarter, seventeen were subsequently made prisoners. The garrison of the castle directed a fire of shot and shells against the Greeks posted on the neighbouring height of Tourlotti. On the 24th, every thing was quiet till mid-day, when the Ottomans sallied out, penetrated to the bazar, and retreated to the fort with little loss, after a slight engagement. On the 26th, the Turks bombarded the town with vivacity, and continued their fire all next day. The citadel, situated close to the sea, (whose waters can be introduced into its moat,) supplied with cisterns, with abundance of provisions, and a strong garrison, had nothing to fear from the insurgents, who endeavoured unsuccessfully to tempt the Pasha, by offering him an advantageous capitulation. Lycurgus having appointed seven new ephors, these undertook their functions with active zeal. Cannon were brought from the adjacent isles,

and the Greeks erected batteries at Tourlotti, near the
custom-house, and on the beach ; their guns, however,
were of too small calibre to breach the walls of the
fort.

Logotheti and Bournia soon began to observe each
other with a jealous eye, and to agitate unpleasant
discussions.   The Samian wished to give the law, and
to exact heavy contributions ; while Bournia pretended
to the chief authority within his native island.   Their
discord naturally had a discouraging effect on the
Sciotes.   But the time for regret and reflection was
past ; the ephors therefore sent two deputies (Ram-
phos and Glarakis) to implore aid from the government of Corinth, which granted them two mortars,
five heavy battering guns, and several foreign officers
of merit ; unfortunately so much delay intervened,
that this succour came too late.   The Grecian squadrons
ought instantly to have left their havens, and cruised
in force around the island ; but absurd procrastination
defeated the sole possible chance of saving the Sciotes.
During the last days of March, and the beginning of
the next month, things remained in the same state ;
the two parties occasionally cannonading, and the
Greeks throwing up breastworks, from behind which
they galled the besieged with musketry.

Meanwhile the rebellion of an island that it prized
so highly extremely incensed the court of Constantinople, apprehensive lest the Christians in Lesbos, who
are numerous and bold, should follow its example, and
thus extend the seat of war to the vicinity of the capital.   The Capitan Pasha received instructions to put
to sea immediately, and the petty governors of Anatolia were ordered to forward their contingents with
the utmost expedition to Tchesmè.   Never were firmans obeyed with more alacrity ; intelligence of the
revolt of Scio excited a very strong feeling throughout

Asia Minor, detachments of troops covered the roads, and the ancient fervour of Islamism seemed to revive. Old and young flew to arms, and a regiment of infantry, composed entirely of Imams, was seen to march through the streets of Smyrna in grave and silent procession; a novel spectacle, which drew tears from the eyes of the Moslems. It would, nevertheless, be an error to suppose, that affection for their religion and empire were the only springs that induced the Asiatic Turks to move so promptly. Samos lay nearer to the continent than Chios, and its inhabitants had given infinitely greater cause of offence; but they were poor and brave: the Sciotes, on the contrary, were the richest and most effeminate of Rayahs. Hence, whenever it was proposed to invade the former, prudence effectually tempered Mohammedan enthusiasm; in the case of the latter, there was little chance of an obstinate resistance, and the certainty of an immense booty. If fanatics led the van of the dense columns that took the direction of Tchesmè, ruffians and vagabonds filled the centre, and brought up the rear.

Expecting hourly the approach of the Sultan's navy, menaced by an army of thirty thousand Ottomans assembled on the opposite shore, disguising real terror under a mask of confident resolution, the insurgents were faintly pressing the siege of the castle, when, on the morning of the 11th of April, the Capitan Pasha, Kara Ali, appeared off the island with a fleet of six line-of-battle ships, ten frigates, or large corvettes, and twelve smaller vessels of war. The Greek blockading squadron, which counted fourteen brigs and six schooners, (mostly Psarrians,) immediately fled; and the grand admiral, stretching his line along the coast, communicated with Vehib Pasha, and obtained precise information respecting the posture of affairs. Indeed the Greeks left him no room to doubt their intention

of braving him ; for, on descrying his armament, they
redoubled their fire against the citadel, and cannon,
placed at intervals along the heights, opened on his
ships. A Turkish felucca of two guns and eighty men,
having got too near the land, struck on a shoal, and
almost the whole of its crew was picked off by the
enemy's musketry. Kara Ali then ordered a disembarkation, and several thousand men landed under
cover of the artillery of his fleet ; at the same instant
Vehib Pasha made a sortie with his garrison, and a
flotilla of boats continually transported troops from
the camp of Tchesmè. The Turks rushed into the
town, and, after a combat of short duration, carried
sword in hand the height of Tourlotti, and the hostile
batteries. The city then displayed a scene, which might
be aptly compared to the sack of Tripolizza. Mercy
was out of the question, the victors butchering indis-
criminately all who came in their way ; shrieks rent
the air, and the streets were strewed with the dead
bodies of old men, women, and children ; even the
inmates of the hospital, the madhouse, and the deaf
and dumb institution, were inhumanly slaughtered.
Flames first bursting from the church of Tourlotti
gave the signal for a general conflagration, which raged
the two following days, and devoured one of the finest
cities in the Levant. Nevertheless, in the midst of
this fearful catastrophe, the Ottoman generals caused
the houses of the European agents to be respected, and
posted guards at the consulates, where the Catholics,
and great numbers of Greeks, found an asylum. It is
thought that 9000 persons of every age and sex were
slain at the storming of the town.

On the 16th the disorder had somewhat abated, as
the soldiers could no longer discover among the ruins
either victims or plunder, the very graves having been
rifled. Fresh hordes were constantly pouring in from

Anatolia, and a vast mass of Turks overran the surface
of the country, and spread fire and sword through the
villages and monastic retreats. Avarice now contended
in their minds with cruelty, and, instead of killing the
Christians without distinction, they reserved the women
and children, in order to sell them as slaves. In the
interior some fighting occurred; and at Vrondado and
Thymiana, the insurgents are said to have made an
honourable stand. It is not less true, however, that
the majority of the Sciotes either suffered themselves
to be slain or bound like sheep, or else dragged on a
miserable existence in mountains and caverns, seeking
an opportunity to escape by sea, as many of them did,
in boats that came to their rescue from Psarra, Tinos,
and other insular ports.

Desirous of preserving the district that furnished
mastic to the Seraglio, and satiated with the torrents
of blood that had flowed for six days, Kara Ali transmitted an application through Vehib Pasha to the English consul Guidici, the Austrian consul Stiepevich, and
Monsieur Digeon, agent of France, requesting them to
propose an amnesty to the insurgents. Severe, but (as
we apprehend) unfounded, obloquy has been cast upon
those functionaries, for acceding to his request. Unless
convinced that the Ottoman commander did not intend
to keep his word, what man of common humanity could
have rejected the only remaining prospect of saving
the wrecks of a population, which was evidently incapable of defending itself? To us the sequel seems to
prove that the Capitan Pasha was sincere, and it will
surely be admitted that the consular agents could not
have foreseen the extraordinary event, which, two
months after, rendered the amnesty nugatory. On the
17th they set out on their mission, bearing with them
an imperial firman, offering pardon to the Sciotes on
their unconditional submission, and a letter signed by

the Archbishop Plato, and the hostages confined in the
castle, begging them to surrender at discretion. Owing
to the prodigious confusion that prevailed among the
troops, Messieurs Digeon and Stiepevich alone succeeded in reaching the Christian quarters, with considerable personal risk; they returned on the 22d,
accompanied by the Primates of the twenty-two mastic
villages, and a train of mules loaded with arms.   The
Pasha gave these suppliants a favourable reception,
and charged Elez Aga, a chief distinguished for generosity and probity, with the difficult task of sheltering
their district from the exasperated soldiery.

All resistance then ceased, and Logotheti and Bournia evacuated the isle, in which they could no longer
remain with safety, the peasants of the village of
Pyrghi having seized and delivered to the Turks a detachment of thirteen Samians. On arriving at Psarra,
Lycurgus was arrested, and threatened with a capital
prosecution, as the author of so astounding a calamity;
for the Psarrians, partly indebted for their prosperity
to the commerce of Scio, had never approved the rash
plans set on foot for propagating insurrection there.
However, the accusation was dropped, and Lycurgus
ultimately regained his influence at Samos.   There is
not in modern annals so frightful an example of the
horrors of war as that presented at Chios : it recalls
us to those dark epochs, when barbarous myriads
rushed down on the civilized world.   If it was easy
for the Porte to instil into her Asiatic subjects a thirst
of vengeance, it was impossible for her to check their
career, and stay the inundation.   After the complete
subjugation of the surviving inhabitants, not a day
passed on which new bodies of Anatolian volunteers
did not march into Tchesmè, whence they were wafted
to the island ; the sight of others who had gone before,
returning with slaves and valuable spoil, stimulated

their impatience, and for upwards of a month 30,000 ferocious Turks roamed about the country, hunting down miserable fugitives, and gleaning the fragments of their poverty. Elez Aga protected the mastic villages from their irruption, but four other cantons, that had equally shared the benefit of the amnesty, were ravaged by the unruly troops. A populous city, forty-six flourishing villages, and many splendid convents, reduced to ashes, attested the fierceness of Mohammedan revenge; and it was calculated at the end of May, that 25,000 Chians had fallen by the edge of the sword, and 45,000 been dragged into slavery: among the latter were the females and children of the best families. Not a few captives owed their liberation to the charity of strangers, and particularly of the merchants of Smyrna, who, in these melancholy circumstances, forgetting their enmity to the Greeks, ransomed a multitude of prisoners; but this was, comparatively speaking, a small portion: whole cargoes were shipped off to Constantinople, Egypt, and Barbary, and for a long period the slave market at Smyrna displayed the bustle of active trade, and attracted Moslem purchasers from all parts of Asia Minor. The Capitan Pasha at one moment forbade the exportation of this merchandise, but as the soldiers began to put their prisoners to death, he judged it better to tolerate the abuse. About 15,000 Sciotes, mostly in a state of total destitution, escaped after the landing of the Turks: the majority of them first reached Psarra, and that place not having the means to subsist them, were conveyed to other points of Greece; suffering, as they universally did, from wounds, disease, or at least hunger and nakedness, their wretched plight excited the deepest compassion. Families once opulent, and nursed in luxury, were fain to court the shelter of a ruined hovel, and to crave a morsel of bread, and many of the young

women, mutilated by sabre cuts, bore testimony to the
enemy's brutality. Yet this brutality was more ex-
cusable than the infamous speculation of some Greek
islanders, who, profiting by their early arrival, admitted into their barks none but those who could
pay them. It was reckoned, moreover, that 5000
Sciotes were absent when the revolt began, and that
15,000 still existed in the mastic villages. Those
who fled to the consulates were saved from death or
slavery; but report states that the rich were obliged
to buy very dear the safeguard afforded them, and it
is added, that the Neapolitan consul Bogliaco exacted from females compliances of a more humiliating
description: we do not vouch for the perfect accuracy
of such charges, although all Greece proclaims them,
and with too much appearance of truth. The Capitan
Pasha, who had proved in the previous campaign that
the bent of his inclination did not lie towards fighting,
now assumed a semblance of humanity, deploring the
misfortunes of Scio, and declaring that if the other isles
would send in a simple act of submission, his fleet
should immediately return to the Dardanelles. It
would be unfair to attribute either to him or to Vehib
Pasha all the horrors that had taken place, since we
know that Turkish troops, once let loose, do not listen
to their general's voice; but it would be equally beside
the purpose to give him credit for feelings of humanity.
Hundreds of prisoners, who had attained to the age of
puberty, were, in obedience to his orders, slaughtered
from day to day, so that the town and the beach resembled a vast collection of shambles. A party of soldiers having broken into the mastic villages, and carried
away eighty-seven persons, the grand admiral effected
their liberation, but had not authority enough to punish
the ringleader in this outrage, a ruffian of Smyrna,
named Yussuf Bayraktar. If the islanders had ever

been disposed to confide in Kara Ali's insidious promises, he committed an action at the commencement of May which must have opened their eyes, and dispelled the most distant idea of an accommodation. We have seen that in 1821 the Motesellim had taken hostages, whose number was augmented by degrees to fourscore. Vehib Pasha subsequently despatched four of them to Constantinople, but when the Samians disembarked he still kept in custody seventy-six of the principal citizens, including the archbishop and the heads of the clergy.* These men were clearly innocent: so far from stimulating rebellion, they had done all in their power to prevent it, and had by their letters contributed to the pacification of the Masticokhoria, and to Logotheti's expulsion. Yet as soon as they had performed that service, they were executed with every mark of ignominy, and their remains thrown into the waves, where, with shoals of other dead bodies, they floated around the Ottoman vessels. There is reason to believe that a direct order from the Sultan prescribed this atrocity, because at the same time the four hostages at Constantinople, and seven or eight Sciote merchants settled in the capital, were put to death. The flimsy allegation brought forward to justify the perpetration of so shocking a piece of barbarity, was, that two primates, sent into the country by Vehib Pasha, when he learned Lycurgus's approach, to calm the minds of the peasants, had joined the insurgents; as they could not help doing, their retreat to the castle being cut off by the precipitate flight of the Turkish detachments.

While at Scio the Moslems were thus gorging themselves with spoil and carnage, the narrative of its sufferings covered Greece with mourning: sorrow soon

* Some accounts state them at 120.

gave place to indignation, and the seamen prepared
signally to avenge the massacre and slavery of their
brethren. The Hydriotes and Spezziotes quitted their
ports on the 5th of May, and on the 10th the whole
fleet having rendezvoused at Psarra, proceeded in quest
of the enemy. The greatest strength of the united
squadrons in this expedition amounted to fifty-six vessels of war, (the largest carrying twenty guns,) and
eight fire-ships: they were commanded by the three
Navarchs, Andreas Miaulis, Nicholas Apostoli of
Psarra, and Androuzzo of Spezzia, and had on board
several foreign officers of marine and artillery.* Hydra
being superior to the two confederate isles in wealth,
population, and the number of its shipping, they paid
it the compliment of considering its Navarch as admiral of the combined fleet: there did not however
prevail the least subordination, the admiral being
forced on every occasion to take the advice of his captains, and the latter to consult their crews. A thousand
obstacles to success were created, moreover, by the
mutual jealousy of the islands, as well as of the factions
that divided each of them, and particularly Hydra.
Had union and obedience consolidated the Greek navy,
there is no saying to what extent they might have
pushed their triumphs over their clumsy and pusillani-
mous opponents. Jachomo Tombazi, although a brave
and respectable man, had not given satisfaction to his
countrymen, who alleged that he wanted firmness, and
was harsh in his deportment to the sailors: if they
were unjust towards him, they repaired their fault by
electing in his stead Miaulis, whose cool intrepidity,
sincere devotion to the cause of freedom, primeval sim-

---

* It was then that the English captain, Frank Abney Hastings,
commenced that course of honourable service, which must ever connect his name with the emancipation of Hellas.

plicity of manners, and undoubted probity, have acquired for his name esteem as general as deserved, both
in Greece and in Western Europe.—(Vide Appendix.)
For several days they cruised between Psarra and Chios,
observing the enemy, landing small parties, and rescu-
ing the greatest possible number of Sciotes, who crawled from their lurking-places on perceiving the friendly
vessels. The Capitan Pasha affected to pay little attention to the Greek squadrons: he, indeed, once or
twice got under weigh with his fleet, but always returned to the anchorage after exchanging a few shots.
On the 22d of May began the Ramazan, a season during which the Moslems are unwilling to be disturbed,
and therefore the destruction of the revolted isles was
put off till its conclusion. The insurgents, however,
did not allow them to pass in quiet this Mohammedan
Lent: a council of war being held on the 30th on
board their Navarch's brig, they resolved to hazard an
attack. At eight o'clock in the evening of the 31st,
Miaulis entered the channel with fifteen ships of war
and three fire-ships, while the rest of the squadrons
formed in his rear a line extending from the northern
cape of Scio to the coast of Asia. The Turkish frigates
that were under sail at the mouth of the strait having
fired alarm guns, their fleet cut their cables and cleared
for action with extreme haste and confusion. Four
brigs (those of Miaulis, Saktouris, Skourtis, and Tza-
mados) engaged for near an hour the Capitan Pasha's
eighty-four gun ship, without being materially injured,
so ill did the foe point his cannon. Kara Ali had a
narrow escape from a brulot, which passed close under
his poop, and would have burned him had the train been
kindled a little later. Seeing that the attempt had
failed, and pressed by an irresistible force, the Greeks
beat out of the strait by the same pass through which
they had entered, and the Turks, after cannonading

heavily all night, left it by the southern channel, so that
next morning they again neared each other, and renewed a partial and innocuous action.   The islanders
went back to Psarra, and the Ottoman admiral, proud
of having made a show of pursuit, took up his old
station.

Immediately after this affair, Vehib Pasha was (for
what reason we know not) deposèd on the 3d of June,
disgraced, and succeeded by Abdi Pasha.   Chios had
become comparatively tranquil, only three or four murders occurring daily : the mastic villages were still
respected, and carefully guarded by Elez Aga, and they
had the farther advantage of being exempt from a ma-
lignant fever, which, arising from the stench of so
many unburied bodies, raged among the Turks.   Nevertheless troops continued to arrive from the interior of
Asia, as though the isle had been an inexhaustible mine
of wealth.   Reinforced from Constantinople, the Capitan
Pasha's fleet amounted, June the 16th, to thirty-eight
sail ; a fresh accession of force was promised him from
the same quarter, and he expected besides to be joined
by a powerful squadron from Alexandria, as soon as it
should have accomplished its primary object of transporting an Egyptian army to Crete.   The fast of Ramazan ended on Wednesday the 19th, and the Grand
Admiral celebrated, on the night of the 18th, by a
splendid entertainment, the approach of the moon of
Bayram, which he was not fated to behold.   Surrounded
by the blood-stained trophies of Scio, he had forgotten
the vicinity of the Greeks, who, since their previous
failure, lay in the harbour of Psarra, meditating a plan
for his discomfiture.   We have now to narrate one of
the most extraordinary military exploits recorded in
history, and to introduce to the reader's notice, in the
person of a young Psarriote sailor, the most brilliant
pattern of heroism that Greece in any age has had to

boast of; a heroism, too, springing from the purest motives, unalloyed by ambition or avarice. The Greeks
were convinced, that if they did not by a decisive blow
paralyse the Turkish fleet before its junction with that
of Egypt, their islands must be exposed to imminent
danger: it was proposed, therefore, in their naval council, to choose a dark night for sending in two brulots
by the northern passage, while at each extremity of
the strait two ships of war should cruise in order to
pick up the brulottiers. Constantine Canaris of Psarra,
(already distinguished by his conduct at Erisso,) and
George Pepinis of Hydra, with thirty-two bold companions, volunteered their services; and having partaken
of the holy sacrament, sailed on the 18th in two brigs,
fitted up as fire-ships, and followed at some distance by
an escort of two corvettes, a brig, and a schooner.
They beat to windward in the direction of Tchesmè,
under French and Austrian colours, and about sunset
drew so nigh to the hostile men-of-war, that they were
hailed, and ordered to keep off: they tacked accordingly, but at midnight bore up with a fresh breeze,
and ran in amongst the fleet. The Psarriote brulot,
commanded by Canaris, grappled the prow of the admiral's ship, anchored at the head of the line, a league
from the shore, and instantly set her on fire; the
Greeks then stepped into a large launch they had in
tow, and passed under her poop, shouting, " Victory to
the Cross !" the ancient war-cry of the imperial armies
of Byzantium. The Hydriotes fastened their brig to
another line-of-battle ship, carrying the treasure and
the Reala Bey's flag, and communicated the flames to
her, but not so effectually, having applied the match a
moment too soon; they were then picked up by their
comrades, and the thirty-four brulottiers sailed out of
the channel through the midst of the enemy without a
single wound; they had, however, in their bark a

barrel of gunpowder, determined to blow themselves up rather than be taken. While they departed full of joy and exultation, the roads of Scio presented an appalling sight. The Capitan Pasha's ship, which in a few minutes became one sheet of fire, contained 2286 persons, including most of the captains of the fleet, and unfortunately also a great number of Christian slaves; not above 180 survived, for the guns going off deterred boats from approaching, and two of those belonging to the vessel foundered, from being overloaded with men endeavouring to save their lives. Although the Reala Bey's ship got clear of the Hydriote brulot, and the flames were extinguished on board of her, yet she was so seriously damaged as to be unfit for ulterior service ; and the brulot, driving about the roadstead in a state of combustion, set fire to a third two-decker, which was likewise preserved through the exertions of its crew. Overwhelmed with despair, the Capitan Pasha was placed in a launch by his attendants, but just as he seated himself there, a mast falling, sunk the boat, and severely bruised him ; nevertheless expert swimmers supported Kara Ali to the beach, only to draw his last breath on that spot where the Sciote hostages had suffered !

For three quarters of an hour the conflagration blazed, casting its light far and wide over the sea and the coast of Asia, and alarming even the city of Smyrna, whose inhabitants contemplated with wonder a bright streak in the south-western sky : at two o'clock on the morning of the 19th, the flag-ship blew up with a dreadful explosion. It would be difficult to paint the consternation of the Turks : all their vessels cut their cables, some running out of the southern channel, others beating up towards the northern ; if the Greek squadrons had been at hand to take advantage of their confusion, the Sultan's armament might have been annihilated.* Within the isle the disorder was not less: when the Admiral's ship exploded, the Mohammedans uttered lamentable cries, and most of them bent their bodies to the earth. Abdi Pasha spent the rest of the night watching by the mortal remains of the Capitan Pasha, which were interred before noon. This melancholy ceremony wound up to the highest pitch the fury of the Ottoman troops; 20,000 of them rushed into the mastic villages, killing or enslaving the people, and in spite of the resistance of Elez Aga, the 19th day of June consummated the ruin of Scio. In the month of August, the total number of Christians living on that island did not exceed 1800, and the most populous village had only twelve indwellers.

From such desolation we turn with pleasure to a subject worthy of delight and admiration ; the triumphant return of Canaris and his valiant companions. It was a proud day for Greece, when those intrepid men, entering the Psarrian harbour amidst the firing of cannon, ringing of bells, waving of banners, and the acclamations of the seamen and citizens, doffed their slippers, and walked in silence to a neighbouring church, to render thanks to Providence, which had granted to thirty-four champions so signal a victory over the Infidel host. Their success dispelled every gloomy idea from the breasts of the islanders, and carried terror into the hearts of the Turks, whose navy fled to Mitylene and Tenedos, cautiously avoiding the vessels it met, lest any of them should be a brulot. On the 21st the Greeks pursued, watching a propitious opportunity of again attacking their enemies in the same way. The morning of the 27th, being, as they wished, thick,

* If we may credit Tombazi's MS. Journal, one of their frigates was lost the same night.

rainy, and squally, they prepared to assail them with
two fire-ships in the port of Lesbos; but just as they
were upon the point of doing so, the weather cleared,
the Turks got under weigh, and the Christians put back
to Psarra. On the 29th, sixty-two sail of Greeks traversed the Canal of Scio, exchanging several hundred cannon-shots with the castle, and anchored next day at
Psarra, where they lay till the 5th of July; they then
went to seek the foe at Tenedos, but found that the
Moslems had retired within the Dardanelles. The
concluding part of this cruise was not very honourable
to the Hellenic marine; after pushing on two fire-ships
close to the Thracian shore, the vessels destined to support them would not proceed, because the wind having
shifted to the south, the sailors were afraid lest the
enemy (whose movements they did not precisely
know) should get the weathergage of them, and cut
off their retreat; and Tombazi attempting to capture
some small craft hauled under a promontory, the Turks
from the land above saluted him with such sharp volleys of musketry, that his men ran below, and but for
the courage and seamanship of Captain Hastings, his
schooner would have been stranded. About the 20th
of July the independent squadrons steered homewards.

The Porte filled up the vacant post of Capitan
Pasha, by nominating to that office Kara Mehemet,
commandant of the forces at Patrass, and ordered the
fleet to go thither, and take on board its new admiral.
It weighed anchor from the Hellespont, July the 12th,
and shaped its course to the south, its strength then
consisting of fifty-four ships of war, of which four were
two-deckers. At the same period, the armament from
Alexandria under the Capitana Bey, having disembarked troops in Crete, and captured on its passage a few
small Greek vessels, (whose captains were put to death,
and their crews loaded with irons,) arrived at Scio, to

the number of forty-two sail : the two fleets effected
their junction, and went together to Patrass.   The
Egean Sea was thus for a season relieved from the enemy's presence ; but a fresh scourge, the plague, afflicted
Tinos, and thence spread its ravages over the Archipelago and into Attica. Most of the isles had accepted
without hesitation the Eparchs appointed by the Central Government, but all were not equally well pleased
with their magistrates ; the Prefect of Tinos gave
general satisfaction, but those of Naxos and Andros,
provoking commotions by their avidity, were very
roughly handled.

APPENDIX

TO

BOOK II.—CHAP. II.

---

*Short Biography of Admiral MIAULIS.**

ANDREAS MIAULIS, son to an Euboean merchant named Demetrius Vokhos, was born at Hydra, and at seven years of age went to sea as cabin-boy on board a ship belonging to his father, and commanded by his elder brother. While yet a boy, he showed his natural courage, and in that respect was superior to others of his own age : he was lively, choleric, and obstinate. When he was eighteen years old he married Irene, daughter to a worthy priest of Hydra, and his brother falling sick, he took the direction of his father's vessel, and made a fortunate voyage. Reflecting, on his way home, that his brother on his recovery would resume the command, and wishing to be independent, he resolved to go to Smyrna and purchase a vessel for himself. He did so, and bought of a Cretan Turk a kind of bark, called a saitta; (rigged like a brig forward, with a lateen sail abaft ;) but being yet inexperienced, he made a very bad bargain, and perceived in returning to Hydra that his vessel was old and exceedingly leaky. He did not dare to present himself before his father, who was so much incensed that he would hold no communication with him ; however, he was at length prevailed upon at the instances of relations and friends to pardon his son, and give him the means of prosecuting his voyages. His ventures were happy, and he raised himself in his father's esteem above his other brothers. On one occasion, he fell in, off the Isle of Prote, (a little to the north of Navarin,) with a Maltese piratical brig, and being chased, ran his saitta ashore. His crew, being frightened, left him, except his two younger brothers, to whom he gave his money, and desired them to save themselves with the other sailors. He remained alone, unwilling to abandon his vessel, and thinking, when the pirates found nothing, they would not molest him. They approached,

---

* Written by his son, Antonio Miaulis, captain of the Hellas frigate.

anchored, and seeing him stand on the poop, ordered him to come aboard in his boat ; he replied, that he was alone in the vessel. The pirates, suspecting a trick, surrounded the saitta with their boats, and kept up a warm fire of small arms ; until, being convinced there was no one else there, they boarded, beat him severely to oblige him to confess where the money was deposited ; and finally brought him before their captain, to whom upon being questioned he told the truth. The Maltese desired him to write for cash to ransom his saitta, but Miaulis begged permission to go to the neighbouring villages, where he might perhaps borrow the sum required. They granted that request, threatening to burn his saitta if he did not return within three days. Miaulis, unable to stand on account of the blows he had received, crawled to a village, and was kindly treated by a bishop of his acquaintance. Ere the prescribed term expired, another bark came ashore to escape the pirates, and the bishop having sent some Albanian soldiers to defend her, the Maltese, repulsed in two attacks, although they succeeded in a third, yet were afraid to remain longer, and seeing several fishing-boats, which they supposed to be full of troops, cut their cable, and went to sea, leaving the two barks ; thus Miaulis recovered his saitta, and returned to Hydra. He afterwards built another on the coast of Euboea, and with the profits he gained bought a Genoese vessel, and in her traded to great advantage. Finally, he built at Venice a large and beautiful ship, and put all his property on board of her ; but sailing to Cadiz with a cargo of grain on his own account, he lost her on Tarifa. Not discouraged, he went to seek assistance at Genoa, where one of his commercial friends, named Risatis, lent him 8000 dollars, with which he bought a new ship, called the Hercules, of 9000 kiloes burden (above 250 tons), paid his debt, and re-established his fortune. A merchant of Malta, (Thomas Wilson by name,) knowing his worth, took him into partnership, and intrusted him to sell goods in different ports of Turkey. With the Hercules he fought and beat off a French brig of 14 guns between Majorca and Algiers. He was once taken by Nelson, who, pleased with his frankness, released him, as is described in Mr Emerson's work. About 1812, he built a brig, called the Mars, and gave the command of her to his eldest son Demetrius. In 1817, he retired from active life, intending to spend the rest of his days in repose ; but in 1821, he hastened to obey his country's summons.*

---

* Once at a critical moment, when the seamen refused to embark, Miaulis, lame, and suffering from a fit of the gout, caused himself to be carried on his bed through the streets, and on board of his brig ; the refractory mariners rushed after him, and the fleet put to sea.

Miaulis is naturally brave, active, diligent, and skilful in nautical affairs ; his moral character is marked by deep thought, decision, steadiness, and patience. His education was neglected, but his talents are of a superior order, and age has not impaired his fire and energy. He conforms to the manners and customs of those whom he associates with, delights in doing good, and shuns every thing contrary to established laws and institutions.

CHAP. III.

Campaign in Epirus—Operations in Eubœa, Macedonia, and Northern
Greece, till the middle of July 1822.

SECTION I.

THE repulse of the Greeks at Arta (related in the
preceding book), accompanied as it was by the defection of the Mohammedan Beys of Epirus, who had
hitherto propped his sinking fortunes, sealed the doom
of the able and infamous Satrap of Yannina. Provided
even to superfluity with money, ammunition, and
stores, he might, perhaps, notwithstanding the loss of
two out of the three fortresses that formed his system
of defence, have wearied the Serasker's perseverance,
if his garrison had remained firmly attached to the interest of their veteran general.   But his Albanian soldiers had already manifested a degree of fidelity and
constancy unusual among their tribes : a prey to disease and ennui, they sighed for the air of the mountains ; and his engineer, Caretto, by going over to the
imperial camp, afforded an example of desertion, which
was almost universally copied.   In the first days of January, the Sultan's troops occupied, without bloodshed,
the Castle of the Lake. Ali, however, retiring with thirty-
five followers (five of whom were Souliote hostages)
to an inner redoubt, which contained his treasure and
powder magazine, and threatening to blow up the fort,
Khourshid Pasha felt that his victory was not yet ac-

complished. A moment's despair might deprive him
of the gold and the head of the rebel, the trophies he
coveted most ; he therefore had recourse to fraud and
perjury, thus combating Ali with his own favourite
weapons. Withdrawing his soldiers from the castle,
he presented to the fallen Satrap a paper, signed by himself, and his principal officers, in which they engaged
to intercede with the Sultan to spare his life, and assign him a retreat, where he might pass the evening
of his days unmolested. It seems incredible that a man
of Ali's experience and capacity, should have been
duped by so shallow an artifice ; yet, instead of illus-
trating his end, and disappointing the cupidity of his
foes, by a memorable act, he clung to the love of life,
hearkened to the delusion, and allowed himself to be
removed, with his wife Vassiliki, the Souliote hostages,
and a few faithful attendants, to an islet in the lake,
where a summer-house had been prepared for his reception. There he lingered for a short space, tormented by conflicting passions, until he voluntarily bereft
himself of the last pledge of safety. On his departure
from the castle, he left to guard the powder magazine
a young Albanian of Chamouria, named Fehim, as
much devoted to his master's will, as the Imaelians formerly were to that of their Prince, termed by the crusaders the Old Man. of the Mountain : yielding to im-
portunate solicitation, he caused this vigilant guardian
to extinguish the port-fire, that was constantly burning by his side. Before transmitting an order to that
effect, he consulted the persons about him, whether it
would not be better to give a signal for exploding the
fort ; but they opined that the time for doing so was
past, and that he ought to have buried himself in the
ruins, rather than capitulate.* Several Pashas and

* Several versions have been published of the story of Ali Pasha's
death ; the present account was communicated by one of the Souliote

great officers came, on the 2d of February, to visit him in the islet: Ali, suspecting treachery, put his train under arms, and admitted them with caution to an interview, which terminated amicably. They presented themselves again on the 5th, when just as he was turning to marshal them into the Kiosk, after the first compliments were over, Mehemet Pasha, drawing a pistol, shot him in the back: a cry of treason being raised, firing continued on both sides, until it was announced that Ali, pierced with thirteen balls, had expired, upon which his attendants surrendered. The Satrap's head, borne in triumph through the Ottoman provinces, and exposed to the gaze of the people of Constantinople, excited unbounded joy among the Mussulmans, who hated him as the ally of infidels: his two recreant sons, Moukhtar and Veli, were, with their male children, massacred soon afterwards at Kutaieh. Never was a ruler more detested during a long and prosperous reign than Ali Pasha, and yet, by a strange, although not uncommon change of sentiment, the Greeks now speak of him with respect; and the Albanians and Epirotes regret him, thinking his regime less insupportable than the anarchy which preceded and followed it. Those who mainly contributed to his destruction, had little reason to rejoice : Khourshid, indeed, was at first recompensed with extraordinary honours, quickly tempered by vexatious enquiries about Ali's treasures, and harsh reproaches; all his subsequent enterprises were unfortunate, and ere many months elapsed, his hoary head went down with sorrow to the grave. Ismael Pasha (Ali's capital enemy) underwent a worse fate : disgraced after the affair of Arta, and exiled to Demotica, he was there decapitated by the Sultan's order, on the 1st of November of the

hostages. We cannot say which is most correct, but it is certain they differ only in minute details.

same year, and his features, stiffened in death, were
placed in the niche of the Seraglio gate, which had held
those of the Epirote Satrap. Having slain the arch-
rebel, and pacified Mohammedan Albania, Khourshid
Pasha had fulfilled half of his instructions; and the
Porte now demanded at his hands the punishment of
the Christian insurgents, and the conquest of Greece.
Unwilling to leave a hostile force in his rear, he determined to begin by attacking the Souliotes, whom he
looked upon as his bravest adversaries ; supposing that
after their extirpation, he could soon impose the Ottoman yoke on the unwarlike Peloponnesians.   The
money found in the treasury of Yannina, enabled him
to make great levies of Albanians, but he did not commence his operations against Souli, until the close of the
negotiation for the ransom of his harem, which was
restored to him at Prevesa, on the 2d of May.   In the
early part of spring, some detachments of his troops,
attempting incursions on the coast of Acarnania, were
generally beaten, and the sole advantage accruing to
him in that quarter, was the recovery of the small forts
of Playa and Tekè, destitute alike of guns and ammunition.

The Souliotes, expecting to be attacked, cheerfully
prepared for the encounter, and took their measures
with skill and judgment, entrenching the chain of
strong and rugged posts that cover the approach to
their lofty citadel of Kiapha. Their warriors did not
exceed 4000, recruited from various cantons of Epirus,
not above one-sixth being genuine Souliotes.   The
Turkish army, stated at 17,000 men, with a train of
field artillery, advanced against them, under the command of Omer Vriones, who had for his lieutenants
Tahir Abbas, Hagos Bessiaris, and Elmaz Bey, the
three Albanian chiefs who betrayed the Greeks at Arta.
On the 28th of May, his vanguard skirmished with the

Christian outposts, and from the dawn of the next day, until the evening of June the 5th, there was a continual succession of bloody combats. As the reports of these affairs are evidently full of exaggeration, we must be content to give a superficial view of them, and to mark the result.* Both parties showed great courage and perseverance ; the advanced positions were frequently taken and retaken, and the Turks even penetrated to the village of Souli ; but after eight days of severe fighting among rocks and ravines, the Souliotes, better acquainted with the country, and contending for their existence, religion, families, and all that is dear to man, by a desperate effort, drove back the enemy, with a heavy loss in killed and wounded, besides the capture of cannon, standards, &c. On the 7th, Khourshid arrived in person, with a reinforcement of 3000 soldiers, and immediately sent a message to the Christians proposing a pacification, on condition that they should resign to him their castle, together with Hussein Pasha, Ali's grandson, and accept another territory in exchange, with an indemnity of 6,000,000 of piastres. He granted them three days to reflect on his proposition, and, as they rejected it, hostilities recommenced on the 10th. In a fresh series of violent actions, victory was long doubtful, and the situation of Souli appeared so critical, that the women armed themselves, and fought by the side of their husbands and brothers. At length, on the night of the 13th, the Souliotes, acting on the offensive, routed the Turks, chased them from all the posts they had occupied, forced the head-quarters of Omer Vriones, and took his secretary, papers, baggage, and war-horse. Although the nature of the ground was much in favour of the Christians,

* To judge of their veracity, it is enough to mention, that, in the engagement of May the 31st, they make the Turks lose 2500 men, and the Souliotes 60 men and women.

yet too great praise cannot be given to their vigorous
defence. We have been assured that they owed their
success chiefly to the well-planned and furious nocturnal assaults they made on the Ottoman tambourias.
Having witnessed the defeat of his troops, and learning
that his own Albanian mercenaries were conspiring
against him, the aged Serasker returned on the 14th to
Yannina, and soon after set out for Larissa, in Thessaly, to assume the command of an army assembling
there for the invasion of Peloponnesus. To Omer
Vriones, who had been appointed Pasha of Yannina, he
committed the conduct of the war against Souli; and
the latter, desisting from useless attacks, adopted the
system of investing that group of mountains, trusting
to the slow but sure process of a blockade. While the
Sultan's Generalissimo was turning his back upon Epirus, Mavrocordato was in full march towards that
province. On the 3d and 4th of June, he disembarked
his army of 700 regular, and twice as many irregular
troops, at Messalonghi, where the inhabitants, who at
all times saw him with pleasure, and now flattered
themselves that his presence would screen them from
the enemy's insults, received him with acclamations.
The president, whose education and habits were by no
means of a military complexion, seems to have had no
fixed plan, beyond an anxious desire to relieve Souli,
and a vague idea of transporting the theatre of hostilities as far as possible from the Hellenic frontier. He
had vastly overrated the forces he would be able to
dispose of, presuming that the militia of the country
would flock around him, and confiding in the assurances of his colleagues, that they would send after him
a considerable corps from the Morea. Through his reliance on their fallacious promises, he weakened himself in the beginning of the campaign, detaching Kyriakouli by sea, with 500 Mainatts and Peloponnesians,

to effect a landing on the coast of Thesprotia, near Parga, and endeavour on that side to open a communication with the Souliotes. Having made arrangements for the internal administration, and for supplying his army with provisions, Mavrocordato marched on the 13th, and two days after, crossing the Achelous at the ford of Stratos, entered Acarnania. During his stay at Messalonghi, some companies of Armatoles joined him, and orders were despatched to the captains to meet him with their bands at the valley of Laspes, where but a small part of the expected reinforcements came in. After a halt of three days, he advanced to Caravanserai, on the Ambracian Gulf, and embarked his artillery, composed of two fieldpieces, and his baggage, in the flotilla of Passano, who landed it at Coprena, on the northern shore. That Corsican, defeated the year before at Vonizza, had again fitted out as gunboats two fishing launches, and arming them with three-pounders, cruised in the gulf, and harassed the Turks of Prevesa. The infantry, marching by roads almost impracticable, traversed the district of Valtos, and the defiles of Makrynoros, and arrived on the 21st at the village of Combotti, which they found occupied by the Acarnanians of Varnakiottis. Gogos Bakoulas was posted at Petta with a few hundred Armatoles of Radovich, while the captain, Andreas Iskos, blockaded Vonizza.

On the morning of the 22d, General Normann going on with a party to reconnoitre, returned hastily to the camp, and announced the approach of 500 Turkish horsemen, who had moved from Arta for the same purpose. The Greeks immediately stood to their arms, and a smart skirmish ensued, in which the Ottoman cavalry was repulsed with loss, and pursued at the point of the bayonet almost to Arta, by the impetuous Philhellenes, who, if the enemy had taken the obvious and ordinary precaution of placing some Albanian infantry in the thickets behind their horse, would most likely have been entirely cut off. As it was, the result of this trifling affair did not improve Mavrocordato's situation ; neither could he disguise from himself the inadequacy of his means for any offensive operation. Instead of 8,000 men, he had hardly 3,000, daily diminishing through desertion, in consequence of the difficulty he experienced in procuring them food. Every courier who stole through the hostile lines, brought dismal accounts of the distress of the Souliotes ; and the numerical strength and able dispositions of Omer Vriones, precluded the possibility of succouring them. Establishing his head-quarters at Variades, a central position betwixt Yannina, Arta, and Souli, and leaving Tahir Abbas to guard the banks of the Acheron, Omer intrusted the defence of Arta, and the entrenched Han of the Five Wells to Reshid Mehemet and Ismail Pliasa Pashas. Other detachments observed the sea-coast of Thesprotia, and kept in check the Laconian Captain Kyriakouli.

The formidable aspect of the Mohammedans was not the only circumstance that disquieted the mind of Mavrocordato ; disappointed by the little enthusiasm manifested in Etolia and Acarnania, he saw reason to suspect the fidelity of Gogos Bakoulas. Gogos, a man of seventy years of age, alternately a robber and captain of Armatolic militia, had spent his life in fighting for and against the Turks, and was reputed the bravest and most expert warrior in Roumelia ; but he was an avaricious and unprincipled ruffian, stained with the assassination of Mark Bozzaris' father, a crime committed at the instigation of Ali Pasha. Nevertheless, the Armatoles greatly looked up to him, especially after the proofs of valour and capacity he had shown at the combats of Langada and Petta. Caring deeply for his own

interest, and indifferent to every thing else, Gogos maintained a constant intercourse with the Turks, receiving
from them abundance of provisions, which he sold at
an extravagant price to Mavrocordato's soldiers, and
engaging in return to betray his countrymen. To the
latter, he boasted of his dexterity in duping the Moslems, and indeed there can be no doubt he was playing
a double game, waiting the turn of events, and determined to follow such a course as his own private advantage might point out. What rendered him more dangerous was the personal attachment of his troops,
accustomed to obey him from a period anterior to the
Greek revolution. The Europeans about the President, ignorant of the ideas and usages of the East, where
scarcely any kind of lucre is thought disgraceful, and
treachery is a venial and familiar occurrence, proposed
that he should be arrested ; but Mavrocordato durst
not venture upon such a measure, which would have
disgusted all the captains of Western Greece ; he was,
moreover, inclined to think that Gogos was really
deceiving Turkish credulity. Besides, there were not
sufficient grounds for convicting him, since the habit of
conferring together, and corresponding in the intervals
of hostility, was sanctioned by the practice of both
Greeks and Ottomans.

After the skirmish of the 22d, tranquillity reigned
for some days on the Epirote frontier, the Christians
being too weak to stir from their position, and the
Turks negotiating with Gogos, whose defection they
wished to secure before attempting any thing of importance. The ardent spirit of Mark Bozzaris could
not brook this inaction ; knowing how much his Souliote brethren were pressed, he resolved, if possible, to
penetrate to their mountains, and Varnakiottis and
Vlakhopoulos, agreeing to accompany him, they set
forward on the 3d of July. To cover their march, and

distract the enemy's attention, Mavrocordato, on the 4th, altered the disposition of his forces : General Normann advanced to Petta, at the head of the Philhellenes, the Greek regulars, and the Ionians ; and the President, with the Peloponnesians, retired to Evangelistra, near Langada. As those two points are at a distance of three leagues, Captain Alexander of Anatoliko was left with 100 men at Combotti, to keep up the communication. Henceforth misfortune attended the insurgents ; the day they were executing these movements, they witnessed from the heights the destruction of Passano's flotilla, which had hitherto given them command of the upper part of the gulf. Attacked by three heavy Turkish gun-boats from Prevesa, the Corsican, with his Lilliputian cannon, long contended against their 48-pounders, until his slight barks were put entirely hors-de-combat ; a calm hindering him from running them ashore, he endeavoured to escape in a skiff, which was sunk by a shot, and the conquerors seized Passano and several of his sailors in the water. The latter they impaled at Prevesa, and threatened their commander with the same fate ; intimately acquainted, however, while in Ali Pasha's service, with many men of note in Albania, he was ultimately released from captivity through the interference of Reshid Pasha, his wife having paid his ransom. Mark Bozzaris had no success in his expedition, encountering every where insuperable obstacles ; after various marches and counter-marches, and failing in an attempt to surprise some Mohammedan Beys, in a village near Yannina, the Greeks (800 strong) were assailed on the 12th at Plakka, by a superior body of Albanians, who pierced their centre, under Varnakiottis, defeated and dispersed them. According to the statement of one of their own chiefs, about 40 were killed ; the rest gained the mountains, and on the 15th re-entered the camp of Petta.

I

Meanwhile the conduct of Gogos was becoming more and more scandalous ; not satisfied with monopolizing the trade in provisions, he, to increase his profits, raised or lowered the relative value of different pieces of coin in an arbitrary manner, and his intercourse with the Turks was unremitted. It seems probable that at this period he fully arranged matters with them, induced as well by the evil prospects of his countrymen, as by aversion to his western auxiliaries. The old prejudices of the Byzantine Greeks against Franks, were still alive among the wild mountaineers of Roumelia, who, esteeming themselves the first of warriors, perceived, with surprise and indignation, that the strangers looked upon them and their military qualities with too undisguised contempt. Semi-barbarians invariably abhor those who excel them in arts, education, and refinement ; thus the dress, manners, and languages of the West were wormwood to many Palikars, who did not scruple to say, that they preferred the Turkish institutions. Their dislike extended even to Greeks brought up in Europe, or European fashions, and both Ypsilanti and Mavrocordato might have fared better had they set cleanliness at nought, thrown away their coats and epaulets, and decked their persons in a dirty Albanian dress, garnished with enormous knife and pistols, which, as well as a profusion of hair and beard, and a swaggering mien, too often cloaked among the insurgents, rank cowardice, and consummate baseness. These remarks do not merely apply to the moment in question, but will offer a key to sundry incidents that happened later. A circumstance occurred at this time which enhanced the President's mistrust of Gogos. That chieftain had placed in ambush, to his extreme right, and near the river of Arta, a party of men intended to prevent the enemy's foragers from carrying off his flock of sheep which pastured in the rear. Although

it appeared that nothing could pass, and the sheep were
not molested, yet one day when there was reason to
suppose that Mavrocordato's quarters were very weakly
guarded, they were insulted by a column of Albanians,
and he would have been killed or taken, but for the
happy accident of Captain Makrys having just before
unexpectedly joined him with his corps; a reinforcement which obliged the intruders to fall back.

General Normann exactly obeyed his instructions to
remain on the defensive; he could not, however, restrain the mad temerity of Dania, seconded as it was
by the impatience of the Philhellenes. Petta is not a
league from Arta, and being seated on the edge of a
chain of hills, overlooking the plain, the exercises and
sports of the Ottoman horse were thence clearly descried, and were considered by the Franks as a sort of
challenge. Gogos, informed that a detachment of Arnauts was gone out to the northward of the place, persuaded Dania to march in pursuit of them, representing
their number to be much smaller than it really was,
furnishing guides, and promising to send him provisions regularly. In spite of Count Normann's disapprobation, the leader of the Philhellenes, with his own
two companies, and the Ionians of Captain Pannas, proceeded on this rash and absurd enterprise, ascended the
banks of the river of Arta, and passed the night of
July the 7th at the village of Plakka, where the party
they were in search of had been a few hours before.
On the 8th they forded the river, and at nightfall,
after a very fatiguing march, reached the lofty hamlet
of Vronzza, where they would have surprised the Albanians, had not their guides, (friends and relations of
Gogos,) by discharging their muskets, alarmed the latter, who decamped with precipitation. As Vronzza
overlooks the high-road from Arta to Yannina, Dania
halted there, although his soldiers were forced to sub-

sist upon ears of maize roasted on hot embers, Gogos having forgotten his promises, as soon as he thought he had led them into a trap whence they never could extricate themselves. According to all reasonable calculation, the Ionians and Philhellenes, so rashly thrown forwards in the midst of the Ottoman divisions, should have been cut to pieces; but it was not so; they remained unmolested, and even destroyed several parties of Turks, who fell into their ambuscades, not dreaming of an enemy being in their rear. At length a positive order from General Normann recalled them to Petta, whither they arrived on the 15th, some hours after Mark Bozzaris. On the same day, John Colocotroni, summoned by a pressing message, in consequence of the dispersion of his father's forces before Patrass, quitted Mavrocordato's head-quarters, and returned to Peloponnesus.

The Turkish generals had at first conceived exaggerated notions of the strength of their opponents, until they acquired precise details from the confession of an Italian officer named Monaldi, who, straying from the camp of Combotti, was seized by the Albanians. Reshid, and Ismael Pliassa Pashas, then began to meditate a serious attack, and with that view collected troops from Yannina and Prevesa; it was a knowledge of their intention, communicated by Christians of the country, which induced General Normann peremptorily to recall Dania from Vronzza. Unable to act offensively, the President could desire nothing better than that the foe should assail his army in a good position; but then he ought to have come up in person and concentrated every man he had, instead of resting behind with his body-guard, at such a distance that he could give no support to those who were engaged :* we may add, that

* As Mavrocordato's conduct on this occasion has been inveighed against by his enemies, the author took the liberty of mentioning the

the opportune arrival of Bozzaris and Dania, the day previous to the action, was a piece of singular luck, that the Greeks had no right to reckon upon.

Petta stands on an elevated neck of land joining two ridges of hills, of which the one in front of, and rather lower than the village, is 600 yards long; the other behind is higher, and far more extensive. It was on the first that Gogos so gloriously repulsed the Turks in 1821 ; however, he had intrenched himself, a precaution which the Philhellenes despised. In a council of war held on the 15th, and attended by General Normann, the Colonels Dania and Tarella, Lieut.-Colonels Gubernati and Stietz, the Chef-de-bataillon Kazzopoulo, and the Captains Gogos, Bozzaris, Vlakhopoulos, Varnakiottis, and Spiro Pannas, it was decided that the regulars should occupy the first, and the irregulars the second line : Tarella, Stietz, and Bozzaris, opposed this arrangement, and as military men their judgment was certainly correct ; but considerations of honour and expediency induced the majority to solve the question otherwise, and most unfortunately the key of their position was intrusted to the perfidious Gogos. The regular troops guarded the Mamelon in front of Petta, the two Greek battalions of Tarella being posted on the right, with two fieldpieces served by ten Philhellenes under the Swiss lieutenant Vrendlie ; the companies of Philhellenes to their left, at the most dangerous point ; the Ionians were ranged as sharpshooters to the right of, and rather in rear of, Tarella's corps. The second ridge, which commands the other, was assigned to the Etolians, Acarnanians, and Epirotes ; Gogos being stationed to the right, Vlakhopoulos and Varnakiottis in

subject to him ; in explanation, the Prince assured him, that he was not (as reported) at Langada, but at Evangelistra, two leagues nearer to Petta, with a part of his staff, and little more than 200 soldiers, commanded by Theodore Grivas and Kanellos Delhiyani.

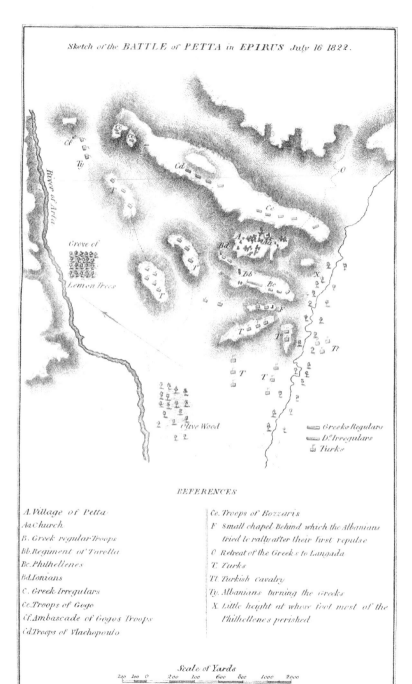

Sketch of the BATTLE of PETTA in EPIRUS July 16 1822.

River of Arta

Grove of

Lemon trees

Olive Wood

Greeks Regulars
Dº Irregulars
Turks

REFERENCES

A. Village of Petta
Aa Church
B. Greek regular Troops
Bb. Regiment of Tarella
Bc. Philhellenes
Bd. Ionians
C. Greek Irregulars
Cc. Troops of Gogo
Cf. Ambuscade of Gogos Troops
Cd Troops of Vlachopoulo

Ce. Troops of Bozzaris
F. Small chapel Behind which the Albanians
   tried to rally after their first repulse
O. Retreat of the Greeks to Langada
T. Turks
Tt. Turkish Cavalry
Ty. Albanians turning the Greeks
X. Little height at whose foot most of the
   Philhellenes perished

Scale of Yards

200 100 0   200 100 600 800 1000 2000

Engraved by J. Moffat.

the centre, and Bozzaris on the left. Thus disposed,
the Greek army, amounting to between 2000 and 3000
men, passed the night of the 15th under arms. At
daybreak on the 16th, the Turks appeared in great
force, covering with their masses all the lower hil-
locks; eye-witnesses computed them at 10,000, chiefly
Albanian foot soldiers. They were drawn up in the
form of a crescent, whose right horn of 600 horse
stretched away as far as the road leading to Combotti.
A large body of infidels made a vigorous attack upon
the first line of the Christians, but, being received at the
distance of 100 yards with a heavy and well directed
fire, was driven back with slaughter, and in confusion ;
returning to the charge they were again repulsed, and
their left wing, under Ismael Pliassa, had no better
success in an onset upon the centre of the Greek second
line. In spite of the fury and obstinacy of the Albanians, victory for two hours inclined to the side of the
Hellenes, when, either through one of those chances
which exercise such an influence over the fate of battles,
or the blackest treachery, fortune suddenly changed.*
A column of the enemy's infantry having attempted to
turn the right of the Christians, Gogos' soldiers, who

* All the surviving Europeans, who could not observe what was
occurring on the extreme right, expressed themselves convinced that
Gogos purposely lost the battle; the Greek captains, and even Mavrocordato, (although they cannot deny his criminal correspondence
with the Turks,) rather attribute the defeat to accident. A moment
previous to the catastrophe, Vlakhopoulos was conversing with Gogos,
who in answer to the former's enquiry, assured him the peak was properly guarded ; he then walked up the hill, mounted his horse, and
rode off, while at the same instant about fifty Arnauts, with a dozen
of little flags, appeared at the top. Vlakhopoulos, lamed by a fall,
escaped through his knowledge of the Albanian tongue, and that similarity of dress which occasioned continual mistakes ; as they took him
for an officer of their own nation, he, with two of his men, got into a
woody dell and lay hid till night.

were in ambuscade, allowed about 60 of the foremost
to pass, and then pouring in a volley, dispersed the
main body. Those in the van, seeing their retreat cut
off, and anxious to escape, climbed the dominant peak
where Gogos had stationed only a few peasants of
Petta, although he pretended to his colleagues that it
was guarded by his son with 100 picked men. As
soon as Mohammedan bayraks crowned the summit,
the Greeks lost courage, Gogos betook himself to flight,
and the whole cloud of barbarians rushed forwards
simultaneously; Vlakhopoulos and Bozzaris were routed, the enemy advancing along their position, and the
first line saw itself outflanked and turned. The Ionians
and the Greek regulars, who had hitherto fought bravely, gave way, Tarella was slain, and the rear companies
of his regiment exterminated in the village; the sick
also were slaughtered in a house which served as a
hospital, the surgeon Treiber saving himself with difficulty by leaping out of a window, while the Turks
were breaking open the door.

Endeavouring to retire when it was too late, and the
Moslems already masters of Petta, the Philhellenes,
surrounded on all sides, opposed a desperate resistance
to assailing thousands. Two-thirds of those veterans, as
well as their colonel, Dania, fell amidst heaps of Albanian dead; and only 25, cutting their way through, were
saved by the troops of Gogos, who from Mount Skouli-
karia fired upon their pursuers. One-half of the Ionians,
and one-third of the regular regiment, (including its
colonel and 16 officers,) remained on the field of battle;
among the survivors of this bloody fight were, General
Normann, slightly wounded by a shot in the breast, and
Captain Pannas. On the whole, we may estimate the
loss of the Greek army, in killed, at 400, and that of the
Turks at 600. The victors bore off as trophies, two
fieldpieces, and the banner of the Philhellenes; but

the young officer and men who served the former died on their guns; and the standard-bearer only resigned his flag with his life. Very few were taken prisoners, and, after enduring every sort of ill treatment, were beheaded at Arta; two alone escaped that fate, one a Prussian, having some knowledge in surgery, and Lieut.-Colonel Gubernati, who once commanded the regular troops of Ali Pasha, and now effected his eva‑sion, doubtless through the attachment of some of his old comrades.

During the battle of Petta, an Ottoman column marched upon Combotti, and burned the village, Cap‑tain Alexander being too weak to resist; this circum‑stance obliging the vanquished party to retreat to Lan‑gada, along a rugged and circuitous path, the Turks, by an active exertion, might have annihilated them, and seized the defiles of Makrynoros: but, as usual, they slumbered after victory, and evacuated Petta next day.*

Great was the grief of the President when the dis‑comfited chiefs presented themselves before him. Var‑nakiottis hung down his head, and seemed reluctant to enter the tent, until pushed in by Bozzaris, who, con‑scious of having always done his duty, would not quail under adversity. Gogos came with the rest, excusing his flight, and asserting his fidelity; however, two days after, he went over to the Mohammedans.

On the 18th, the President abandoned Langada, and

* May we be permitted to narrate here a trivial anecdote, which will perhaps interest some readers? At noon, on the 16th of July, as Mavrocordato sat at dinner with his suite, at Evangelistra, Theodore Grivas, examining the shoulder-blade of a sheep, according to a me‑thod of divination practised in the East, declared that their friends had experienced a bloody defeat; this caused some mirth at the seer's expense, until a horseman, while they were yet at table, brought news of the fight. Such casual verifications confirm and perpetuate popu‑lar superstitions.

leaving a detachment of irregulars to observe Makrynoros, fell back by Makhalè and Vrakhori to Messalonghi, where terror and discouragement had entirely
paralysed the minds of the people. Mavrocordato having ordered some pieces of artillery to be mounted on
carriages in that town, sent one of his adjutants (Raybaud) to convey them to the camp ; but so difficult was
it for men nursed in slavery to raise their ideas above
petty calculations of gain and loss, that the Primates
spent the whole day of the 16th in disputing with the
workmen, and ended by refusing to pay a miserable
sum of 700 piastres. When the overthrow of Petta was
confirmed, the principal citizens thought of sheltering
their persons and fortunes in the Ionian Islands, and
several of them actually fled to Kalamos. At this critical juncture, the appearance of the grand Ottoman
fleet, steering towards Patrass, and extending its immense line of 96 sail, from the shore of Peloponnesus
to that of Etolia, rendered the sea as dangerous as the
land. The President felt, with reason, the utmost solicitude for the safety of Messalonghi and Anatoliko,
well knowing that on their preservation depended the
existence of an insurrection in Western Greece ; he
therefore hastened thither, animating the people by his
presence and the accession of 400 regular soldiers,
the remains of the two disciplined battalions, and the
skeleton of the Philhellenes ; the first commanded by
Gubernati, the second by Raybaud. Although lagoons
and shallows absolutely prevented ships of war from
approaching Messalonghi, the new Capitan Pasha, Kara
Mehemet, sent in a bullying letter, in which he threatened to destroy the town, by landing 20,000 men at
Krioneri, three leagues to the east of it ; however, he
did not attempt to execute his menace, choosing rather
to cruise peaceably, and amass money, by selling to
mercantile vessels permission to trade with the Greeks.

On the 9th of August, a solemn service was performed at Anatoliko, in honour of the brave men slain
at Petta, Mavrocordato attending its celebration, with
all the ecclesiastical, civil, and military authorities.
This was the last occasion where the Philhellenes, embodied at Corinth, assembled as a corps. Tired and
disgusted with the service, most of the European volunteers immediately afterwards asked and obtained
leave to quit the country. The President was able, for
some time longer, to keep with him the regular regiment, though in a state bordering on dissolution, thinned by desertion, unpaid, and almost naked. At length,
the officers and soldiers who still adhered to their colours, resolved to retrace their steps to Peloponnesus,
and, accomplishing a painful and tedious march along
the northern coast of the Gulf of Lepanto, reached
Athens, (September the 25th,) and once more put themselves under the orders of Prince Ypsilanti.

Scarcely had the sympathy excited by the mournful
ceremony of the 9th time to dissipate itself, when it
was awaked again by the funeral obsequies of the Laconian leader, Kyriakouli.

When Mavrocordato marched in June, Kyriakouli
sailed to the coast of Thesprotia with fifteen barks,
250 Mainatts, and as many Arcadians, lent him by
Kanellos Delhiyani, and posted himself at a place
called Splanga, where he was joined by a few Souliotes.
Omer Vriones having detached a superior force against
him, he could not advance into the country, but repelled several attacks upon his position. In the last
of these engagements, (fought on the fatal 16th of
July,) he was struck on the head by a musket ball,
while looking over the parapet of his tambouria, and
instantly expired : Greece certainly lost in him one of
her most skilful and dauntless warriors. By a singular
coincidence, Ahmed Kihaya, his old antagonist at Val-

tezza and the siege of Tripolizza, was killed in the same skirmish. After the death of their commander his companions evacuated Splanga, and transported his body to Messalonghi, where it was interred with every military honour.

SECTION II.

ON the opposite side of European Turkey, in the fertile Pierian vale, and the ridges of Olympus shaded by thick forests, dwelt a race of Macedonian Armatoles, proud of their name and their numbers, and greatly dreaded by the Mussulmans; yet, notwithstanding their high reputation, the Olympians were very unfortunate, and none of the partial revolts that broke out was more quickly or easily suppressed. Their measures indeed were ill chosen, for they lay still in the former years while the peasants of Chalcidice were employing the Ottoman forces of Macedonia, and declared their rebellion at the precise moment when Aboulaboud Pasha had taken Cassandra by assault, and Athos by capitulation. Being in want of ordnance and ammunition, they sent a deputation to Ypsilanti, who gave them three pieces of artillery, and engaged Raybaud and other European officers to serve in Macedonia: but he committed an error in intrusting the conduct of the expedition to his aide-de-camp, Sala, a man of an indolent and listless disposition. As it was only in the Archipelago that workmen and materials could be procured for mounting the guns, Sala and Raybaud proceeded to Tinos, where the latter, labouring with his usual zeal and assiduity, rendered the ordnance effective; while the former, wandering from isle to isle in quest of pleasure and vain ostentation, wasted upwards of three months, until all his associates, (except one Polish officer,) wearied of his interminable delays, left so dilatory a leader. Had he been more active, it must be confessed that a small supply of men and a few guns would not have much increased the positive strength of the Olympians, but might have produced a moral effect. Besides Sala's misconduct, there were other circumstances adverse to those mountaineers; all the districts did not rise, owing to a discordance of opinion among their captains, and they were drained of 1000 soldiers whom the Psarriotes had taken into pay.

The tract of country where this short campaign was carried on, and in which Perseus contended for his kingdom with the Roman Consuls, extends betwixt the rivers Axius and Peneus, is washed by the Thermaic Gulf, and intersected by the Haliakmon and many smaller streams, falling down from Olympus to the sea. Its population is almost exclusively Greek, while to the north and south of the above-mentioned rivers, Turks are numerous; and to the west, at the back of the mountain, is a region inhabited by Bulgarians, who, although wishing success to the Greeks, declined openly to espouse their cause. The plan of the Armatoles was, to occupy the three points by which alone their territory is accessible, viz. the bridge over the Vardar, the straits of Tempe, and the defiles of Castoria: they were commanded by the Captains Kara Tasso and Diamantis, and by Zaphyris primate of Naousta, the man who, in November 1820, assassinated an emissary of Alexander Ypsilanti, and delivered his papers to the Roumeli Valesi. Having considerable masses ready, the Turks at once moved against them from Macedonia and Thessaly, and, although repulsed at first in two or three petty actions, ultimately triumphed completely. An Ottoman division from Larissa forced the valley of Tempe, and crossing the

Peneus, ravaged Pieria, and opened a communication
with Aboulaboud Pasha, a formidable foe, equally expert in war and policy. Marching on the 1st of April
with an army of near 15,000 men, that Vizier swept
all before him; the city of Kara Veria surrendered
without resistance, and on the 23d he appeared before
Naousta, a town of 2000 houses, eighteen leagues to
the south-west of Salonika. Here he was bravely
withstood, the place being defended by Kara Tasso
and Zaphyris. Following the same system as at Cassandra and Athos, he twice summoned it, but the Armatoles having massacred three priests and a Turkish
officer, who bore the summons, he stormed and burned the town, putting to the sword 4000 Greeks, without distinction of age or sex. His cavalry pursued
the fugitives, made a great carnage, and slew the chief
Zaphyris, whose head and flag were presented to the
Pasha. The victorious Moslems committed horrible
cruelties; 120 towns, villages, and farms of the district of Olympus, were laid in ashes, and the surviving
Christians driven into the most impervious wilds.
There is one remarkable proof of vindictive ferocity
that we cannot pass over in silence. A band of Jews
attended the Pasha's camp voluntarily, in the capacity
of executioners, allured merely by the pleasure of butchering with clubs the Greek prisoners, whom Aboulaboud gave up to them in droves. One of those
execrable savages afterwards boasted that in a single
day he had with his own hands slaughtered 64 victims. It is said that there were 600 of them, but if
all had been as active as the individual just quoted,
the whole population of Macedonia would not have
sufficed for their gratification. The Hebrews thus
barbarously avenged the equally inhuman treatment
of their sect at Tripolizza. During these calamities,
Sala, sailing from Myconos in a Psarrian brig, arrived

on the coast, and landed at Milias, in the vicinity of Dium, ordering the vessel that brought him to remain at hand till he should establish an intercourse with the people of the country. On the evening of next day, about 200 Olympians having ventured down from the hills, and joined him, he disembarked his guns, (two of which were brass six-inch-howitzers,) and his stores, consisting of powder, cannon-balls, and Ypsilanti's proclamations. On the following morning, the Turks, attacking him with superior numbers, cut most of his party to pieces: some got on board the brig, while Sala, and the Pole Leczinski, fled to the mountains, and thence traversing Thessaly on foot, hiding themselves in the daytime, and journeying at night, suffering from fatigue, hunger, and continual apprehension, were happy enough to gain the Hellenic frontier near Karpenizza; Sala reached Corinth thirty-five days after his defeat.

Aboulaboud Pasha returned on the 7th of May to his palace at Salonika, where he utterly divested himself of the mask of clemency he had affected to wear. Not content with putting to a cruel death thousands of male captives, he caused the wife of Kara Tasso, and many other females, to expire in the midst of tortures: even the innocent hostages of Mount Athos perished, although, since the capitulation, their monasteries had given no grounds of offence. Such was the last bloody act of the revolutionary drama played in Macedonia, for if any bands of insurgents still lurked in the woody recesses of Olympus, they could only be looked upon as companies of outlaws. Kara Tasso and Diamantis retreated towards the Pagasetic Gulf, and prosecuted a partisan warfare: the former, when subsequently obliged to quit the mainland, crossed over to the isles of Skopelos and Skiathos, which became the head-quarters of the Olympians.

Inflamed with the direst spirit of revenge for the murder of his wife, Kara Tasso was never afterwards known in any instance to give quarter to a Mohammedan. Diamantis went to Euboea, and was invested with the command of the northern part of that extensive, fertile, and important island. A glance at the map will show how admirably Euboea is situated for bridling Attica and Boeotia, and that the ancients were right in considering the city of Chalcis as one of the keys of Greece. Possessing at Negropont a bridge over the Euripus, and a secure outwork in the castle of Karababa, the Ottomans could scour the rich fields around Thebes and Livadia, and all the Attic coast, as far as Cape Sunium, was exposed to invasion from Carysto. Although neglected and ill cultivated, the island is of great intrinsic value, for, being favoured with a good soil and plenty of water, it produces much corn and wine, without taking into account its forests and marble quarries. The Euboean peasants were among the foremost to take up arms, but scattered as they were, in defenceless villages, they could only, as opportunities offered, annoy an enemy from whose sorties they endured more evil than they inflicted. At the beginning of 1822 the Greeks resolved to undertake its conquest in earnest, and to apply themselves to the reduction of Carysto, the weakest of its two fortresses. Troops were therefore despatched from Peloponnesus, Roumelia, and the Egean Sea, but there was a want of concert and arrangement in their movements. Elias, son to the Bey of Maina, sailed from the Piraeus on the 14th of January with 600 Mainatts and Moreotes, and disembarked near Carysto. On the 24th he was surprised in the village of Stura by a body of 1000 Turks; his soldiers, who had dispersed for the purpose of plundering, fled, and the Beyzade, with a handful of his friends, was surrounded in a mill, which they defended as long as their ammunition lasted. Perceiving that all his companions had fallen, and that the Moslems, anxious to secure a prisoner of such distinction, respected his life, the young and valiant Elias plunged a dagger into his own bosom, and died universally regretted for his patriotism and noble character. This defeat, which was reported to have cost them 150 men, did not induce the Greeks to give up their design on Eubœa: Kyriakouli rallied the Mainatts, Odysseus came to his aid with 600 Roumeliotes, and the Bishop of Andros conducted thither a larger body of troops levied in the Archipelago. During a part of February they observed Negropont, and blockaded Carysto, until bad weather, scanty provisions, and fevers proceeding from those causes, forced them to break up their camp.

The preparations of the Turks at Zeituni attracted Odysseus towards Thermopylæ, and in the first days of March the islanders returned in wretched plight to Tinos. Affairs in Eubœa then went on as they had done before the expedition; that is to say, the Christians were masters of the mountains, the Turks of the towns and plains.

Thessaly was in a state nearly similar, although its revolt had not been so openly pronounced; the cities were occupied by Moslem garrisons, while parties of mountaineers from Othryx, Oeta, and Pelion, made incursions on all sides : their ravages, joined to those of the Ottoman soldiery, converted into a desert the fruitful district of Pharsalus. Mahmoud Pasha of Drama, commanding the Sultan's army in Thessaly, advanced on the approach of spring to the banks of the Sperchius, which separated the posts of the two nations; although beyond its stream, the Turks held the town of Neopatra, or Patradjik, supposed to be the ancient Hypata.

We shall here pause for a moment to enquire into the condition of the people that dwelt near the frontiers, and who were supporting the charges and tasting the miseries of war.

With regard to Eastern Greece, we derive authentic information from the journal of the court of Areopagus,* a tribunal specially instituted to hunt out and rectify abuses. The faithful picture it draws of Phocis, Locris, Bœotia, and Eubœa, is extremely gloomy; living in constant fear of a surprise from the Turks of Zeituni and Negropont, ready to abandon their houses at the least alarm, the wretched inhabitants were obliged to supply from their impoverished substance the necessities of the Greek troops, the central government contributing nothing. Nor was this all they had to complain of, for the captains too frequently tyrannized over the peasants in a most shameful manner. The worst of those local despots was Panourias, commandant of Salona, whom some writers have elevated into a hero, but who was in fact an ignoble robber, hardened in evil. He had enriched himself with the spoils of the Mohammedans of Salona and Vostizza, yet he and his retinue of banditti compelled the people to maintain at free quarters their idleness and luxury, exacting not only bread, meat, wine, and fodder, but also sugar and coffee. Hence springs a reflection that the Greeks had cause to repent their early predilection for Klefthes, or predatory chiefs, who were almost all (beginning with Colocotroni) infamous for the sordid perversity of their dispositions. We have no reason to think that Western Greece was better off than the sister province; but in Peloponnesus and the Archipelago there was less suffering and greater tranquillity.

* Written by Neophytus, Bishop of Talanta, who was kind enough to put it into the author's hands.

As the agglomeration of Ottoman troops in the valley of the Sperchius threatened an invasion on the side of Thermopylæ, the captains of Eastern Hellas, consulting with the Areopagus, deemed it expedient to anticipate the enemy, and to assemble in Epiknemidian Locris the utmost strength they could muster. Fixing their residence at Livadia, the Areopagites exerted themselves in procuring ammunition and provisions, and notwithstanding the deficiency of their funds, engaged the services of 30 vessels and large boats, which transported the division of Odysseus from the north of Eubœa to the opposite mainland. The Hellenic Government had decreed that 3000 Peloponnesians should march to the confines of Eastern Greece, but not above 700 actually went there, under the orders of Nikitas, and Zakharopoulos of Mistra. After their arrival, Odysseus, in his official report, stated his army at 8000 men, from which we may without scruple subtract upwards of one-third. In a council of war, held at Paleokhori, it was resolved to distribute the troops into two bodies; that the first, led by Odysseus, Dyovouniotis, Nikitas, and Zakharopoulos, should act against Zeituni; and the second under Ghouras, Kontoyani, Panourias, &c. against Patradjik. On the evening of April the 12th, Odysseus went with his division on board of the flotilla, and crossing the Malian Gulf, approached next morning the village of Stellida to the east of Zeituni. A small party of Turks endeavoured to hinder their landing, but the Greeks, as fast as they got ashore, took post behind the rocks, and firing from thence checked the enemy, until their disembarkation was completed. They then carried the village, and exterminated the Moslems, by burning the houses where they had shut themselves up: the Christian families of Stellida were sent to the other side of the gulf. On Sunday the 14th (the Greek festival of Easter), the

Knasnadar, or treasurer of Bayram Pasha, advanced
from Zeituni with troops and artillery, in order to dislodge the insurgents, while Odysseus, expecting a vigorous attack, intrenched himself at Agia Marina, another village near the sea.   Nikitas and the Peloponnesians repulsed the Knasnadar with loss, but in the ensuing night they abandoned Stellida, and cutting their way
through the enemy, rejoined Odysseus at Agia Marina;
60 Greeks were killed, and Dyovouniotis passed over
to Euboea, with 95 wounded, 15 of whom died shortly
after.   Unable to storm the position of Agia Marina,
the Turks opened trenches against it, erected a battery,
and gained ground foot by foot. The Greeks defended
it for 15 days, until, disputes breaking out among their
generals, Odysseus proposed its evacuation. The Areopagites hastening thither, opposed this with all their
might, and one of them, Drossos Mansolas, had a violent altercation with the Stratege ; for, being a native
of Thessaly, he considered the occupation of Agia Marina to be important, inasmuch as it would encourage
his countrymen. Odysseus, however, persisted, and
having set fire to the village, reimbarked his army, and
landed near Mendenizza, where many of the soldiers
deserted, and returned home.   Meanwhile, the column
on the left had not as yet made any impression upon
Neopatra; but being reinforced by Nikitas in May,
it had a brilliant affair with the enemy. Two thousand men, marching from Salona to Patradjik, cut to
pieces 200 Turks, stationed outside of the town, stormed the castle, and put the garrison to the sword : half
the place was now in their possession, but the Mussulmans still resisting in some buildings, afforded time for
succours to arrive from Zeituni. The first detachment
met with a repulse, but a second, reckoned at 3000
cavalry and infantry, compelled the Greeks to retire to
the mountains of Aetos. During these operations on

the borders of Thessaly, two distinguished Philhellenes
lost their lives ; the Danish Count de Quelen, (a young
man of rare merit,) slain by a cannon-ball; and Heyne-
man, a Prussian, shot while rushing sword in hand
upon a Turkish tambouria.

The insurgents having thus failed in their attempts
to drive Mahmoud Pasha from the bank of the Sperchius, both parties rested for a time in observation ;
the Turks not being yet fully prepared, and the Greeks
torn by dissension. Their bickerings were then in a
great degree ascribed to the presence of Demetrius Ypsilanti, whose principal motive in coming to Roumelia
was to gain partisans, and organize an opposition to
the existing government. Inflexibly wedded to every
idea he had once taken up, the Prince imagined that
the title conferred upon him by his brother Alexander,
gave him a clear right to the dictatorship of Greece,
and he looked upon his competitors, Mavrocordato, Negris, &c., as rebels and traitors. The persons that habitually attended him, although (excepting Vambas)
they had few good qualities to recommend them, nevertheless possessed art enough to sow disaffection, and
depopularize the executive body and the Areopagites.
The latter, on learning Ypsilanti's intention of visiting
Eastern Greece, sent three remonstrances to the government representing the bad consequences likely to result
from it, but they were not heeded. Prince Demetrius
seems to have entertained hopes of bringing over to his
interest Odysseus, a deeper and more crafty politician,
who was then on ill terms with the ruling party. It
will be proper to delineate at some length the character
of this last-mentioned personage, a perfect master in
the science of dissembling, and who thereby acquired in
the world a reputation for probity, which he was nowise
entitled to. His father, Androuzzos, a famous captain
of outlaws, and a native of Martano, in Opuntian Lo-

cris, fled from his country to Prevesa, after the insurrection of 1770, and being ultimately surrendered to
the Turks by the republic of Venice, died in confinement at Constantinople : his mother was born at Prevesa, where Odysseus first saw the light in 1790.   At
the age of twelve, he lost his father ; and six years later,
his mother having no other children, contracted a second marriage with a medical practitioner named Philip Komano : however, the young Odysseus found a
friend and patron in Ali Pasha, who, struck with the
celebrity of Androuzzos, inscribed his son among the
pages of his court, and had him brought up in the palace of Yannina, a school where only vice could be
learned.   Having given signs of a bold and boisterous
spirit, the youth drew the Satrap's attention, and was
sent by him, at the head of 100 men, into the territory
of Livadia, in order to suppress the noted robber Panourias.   In this commission he succeeded, for having
surprised in a cavern the wife and children of Panourias, the latter went to Yannina, submitted to the Pasha,
and was pardoned.   The marked favour of Ali, as
well as his own natural arrogance, is said to have roused
against Odysseus feelings of resentment in the breasts
of the tyrant's sons, Moukhtar and Veli ; but their
father judging him to be a person altogether devoted
to himself, and capable of rendering service, appointed
him captain of Armatoles, in the provinces of Livadia
and Talanta, which he was endeavouring to wrest from
the Pashalik of Negropont, by fostering intrigues among
the Primates.

Invested with almost unbounded authority in Bœotia,
Odysseus soon showed the effects of a corrupt education
engrafted on a violent and headstrong disposition, indulging, after the example of his master, the passions of
cruelty, lust, and avarice.   His character was a com-
pound of the Greek and Albanian, with the evil quali-

ties of both prominently displayed, without that respect for their faith which is almost universal among the former race. He scoffed at religion, and despised and insulted the priests, differing in that particular from his prototype Ali Pasha, who always affected profound veneration for the superstitions of his subjects. Blood-thirsty, vindictive, and treacherous as an Arnaut, Odysseus surpassed in subtilty and falsehood the most mendacious Greek; he was endowed with an uncommon share of finesse and sagacity, and could at pleasure put on the semblance of virtue. His personal courage was doubtful, and his mistrust excessive, insomuch that he did not dare to disclose where he intended to sleep. With regard to bodily qualifications, he had a robust and vigorous constitution, an imposing presence, and incredible swiftness of foot, having more than once outstripped a horse in running; it is a fable, however, that an exploit of that sort introduced him to Ali Pasha's notice. Delighted with the conduct of his lieutenant, the Satrap of Yannina selected a wife for him out of his own harem, (a beautiful girl of Kala-rites, named Helena,) and obliged the inhabitants of Livadia, Talanta, and Salona to furnish a marriage por-tion, amounting it is said to the value of half a million of piastres. Soon after his nuptials, war began between the Sultan and the Pasha, when the people of those districts which had groaned under the administration of Odysseus rose against him, and chose for their leader Captain Diakos of Loidoriki. At the same time a Turkish corps marching upon Livadia, under Pehle-van Baba Pasha, the citizens drove Odysseus away: he fell back upon Yannina, and thence repaired to the island of Ithaca. Returning to the continent at the commencement of the revolution, he threw himself into the mountains, collected partisans, and on the death of Diakos assumed the command in Eastern

Greece. Odysseus never felt a spark of enthusiasm for
the cause that he embraced ; his prime object was to
avenge himself of the people of Livadia, and this he
accomplished in the two subsequent summers, by putting to death several men of the first families ; his next,
to erect a principality for himself, and to that end he
constantly strove to delude both Greeks and Turks by
letters and protestations, sometimes asserting that he
was fighting for liberty, at other times to punish the
assassins of Ali Pasha, or to obtain redress from the
Sultan. He of course saw, with displeasure, a shadow
of regular government established at Corinth, and was
very jealous of the Areopagus, a tribunal mostly composed of sincere patriots.   Pretending to be disgusted
at the disorder in the army, after the late combats near
Zeituni and Patradjik, he sent his commission of Khiliarch to the Areopagus, with a letter, stating, that he
was resolved to resign the command, and go back to his
family at the expiration of five days. The Areopagites
ordered two captains (Lyapas and Triandafilos) to take
charge of the troops ; but they soon discovered that
Odysseus, far from departing, was busily fomenting a
mutiny among the soldiery. Upon their report, the
Executive despatched Alexis Nouzza, ex-primate of
Zagori, and Christos Palascas, a Souliote, educated in
the service of England, to take cognisance of these
troubles, and invite Ypsilanti to return to Peloponnesus, and discharge there the duties of his office, as president of the legislative body. On their arrival at
Livadia, a great council was held, at which two members of the Areopagus (Anthimos Gazi and George
Ainian) assisted ; the jarring chieftains agreed to a
compromise, and the government commissioners retraced their steps to the Morea, in order to give an
account of what they had seen and heard ; but Ypsilanti refused to accompany them. In a little while

faction was again at work, and many of the inferior
officers drew up a remonstrance against Ypsilanti and
Odysseus, protesting they would no longer serve with
the latter.   About the middle of June, the Executive
sent back Nouzzas and Palascas to Eastern Greece,
with public instructions to the following purport ; that
the first should manage the revenue of that province,
while the second put himself at the head of the militia ;
and that they should summon Odysseus to compear,
and justify his conduct at the seat of government.
There is reason to think that his life was aimed at, and
that a sum of 5000 piastres was offered to Ghouras for
the head of his general : Odysseus certainly apprehended treachery, and took his measures accordingly.
Meeting Nouzzas and Palascas at the village of Dracospilia, in the territory of Mendenizza, he saluted
them amicably, entertained them to supper, and dismissed them with their suite of ten persons to pass the
night in a small church.   Then calling together his
soldiers, he asked them whether they wished to be
commanded by him, or by the new comers ?   On their
replying that they would obey him alone, he told them
to do what they would with his enemies.   They hereupon instantly assaulted the church, and in spite of the
resistance of those within dragged them out, and cut
them to pieces.   It is said that Nouzzas had twice
saved Odysseus at Yannina by his intercession with
Ali Pasha, and that Palascas had once been his intimate
friend.*   Some persons suspected that Ypsilanti was
privy to their assassination ; but it was an action so
foreign to his principles, that we do not in the least
credit the accusation.   He was then, June the 20th,

* Odysseus, long afterwards conversing with some Philhellenes
about the death of these men, remarked, " If I had not killed them,
they would have killed me."

encamped at Velizza, not far from Dracospilia, and immediately afterwards proceeded by the road of Dystomo
to the coast, and crossed over in a boat to Peloponnesus. The murder of the government commissioners
produced total anarchy in Eastern Greece; the Areopagus fled to Salona, the troops dispersed, and confusion reached its acme, just as an Ottoman army was
preparing to rush down upon the province.

SECTION III.

GREAT tranquillity prevailed at Athens during the
first two months of the year 1822 ; the Turks having
walled up the gate of the Acropolis could not attempt
a sortie, and the Greeks seem to have laid aside all
idea of an active siege. Scarcely was a cannon heard,
and even musket-shots became rare ; the bazars were
frequented, and the people of the town repaired their
houses and brought their families. On the 9th of
February, the new court of Areopagus made its appearance there, and after nominating twelve Ephors, continued its progress into Roumelia. In March, however,
the aspect of things underwent a change : the Athenians lost patience, and dreading lest with the approaching fine season a Turkish force should come to blast
the prospect of regaining their citadel, as Omer Vriones
had done in the past summer, determined to try the
effect of a bombardment. Having applied to the Executive, they on the 10th received from Corinth two
mortars, with 200 shells ; and the war minister, Colletti,
directed Monsieur Voutier to superintend the siege. On
the 12th, Prince Ypsilanti visited Athens with an
escort of 100 men, and on entering the gate was saluted
by the Turks with two cannon-shots ; he staid one
day, and then pursued his march towards Thermo-

pylæ. The Greeks placed the two mortars in battery
on the 17th, at the height of the Areopagus, and on the
22d opened their fire, throwing a shell every half hour ;
but 30 was the largest number discharged in any one
day. As they were not always very skilfully thrown,
they destroyed several of the inhabitants by passing
over the fortress, while they did little harm to the
enemy. On the 29th, twelve Philhellenes came from
Corinth with twenty bombs ; but the stock of those
projectiles being nearly exhausted, the mortars were
henceforth only occasionally discharged. The Athenians perceiving the inutility of their bombardment,
began again after Easter to sink a mine under the two
outer enceintes near the gate. They sprung it at daybreak of April the 30th, overturned a bastion, and blew
up about a dozen soldiers of the garrison : 700 Greeks,
headed by twelve European officers, immediately
advanced to storm, but were stoutly repulsed, losing
four killed, and twelve wounded ; the Swedish captain,
Stralembergh, was slain, and two other Philhellenes
slightly hurt. With remarkable perseverance the besiegers commenced working at a new mine, which was
never finished, for various indications rendered it more
than probable, that the citadel must soon fall into their
power. Provisions and ammunition were abundant
within it, but thirst was fast breaking the garrison's
spirit. Since November the Turks were deprived of
the well of the Serpendje, the cisterns were now emp-
tied, and as though Heaven had declared against them,
not a drop of rain moistened the Acropolis for several
months—a circumstance the more astonishing, since the
rest of Attica was refreshed by copious showers, and it
even rained once or twice in the town of Athens. On
the 13th of May, a Mussulman deserter, letting himself
down from the wall, informed the Christians that his
countrymen were brought very low, by a scarcity of

water, and an epidemic malady; on the 27th a Greek
prisoner escaped in like manner, confirmed this intelligence, and added, that the besieged were quarrelling
among themselves. A Greek and a Turk, sent by the
garrison to implore succour from Negropont, were
intercepted by the insurgents on the 13th of the ensuing month, and the same night, two Mohammedan
women, prompted by despair, got out of the fortress ;
their concurring testimony left no doubt of the enemy's
extreme distress. At length, on the 18th of June, two
considerable Agas mounted the rampart, and demanded
a parley with the Athenian Ephors. The Moslems
insisted at first, that the European consuls, on whose
honour they relied, should guarantee the conditions of
surrender ; although those magistrates of course did
not venture to go so far, they yet promised to use their
utmost efforts to have the treaty observed. On the
21st, the following terms of capitulation were signed
in the Austrian consulate, and, at the express desire of
the Turks, in presence of the Austrian, French, and
Dutch consuls.

I. The life and honour of every individual belonging
to the garrison shall be safe.

II. The Turks shall give up to the Greek government half their money, plate, and jewels, and retain
the other half.

III. They shall each keep three suits of clothing.

IV. Any Turks wishing to remain in the city shall
be free to do so, and those who desire to embark, shall
be provided with a passage to Anatolia in European
ships.

V. A quarter of the city shall be assigned them to
inhabit until their departure.

VI. All their immovable property shall belong to
the Greek government.

VII. To-morrow the Greek troops shall take possession of the fort.

The Archbishop, having assembled in his house all the primates and captains, made them swear on the Gospels to observe the articles of this capitulation, after which he subscribed it. On the morning of the 22d, the Athenians occupied their citadel, reaping the fruits of seven months' perseverance, and hoisted the national flag with a salute of five guns : the Ottoman Disdar surrendered his keys to the Archbishop, and the latter handed them over to Captain Panaghy Ktinas, who was named provisional commandant, but lost his life on that very day, in the midst of rejoicing, by the explosion of a cannon he was ramming down. It is asserted by persons worthy of credit, that during the two sieges of the Acropolis near 300 Greeks were killed. The Turkish prisoners amounted to 1150, of whom only 180 were fit to bear arms, the rest being old men, women, and children ; they were almost all sick, and sixty of them died within a few days after their surrender. Besides arms, precious garments, and a great quantity of copper, there were found in the castle 10,000 kiloes* of grain, 30,000 okes of cotton, as much hemp, forty kantars † of silver, many jewels and pearls, 100,000 piastres in money, and abundance of butter, cheese, and honey. The Athenians had now an opportunity of distinguishing themselves, by giving to the other Greeks an example of good faith and generosity, not less conducive to their reputation, than advantageous to their cause. Such behaviour would have made an impression in Europe, and put to silence their political adversaries, who were continually exclaiming against the perfidies they had already been guilty of ; it would have helped them more than many

---

* Of 22 okes each.   † Of 44 okes each.

victories. The best and wisest men at Athens were sincerely anxious that the faith they had pledged should be kept inviolate ; but there was a more numerous party, guided by feelings of revenge and fanaticism, that had very different intentions. Unfortunately, the alarming turn that affairs took at that moment in the neighbouring provinces, aided the criminal designs of the more cruel and treacherous portion of the Athenian people and soldiery. On the 22d and the following days the Turks came down to the town, where they were mostly lodged in the Vayvode's palace ; as, however, the Greeks began on the 24th to infringe the capitulation by massacring two women and two children, the consuls, with a foresight too well justified by the sequel, wrote to Syra to solicit the presence of any European ships of war which might happen to touch there. About the same time peremptory orders were transmitted by the Greek government, enjoining the Ephors to freight merchantmen, and send the prisoners away. Accordingly a contract was signed (July 7th) with a French and an Austrian captain, who agreed to carry the Turks to Tchesme at the price of twenty-five piastres a-head, to be paid in old copper. In order to remove all difficulties, the French consul generously offered to contribute 2000 piastres for the passage of indigent Moslems ; but it soon appeared too evident that the Ephoria was not acting with sincerity. On the 9th there ran a rumour, that a strong Turkish army had reached Zeituni, and this report inflaming the populace, put the captives in peril ; the consuls did all they could to ensure their safety, and next morning came to an understanding with the Ephors, that 250 of them should be embarked on the 11th. Hardly was this arrangement concluded, when intelligence was published that 20,000 Ottomans had forced the straits of Thermopylæ, and were marching upon Thebes and Athens. Consternation pervaded the town, the women and children fled towards Salamis, and the soldiers, headed and incited by Captain Leckas, taking advantage of the general dismay, and favoured by the shameful indifference of the municipality, commenced an indiscriminate massacre of the prisoners. Four hundred of them were put to death, and the others would have shared the same fate, had not they been protected in the consulates, whose sanctuary the assassins were with difficulty persuaded to respect. The three consuls, Messieurs Gropius, Fauvel, and Origone, displayed much resolution; alone, however, with no defence save that of their flags, surrounded, insulted, and menaced, they would not long have been able to hold out, if happily the French schooner of war Estafette had not cast anchor in the Piræus on the 15th of July. The spirited remonstrances and gallant bearing of Monsieur Hargous, who commanded her, overawed the cowardly brutality of the Greek troops, and the base tergiversation of the Ephoria; with two of his officers and seven seamen, he escorted sword in hand to his vessel fifteen of the principal Turks, as well as their families. Perceiving that the popular effervescence was becoming more violent, and that the French consulate was in danger of being forced, he blockaded the Piræus, then full of barks ready to convey the Athenians to Salamis, neither did he allow a single boat to pass, until assured that all the prisoners in the consulate should be delivered up to him. During the discussion, arrived the French corvette L'Active, commanded by Monsieur Reverseaux, who lost not an instant in repairing with a small detachment to Athens, where he rescued and bore off a number of Mussulmans, in defiance of the clamour of 2000 irregulars, who hung around his party, but did not dare to fire. The conduct of those two officers afforded a striking contrast to the meanness, ferocity, and treachery of the insurgents.   On the night of the 16th, the Active and Estafette sailed away, carrying with them 325 Turkish men, women, and children, whom they landed at Smyrna. About 250 still remained in the Austrian and Dutch consulates ; frequently exposed to imminent risk, from the ungovernable fury of a lawless soldiery, and of depraved and barbarous captains, they owed their existence to the vigilance of the consuls, who shipped them off to the coast of Asia as opportunities offered. It was not till the 10th of October (1823) that the last of them departed.   The slaughter of July the 10th at Athens was perhaps the most odious act of cruelty and breach of faith that the Greeks committed throughout the war ; not done on the spur of the moment, or in the heat of battle, as at Navarin and Tripolizza, but after fifteen days of cool reflection.   In vain hath it been alleged, that the enemy's approach rendered the destruction of the prisoners a necessary measure of precaution, since they were sick, unarmed, mostly of the feebler sex, and vessels were waiting to take them away. Equally futile would it be to cast all the blame on the Sciote and Aivaliote refugees, although it is positively true, that they, as well as some Ionians, were continually haranguing the troops, and exhorting them not to spare a single Mohammedan. A declaration of one of the captains, who several days before told the Dutch consul that it was useless for him to undergo so much trouble in procuring ships, because the Turks would never embark, proves that the deed was premeditated, being indeed part of a system adopted by the worst and most degraded Greeks, of exterminating, *per fas et nefas*, every disciple of Islam who fell into their hands.   Yet those very persons were the loudest in their complaints of Turkish inhumanity, and in affected zeal for their own religion which they so deeply disgraced. All we can say in extenuation is, that the worthiest Athenians looked on the transaction with horror and detestation, and by their exertions saved many victims.

APPENDIX

TO

BOOK II.—CHAP. III.

(No. I.)—*List of Turks saved by the Consuls at Athens, and sent to Smyrna.*

325 per French corvette Active, and schooner Estafette, July 16, 1822.
  11 per Austrian brig Montecuculi,   .   August 12, 1822.
  32 per Austrian merchant brig,   . .   August 21, 1822.
  12 per English sloop of war Rose, . .   August 30, 1822.
  33 per French corvette Active,   . . September 30, 1822.
  61 per French corvette L'Arriège,   .   January 20, 1823.
  29 per do.   do.   do.,   . .   March 22, 1823.
  11 per Austrian brig Veneto,   . . .   July 12, 1823.
  31 per English merchant brig Jane, . September 25, 1823.
    5 per Austrian merchant brig,   . . October 10, 1823.

550

The Turks in the castle at the period of its surrender amounted to 1150; of these, however, sixty died immediately, and several women and children either voluntarily remained with the Greeks, or were concealed by them, so that about 500 came to a violent death at Athens or Salamis.

(No. II.)—*Paper communicated to the Author by Signor Origone, Vice-Consul of his Majesty the King of the Netherlands at Athens; translated from the Italian original.*[*]

In the work written by Monsieur de Pouqueville, and entitled a History of the Regeneration of Greece, I have read the following sentence :—" They (the Greeks) would not have proceeded to this extremity, had it not been for the intrigues of the Corsican Origone,

[*] We insert this document in justice to a highly respectable and inoffensive individual, who has been cruelly calumniated by Monsieur Pouqueville.

consul of Holland. Every day, under cover of a flag which he dishonoured, he, by signals, gave the besieged notice of the operations of the besiegers, whether they were working at a mine, or preparing attacks, which, by hastening a capitulation, would have spared many misfortunes to those whom he served with so much zeal." As it is beyond a doubt that this passage is an outrageous insult, not only to me personally, but also to the office I held, in quality of consul to his Majesty of the Netherlands, my honour obliges me to point out how much Monsieur de Pouqueville is deceived. I have too great respect for that gentleman to impute to malevolence so gross a calumny, and I rather wish to believe, that the accounts transmitted to him on Greek affairs have been tainted with that spirit of party which for eight years has afflicted this unhappy country, and that he has thereby been induced to credit what he never ought to have believed regarding a person with whose sentiments he is well acquainted. Faithful to the principles of humanity, and to the instructions of his Majesty the King of the Netherlands, I always observed the strictest neutrality towards the belligerents, but did whatever I could to alleviate the miseries of war. In proof of this assertion, I am able to cite various Greek families redeemed from slavery at my expense, the gratuitous distribution of grain to women in a state of destitution ; and lastly, the fact, that for two whole months the consulate was open to hundreds of poor people who had no refuge but the Dutch flag.

Men rarely enter into intrigues without having some interest in view ; now, I ask what interest I could have in the cause of the Turks ? As Dutch consul, I neither could nor ought to have interfered in such affairs, nor have departed from the line marked out by my government : as Origone, a private individual possessing property in Attica, it was my interest to see the scourge of war removed as soon as possible from that country, and what surer way was there of obtaining my wish than the surrender of the citadel of Athens ? Would this were the only mistake Monsieur Pouqueville had fallen into ! Unfortunately, his book being drawn from materials of no better a texture, is full of similar incorrect details.

So much for facts ! As for the epithet of Corsican, which he applies to me as a term of reproach, Monsieur de Pouqueville ought to recollect, that, if it had not been for another Corsican, he would never have attained to a rank he does not show himself worthy of.

(Signed)   ORIGONE.

NAUPLIA, *December* 1828.

CHAP. IV.

Grand Expedition of the Turks against Greece—Invasion of Peloponnesus—Military and Naval Operations in Argolis and the Argolic Gulf, until the end of September.

SECTION I.

THE storm which had so long been gathering, and
whose approach had been hitherto retarded by a com-
plication of events, at length burst upon Greece at a
moment when she was ill prepared to resist its shock.
From Thrace and Macedonia, the banks of the Danube
and the Strymon, the Sultan's troops traversed the
plains of Thessaly ; while the navies of Turkey, Egypt,
and Barbary, were shaping their course towards the
Gulf of Patrass.   Although these movements were
ostentatiously bruited abroad with a view of intimida-
ting the insurgents, yet neither the voice of rumour,
nor a succession of alarming reports from the frontiers,
could rouse the Greeks, until the enemy had reached
the heart of their country. The fleet had just returned
into port, Eastern Greece was disorganized, and almost
in a state of rebellion ; Peloponnesus slumbering, the
President Mavrocordato waging a disastrous warfare
in Epirus, and the other members of government fond-
ly awaiting the surrender of Napoli di Romania, and
taking a list of its spoils.
On the 27th of June, the Roumeli Valesi, Khourshid
Pasha, arrived at Larissa, and immediately ordered the
corps that was lining the Sperchius to commence offen-

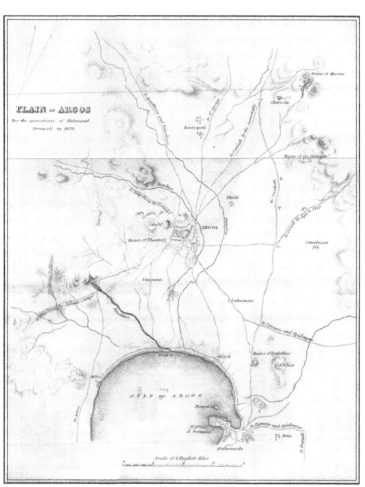

PLAIN of ARGOS

for the operations of Mahmoud
Dramali in 1822.

Ruins of Mycene

Charvatia

Kutzpoeli

to the peninsula

to Corinth by the peninsula

Ruins of the Heraeum

Inakhos

to Tripolizza (a Tenia)

Phuck

to Corinth

Citadel

ARGOS

to Corinth by Agios Oros

Ruins of Theatre

Omorbacan

Vineyards

to Splade camp

to Lelevanara

Kranni

to Leonara and Epidaurus

Genia

Kivek

Ruins of Tyrinthus

Mills

StElias

GULF of ARGOS

Honrda

NAPOLI
& Romania

to Myloi

to Argive and Epidaurus

Aria

to Corinth

Palamede

Scale of 4 English Miles

Engraved by J. Walker

sive operations. It was commanded by Mahmoud Dramali (who had for his lieutenants two viziers, and five
or six pashas of two tails), and having been gradually
reinforced, was said to reckon 30,000 men. The majority of the Greeks declare, without hesitation, that it
amounted to 45,000 ; but we believe that its numbers
in reality did not exceed 20,000.* It consisted chiefly
of cavalry ; but was likewise furnished with a body of
Albanian infantry, a detachment of gunners with a
small train of field artillery, and attended by an immense herd of sumpter-horses, mules, and camels.
Oppressed by the infirmities of age, Khourshid proposed to spend the summer at Larissa, whence he could
superintend the campaign in Greece and Epirus, and
support Dramali with reinforcements and supplies.
About the 5th of July, Mahmoud Pasha crossed the
Sperchius, seized the defiles of Oeta, and penetrated to
Livadia without opposition ; Odysseus having withdrawn into the mountains of Doris two days prior to
his advance. The retreat of the Greek Stratarch was
then generally attributed to treachery, and the magnificent offers of Khourshid. It is no secret that Odysseus was in the habit of corresponding with the enemy,
but he knew the Turks too well to trust them ; and certainly could not, at the head of his 3000 irregulars,
have attempted to stop their march with the least
chance of success.† On the 12th, the Ottomans entered and burnt Thebes, the bishop and inhabitants

* The commissary-general, Kara Osman Oglou, stated it to Mr
Green at 23,000 soldiers, receiving 28,000 rations. Another Turkish
officer assured a friend of the author, that there were not above 15,000
combatants, and 3000 camp followers ; however, they had with them
more than 30,000 horses.

† Talking of this business, Odysseus used the following expressions : " They say, I ought to have fought the Turks ; now I had not
4000 men under my command, not 400 good soldiers, and not 40 to
whose courage I would trust my life."

flying before them; terror preceded their van; and
from Bœotia and Megaris, the trembling Greek population flocked into the isle of Salamis, where the Areopagites also took shelter in the convent of Phaneromeni; those who could not gain that asylum in time,
hid themselves among the hills. Finding the passes
of Cytheron unguarded, the Turks rapidly advanced
to Megara and the great Dervend, which was occupied
by 1000 Peloponnesians under Sekeris, Riga Pala-
mides of Tripolizza, and Agalopoulos. Had this corps
showed the least resolution, the enemy's progress might
have been impeded; intimidated, however, by the sight
of the infidels, and the sound of their artillery, the insurgents fled in confusion, leaving open the road to
Corinth.

The Hellenic government had confided the defence
of the Acrocorinthus to a priest named Achilles (a
client of the Notaras family), with a garrison of 300
men, and provisions for three months; the commandant was esteemed a man of courage, and would, perhaps, have held out, if his soldiers had not abandoned
him. Terrified at the idea of being enclosed by the
Turks, they deserted in small parties, and Achilles,
with the few who remained, thought proper to go off
during the night, and soon after shot himself in a fit
of despair. Amidst the hurry of the evacuation, Kyamil Bey was forgotten; but unfortunately, a soldier
recollecting that the Bey was left behind, turned back,
and firing at him through a cranny in the door of his
chamber, laid him dead on the spot. His wife, sons,
and surviving servants, regained their liberty, and went
to Constantinople. The joy of Mahmoud Pasha was
equal to his surprise, when, on approaching Corinth,
he learned from the lips of a female slave, who hastened
to meet him, that the Greeks had quitted the fort.
Finding himself, at the end of a bloodless campaign

of ten days, master of the Acrocorinthus, it is no wonder if he expected easily to complete the conquest of
the Peninsula. Nevertheless, he already began to experience the bad effects of having marched too fast,
without taking any precaution to secure his communications. Megaris was strewed with the carcasses of his
beasts of burden ; and on the 16th, while he was celebrating the occupation of Corinth, a body of militia,
belonging to the villages of Kondoura and Villia,
defeated a convoy on its way to join him, killing 20
Turks, and capturing two pieces of brass ordnance, and
60 loaded mules. His lieutenants advised him to halt,
and wait the arrival of reinforcements and supplies
promised by Khourshid ; but he answered that he was
in no fear of starving, as long as the Greeks had any
provisions : indeed, it cannot be doubted that he was
right in pushing on to Napoli, and that his subsequent
reverses arose from his neglecting to guard the defiles
between Corinth and Argos, and from the dilatory and
injudicious movements of the fleet, which frustrated
his hopes of naval co-operation. With so much rapidity
did the Ottoman general press forwards, that the Greek
government was at the same instant informed of his departure from Zeituni, and the loss of the Dervend : this
last piece of intelligence, brought by a mass of flying soldiers, had scarcely transpired, when it was announced
that Corinth had fallen. Some Hydriote and Spezziote
vessels lay in the gulf, ready, at the expiration of another
week, to carry away the garrison and inhabitants of
Nauplia, while the executive and legislative bodies resided at Argos, which was crowded with troops and refu-
gee families, from different parts of Greece. The unexpected approach of the Turks filled this multitude with
extreme consternation : the military men, who had assembled for the purpose not of fighting but of plundering, mostly dispersed ; and so utterly panic-struck

were the insurgents, that 40 horsemen, sent from the
Isthmus by Dramali, entered Napoli on the 18th, encouraged the Disdar with assurances of speedy relief,
and returned to the Pasha's camp, without a hair of
their heads being hurt.   Wanting confidence in themselves, and sharing the universal dismay, the members
of government thought of retiring to Tripolizza, and
deliberating in concert with the Peloponnesian Senate;
but as the latter rejected their overtures, the sole remaining resource was, to hurry to the Mills, and go on
board the vessels anchored there : the people of Argos
took the same direction, and the road to Lerna was
covered with thousands of fugitives.   In this crisis,
the Mainatts, who would have reputed it a disgrace to
have gone back to their mountains as poor as they left
them, determined to indemnify themselves for the disappointment they had experienced, with regard to the
wealth of Nauplia.   Not content with ransacking the
houses at Argos, they placed ambuscades on all the
roads, and stripped their countrymen without the least
compunction, or making any exception in favour of
the senators and ministers.

Nor was this all; seeing a vast crowd collected at
the Mills, and detained as well by the paucity of barks,
as the extravagant demands of the seamen, the Laconians suddenly raised a cry of Turks ! that in the
flight, which was sure to ensue, they might have a
fresh opportunity of exercising their talents for pilfer-
ing.   Many of the poor people in their anxiety to escape plunged into the sea ; when they succeeded in
embarking, they found themselves a prey to the avidity
of a new set of harpies, the Hydriote and Spezziote
boatmen, who violently seized the last fragments of
their property, and deposited them on distant points of
the Morea and the Archipelago, without any means of
subsistence save casual charity.   While such scenes of

timidity and shameless rapine dishonoured Greece, and seemed to prove that her sons neither deserved nor were capable of acquiring independence, Prince Demetrius Ypsilanti displayed a bright contrast, and summoning up an energy supposed to be foreign to his character, did every thing that courage and prudence could inspire for the salvation of his country. Rallying around his person a few hundred soldiers, his first care was to consume with fire the standing corn in the plain of Argos, and to destroy every sort of provision in the town and villages ; then devoting himself to the cause of Hellas, he ascended to the ruined fort of Larissa, carried up as much food, water, and ammunition as the shortness of time would allow, and heaped up loose stones against its numerous breaches. His object was to amuse the Turks until the arrival of Colocotroni, on whom the eyes of the nation were fixed, and who was advancing by forced marches, having received from the Moreote Senate the brevet of General-in-Chief.

Whilst Ypsilanti was making these dispositions for a defence of a few days, the Turkish vanguard entered the plain on the 23d, and Dramali, who followed two days after, with the main body and the baggage, despatched Ali Pasha (formerly Bey of Argos) with a corps of cavalry to Napoli, where the inhabitants expressed their satisfaction by firing a salute of 500 guns. The Greek scribes, on the earliest intimation of a change of circumstances, endeavoured under various pretexts to get out of the place, but many of them were arrested, and added to the number of hostages. Nicholas Stamatelopoulos, who had so long and so strictly blockaded the fortress, withdrew to Lerna, and his soldiers mostly retreated to the monastery of Avgo (or the egg), on the road to Kranidi : Petro Bey encamped at the Mills, close to the sea-shore.

The plain of Argos stretches nine miles in length,

in the direction of north and south, from the mouth of
the defiles leading to Corinth, to the head of the gulf,
and about six miles in breadth.   There is a space of
three miles from the 'town to the sea, and a straight
line drawn betwixt them intersects nearly midway the
road along the beach from Napoli to Lerna, each of
which points is two leagues from Argos. During half
the year, all the lower part of the plain towards the
gulf is a swamp, but in the summer heats there are
only marshy ditches ; the upper part near the hills is
firm and dry at every season. Argos is at a mean distance of 27 miles from Corinth, Tripolizza, and Epidaurus, and taking it as a centre, we may enumerate the
following issues from its basin :—1. On the north to
Corinth, by the defiles called Dervenakia, leaving Mycenæ to the right hand.—2. On the north-west to Corinth, by the large village of St George and the ruins
of Nemea.—3. On the north-east to Corinth, by the
defile of Agion Orós, leaving Mycenæ to the left hand.
—4. On the east through an open valley to Epidaurus,
having Mount Arachneus to the left.—5. Along the
eastern shore of the gulf to Kranidi and Hermione.—6.
Along the western shore of the gulf to Astros, and into
Laconia.—7. Up the bed of the Inachus, and over Mount
Artemision, by Torniki, to the plain of Tripolizza.—
8. By the pass of Portus into the plain of Tripolizza,
near the ruins of Mantinea.—9. On the south-west to
Tripolizza, by the old road of Tegea, across Mount
Parthenius.   The town of Argos covering a wide
space of ground, had before the war a delightful appearance, being interspersed with gardens full of orange,
lemon, fig, and mulberry trees : it is sheltered on the
north and north-west, by the conical rock of Larissa
(whose summit is at an elevation of 900 feet above the
level of the sea), and the flat-topped hill of Phoroneus ; passing along the base of the latter, the broad,

white, and stony bed of the Inachus skirts the town.
There is seldom a drop of water in its channel; but
after heavy rains, or the melting of snow, it rolls a
fearful torrent, sweeping every thing before it. The
citadel of Larissa, or Aspis, founded in remote antiquity, still shows traces of Hellenic architecture,
although the modern works forming three lines of
ramparts, and as many separate castles, are almost
entirely Venetian. Were its beautiful cisterns repaired, it would be a strong fort, since, owing to its
height, neither cannon nor mortars can make an impression, and it is not easy to block it, because the peak
on which it stands communicates with Mount Chaon,
and other hills running up to the great Arcadian chain.
At a short league from Argos, on the high-road to
Tripolizza, from beneath the rocky roots of Mount
Chaon, and overarched by a spacious cavern,* bursts
forth the river Erasinus, a clear, deep, and copious
stream, supposed to drain off the waters of the lake of
Stymphalus. It is immediately dammed up by a stone
dike, with five apertures, directing the river into as
many channels, confined by walls, and crossed by sundry little bridges, at a hamlet called Kefalaria, just below the point of separation; after winding through the
plain, turning a variety of mills, and replenishing the
ditches which intersect the vineyards of Argos, its
main branch falls into the sea, at a place termed Ge-
phyri (or the bridge) between Napoli and Lerna.
Those who go directly from Nauplia to Tripolizza,
land at the small village of the Mills, a row of buildings on a narrow slip, compressed betwixt the gulf
and the celebrated marsh of Lerna, in the midst of
which is the unfathomable Pool of Halcyone: an immense body of fresh water here rushes from the swamp

---

* In this cave the ancients sacrificed to Bacchus and Pan; it now
contains a chapel dedicated to St Sophia.

into the sea, its course not exceeding a few yards. The Argos road turns this bog, passing along the foot of a stony height (where there are some remains of an old castle), within musket-shot of the Mills, and ascending for four leagues, rejoins, near Agladocampos, the route from the former town to Tripolizza. A mile to the east of the Inachus, another lesser river, the Panizza, dry for nine months of the year, comes down from the mountains of Portus, and loses itself in the wet ground, near the gulf.

The first resistance Dramali met with was at Kouzzopodi from a party of Mainatts under one of the Bey's sons, who bravely defended an old church, and then effected their escape in the night. As Ypsilanti had calculated, Larissa attracted the whole attention of the Turks, and instead of proceeding, as they ought to have done, to the Mills, and seizing the Greek magazines, they, on the 26th, drew the bulk of their army round Argos, dislodged the insurgents from its houses and gardens, after a great deal of desultory firing, drove them to the castle, and sent in a summons to surrender. Prince Demetrius received the bearers of this proposal with apparent indifference, regaled them out of the small stock of luxuries reserved for his own table, and declared his resolution of holding out for six months. As he did not conceal his name, the Ottomans were entirely possessed with the idea of taking so important a personage, whom they looked upon as the author of the war; they placed their train of six field-pieces on the hill of Phoroneus, and thence threw shot at the monastery below the castle, where Ypsilanti had stationed 100 men, while around Larissa a continual roll of musketry was kept up day and night. At the same time, Colliopoulo, sent in advance by his brother-in-law Colocotroni, reached the Mills, at the head of 1200 soldiers, and marching towards Argos without the least delay, engaged in a skirmish, which produced no result except the loss of a score of lives on each side. On the 28th, a boat from Spezzia brought the alarming intelligence that the grand Ottoman fleet had been seen off Hydra, steering towards the Argolic Gulf. The shock caused by such information was too severe for the nerves of the Greeks, and there was reason to apprehend a general dispersion ; the vessels, on board which the members of government were embarked, got under weigh, and one of them sailed as far as Port Tolon, when it was fortunately hailed by a Hydriote brig, whose captain assured the government that the armada had stood on its course to the S.W. and doubled Cerigo ; thereby casting away the fairest opportunity that ever offered itself for the subjugation of Greece. So deeply did the Peloponnesians despond at the period of Dramali's invasion, that all their primates and generals, with the solitary exception of Ypsilanti, coincided in an opinion emitted by Krevatas of Mistra, that there remained no hope for them but in the protection of England. Two Senators (Poniropoulos of Pyrgos, and Zaffiropoulos) undertook therefore a journey to Zante, where, in the lazaretto, they had repeated conferences with an Ionian protopapas named Garzzouris. Their mission, which gave birth to a thousand reports of English intrigues, led to no arrangement ; nevertheless, it was useful to the Hellenic cause by encouraging the people, and served to mark that propensity to British connexion which the notables of the Morea have ever cherished.

Besides Prince Demetrius Ypsilanti, there were shut up in Larissa, Colocotroni's eldest son Panos, who was then Politarch* of Peloponnesus, two sons of Petro Bey, and 800 soldiers. Not knowing how long their resources might last, and anxious to relieve them, the

---

* Commandant of the Military Police, or Gendarmerie.

Greeks determined to hazard an attack, and to commence it in the evening when they thought the enemy's cavalry would be less formidable. Accordingly,
Colliopoulo moved at sunset of the 29th, and the fire
was maintained till past nightfall; the Peloponnesians
at length gave way, and were pursued to the Erasinus,
but Ypsilanti, Panos Colocotroni, and the Beyzade
George, profited by this diversion to get out of the
castle with fifty men, and repaired to Lerna, leaving the
Beyzadè John to defend Larissa. About eighty Greeks
were killed in the affair, the Turkish horse that followed them doing very little execution, and hardly
making use of their sabres.   The Christians ascribed
their defeat to the cowardice of a priest carrying a
standard, who turned his back and fled; for which
misconduct he was shot next day.   Immediately after
this engagement, Colocotroni descended from the mountains of Tripolizza with 2000 men, and by the activity
and energy he manifested, and the air of confidence he
put on, infused courage into the insurgents.   He despatched on his march couriers to all the districts of the
Morea, ordering them to forward their contingents,
and threatening a terrible chastisement in case of disobedience: this measure, joined to the return of many
Mainatts and other deserters, who had gone to lay up
their booty in places of security, having enabled him to
collect 7000 soldiers, he resolved to give battle to the
enemy.   On the evening of the 1st of August, Ypsilanti led the troops from Lerna, to Colocotroni's camp
at Kefalaria, and before daylight on the 2d, the whole
advanced towards Argos, and repulsed the hostile outposts to the entrance of the town.   The Turks pointed
their artillery against them, and the action was warm,
especially in the vineyards; it did not, however, last
very long, for Colocotroni, who was posted on a hill to
the left of the highway, having commanded his body-

guard to fire a volley, the Greeks below, supposing that
the Moslems had gained their flank, instantly fled, and
were chased by cavalry almost to the Mills, which the
conquerors might easily have taken had they not been
deterred from attempting it by a discharge of musketry
from the neighbouring tambourias : 125 Peloponnesians were slain, and Ypsilanti, who always fought
in the front, being obliged to dismount in order to cross
a ditch, was in great danger of being made prisoner.
As the Turks were satisfied with remaining masters of
the field, this action wrought no change in the relative
situations of the two parties ; a considerable body of
Greeks, indeed, went off to their villages, but reinforcements from the interior of the Morea supplied their
place ; Colocotroni kept up the spirit of his men, and
his dispositions were extremely judicious. Resting his
right flank on the Mills, he posted his left wing (where
the bulk of the army was) behind a rampart of stones,
among the craggy roots of Mount Chaon, and just in
front of the fount of the Erasinus ; similar intrenchments were thrown up on the bank of the river, at the
small bridges, and along the dikes. A detachment
held an isolated tumulus about a mile in rear of his
left, where a path branches off to Torniki, and other
little corps watched the mountain passes leading into
Arcadia by the Artemisian ridge. He thus commanded
with his wings the two high-roads from Napoli and
Argos to Tripolizza, while the Erasinus covered his
front, and being lined by companies of sharpshooters,
presented, as well as the vineyards and muddy ditches,
an impenetrable obstacle to the enemy's horse. His
magazine was at the Mills, where the Greeks had previously deposited a cargo of corn, taken out of a Maltese prize. The numbers of his army fluctuated from
6 to 10,000, but 8,000 rations were given out daily.
In this position the Peloponnesian general waited for

the retreat of the Turks, which he foresaw must soon
happen, and then he hoped to be able to strike a decisive blow.   Mahmoud Pasha had brought with him a
large stock of live cattle, but, besides sharing it with
the starving people of Napoli, his followers so lavishly
wasted their resources, that meat was sold in the town
at ten paras an oke ; and the insurgents having removed or destroyed every kind of grain, the country furnished only unripe grapes.   The excessive use of this
fruit produced fevers in his army, and the soldiers,
straggling through the vineyards, continually fell into
ambuscades laid for them by the Greeks.   Thirst likewise afflicted the Mussulmans, for the remarkable sul-
try summer of 1822 dried up most of the wells and
springs in Argolis.   Still more intolerable was the disorder arising from the pride and indiscipline of a multitude of Beys of Thrace, Macedonia, and Thessaly,
who, with their vassals, composed the Serasker's brilliant cavalry ; little disposed to obedience, they were
always ready to fight with each other, and once, at least,
a quarrel about the distribution of rations brought on
something like a regular engagement amongst them.
They did not, however, show so much pugnacity in
their operations against the rebels, a circumstance attributed to the severity of Dramali, who, displeased with
the conduct of his troops at the attack of Argos, and
with their wandering in the vineyards, killed three of
them with his own hand, and thus rendered himself
hateful in their eyes.   Some of his foraging squadrons
scoured the road to Epidaurus, and burned Ligourio,
and several convents, but such exploits availed him
little.   With Northern Greece the Pasha had no longer
any communication, for the Megarians had reoccupied
the grand Dervent, and even the Isthmus was infested
by foes : Nikitas, on his return from Roumelia, traversed it without opposition, almost treading on the heels

of the Turks; and Emanuel Tombazi sailed up the Saronic gulf with a Hydriote flotilla, landed at Cenchreæ, and seized all the corn in the warehouses there, regardless of the garrison of the Acrocorinthus. Hitherto, since the capitulation signed on the 30th of June, no hostilities had passed betwixt the forts of Napoli and the castle of the Burj, in spite of Dramali's reiterated injunctions, and a strong inclination on the part of the Greek government to set fire to the city.

Captain Jourdain, a Frenchman who pretended to great skill in pyrotechny, had promised the Executive Council, that he would accomplish their design by means of incendiary balls of his invention, and was in consequence appointed commandant of the Burj, the Philhellenes Hastings, Hane, Anematt, and Jervis, volunteering to assist him, and act under his orders. While he was busied in preliminary arrangements, an alarm arose as to the coming of the Ottoman fleet, whereupon the doughty Monsieur Jourdain jumped into a boat, and appeared no more at the Burj, where the direction of the artillery devolved upon Captain Hastings, a man of a firmer mind. On the other side, Dramali insisted that the Nauplians should send him the heads of the Greek hostages, and should batter the insular castle, whose garrison he endeavoured in vain to buy over by the offer of 150,000 piastres. To enforce his commands, he went from Argos with an escort of 300 men to the gates of the town, intending to enter it; but as the citizens refused to admit more than fifteen of his attendants; he desisted from that purpose, and pitched his tent at the village of Aria, outside of the wall. Nevertheless he succeeded in obliging the governor Ali Pasha to break the tacit armistice which he had been observing. The 1st of August was spent in preparation, and at daybreak on the 2d, a heavy cannonade commenced, and was answered with spirit from thirteen guns and a mortar,

mounted on the Burj ; the fire ceased at noon, began
again towards evening, and continued till it was dark.
At eleven o'clock, however, the Hydriote captains Sakh-
touri and Bulgari arriving in a pinnace, advised the
garrison to fire as much as possible during the night,
to annoy the Nauplian Turks, who were known to be
averse to this violent step of Dramali : accordingly a
hot cannonade was renewed for upwards of an hour.
The 3d and the two following days presented an exact
repetition of the scenes of the 2d, the Greeks pointing
all their shot against the houses, which suffered very
much, so that on the forenoon of the 3d, some of the
inhabitants called to the Christians from the nearest
point, begging that their dwellings might be spared,
since the firing was altogether the work of Mahmoud
Pasha, and contrary to their inclinations. On the side
of the Turks the cannonade gradually slackened, and
entirely ceased on the 6th, when they requested a ces-
sation of hostilities ; but this the insurgents refused,
and fired the whole day, without receiving a single shot
in reply. During the interchange of bullets, the ramparts of the Burj sustained considerable injury, and
three pieces of artillery were dismounted on the 2d and
3d : of the Kranidiote soldiers who defended it, none
were killed, and only two wounded. While the contending parties were thus burning powder at Napoli,
the Ottomans obtained their darling object, the occupation of the citadel of Argos ; his provisions and water
being at an end, John Mavromikhalis abandoned it in
the night of the 3d, and, favoured by a false attack, rejoined his friends with little loss. It was reported that
the Greeks owed their escape to the avidity of the Albanians, who, eager to be the first in plundering the fort,
allowed them to pass. The Turks expected to find in
Larissa copious supplies, and their disappointment was
extreme on discovering that it was quite empty, and

perfectly useless to them ; upon which they began to
go off in bands towards Corinth. Afraid of famine,
weak in infantry, harassed by affairs of outposts, and
not conceiving himself strong enough to force Colocotroni's lines, Dramali resolved to fall back upon the Isthmus, and to await there the Capitan Pasha's appearance
on the eastern coast of the Peninsula. Quitting therefore the village of Aria on the 5th, he retraced his steps
to Argos, sending at the same time his Greek secretary
to the head-quarters of the Christians to propose an
accommodation ; but the insurgents listened with disdain to the words submission and amnesty, and detained
the messenger. Suspecting his design from certain indications confirmed by the reports of prisoners and deserters, the vigilant Colocotroni adopted measures for intercepting the enemy's retreat, and marched in person
at the head of 1000 men to St George, while Ypsilanti,
Nikitas, and Dikaios Papa Flessa, went with 2000 or
3000 more to post themselves in the passes of Dervenaki
and Agion Oros : Petro Bey remained to command the
troops at Lerna, chiefly consisting of Mainatts and
Kranidiotes.

The canton of Argos is separated from those of Corinth, Sicyon, and Phlius, by a hilly belt on one side
touching the Saronic Gulf, and on the other connected
with Mount Cyllene, and the summits about the lake
of Stymphalus : the south-eastern exposure is stony, but
to the north it is a white, rotten, chalky soil, disfigured
and hewn into precipices by the torrents which are
always washing portions of it away. Although we have
already recapitulated the roads, or rather mule-paths,
between Corinth and Argos, yet we shall now dilate
further on that subject. The most circuitous but most
commodious path issues from the plain at its north-
western corner, crosses some open hills, and descends

on the village of St George, in a long valley noted for
the extent of its vineyards, and the quality of its red
wine ; * travellers then turning to the right pass by the
ruins of Nemea, under Mount Apesas, remarkable for
its table top, and near Cleonæ enter the labyrinth of the
Aspra Khomata, or white lands, mentioned above : the
whole distance to Corinth this way is about ten hours.
The second and more frequented road offers two hours
of plain, and two of narrow defiles called the Dervenakia, where, among rocks and trees, there is a choice of
two paths ; one at the bottom of the valley, in the bed
of a brook, the other, termed Agio Sosti, winding pain-
fully along the flank of the rugged acclivity above : on
leaving the pass, there is the pleasant vale of St Basil,
where this route joins the former one. To the east a
third road goes directly from Napoli to Corinth, by the
village of Birbati, and the Kleisura or Agion Oros ;
this last is steep, rough, and ill calculated for horsemen.

Mahmoud Pasha having through a fatal oversight
omitted to occupy these straits, the Greeks by a flank
march got there before him, and enhanced their natural
difficulties by felling trees, and piling up stones. The
Serasker encamped on the evening of the 5th at the
village of Hirvati (close to Mycenæ), preparing to execute his retreat next day, and hardly, as it would seem,
anticipating resistance. His Albanian infantry took
the road of St George, and with their usual sagacity
keeping the mountains, and avoiding beaten paths,
reached Corinth in safety, losing only three men who
missed their way : the cavalry was less fortunate. Before day broke on the morning of the 6th, the head of
the Ottoman column penetrated into the Dervenakia,
and had almost got through to the plain of St Basil,

* At the upper end of this valley, are traces of the city of Phlius.

when it suddenly encountered Nikitas and Ypsilanti,* whose troops showered down musket-balls upon the enemy from behind the overhanging rocks : the struggle was most violent on Agio Sosti, where Nikitas fought in person, and where the two parties came to action sword in hand around a leading Mohammedan standard. The Turks, however, suffered more from their own weight and impatience to emerge out of fire than from the blows of the insurgents, for their horsemen crowding blindly on each other, numbers rolled down the precipices. Many nevertheless, although dismounted, succeeded in breaking through to Cleonæ, and their rear turned back towards Argos, leaving the defile encumbered with arms, horses, and dead bodies, whose mouldering bones still arrest the traveller's attention. Learning the disasters of his vanguard, Dramali halted for that and the ensuing day at Mycenæ, while the commandant of Corinth endeavoured to clear the road for his general, by bringing, on the 7th, three pieces of artillery to the plain of St Basil, and ineffectually cannonading the Greek position at Agio Sosti. On the 8th the Serasker essayed the passage of Agion Oros, which was guarded by the Archimandrite Dikaios. Here he experienced heavier misfortunes, for Ypsilanti and Nikitas having by a flank movement joined Papa Flessa, they disposed an ambuscade in the narrowest part of the Kleissoura, and had Yatrako done his duty, and come up in time, it is probable that very few Moslems would have escaped. This, like the previous affair, was rather a massacre than a battle, the cavalry defiling under the musketry of the Greeks, and whole squadrons tumbling headlong into the abyss beneath them.

* It is evident that on this, as on many other occasions, fortune was highly favourable to the insurgents ; for Ypsilanti assured the author, that being on his march to Megaris, he unexpectedly met the Turks in the Dervenakia.

Surrounded by a troop of faithful attendants, Dramali himself passed the danger, amidst the hootings and taunts of the Peloponnesians, who recognised him, and with the loss of his sword and turban : another Pasha of two tails, from the vicinity of Serres, was shot by a soldier at the moment Nikitas was stepping forward to take him alive, and his head sent to the Hellenic government.   It is no wonder that in the plenitude of exultation the insurgents exaggerated the slaughter of their foes, stating it at 5000, and allowing on their own side but 47 dead and wounded.   In the actions of the 6th and 8th of August, about 2000 Turks were killed, including a good many camp followers ; in other respects their losses were immense, consisting of the treasure of the army, all its baggage, 400 cavalry horses, 1300 sumpter-horses and mules, and from 500 to 700 camels taken, - besides a vast number of horses slain.   The captors afterwards sold camels at half-a-crown a-head, and fine steeds at the price of a few shillings, and for a month the towns of the Morea resembled auction marts, rich dresses and arms being hawked about the streets from morning till night.   This prodigious booty assisted the evasion of the Ottomans, as the Greeks eagerly threw themselves on the baggage which came in the rear ; 300 horsemen, who guarded it, being unable to pass, fell back under the walls of Napoli.   Mahmoud Pasha had brought with him six six-pounder brass guns, one of which he conveyed to Nauplia, and the other five, abandoned at Argos, were immediately sold to the brothers Condouriotti.   Too happy to gain Corinth, with the wrecks of his army, the Serasker encamped there, and applied for succour to the Capitan Pasha, and Yussuf, governor of Patrass and Lepanto, representing that he was very short of provisions : they accordingly sent him five transports loaded with wheat and rice from Constantinople and

Alexandria. As was customary after victory, most of the Greek troops dispersed in order to sell their plunder; Ypsilanti and Nikitas crossed from Piada to Roumelia, the former having, at his own request, been intrusted with the defence of the Dervend, and the brother of the latter, Captain Nicholas, drawing together 800 men, resumed the blockade of Napoli di Romania. As the garrison was strengthened by a corps of cavalry cut off from Dramali's main body, Ali Pasha, who commanded there, attempted to hold the adjacent plain, its possession being necessary to afford his horses fodder. This occasioned frequent skirmishes, almost invariably to the disadvantage of the Mohammedans. The Greeks however met with a check on the 20th, when, in spite of the fire of two gunboats, one of their outposts was overpowered and pushed into the sea, losing 30 men. On the 26th the Turks venturing in force beyond Tyrins, all the troops of Captain Nicholas, and those of Petro Bey about Lerna and Argos, alarmed by a signal from the Burj, advanced to attack, and after a smart musketry fire, compelled them to retreat, the enemy's numerous cavalry being deterred from charging by the appearance of a small party of Greek officers mounted on horses recently taken. Nicholas, who was always distinguished for daring valour, alone killed five or six Mussulmans, but unluckily attaching himself to the pursuit of one extremely well-dressed and equipped, and seizing his bridle, the Turk in despair drew a pistol and shot him through the head. His death damped the joy of the insurgents, who otherwise would have had reason to be pleased with their success, since, at the cost of two killed and five wounded, they drove the Ottomans under their batteries, and brought in 26 heads, 20 horses, and several mules and camels.

Captain Staicos of Dimizzana assumed in place of Nicholas the direction of the blockade, and performed that service with great care and diligence. At this period the plain of Argos, having been for a month the theatre of continual combats, was strewed with hundreds of human trunks in a state of corruption, while the dissevered heads were laid in heaps at Napoli and Lerna. The members of the Executive and Legislative Councils, who had rarely trusted their persons ashore for fear of the Turks and of Colocotroni, tired of so monotonous a life on shipboard, now transferred the seat of government to St John of Thyrea, near Astros, and languished there unnoticed. The happy result of his defensive operations, exalted the reputation and redoubled the power of their antagonist General Colocotroni: his name became a sort of talisman, the people every where sung ballads in his honour, his political adversaries humbled themselves before him, and for some months he was absolute in the Morea. To his credit, however, it must be said, that the sole revenge he exacted from the jealous and now trembling primates, was limited to affrighting them by a haughty and menacing demeanour. From St George he moved to Souli, a village of Sicyonia, on the edge of the plain stretching towards Corinth; here a detachment of his troops was beaten on the 22d, in a partial engagement with those of Dramali, whose horse falling in amongst them on level ground, sabred a great number of soldiers, as well as their chief, Anagnosti Pettimezà. Judging, nevertheless, that the Serasker would not be tempted to quit the shore of the gulf, and hazard a march into the hilly country, Colocotroni went (September the 7th) to Tripolizza, where the inhabitants marked their grateful sense of his exploits by giving him a brilliant reception.

SECTION II.

THE grand Turkish fleet, after its junction with that of Egypt, sailed to Peloponnesus, and passed within sight of Hydra, just as Mahmoud Pasha was executing his invasion of Argolis, when the approach of a few ships might have decided the fate of the Revolution. Peaceably navigating, without a thought of the great things they could have effected, the Mohammedans, in the first days of August, received on board their new admiral, Mehemet Pasha. Since Colocotroni's departure in June, Patrass had not been molested, and if a small corps of insurgents under Zaimi and Londos showed itself on the neighbouring hills, it was rather with a view of protecting their own lands and villages than of annoying the garrison. Elated by the first reports of Dramali's progress, Yussuf Pasha undertook an expedition up the Corinthian Gulf, and landing at Vostizza, destroyed a one-gun battery. Ere long more desponding accounts arrived, and the Serasker, forced to retrograde, craved succour from his colleagues, who were anxious rather to enrich themselves than to preserve his army from ruin: love of money was uppermost in their minds, and they heeded not the public service. While they obliged the Sultan's troops to purchase bread extracted from the imperial magazines, they, on the payment of a stipulated retribution, opened to speculators from the Ionian Islands the ports of the gulf they were professing to blockade, thus enabling the Greeks to dispose of the currants, which otherwise would have been of no value to them. All parties, whether Christian or Mohammedan, were well satisfied with this convenient arrangement, except the famished soldiers, who gradually exchanged their arms for food. But such lucrative repose could not last for ever; it was urgent to do something for the relief of Napoli, and therefore the Capitan Pasha weighed anchor from Patrass on the 8th of September, and steered for Cape Malea, near which he was detained by contrary winds. The Greeks were aware of his approach, and twenty Psarrian vessels having joined those of Hydra and Spezzia, the combined fleet, of near 60 sail, cruised at the mouth of the Argolic Gulf, under the orders of Miaulis: as an attack was apprehended on the town of Spezzia, which is incapable of defence, its population emigrated to Hydra, and Panos Colocotroni, with 300 men, occupied the empty houses.

At sunrise of the 20th, the Ottoman navy of eighty-four ships of war was descried in the south-west quarter beating up towards the isles, and next morning it was within a league of Spezzia, extending at least fifteen miles from van to rear. The islanders disposed their fleet in two divisions; eighteen armed vessels and eight fire-ships formed three lines in the strait before the town, while another squadron, ranging along the south coast of Hydra, manœuvred in such a way as if possible to draw the enemy into the channel betwixt Hermione and Hydron.* On the 21st, the Turks cannonaded for six hours, but at too great a distance to produce the least effect, and the calmness of the weather rendered nugatory the efforts of the Greek brulottiers. During the combat (if that word may be applied to an useless consumption of ammunition), all the Hydriotes who were not employed on board remained under arms, as well as the people of Castri and Kranidi, on the opposite shore of Argolis, and in the night hundreds of watch-fires blazing along the hills terrified the Capitan Pasha, who had his predecessor's catastrophe for ever present to his imagination. Be-

---

* A desert islet formerly called Hydrea, to the north-west of Hydra.

sides their fear of brulots, the detached rocks scattered about the isles disconcerted mariners like the Turks, scarcely able to work their ships in the finest weather and the smoothest sea. A two-decker actually grounded on a reef to the south of Hydra, but being lightened of her guns, floated off again. The day of the 22d passed in inactivity, but on the following night a false alarm that the enemy had landed, caused great commotion at Hydra.

On the 23d, the Capitan Pasha once more drew near Spezzia, without committing any hostility, and on the 24th he proceeded towards Napoli di Romania with his whole fleet ; the Greeks pursued, hoping to assail him with advantage at the bottom of the gulf, where they had some fire-ships ready. Nothing, however, could now have prevented the Ottomans from revictualling the fortress, had any man but Kara Mehemet been at their head : but that despicable dastard, frightened by the account which a negro escaped from Hydra gave of the preparations made to burn him, shortened sail within sight of the place on the 25th, and despatched thither an Austrian merchantman laden with maize flour, and having on board a Turkish officer, the bearer of letters, written in a style of bombast, that contrasted singularly with the poltroonery of their author. A Greek fire-ship issuing from Port Tolon, and a gun-boat attached to the Burj, captured this transport under the eyes of fourscore ships of war. Without risking another attempt, the Grand Admiral thought only of extricating himself from the gulf, which he effected on the 26th, after a distant cannonade with the van of the insurgents, and standing to the north-east, disappeared on the 27th, and went to refresh his crews at Suda, fairly giving up the important object of his expedition. His fleet came out of the gulf in such loose and straggling order, that the Greeks,

by a little boldness, might easily have cut off the rear
division, and attacked it with their fire-ships ; but they
did not venture to bring their small vessels into contact
with the enemy's floating castles. In the running
fights that occurred, two Hydriote sailors lost their
lives, and only a few were wounded, for the firing was
quite out of range: a Barbary frigate having by mistake bore down upon and boarded a brulot, the Greeks
lighted the train, whereby 50 Moslems perished in the
flames, and the frigate's sails were burnt. From the
period when Mahmoud Pasha evacuated the plain of
Argos, the best understanding had subsisted between
the garrison of Napoli and the handful of Moreotes
established in the Burj ; the latter, indeed, in defiance
of their government, carried on with the former a very
profitable trade, selling to their foes provisions and
luxuries, which they consigned every morning to the
captain of the port, an Algerine, who acted as factor,
his daily visits being cloaked under the pretext of
receiving rations for the Christian hostages confined in
the place. Intelligence of the Capitan Pasha's arrival
interrupted this shameful traffic, and disturbed the
Greeks so much, that all of them left the fort, except
two old men, one a Hydriote, who had served many
years as an artilleryman in the French Imperial Guard,
the other a Spezziote : these two veterans, and a young
English Philhellene (Mr Hane), for 48 hours constituted the whole garrison. At length a Zantiote
captain reinforced them with twenty Ionian seamen,
and was followed by Michael Gramzi, a Chimarriotte,
with a score of soldiers. Hearing the sound of cannon
in the direction of Spezzia, the Turks opened their
batteries against the Burj ; shells were thrown on both
sides, and as long as the fleet hovered in the neighbourhood, the firing was brisk, until the Nauplians being
convinced that the prospect of relief had vanished, these

mutual hostilities ceased by common consent, and were not again resumed : the town was a good deal injured, and if the Turks had pointed their guns with tolerable accuracy, they would have converted the insular castle into a heap of rubbish, as its works were beginning to give way.*   Connected with this part of our subject is an incident, which must not be buried in oblivion, since it very nearly led to serious consequences, and tended to stain the honour of the French flag.   In the spring of 1822, an Italian merchant-captain having got French papers and colours, loaded his brig, called the Listock, with corn, and seeking a market, as he alleged, anchored at Monemvasia, where the governor, John Mavromikhalis (a brother of Petro Bey), confiscated both vessel and cargo.   The reason the Mainatt assigned was, that the Italian had offered him a sum of money to betray his fortress to the Turks.   This accusation the skipper subsequently denied, with what truth we shall not take upon us to pronounce, since on the score of character neither of them would be entitled to a verdict.   The Chancery of France at Constantinople claimed an indemnity for the brig and cargo ; and as the worthy Admiral Halgan had departed from the Levant in April, the business was committed to Monsieur de Viella (Capitaine de Vaisseau), who succeeded him in command of the station.   In the month of August, that officer came up to Napoli, in the frigate

* Mr Green asserts, that the Greeks told him they would have surrendered if the Pasha had continued his tremendous fire much longer: that fire must indeed have been tremendous which never killed a man, and, in August, at half musket-shot distance, dismounted only three out of fourteen guns in four days' cannonading. Although so near, the Turks were seldom able to hit the Burj, and they amused themselves by throwing away shot at passing boats. What he says of the hostages being stuck up on the wall is equally fabulous, for they were not detained in the Burj.

Fleur-de-lis, and at the same epoch Captain Hamilton
visited the gulf in the Cambrian, when the Greek
government sent a deputation to compliment the two
commandants, and beg them not to communicate with
the blockaded fortress. So reasonable a request the
Englishman readily granted, and the Frenchman as
roughly refused, while he demanded 35,000 piastres
for the Listock, and 5000 more the freight of Ottoman
prisoners from Athens to Tchesme. The Hellenes
agreed to pay, and a delay of two months being formally allowed them, the matter was considered as settled. Will it be believed by posterity, that the French
Commodore, mocking his own stipulations, renewed
his threats and importunities ere a month expired, and
chose the 21st of September to present himself with a
frigate, and two other ships of war, in a hostile attitude
before Hydra, at an instant when the Greek and Turkish fleets were cannonading each other, when the men
were at the batteries, and the priests and women pro-
strated at the foot of the altars? The Hydriotes, who
had nothing to do with the affair, requested him to
postpone further discussion, at least till the action was
over; meanwhile a schooner belonging to Condouriotti
neared the port, conveying the Turkish hostages surrendered at Nauplia. It was then, that giving reins to
his passion and ultra prejudices, trampling on law and
justice, and heedless of the lives of the Greek hostages,
which would infallibly have been sacrificed if he had
released the Turks, Monsieur de Viella fired on the
schooner, and sent boats to board her.* Fortunately

---

* On the 25th of October, Monsieur de Viella caused to be published in the Smyrna paper an account of his proceedings nearly coinciding with our statement. In addition to the influence of ultra despotic principles, he seems to have sucked in the venom of the Frank
traders of that city, a caste of men, which, though recruited from Europe, too often loses the distinctive traits of European character, and

for the glory of France, the resolution of the Greek captain frustrated this nefarious design ; he was himself kidnapped on board the Fleur-de-lis, but his crew faithfully obeying the instructions he left them, although a cannon-ball went right through their schooner, landed the hostages in the Morea, declaring they would rather put them to death than deliver them to the French. The Hydriote captain was then set at liberty, and the money being paid in a few days, the Commodore sailed away, pursued by the merited execrations of the Greeks, which will be re-echoed by every man who values reputation and conscience. It is fair to add, that the French government marked its sense of this outrage ; the captain of the Listock was deprived of his papers ; and Monsieur de Viella, whose conduct proved his unfitness for the delicate situation he held, was soon recalled to France.

puts on the softness and crafty malice of Asia; enjoying privileges secured by treaty, they formed a Christian aristocracy, and frequently retaliated on the Rayahs the affronts they experienced from Mussulman haughtiness.

It was not alone commercial jealousy, but likewise an impatience of seeing the Greeks become their equals, that rendered them such bitter enemies to the latter.

CHAP. V.

Operations in Northern Greece till the close of the year 1822—
First siege of Messalonghi.

SECTION I.

IF, in pushing forwards the army of Dramali, Khourshid Pasha reckoned upon the defection or neutrality
of Odysseus, he was grievously dissappointed ; for as
soon as the Serasker swept by, the Greek general again
approached Thermopylæ, and, seconded by Ghouras,
Dyovouniotis of Zeituni, Sifakas of Kravari, Scalza
Dimos, Makriyani, &c., gave sufficient employment to
the Ottoman reserves cantoned along the Sperchius,
by harassing the Turkish posts at Nevropolis, Fontana,
and Gravia, and cutting off their convoys on the roads
to Livadia and Negropont. At the same time the
mountaineers of Pelion, and the Olympian exiles at
Trikeri, once more threatened the town of Volo. The
blockade of Negropont had been raised on the land side
by Captain Minas of Thebes, and a Greek vessel, paid
by the Areopagus, performed so negligently her duty
of cruising in the Eretrian Gulf, that several merchantmen were enabled to throw in supplies of rice and
flour. A new Mutesellim having also entered the city
with 500 troops, the Mussulmans made excursions
from thence and from Carysto, and afflicted the revolted Christians.

In the southern districts of Eubœa, the insurgents
were commanded by Nicholas Griziotti, and by a Scla-

vonian named Vasso; in the northern parts there existed an Ephoria acting in concert with the Olympian Captain Diamantis. Sailing from Egina at the end of July, the Areopagites cruised with two ships of war betwixt Attica and Negropont till the autumnal equinox ; the land operations, being limited to numberless petty skirmishes, were on too insignificant a scale to merit description.

After Mahmoud Pasha's retreat to Corinth, Ypsilanti, being charged with the superintendence of the Megarian defiles, came to Salamis, accompanied by Nikitas, and assuming the command at the Dervend, fixed his head-quarters in a ruined Han of Mount Geranion, and hermetically sealed the Isthmus. While engaged in this service, an occurrence happened that must have been as pleasing to him, as it was unexpected ; the arrival of Colonel Gubernati with the regular regiment, which owed its primary formation to the Prince, and now having marched from Messalonghi, rejoined him ; its strength was, however, reduced from 600 to 200 firelocks. Pressed by hunger, the enemy at Corinth repeatedly attempted to forage the territory of Megaris, but although supported by a light squadron belonging to Yussuf Pasha, they met with little success. A body of Turks, stated at 2000, having landed near Perakhora, October the 8th, Nikitas, at the head of 600 Greeks, charged, and compelled them to reimbark with the loss of 45 killed; of the Christians twelve were slain.

Since the horrid massacre of July the 10th, anarchy reigned at Athens, abandoned by its inhabitants to the guard of 500 soldiers, who, expecting a siege, diligently stored in the Acropolis, wood, grain, and water. As the Ottoman army rushed headlong on Peloponnesus, without paying any attention to Attica, the Athenians, considering all danger to be over for the present,

returned to their houses, and in forty days the city was
again fully peopled.   Unfortunately for public tranquillity, there were in the town and neighbourhood
four or five captains equally obscure, but equally desirous of holding the citadel in their own hands.   After
Captain Panaghy's death, one Spiro Bazziakharia had
been named governor; the jealousy of his compeers
being thus excited, they watched an opportunity, when
he was gone with part of the garrison to bring corn
from Piræus, got into the castle, and shut the gates
upon him.   The distribution of Turkish effects raised
disputes between the citizens and villagers ; sundry
arrests took place, and an Ephor was assassinated on
his way from Salamis.   During Ypsilanti's short stay
in that isle, he endeavoured to compose the differences
which prevailed amongst the Athenians ; and on the
2d of September went in person to the city, followed
by Nikitas, and some detachments of troops from the
Dervend. They immediately published a proclamation,
setting forth, that a considerable corps of the enemy
being arrived at Thebes, it was indispensably necessary
that all of virile age should hasten to defend the
straits on the borders of Attica.

Ypsilanti wished to visit the Acropolis, but the captains commanding there (Leckas and Sari), judging
that his intention was to turn them out, and keep possession of it, refused to let him enter.   The Prince
next day wrote a letter to the garrison, threatening to
burn their houses, and imprison their families, if they
did not deliver up those two chiefs ; to this no answer
was returned. As for the Ottoman column that caused
alarm, it retired to Negropont, after plundering grain
and cattle from the plains of Bœotia. On the 6th Ypsilanti and Nikitas having reiterated their menaces, and
declared they would treat the soldiers in the citadel as
rebels and outlaws, Leckas and Sari replied, that they

could not acknowledge the authority of Moreote Generals, but would refer the whole controversy to Odysseus, whom they looked upon as their superior officer; thus the matter rested. It seems they acted on a secret understanding with the Ephors and principal Athenians, unwilling to resign their Acropolis to Ypsilanti. On the 8th, Odysseus entering Athens, attended by the Captains Ghouras, Minas, Stathi, and Meleti, was saluted by a discharge of cannon and small arms, and Leckas and Sari instantly descended to compliment, and give up to him the keys of the castle. Nevertheless, so marked a preference did not outwardly trouble the harmony that subsisted betwixt him and the Prince; for, on the 18th, they presided together at a popular assembly, where new magistrates were elected.

The French corvette L'Active, and the schooner Estafette, again appeared in the Piræus on the 27th, in order to receive on board the Vayvode's family and other Turks sheltered in the consulates, intending to exchange them for the Greek bishop of Negropont. Ypsilanti and Odysseus consented to this arrangement, but the former departing next day with the regular regiment for Megara, unforeseen difficulties arose. The insurgents forcibly opposed the abduction of six boys and of a man escaped from the Acropolis two months before, and whom the French disguised in European clothes. Being recognised, the latter was thrust into the public prison, and it required great exertion on the part of Monsieur de Reverseaux and his small escort, to save him from being butchered on the spot. It was in vain to represent that the captives in question were doubly entitled to their liberty, from the terms of the capitulation, and the guarantee of the flag of France; the Athenians seemed incapable of comprehending the obligation of an oath. However, the ships having landed a party of men with carriage guns, Odysseus and the Ephors thought

fit to yield, and, to avoid any commotion, thirty-three
Mohammedans were embarked in the night-time. That
aversion to parting with their prisoners so often shown
by the Greeks, did not always proceed (as many readers
may suppose) from a preconcerted design of putting them
to death ; it was more frequently owing to a wish to·
barter them for some of their own friends, and, in the
case of young females, to a passion very different from
cruelty. When one or two interested individuals raised
an outcry, the mob was generally ready to join in the
chorus.

Afraid of the enemy, and oppressed by ignoble tyrants,
whose daily quarrels distracted their country, the inhabitants of Attica and the adjacent provinces determined
to seek repose under the protection of a single sword,
and on the 6th of October solemnly chose Odysseus
military dictator of Eastern Greece, in the presence of
the Bishops of Thebes and Athens, the primates of the
town and villages, and the people at large. The prelates,
after the celebration of divine service, read his diploma
aloud, and girt him with a sabre of honour. The same
assembly abrogated the powers granted the year before
to the Court of Areopagus, perhaps the most virtuous
and innocent council that flourished in Greece during
the revolution, despised by the military for that very
reason, and odious to Ypsilanti, and the son of Androuzzos, because its members were friends of Mavrocordato.
Just previously to its dissolution, this tribunal rendered
a last benefit in preventing a civil war in Euboea between
Diamantis and his inferior captains, incited by the opposite faction. As the Olympian chief turned a deaf
ear to an emissary whom Ypsilanti sent to poison his
mind against the government, he and Odysseus were
henceforth at variance. Ghouras received the command
of the Acropolis, where an important discovery had
lately been brought to light ; some workmen excavating

beneath the grotto of Pan, came accidentally upon an ancient vault containing an abundant source of limpid, though rather brackish water, and Odysseus lost no time in securing this valuable acquisition, by building in front of it a strong and lofty semicircular wall. He likewise caused the fortifications to be repaired, stimulating the citizens to labour by working with his own hands, and wisely demolishing an outer enceinte constructed by the Ottomans, and more prejudicial than useful to the castle's defence.

Dramali's army was now in so languishing a state, that it ceased to inspire apprehension, and the militia of the Dervend being thought sufficient to guard the northern bounds of the Isthmus, Ypsilanti and Nikitas returned to the Morea, with the regulars, and the troops they had brought from that Peninsula. However, on the side of Thessaly, the Turks, who for three months had been content to maintain the line of Oeta, began to operate more vigorously, and a fresh army under Mehemet Pasha overran Phocis, and occupied Salona, after driving Panourias from a strong position in front of it. Report exaggerated this force of the enemy to 12,000 men, mostly Ghegs, a tribe of warriors much feared by the insurgents. Odysseus marched out of Athens (November the 4th) to oppose them with 300 soldiers recruited in the city, and, being joined as he advanced by different captains, encamped near Dadi. Exaggeration was as busy on one side as the other, for the Mussulmans supposing him to be at the head of 7000 men, when he had hardly 1000, called in their detachments and concentrated themselves at Salona. Being better informed, they surprised and routed him on the 13th, taking the village of Dadi, and a convent in which they found the baggage of the Greeks, as well as a number of families : the men they put to the sword, and enslaved the women and children. Captain Minas was slain, Captain Sari made prisoner, thirty of Odysseus's body-guards fell, he lost his horses, and escaped death only through his wonderful swiftness, having run eight leagues across the mountains to Rachova, where he arrived without his slippers, and with his feet terribly bruised and swollen. On the 15th the Turks captured Velizza, and indeed there was nothing to hinder them from pushing on to Athens, had their general been so disposed : but Mehemet Pasha chose the moment of victory for negotiating with Odysseus, and at diplomatic fencing his subtle antagonist foiled him completely.   The first demands of the Turk were, a sum of money, a recognition of the Sultan's sovereignty, and liberty to pass unmolested to the Morea : feigning an inclination to comply, the Greek leader prevailed upon him to accord a suspension of arms for twenty-one days, commencing from the 17th of November.   Odysseus employed this period so artfully, that he persuaded the Albanians in the Ottoman camp to desert the Pasha and take the road to their own country, under an impression that the insurgents having emigrated to the islands, there was no booty to be gotten. Weakened by their secession, and straitened for want of bread and fodder, Mehemet Pasha lowered his pretensions. A Greek band, headed by a certain Papa Andreas, intercepted a convoy of fifty loaded mules proceeding from Zeituni to Velizza; before him was a wasted district, and his soldiers were already glad to purchase wheat and barley from those of Odysseus, at a price fixed by the latter : besides, news of Khourshid Pasha's sudden death added to his trouble.   He therefore consented to prolong the armistice till the following spring (vainly flattering himself that the insurgents would then submit), and withdrew beyond Oeta, leaving troops, however, to insure possession of its culminating points. It was proposed that the Ottoman commanders in Negropont and Carysto should accede to the truce ; but they declined doing so, and war continued as before in Euboea. As soon as the Mohammedan army had evacuated Phocis, Odysseus, dismissing to their homes the contingents of Attica and Boeotia, moved westwards, and entering Kerasova with a very small party of men, rumours of his approach attended by a mighty host contributed to the deliverance of Messalonghi. He visited that place, and then crossed over to Peloponnesus, to assist at the congress of Astros. Eastern Greece enjoyed throughout the winter season comparative tranquillity, and the peasants confiding in the armistice, resided in their villages, and tilled and sowed their lands.

At Constantinople, as at Carthage, ill success hath ever been punished as a crime against the state, and in proportion as Khourshid's former triumphs and inflated despatches had buoyed up the Sultan's hopes, so did his signal failure in the work of subjugating Greece inflame that monarch's anger.* Accused of embezzling the treasures of Yannina, and loitering in inaction at Larissa, involved in the ruin of Khalet Effendi's ministry, the aged Roumeli Valesi eschewed a public execution, by swallowing a dose of poison ; and the Kapigi Bashi, sent to bring his head to the Seraglio, found him a corpse. In the confusion that ensued at Larissa, the Turks broke open the prisons, and Captain Sari, taken at the combat of Dadi, effected his evasion,

---

* Sultan Mahmoud has caused the heads of his most eminent victims to be interred outside of Constantinople, on a spot of ground set apart for that purpose, with splendid tombs, showing, in their relative scale of magnificence, the degree of celebrity enjoyed by the deceased person. There are the mausoleums of Ali Pasha and his family, of the chief of the sect of Abdul Wechab, Khalet Effendi, Ismael Pasha, &c. We have been assured that Khourshid's cenotaph is within a few feet of the earth covering the Satrap of Yannina's skull. Here we see a strange instructor in philosophy, and a stranger method of teaching it !

and to the astonishment of the Athenians appeared in
their city, January 1, 1823, with his fetters still on
his limbs.

SECTION II.

THE result of Mavrocordato's expedition delivered
Epirus to the Turks, and laid open Acarnania and
Etolia to an invasion which those countries seemed
nowise able to resist.   It would probably have been
undertaken at the end of July, if Omer Vriones had
not been fully bent upon first reducing Souli, and ex-
tinguishing that focus of rebellion.   Informed of the
events of Plakka and Petta, and of Kyriakouli's death,
the Souliotes, despairing of relief, saw before them the
cheerless prospect of famine.   Here we may naturally
ask, how it happened that the immense stores deposited
at Kiafa by Ali Pasha, should have been so soon exhausted ?   To this question the Souliotes reply, by
enumerating the thousands of Christian families that
lived under their safeguard, and at their expense :
other Greeks of sense and penetration, from whom the
truth could hardly be concealed, whisper that the Souliotes sold their magazines, and popular songs plainly
stigmatize Nothi Bozzaris and Kouzzonikas. However
that be, the English consul at Prevesa (Mr Meyer)
having offered his mediation, it was accepted, and on
the 9th of August, four Souliote deputies signed a capitulation at his house, with Omer Pasha's commissioners.   Its conditions, advantageous and honourable
to the besieged, were faithfully observed ; yet we cannot be blind to the motives which induced the Anglo-
Ionian authorities to interfere, namely, a desire to put
Souli into the hands of the Turks, and thereby enable
them to march against Western Greece.   The Souliotes

stipulated for a delay of six weeks, a sum of 200,000 piastres, permission to depart with colours, arms, and baggage, a temporary asylum in Cefalonia, and unrestricted liberty to go afterwards wheresoever they pleased. British agents guaranteed the treaty, and on the 16th of September, two English transports, escorted by two brigs of war, conveyed them to Assos. No more than 320 fighting men, and 900 women and children, embarked, their Epirote auxiliaries having dispersed and returned to their cantons. Before they went on board, the English officers had a violent dispute with Omer Pasha respecting the payment of the 200,000 piastres, and giving back the Turkish hostages, one of whom was the Pasha's nephew : it is a fact that the Souliotes at last lent him the money, and were repaid through Mr Meyer at Prevesa ; so well do Albanians understand each other !

Meanwhile, Omer Vriones was carrying on intrigues with the Armatolic captains of Acarnania, several of whom were ready enough to imitate Gogos Bakoulas, enjoyment of the military fief overweighing, in their selfish minds, graver and nobler considerations. George Varnakiottis, captain of Xeromeros, had never been sincerely attached to the doctrines of political regeneration predicated by the Hetœria, and he felt hurt at Mavrocordato's preference of his rival Tzongas, captain of Vonizza, a man of greater worth as a soldier and a citizen. By corresponding with the enemy about an exchange of prisoners, and matters of a similar stamp, Varnakiottis gave grounds of suspicion ; but the President, not having the power to coerce, was obliged to employ, caress, and appear to trust him. Ever fertile in expedients, he even strove to turn to advantage that chieftain's intimacy with the Turks, by encouraging him to feign an intention of submitting, and thus, like Odysseus, to temporize and delude them. A letter was

written by the municipality of Messalonghi to Varnakiottis, expressly declaring that the safety of Western
Greece required his entering into negotiation with the
Ottoman generals (Vide Appendix) ; but the stratagem
recoiled on the heads of its inventors, for, thinking he
had now got a sufficient guarantee against future prosecution, he played the part of Vladimiresko, and went
over to the Moslems in good earnest.* Steeling his
breast against adversity, Mavrocordato quitted Anatoliko on the 12th of August, and proceeding towards
Vrakhori, busied himself in visiting the camps, reor-
ganizing the militia, strengthening the posts that blockaded Vonizza, calming the fears of the population, and
arranging a system of defence. In the midst of these
occupations, he learned at Stanna, on the 16th of September, that Varnakiottis had joined the infidels, and
disseminated copies of a proclamation, inviting the inhabitants of Acarnania to accept an amnesty. As the
traitor had extensive ramifications in that province,
where his relations and clients were very numerous, he
drew over to the side of the Turks John Rhangos, and
a portion of the Armatoles : the troops encamped before Vonizza disbanded, and those Acarnanians who
rejected his criminal proposals, either fled to the mountains, or took refuge in the isle of Kalamos, a dependency of the Ionian republic. The captains of Etolia
still remained faithful, and the enemy delaying his invasion, the President endeavoured, in conjunction with
Bozzaris, Makrys, and Tzongas, to rouse the peasantry,
and fortify the passes of the woods, rivers, and hills.
Although the year was far spent, and the rainy season
close at hand, the Serasker, Omer Pasha, expected to

* In 1830, Varnakiottis brought this document to Argos and
Nauplia, and at Capodistria's secret instigation attempted to raise an
action at law against Mavrocordato, for having persecuted him unjustly;
however, the thing was too glaring, and would not do.

finish a long and prosperous campaign, by the entire conquest of Western Greece. Assembling his forces at Arta, he advanced, in the middle of October, at the head of an army of 10,000 or 12,000 men (mostly Albanians), with a train of artillery, and a corps of cavalry, under Reshid Pasha. Guided by Varnakiottis, he traversed the unguarded straits of Makrynoros, forded the Achelous, and moved rapidly on Messalonghi; Mavrocordato retiring before him, and the Etolian levies dispersing at his approach, after burning the town of Vrakhori.

The officers who formed the President's staff, besought him to abandon altogether a district, where his wisest plans were for ever frustrated by base ingratitude. " The natives of these provinces do not deserve that we should sacrifice ourselves for their sake, but if I go away, they will submit, and the Albanians pouring into Peloponnesus, through Patrass, that peninsula, already hard pressed, must be overwhelmed; it is here that we ought to lay down our lives!" Such was the magnanimous reply of Mavrocordato, who, on the 27th of October, threw himself into Messalonghi. At the same time, the Ionian government, departing from its rigorous maxims of exclusion, politely offered him an asylum in the lazaretto of Zante ; a stroke of finesse which could make no impression on a character like his. Had he embraced a less honourable resolution, it would have been somewhat difficult to withdraw ; for Yussuf Pasha commanded the sea, and an Ottoman corps having penetrated to Salona, herds of fugitives from Eastern and Western Hellas met on the road leading from thence to Messalonghi, and by their mutual lamentations, converted into despair the hopes each had entertained of reaching a place of safety. So rapidly did the Mohammedans march, that before Anatoliko they very nearly intercepted the retreat of Mark Bozzaris,

the Ghegs having turned him, while the cavalry hung
on his rear ; he got into Messalonghi with the loss of
thirty men ; but a good many women, working in the
fields, were surprised and captured by the Turks. Nothing could at first sight wear a more desperate appearance than the President's determination to stand a
siege in a little town, built on a mud bank, level with
the waves, protected merely by an unfinished ditch,
seven feet wide, and five deep, with a parapet of stones
and earth, four feet high, and two and a half in thickness; add to this, that the absurd developement of its
lines would have needed a garrison of 4000 soldiers,
and Mavrocordato had only 380, thirty-five of whom
were Souliotes of Bozzaris. His train of ordnance
comprehended fourteen old iron guns, with powder
enough for one month's consumption, and his magazines were pretty well stocked with maize flour. The
Mussulmans showed themselves on the 6th of November, but, through a mistake, their columns marched past
Messalonghi, and rendezvoused at Krioneri ; next day
they returned, encamped before it, and made a feeble
attack upon the Greek lines, as if to try their strength.
Omer Vriones ought instantly to have risked a general
assault, which, in all probability, would have succeeded;
such was the advice of Reshid Pasha, but the Serasker
would not listen to him, for Eastern generals are commonly averse to storming towns, if they imagine there
is any chance of their surrendering ; because, in case
of an assault proving fortunate, the booty falls a prey
to the soldiers, instead of filling their own coffers. To
render the blockade complete, Yussuf Pasha detached
from Lepanto two brigs and a schooner of war to
cruise before the small insulated fort of Vassiladi, situated at the mouth of the main channel through the
lagoons, five miles below Messalonghi. The enemy's
hesitation encouraged the garrison, which, directed by

European officers,* sedulously improved its means of defence, by repairing the parapet, making grape-shot out of old shells, piercing with loopholes, and connecting by a fosse two chapels within the gate, and arming two launches, as gun-boats, to flank the extremities of the wall. A reinforcement of men arrived from Anatoliko, and to deceive their adversaries, the Greeks planted along the rampart a row of bayonets stuck to the ends of poles, as though there had been in the place a body of Franks.

After all, the unbounded confidence of the besiegers, and the discord and jealousy of their Pashas, served the Christians better than any labour or stratagem. Never doubting that the town must fall, persuaded that it contained considerable wealth, and knowing that it held Mavrocordato, whose head would be a most acceptable present at Constantinople, each wished to vindicate to himself the achievement of so shining an exploit. Omer Vriones began a negotiation with Mark Bozzaris, who pretended to be willing to come to terms, and Yussuf Pasha, ever at enmity with his colleagues, opened a separate treaty. The President adroitly availed himself of the rivality of the Ottoman generals, communicating Yussuf's propositions to the Serasker, who was indignant at the idea of seeing his promised conquest snatched away by the commander of a small naval force. Although these delays and the heavy rains of autumn retarded the besiegers in their operations, they nevertheless constructed batteries armed with 24-pounders and howitzers, and plied the garrison with shot and shells; but the Greeks, who dreaded an assault, beheld with indifference, and even satisfaction,

* Count Normann, Messrs Voutier, Graillard, Daniel, Reineck, and Bringeri; the four last alone saw the commencement and conclusion of the siege.

this discharge of projectiles, since the methodical way
in which the enemy was proceeding, afforded their
countrymen time to come to their assistance.

Meanwhile the islanders and Peloponnesians, elated
at the result of their struggle with Mahmoud Dramali
and the Capitan Pasha, responded with alacrity to
Mavrocordato's earnest application, and on this occasion, at least, their measures were prompt and effectual.
A Hydriote squadron of seven sail hastened towards
Etolia, while Petro Bey, Zaimis, Londos, and Kanellos Delhiyani assembled troops in Achaia and Elis.
Day after day, every eye in Messalonghi was anxiously
turned upon the sea, seeking to discern a sail in the
horizon ; at length, on the 20th of November, some
movements were observed in the blockading squadron,
indicating an intention of getting into the Corinthian
Gulf, and shortly after six vessels appeared advancing
with a fair wind from the south. One of the Turkish
brigs, too far to leeward to fetch Patrass (the Sirocco
invariably blowing strong out of the gulf), was brought
to action by the islanders, and after gallantly sustaining an unequal contest, ran into Ithaca in a sinking
state, with loss of her mainmast, and one-third of the
crew: on the morning of the 21st, the garrison descried,
with transports of joy, the Hydriote squadron anchored
near Vassiladi. The navigation was thus free, and in
the course of a few days, a ship from Leghorn, laden
with ammunition, touched at Messalonghi ; but the
flotilla had as yet brought no troops, and the Turks
might still have stormed the place, if a sudden and
energetic resolution had been compatible with their
sluggish natures. To confirm them in their slow
system, Mark Bozzaris came under a verbal engagement to surrender, if he was not relieved within a certain number of days. General Normann, worn out by
a lingering fever, expired at this interesting moment,

and was buried in a tomb adjoining that of Kyriakouli ;
he had served with distinction in the great continental
wars, and in Greece his courage and honesty gained
him the attachment of the Philhellenes, as well as
Mavrocordato's esteem.

On the 23d, four Hydriote brigs sailed to Klarenza,
whence they speedily returned with 600 soldiers, commanded by Petro Bey ; Bozzaris then abruptly broke
off his conferences with the Albanians, and the new
comers revealed their presence by frequent and vigorous sorties, insomuch that the Bey was obliged to
restrain their ardour. Omer Vriones, who, with 10,000
men, the flower of Albania, at his back, had sitten still
for three weeks, gazing at a mud wall defended by 500
Greeks, now perceived that his hopes were vanishing
into air. The elements declared against him, and torrents of rain inundating the swampy ground on which
he lay encamped, introduced fevers into his army, and
caused him to extend his quarters, Reshid Pasha
moving with the sick and the cavalry towards the
banks of the river Evenus, in quest of purer air, and a
drier situation. These, however, were not the last or
heaviest of the Serasker's mischances ; the crowning
stroke came from a power which cherished for him the
most friendly sentiments. We have seen, that after the
defection of Varnakiottis, a multitude of Acarnanians
fled with their families to the isle of Kalamos near
Ithaca, expecting to receive from the Ionian government that cheap sort of hospitality which it is not the
custom of any nation to refuse. Undoubtedly, with a
view of compelling them to submit, an order emanating
from Corfu prescribed their expulsion, and they were
literally (not figuratively) driven into boats at the point
of the bayonet, and thrown back on a land possessed
by their implacable foes. The authors of this rigour
had ill calculated its effects ; for, stimulated by despair,

and by Mavrocordato's emissaries, the Acarnanians, thus forced into contact with the enemy, formed themselves into guerilla parties, and infested the Ottoman rear. A signal of insurrection being once given, the mountaineers every where descended in arms from their fastnesses, and Omer Pasha's communication with Epirus was intercepted. Furious at so many crosses, he adopted a tardy and violent resolution of carrying Messalonghi by a coup-de-main, when the chances against him were multiplied tenfold, since, in addition to the troops of Mavromikhalis, fresh reinforcements had come from Peloponnesus under Andreas Londos; and the Roumeliote Captains Tzongas, Makrys, and Vlakhopoulos having entered the place by sea, its garrison amounted to between 2000 and 3000 men.

The Serasker planned an attack for the night of January the 5th, the vigil of Christmas, according to the Greek style, supposing that the Christians, being at their devotions, might be taken by surprise. As it is almost impossible to preserve secrecy in irregular armies, his design was imparted to the Greeks by a fisherman, and the Archbishop of Arta granted them a dispensation from the performance of public worship on the above festival. Impressed with an idea that it would be easy to surround and destroy the besieging army, Mavrocordato had induced the Bey of Maina to charge himself with conducting a body of troops by sea, to the mouth of the Achelous, and Mavromikhalis and his forces were already on shipboard, but luckily adverse winds hindered them from setting sail. When, on the 5th, it became certain that the Turks would storm the following night, the President ordered Theodore Grivas (a valiant captain attached to the Bey's expedition) to land again with 250 soldiers, who came apropos as a corps of reserve. At five o'clock on the morning of the 6th, a general discharge from the Otto-

man batteries announced the moment of attack, and
immediately a heavy fire of cannon and musketry commenced on both sides ; a column of 800 Albanians, provided with fascines and scaling-ladders, had crept un-
perceived into the ditch, and 2000 more supported
them. Those who first mounted to the assault displayed great courage, but it was of no avail ; very few
reached the top of the parapet, and the Greeks fighting
in comparative security, and showering down musket-
balls and grape-shot, obliged them to retire. Five or six
hundred Albanians were killed or wounded, and the
proportion of the former to the latter was unusually
large, owing to their masses having received the fire of
the garrison at the very muzzles of the guns ; in proof
of this assertion, we can state, that many of their dead
in the fosse were found to be pierced with seven or
eight balls. The concurring evidence of Europeans
present at the assault, attests that only six of the
besieged were slain, and a writer, highly favourable to
the Turks, and who then resided at no great distance
from the scene of action, reckons the loss of the garrison at less than seventy men *hors de combat.* Two
days after the affair, Petro Bey sailed with 700 soldiers
to Katokhi, captured on his way thither a transport
from Prevesa, bringing supplies of every description to
the hostile army, destroyed a Turkish detachment at
the embouchure of the Achelous, and rallying around
him the Etolian insurgents, occupied the farther bank
of that river. Although the severe check he had experienced precluded all prospect of his taking Messalonghi, Omer Vriones loitered before it another week,
until his faculty of effecting a retreat appeared problem-
atical. Informed by a despatch from Varnakiottis of
the Bey's movement, as well as that Acarnania was up
in arms, and that Rhangos, again changing sides, had
seized Makrynoros, he on the night of the 12th set fire

to his camp, and marched off; the Greeks issuing out next day pursued his rear, put many stragglers to the sword, captured part of his baggage, and disinterred eight pieces of brass cannon, a mortar, and two howitzers, which the Turks had buried. The Serasker found the Achelous swollen by rain to such a degree, that, unable to ford it at Stratos, he was under the necessity of halting amidst the ruins of Vrakhori, and a division of his army attempting to cross on the 2d of February, was repulsed by a nephew of Petro Bey at the head of a body of Etolians and Mainatts, and lost many men killed or drowned. The country about Vrakhori being utterly devastated, the infidels were reduced to such distress, that after eating most of their horses, they fed upon grass and wild herbs. At length the waters having diminished, they passed the river on the 27th, but not with impunity, for the impetuous stream swept away 600 foot-soldiers.*   About the 5th of March Omer reached Karavanserai, and Reshid Pasha Vonizza; the latter arriving first at Prevesa, sent boats full of provisions up the gulf to his colleague, but as soon as they touched the mole, 700 Albanians rushed on board, and without allowing any thing to be landed, forced the boatmen to convey them to Prevesa, whither the Serasker finally withdrew himself by sea, thus quitting, in the guise of a fugitive, provinces that he had trampled on as a conqueror.   Varnakiottis, despised by the Turks, and excommunicated by his own church, hid his shame in the Ionian Islands, and Acar-

---

* A vast number of Albanians had tied on their backs the large metal pots used in Greek houses, and which they had plundered in the villages; of course when the water got in, they were instantly carried down the torrent. Having crossed the river, Omer Pasha conversed in his bivouac with an English gentleman, and affected to treat his disasters lightly, saying, " Messalonghi is a sausage, which I can eat when I please."

nania became once more a member of the Hellenic confederacy.

The fortunate termination of this protracted and sanguinary campaign reflected solid glory on Mavrocordato, whose firmness, perseverance, and dexterous management, retrieved the desperate affairs of Western Greece,
and chased the haughty Vriones, and his formidable
Arnauts, beyond the Ambracian Gulf. As a soldier, the
President could not be expected to shine equally as in
the character of a statesman and politician ; we know,
however, that during the siege of Messalonghi, whenever it was necessary to encourage the troops, he freely
exposed his person to the enemy's fire.

Here we cannot help again adverting to the stupidity and improvidence of the Ottoman generals. While
Mahmoud Dramali lay at Corinth, and Omer Vriones
was besieging Messalonghi, Mehemet Pasha, after defeating Odysseus, occupied the intermediate point of
Salona, within a few miles of the sea, and Yussuf,
tranquil possessor of Patrass and Lepanto, held in his
hands the navigation of the Corinthian Gulf; their
forces exceeded 30,000 men, and the Greeks had scarcely 10,000 opposed to them.   Yet, neglecting the most
ordinary precautions, and each attending merely to
what was directly beneath his vision, they failed in
every enterprise, and saw their armies melt away
through famine and maladies.

APPENDIX

TO

BOOK II.—CHAP. V.

(No. I.)—Letter written by Odysseus to Mehemet Pasha.*

SINCE you ask the reason of our revolt, all the inhabitants of the Sanjak of Negropont, and I among the rest, have resolved to write to your Excellency. The following are the motives which I will now point out to you : the cruelties committed without the knowledge of the Sultan's government; the injustice of the Viziers, Vayvodes, Khadis, and Buloukbashis, each of whom closed the book of Mohammed, and opened a book of his own. Any virgin that pleased them they took by force; any merchant in Negropont, who was making money, they beheaded, and seized his goods ; any proprietor of a good estate they slew, and occupied his property; and every drunken vagabond in the streets could murder respectable Greeks, and was not punished for it. The book of Mohammed allows none of these things, but prescribes blood for blood, honour for honour, money for money ; this precept, however, did not satisfy those functionaries, and therefore they laid it aside, and composed every one his own book, and judged according to it, and to the length of his sword. We are well aware that the great Sultan never knew, nor had an idea of such things, and consequently we sent in numerous petitions, none of which reached him, because those wicked persons had power enough to hinder our memorials from being presented, and thus constrained us to take up arms, and either to perish or free ourselves from such calamities. If it please your Excellency, write a representation to the Sultan, and obtain for us an Imperial edict, that we may be delivered from our ills. We will then sit quietly in our houses, looking after our private affairs, and so things will go better a thousand times than they have done. With

---

* The drift of this letter was to persuade the Pasha, that the Greeks had risen to obtain a redress of grievances, and would lay down their arms if that was granted them.

regard to my capitaneria, my father inherited it from his father through his valour, and I hope to keep it in the same way. I have the honour to salute you humbly.

(Signed)   ODYSSEUS ANDROUZZOS.

NOVEMBER $\frac{15th,}{27th,}$ 1822.

(No. II.)—*Resolution of the Council at Messalonghi, empowering Varnakiottis to negotiate with the Turks.*

Western Greece is now in such a state, that although it might possibly be preserved from invasion by the active zeal of its armed inhabitants, yet since that zeal (without which courage is useless) hath cooled, owing to internal circumstances, no resource is left but by some stratagem to retard the enemy's irruption, until the Greeks be again united. Let this be a pretended treaty of submission, which may be protracted so as to give us time to arrange our affairs advantageously.

With the unanimous assent of all here present, the brave General George, son of Nicholas (Varnakiottis), is, in consequence of the irreproachable character he bears, appointed to conduct this negotiation, doing every thing that his judgment may point out in order to attain the object we have so much at heart; that is to say, to gain time. That once obtained, we shall be enabled to take salutary measures for the future.

(Signed)   ALEXANDER MAVROCORDATO.
                                   CONSTANTINE KARAPASI.
                                   SPIRIDION TRIKOUPI.
                                   SPIROS KOUMOUMALIS.
                                   ATHANASIUS RAZIS.
                                   EVTHYMOS VASSILAKIS.
                                   NICHOLAS KARAPOUNIS.
                                   DEMETRIUS PLATIKAS.

CHAP. VI.

Transactions in the Archipelago and Peloponnesus during the three last months of the year—State of Greece and Turkey at its conclusion—Campaign of 1822 in the Island of Crete.

SECTION I.

AFTER his ignominious flight from the Argolic Gulf, the Capitan Pasha reposed for a week or two in the harbour of Suda, and then reappeared in the Archipelago about the 20th of October, cruising among the Cyclades, and hoping probably that the sight of his armada would frighten some of the smaller isles into an act of submission, which might gain him credit at Constantinople: however, Syra alone sent a deputation of Catholic primates on board his flag-ship. Mehemet Pasha received them with civility, clothed them in pelisses, expatiated on his own moderation and clemency, and expressed astonishment that the revolted islanders persisted in their obstinacy. The Turks indeed deserve due praise for the forbearance they displayed in every campaign towards the helpless population of so many detached rocks that would have offered them a sure prey. There is no doubt that the wreck and horrors of Scio inspired a salutary repentance into the breasts of the Mussulmans; besides the Porte was aware, that if it could once reduce Hydra and Psarra, the Egean Sea would be no longer troublesome to it.

From Syra the Capitan Pasha steered towards Myconè, which the natives mostly quitted, seeking a re-

fuge at Tinos ; 400 men who remained, seemed to
court an attack by their bravadoes and insults to the
Islamite faith. A detachment of 100 Algerines landed
for the purpose of taking cattle, but, being vigorously
assailed by the Myconiotes, were driven off, leaving
seventeen dead behind them, while the Greeks had but
two wounded : the Ottoman admiral did not think
proper to avenge this affront. At Tinos the view of
the hostile fleet excited the utmost enthusiasm, not less
than 7000 men preparing to defend themselves to the
last extremity ; their courage, however, was not put
to the test, for the Turks proceeded to Tenedos, and
anchored there to await the Sultan's orders. At that
insecure roadstead a tempest dispersed many of their
vessels, and immediately afterwards the Greeks struck
one of those blows which give so romantic a tinge to
the history of this war. Two fire-ships, one commanded
by the intrepid Canaris, the other by a Hydriote, and
convoyed by two armed brigs, left Psarra on the night
of the 9th of November, and the following evening
approached Tenedos ; the crews of the brulots wore
Ottoman dresses, hoisted Ottoman colours, and seemed
to be chased by the brigs of war, which bore the independent flag, and fired shot in their direction. The
latter ceased their feigned pursuit at a short distance
from the Capitan Pasha's fleet, thus lulling the suspicions of the Mohammedans, who, delighted at the escape
of their pretended countrymen, called to them to anchor
under their guns. In an instant the Hydriotes ran
aboard of the admiral, and the Psarriotes fastened their
bark to another ship of the line containing the treasure, while Canaris cried out, " Turks ! you are burned
as at Scio." The Capitan Pasha, cutting his cables,
narrowly avoided impending destruction ; the other
two-decker was caught by the flames, and blew up in
half an hour, with a crew of 1600 persons, of whom

not above four or five saved their lives. Under the
influence of panic terror, the navies of Turkey, Egypt,
and Barbary ran into the Dardanelles, where they did
not all reassemble, for since the preceding storm several ships were missing : we are able to account for two
African corvettes, one of which was found by the Greeks
dismasted and abandoned in the waters of Patmos, and
the other lay a total wreck on the strand of Tenedos.
The victors returned to Psarra without having a single
man wounded (the enemy not even firing a musket at
them), and accents of joy resounded throughout the
Egean isles.

A circumstance worthy of attention is, that on the
18th of June, as well as the 10th of November, the
Hydriote fire-ships, although managed with equal au-
dacity, failed, while those of the Psarrians perfectly
succeeded : the difference of result must be ascribed to
the admirable coolness of Canaris, who, in this second
affair, perceiving, after he got into his scampavia, that
the brulot was not properly inflamed; went on board
again and completed his work ; we may assert, that in
the campaign of 1822 his single heart and arm exterminated 3000 barbarians ! The grand admiral's retreat
within the Hellespontine castles, resigning the sea to
the insurgents, alarmed the Mohammedans dwelling
either in islands or on the continental shore. Those
of Scio and Mitylene took their measures as though
they looked for an immediate descent, and at Smyrna
the Pasha deemed it necessary to raise new works, in
order to resist the Psarriotes, who prepared for attack
as well as defence, erecting batteries, and building a
number of fire-ships on an improved construction. On
the 16th of November they disembarked forty heavy
guns and a quantity of ammunition, gifts from one of
their countrymen settled in Russia ; indeed their rocks
actually bristled with cannon. Nevertheless they did

not change their harassing and desultory method of warfare, which was a source of severe annoyance to their foes, whose darling indolence they disturbed by showing themselves continually, and landing in every quarter where there was a chance of easy plunder. In the beginning of December, one of their brulots would have burned a Turkish corvette in the harbour of Follieri, had not the crew of a Russian ship, anchored alongside, roused by their cries the sleeping Moslems; and in the month of February 1823, two Psarrian vessels cut out of the same port an Ottoman bark from Candia. Their cruisers swept the sea from the Dardanelles to Egypt, co-operated with the rebellious Pasha of Acre, and before the end of the year two of their brigs obtained a very rich prize off the coast of Syria, capturing four Turkish djems, whose cargoes were valued at 450,000 piastres.

About the middle of September, four Cassiote privateers undertook a daring enterprise upon the Egyptian shore: arriving suddenly in the roads of Damietta, they surprised thirteen vessels and boats laden with rice for the Sultan's fleet, and found in one of them 1,000,000 of piastres in specie. Selecting three, which they filled with booty, the Cassiotes carried them off, abandoning the others, and it is added, that they left untouched a bark containing goods, which they knew by the mark to belong to Europeans; a rare instance of respect for neutral property!

In the winter season of 1822-3, troubles broke out in various parts of the Archipelago, particularly at Samos and Syra. The disturbances of Samos, which almost assumed the form of civil war, were caused by the return of Lycurgus Logotheti, who, finding the administration in the hands of an adverse faction, collected his friends and partisans, and after some blood had been spilt, replaced himself at the head of affairs.

Syra, an arid rock, possessing nevertheless the advantages of a pure climate, and a spacious haven, was,
before the Revolution, noted only for its sterility, the
droves of swine that defiled its streets, and the number of male and female servants who migrated annually
from thence to Constantinople and Smyrna. Living
by their connexion with Turkey, and unmolested by
the presence of Turks, the Syriotes clung to the Ottoman government, and their fanatical spirit, sharpened
by the rancour of the Catholic priests, confirmed their
allegiance to the Porte. To Greece, shut out from the
Mediterranean harbours, and without an acknowledged
flag, the neutrality of this island was an incalculable
benefit, since it afforded her an emporium and magazine, whence the insurgents drew indispensable supplies
of grain, brought thither from Italy and the Black Sea
by Austrian and Ionian merchantmen. Frequented by
traders of all nations, Syra soon became wealthy, and
its population increased from 4000 to 30,000 souls.
Hydra, Spezzia, and Psarra hitherto respected her
rights, and the Turks, although sensible of the utility
their enemies derived from her commerce, had generosity enough not to destroy attached subjects whom
they could not defend. The native inhabitants, therefore, sheltered themselves under the banner of France,
which has always protected with solicitude the Catholic church in the East. Unfortunately for the Latins,
they could not conceal their bigoted hatred of neighbours, as virulent and bigoted as themselves; they indulged in festivities on every reverse of the Hellenes,
and would not allow the independent flag to be hoisted
on the single Greek chapel in their town.* Hence

* The Syriotes, not content with expressing their joy at the ruin of
Scio, by balls and fêtes, had the infamy to refuse even water to the
miserable fugitives, a fact which gives us the measure of their malice.

sprung a dispute with the crew of a Cefalonian vessel, occasioning brawls and mutual assassinations. In December, a band of Ionians and Greeks of the lesser isles, thinking these quarrels might serve as a pretext for pillaging Syra, came regularly organized for that purpose, in two ships commanded by a Zantiote adventurer named Fazzioli; the people rose against them, and an action was fought, in which near thirty persons lost their lives. Succoured by a detachment from an Austrian pinnace, the Syriotes repulsed the robbers: the latter, however, persisted in their design, and returning on the 22d of February, reinforced by other pirates, and amounting to 2000 men, embarked in a flotilla of sixty boats, rifled and burnt several warehouses at the port, and were on the point of storming the town, when the appearance of the French royal schooner Estafette, saved Syra from plunder and carnage, by obliging the banditti to retreat with precipitation. At the same period intolerance produced likewise disorders at Tinos, where, in consequence of a marriage between two individuals of different sects, the Greeks devastated a Latin village. That island, as well as Zea, Naxos, &c., was afflicted by the progress of the plague, which continued its ravages till the ensuing spring.

SECTION II.

WHILE without they provided for the relief of Messalonghi, the attention of the insurgents within Peloponnesus was again fixed upon Napoli di Romania, which they blockaded by sea and land, waiting patiently for the moment when inanition should compel the garrison to open its gates; well knowing that the stores introduced by Dramali in July, would soon be

entirely consumed.   Had it not been for the shameful
traffic exercised by successive commandants of the
Burj, the fortress must have already fallen, and as before the first capitulation, the Turks, extenuated as
they were, essayed daily sorties in quest of some article
of subsistence, and were as constantly driven back.
The condition and prospects of the Ottoman army encamped at Corinth were not much better; the five
cargoes of wheat and rice sent from Constantinople
and Alexandria, being exposed to the peculation of
the chiefs and commissaries, did not long keep scarcity at a distance, and the measures of the Porte for
feeding its troops in the Morea were rendered nugatory through the avarice of Yussuf Pasha, who, trading at the Sultan's cost, and considering the imperial
magazines as his capital, sold biscuit to the starving
soldiers at the price of a dollar an oke.

With the autumnal rains another scourge visited
this devoted army, which suffered infinitely more from
the unhealthy climate of Corinth, than from famine
and the sword; an endemic distemper cut off the men
by thousands, and closed the mortal career of Mahmoud
Dramali, who expired towards the commencement of
December.* · Notwithstanding the weakness and discouragement of the Serasker's forces, the Nauplian
Turks having discovered means to communicate the
extremity of distress they laboured under, repeated
attempts were made to relieve them, and against all
possible calculation, two of those forlorn efforts attained
in part the desired result. About the 20th of October,
sixty Ottoman horsemen, each leading a mule loaded
with victual, passed through the Greek posts, entered
Napoli, and returned next night to Corinth, with the
loss of one man, although John Colocotroni had a fort-

* To this day the debris of Corinth are strewed with the dry bones
of men and horses.

night before been despatched by his father to occupy the defiles. Provoked at this event, Colocotroni ordered reinforcements to march from all quarters, while the blockading corps was strengthened by the regulars under Gubernati, whom Ypsilanti led back from Roumelia. Barefooted and half covered by the tattered remnants of their uniforms, the soldiers of the regular regiment persevered in serving, chiefly with a view of obtaining shoes and clothes at the enemy's expense, and they were paid only in government paper, which was hardly current at any discount.

On the 6th of November, the vigil of the feast of St Demetrius, when many of the insurgents had quitted their stations to enjoy themselves at home, a second convoy of 160 mules, escorted by an equal number of cavalry, got into the place without opposition. The Greeks determined, this time at least, to prevent their egress; but the Turks, nothing daunted by the immense disparity of force, issued out of the fortress on the following day, and gallantly charging regulars and irregulars near the ruins of Tyrins, cleared the road and escaped to Corinth, leaving two dead behind them. Colocotroni now saw the necessity of going in person to the Dervenaki, attended by his nephew Nikitas, and collecting about 7000 men in the vicinity of Cleonæ, effectually barred the passes. Yet still the fate of Napoli hung upon a thread, for, at the very last moment, the speculation of an English mercantile house went nigh to accomplish an object that baffled the power of Turkey. Two hours before daybreak, on the morning of the 17th of November, the soldiers guarding the Burj perceived a brig standing into the port, and already close to the anchorage. Terrified at the idea of the Ottoman fleet being again in the gulf, they could neither resolve to fire at, nor board her, and she would soon have been moored beneath the batteries of the town,

when at that critical instant, an English Philhellene in
the Burj, persuading two Greeks to assist him, pointed
and discharged a gun with such good aim, that the ball
killed the mate who was at the helm. She then tacked,
and lay to till daylight, when two Greek vessels at the
Mills, and several gun-boats getting under weigh, her
captain supposing the first shot to be owing to a mistake,
and not aware that the insurgents held the Burj, approached it, showing his colours, and hailed that he had
provisions on board. He was answered by a discharge of
artillery, which pierced his brig from side to side, and
at the same time the Turks opening their fire against the
Burj, some of their balls fell close to the English vessel;
the captain then stood out, and was taken by the Greek
cruisers : this prize proved to be the Flora of London,
completely laden with flour, rice, sugar, coffee, and tobacco, and chartered by the Pasha of Smyrna. She
was sent to Castri, and rejoined there by another brig
belonging to the same house, and captured off Spezzia
with a partner on board, a cargo of provisions, and
false papers for Candia. However, as Hellenic blockades were not acknowledged, Captain Hamilton arriving in the Cambrian frigate, compelled the Greeks to
release those two vessels (the Flora and Malvina), and
to promise payment for damage done the former, and
for her cargo which they had unloaded. It seemed to
be the lot of the unfortunate Turks of Napoli to be tantalized with delusive hopes, and we can conceive the
bitterness of their feelings at seeing this last unexpected
succour snatched away when just within their grasp :
as the Flora was hailing the castle of the Burj on the
morning of the 17th, a crowd of women lined the ramparts of the town most advanced towards the sea, and
stretching out their hands, implored the English captain
to enter the harbour, which he might have done if he had
been better acquainted with the nature of the anchor-

age ; for he could have lain secure and sheltered behind the point of Itchkalè.

After eating up every animal in the place, the garrison subsisted on the leaves and fruit of the prickly pear, on grass, and lastly on human flesh ; these aliments causing a fatal sickness amongst them, the streets were filled with dead and dying, and the living, walking about like spectres, had no longer physical strength enough to load and work the guns. No fortitude could endure such misery, and accordingly deserters came out daily, although sure to be massacred. In vain each night they burned on Palamide and Itchkalè rockets, which were discerned from the Acrocorinthus ; their friends indeed at Corinth understood the signal, and endeavoured to penetrate to Napoli with a convoy accompanied by 1500 men, but were repulsed in the defiles of Agion Oros, by Nikitas.* On the 10th of December, the Moslems who did duty in the Palamide, utterly exhausted through starvation, left their station and descended to the lower town, where they remained in spite of the Pasha's offer of 5000 piastres to any soldier who would serve in the upper fortress. A man and a woman coming out on the 11th, communicated this circumstance to Captain Staikos, and the latter, climbing the hill next night at the head of his troops, marched in at the open gate at two o'clock on the morning of December the 12th (anniversary of St Andrew, the patron saint of Peloponnesus), and took possession unopposed of six batteries ; the seventh was locked, and contained a handful of Turks, sick, and consequently too weak to go down with their comrades ; they surrendered, however, before noon. Amidst the gloom of a dark and rainy winter

---

* According to the MS. journal of Captain Hastings, who commanded a small corps in the Dervenakia, this attempt of the Turks occurred on the 17th of December, when the Greeks were already masters of the Palamide.

night, the roar of cannon and musketry, fired from the
Palamide in token of rejoicing, awaked the inhabitants
of Argolis; uncertain what the reason might be, they
waited in suspense, until daylight discovering the Greek
flag flying on that citadel, they saluted it with a triple
round of artillery and small arms from the Burj and the
ships of war ; while the Mussulmans in the town, seeing
their bulwark lost, set up lamentable cries. In the course
of the forenoon, a horseman, riding at full speed to the
Dervenaki, informed Colocotroni of the fall of Palamide,
and at two o'clock redoubled volleys of cannon announced his arrival.* The general immediately proposed a
capitulation to the Turks, who were now glad to accept
any terms he chose to grant them. Instead of the liberal
conditions of the treaty signed on the 30th of June, it
was stipulated that they should deliver up their money,
arms, and valuables, keeping only the clothes they wore,
with a blanket and carpet for bedding ; that the Greeks
should transport them to Asia Minor, and furnish them
with rations till they got there ; moreover, Colocotroni
engaged not to occupy the town until they were all embarked. This last article, although not really dictated
by humanity, but as essential to the prevention of a
general scramble, had the happiest effects, for the Hellenic name was not tarnished by scenes like those of
Corinth and Athens, which could not have been avoided
if the troops had broken in. Under pretence of distributing the booty in equal shares, Colocotroni sent into
the place commissaries charged to register the property
of the Mohammedans, and he thus secured to himself
the far larger and better portion.

Cunning as he was, however, his fair speeches did not
impose upon the sagacity of his countrymen ; on the

---

* Here the old Kleft showed his sordid avarice, giving but one
dollar to the messenger, who had killed his horse !

21st, Nikitas, with 200 men, entered the Itchkalè, and
the whole army flocking from the Dervenaki, and
assembling under the walls, expressed discontent, threatening to storm the town, to murder the Turks, and to
seize their goods. These menaces they would very
likely have proceeded to execute, if Captain Hamilton
had not come up the gulf from Castri on the 24th. By
his urbanity, and the interest he took in their cause,
that officer had acquired great influence over the insurgents, and he always turned it to the most laudable
ends. After a conference with Colocotroni, whose views
from a different motive coincided with his own, but
who nevertheless affected to start difficulties, and to
yield by degrees to Captain Hamilton's arguments, it
was agreed that the Cambrian's boats should be stationed close to the water-gate, and a party of seamen
and marines landed at the battery of the Five Brothers,
where the embarkation of the Moslems was going on.
Four hundred Turks were shipped on board the Cambrian, and deposited at Smyrna, January the 14th, and
900 more went in seven Greek vessels to the neighbourhood of Scalanova ; the governor, Ali Pasha, and
the second in command, Selim Pasha, refusing to put
their hands to the capitulation, were detained with
their suite of 200 persons, but treated with respect,
and allowed a reasonable degree of liberty. During
the last week of the blockade, the principal sustenance
of the besieged consisted of boiled leather ; their appearance was most ghastly, and in a few days not one
would have survived. Their extraordinary obstinacy
arose as well from a fear that the Greeks, incensed at
their violating the previous capitulation, would show
them no mercy, as from reluctance to quit their native
spot : many wept on departing, and some required to
be forced into the boats. Weakened by long absti-
nence, their stomachs were hardly capable of sustaining

nourishment, and several lost their lives owing to the
injudicious kindness of the English sailors, who urged
them to eat their own rations in addition to those
allotted by Captain Hamilton : altogether sixty-seven
died on their passage to Asia, and the fever they had,
infecting the frigate's crew, cost her a few men. It was
remarked, that the rich Turks frequently concluded
particular conventions with Greeks of their acquaintance, revealing to the latter where their treasure was
hid, on condition of receiving back a part ; and that
although the Cambrian was open to them, they generally preferred Hydriote and Spezziote vessels whose
captains they knew : so rooted is Oriental repugnance
to the usages and society of Franks ! Colocotroni
caused the Turkish females to be strictly searched before they went on board ; but as the employment of
men in such a business would have been too shocking
to the ideas of the East, he committed that task to a
Frenchwoman serving as a Philhellene in male attire,
and he thus got a considerable value in jewels. When
the Moslems were all shipped off, he, on the 4th of January, ordered the gate to be unbarred ; the army
then rushed in, and in a few hours the houses were
thoroughly gutted, and the doors, window-shutters,
and furniture carried away. Being resolved to keep
the fortress in his own hands, the Peloponnesian Generalissimo appointed his brother-in-law Colliopoulo military commandant, and introduced a garrison that he
could depend upon. The submission of Napoli di Romania worthily consummated a campaign glorious to
the arms of Greece, since in every province, the enemy,
who brought into play 50,000 soldiers, and 100 ships
of war, met with disgrace and discomfiture ; and the
Christian standard, waving on the towers of Athens
and Nauplia, threw into shade the temporary reoccu-
pation of Corinth, a place which the Turks were not

likely long to retain. It is true that the Sultan's forces
had annihilated Scio, reduced the rock of Souli, and
pacified Macedonia and Epirus, but ensuing defeats
neutralized the moral effect of those advantages, and
the insurgents justly considered the balance of events
to be much in their favour. They celebrated the
destruction of one, and the flight of another Capitan
Pasha, the blowing up of two line-of-battle ships, the
defence of Messalonghi, and the ruin of the armies of
Dramali and Omer Vriones. In the interior things did
not go so well; for the security that reigned in Peloponnesus at the end of 1822, encouraged the growth of
faction. The authority of the provisional government
tottered from the moment it withdrew itself on board
the squadron in the Argolic Gulf, and its subsequent
sojournings, first at St John of Thyrea, and next at
Castri, whither it removed its seat in the beginning of
November, were periods of deeper decline. Its president, Mavrocordato, had dedicated his attention to the
affairs of Western Greece, and the vice-president, Athanasius Kanakares, died at Hermione. Confounded
under Ottoman domination in the servile crowd of
Moreote primates, Kanakares, electrified by the revolution, manifested patriotism and disinterestedness at
an age which is thought to chill such sentiments:
having in two years of administration obtained his
countrymen's esteem, he expired in extreme poverty,
without regretting his former splendid fortune.* Previous to his death, the term for which the government
was elected being near its conclusion, the Executive
published a decree, dated from Hermione, December

* At Castri his finances were reduced to three dollars, one of which
he expended in entertaining a party of English officers who came to
visit the government. The fortune of his family is now partly re-
established, and his son, who resides at Patrass, is much respected in
the Morea.

the 3d, inviting the people again to choose representatives, and convoking the new Congress at Astros. Two parties divided the Morea : 1st, that of the Primates, deducing their pretensions from the Turkish regime ; and, second, that of the Captains, flushed with recent victory. The main distinction between them was, that in fleecing the people, the Kojabashees followed an old routine, while the rapine of the military chiefs was irregular and undisguised by forms ; the first might be compared to foxes, the second to wolves. Colocotroni, the Coryphæus of the latter class, had already begun to lose his excessive popularity ; his brutality and covetous disposition disgusted the higher orders, and the peasants were displeased at the rigour with which he enforced levies and punished desertion.   It hath been suspected, that in these matters he hearkened to the insinuations of some false friends, desirous of sapping his dictatorial power in the Peninsula.   Beyond the Isthmus there was no civil authority capable of making head against the men of the sword : Etolia and Acarnania obeyed the Armatolic captains, each lording it in his petty district, and ready, on the slightest broil, to burst the link of union which Mavrocordato's ability had woven around them ; in Eastern Greece, Odysseus ruled without a competitor.

The Greeks are fond of asserting that few political crimes tarnished their revolution ; they ought rather to affirm that little publicity was given to such delinquencies, for we could easily draw out a long and black scroll. At present we shall cite a single instance which happened in the autumn of this year, and occasioned a sensation for a month or two ; the murder of Krevatas of Mistra, who was shot on his way to Tripolizza—a deed that every one attributed to the ambition and hatred of the rival family of Yatrako.   With regard to the external relations of Hellas, although her cause was still disavowed, and even taxed with the mortal sin of Carbonarism, yet those who scrutinized closely, could perceive an amelioration silently creeping onwards, in spite of the frowns of Princes. When Dramali's incapacity, and the unparalleled misbehaviour of the Capitan Pasha, had rendered abortive the Ottoman invasion of Peloponnesus, the leading men in Greece had leisure to look around them, and to search for protectors and partisans in the West. Learning that a congress of sovereigns and ministers was about to meet at Verona, to pass in review the state of Europe, they immediately believed that their affairs would form the principal subject of its deliberations. The provisional government thought this a fit opportunity to beg the protection of the august monarchs of Christendom, and determined, therefore, to send deputies to attend the Congress, and at least prevent their country from being condemned unheard; for they were not quite free from the fear of foreign intervention. On the 30th of September, Count Andreas Metaxa, and Captain Jourdain, sailed from Hydra for Ancona, and were soon afterwards followed by the Archbishop of Patrass, and a son of Petro Bey, intrusted with a special mission to the Pope, and holding out the old lure of an union between the Greek and Latin churches. Metaxa, being refused passports for Verona, never got farther than the gates of the city, where he landed, and returned to Greece, after protesting beforehand against any decision that might be taken in reference to the Hellenes, without their concurrence: the Archbishop Germanos remained several months in the Roman States, but did not gain a single point. Notwithstanding this contemptuous reprobation on the part of the higher powers, inflated reports of the successes of the insurgents, joined to the indisputable truth, that, instead of flinching from extreme peril, they had warded it off by their unaided

exertions, biassed in their favour every generous breast
in Europe, and (as cabinets in an enlightened age must
be more or less influenced by national feeling) produced a change in the line of conduct adopted towards
them. This showed itself in a matter of vital importance, the recognition of their naval blockades, which,
for almost two years, had been totally disregarded by
some powers, and barely tolerated by others. Hence
resulted doubt and uncertainty, prejudicial to neutral
commerce, and harassing to the European sea-officers,
who could not execute their instructions to the letter,
without outraging justice and humanity. It could not
be expected that the Greeks would be always moderate
and forbearing, when they detected merchant-ships,
with false papers, endeavouring to revictual the fortresses they were blockading, or that they would never
resent the boldness of greedy speculators, who attempted to bully, as well as injure them, under the shelter of
respected flags. Where no rights were acknowledged,
vessels employed in the service of government could
not be distinguished from corsairs, and the insurgent
marine, provoked by the unceremonious usage it frequently experienced, began to conceive, that, in pursuing neutral merchantmen, it was warring against the
friends of the Turks. England first applied a remedy
to so anomalous a position, by recognising the validity
of effective Greek blockades, and the Ionian authorities no longer delivered papers to vessels bound for
Turkish ports in the Morea. Other nations gradually
imitated the example of the queen of the ocean; less
completely, however, because they construed maritime
rights differently. Men conjectured that the alteration in British policy was owing to the death of an
arbitrary and unpopular minister of foreign affairs,
and the accession to office of a more liberal successor:
it perhaps also arose from a conviction, that Greece

having now a chance of final emancipation, the war should be looked upon as a regular and steady contest, and not a short-lived rebellion.

Although the narratives of those mortified Philhellenes, who went home in disgust, were of a nature to discourage such crusades, nevertheless fresh adventurers continually arrived on the scene of action. In the commencement of 1822, ships came to Greece, entirely freighted with military men, most of whom brought only their swords and their uniforms, and consequently were soon reduced to misery. The battle of Petta, and diseases incident to the climate, thinned their number, and many of the survivors left a country where their enthusiasm could not bear up against want and neglect. But the void was quickly filled up, and it often occurred, that champions of liberty, setting their feet on the shores of Hellas, encountered their predecessors departing, whose recitals converted into sad despondency the exaggerated hopes of the former. A certain Kefalas of Mount Olympus, having circulated in Germany a proclamation, addressed to the Germans, in the name of Greece, drew round him 150 young men of that chivalrous nation. Forming themselves into a well-equipped battalion of light infantry, they sailed under his auspices, and touched at Hydra on the 5th of December. Instead of greeting them as they expected, the Hydriote Primates, afraid of the sullen and suspicious temper of their own populace, for thirteen days withheld them permission to land, and then only allowed them to go ashore in small parties. Thence they went to Castri, where they did not fare better, for, at a time when the native troops were in danger of starving, the Greeks could afford nothing to strangers : ere three months elapsed, the corps was dissolved without having seen an enemy, and most of its members bent their course homewards.

The issue of the Congress of Verona seemed to have confirmed the safety of Turkey, on the side of her most dreaded neighbour ; and it was generally believed that an accredited Russian agent would shortly present himself at Constantinople. On the eastern frontier, the Persians still prosecuted hostilities ; victorious in every combat, they advanced within a day's march of Bagdad, and would have taken the city, if the ravages of that terrible distemper, called cholera morbus, had not paralysed their operations. The Porte, at length, seriously occupied itself with this war, and recruits were commanded from the vicinity of Smyrna, to oppose the Persians.

A violent irritation pervaded the empire, on account of the calamitous termination of the Grecian campaign; and the Janissaries, always prone to sedition, murmuring loudly, their discontent could only be appeased with blood. The decapitation of Ismael Pasha, who was offered as a holocaust, did not satisfy them, and the Sultan was obliged to sacrifice his favourite minister to their clamour. In November, the deposition of the Grand Vizier, and the Shekh Ul Islam, were but preliminaries to the disgrace of Khalet Effendi, who, although holding nominally an employment of secondary rank, had for many years governed the Ottoman monarchy. Deprived of his dignity, and banished to Asia, he set out for Iconium, the place of exile assigned him, graced by a numerous suite, and without apprehending any severer sentence, since, besides permitting him to enjoy his fortune, the Sultan gave him an autograph writing, declaring his life inviolable. However, the affection of despots is inconstant, and Khalet Effendi's fate furnished a striking evidence of it. Either intimidated by the cries of the Janissaries, or unable to resist the temptation of appropriating his lately beloved servant's treasure, Mahmoud determined to settle accounts with a bowstring. A firman of death overtook, at Konieh, the man whom his master had delighted to honour, and his head was exposed at the Seraglio gate, with a Yafta, or inscription, accusing him of perversely sowing discord among the true believers. Several functionaries partook his downfall, and were treated with different degrees of rigour, some losing their heads, others merely their offices: the Capitan Pasha was only punished for his notorious misconduct (the main cause of the Porte's reverses in Europe), by a gentle descent from his elevated station, and was succeeded by Khosref Pasha. A fearful misfortune wound up this series of troubles, executions, and intrigues of the palace: on the 1st of March, 1823, a prodigious fire raged in the city of Constantinople, consuming thirty mosques, the beautiful artillery barracks and cannon-foundery of Top Hanè, and 12,000 Mussulman houses; a multitude of persons perished in the flames, and many thousand families sank into utter indigence. As not a Christian or Jewish habitation suffered (the conflagration being confined to the Mohammedan quarters), it made a deep impression upon the sombre and superstitious imaginations of the Turks; they regarded the fire as a judgment; and the story of a vision seen in Arabia, darkened their melancholy forebodings. A fanatic, named Shekh Ahmed, asseverated, that while praying before Mohammed's tomb at Medineh, the prophet appeared, and desired him to reprove the Moslems for their backslidings. Hoping to render his subjects more tractable through the effects of ghostly fear, and thereby promote his intended reforms, the Sultan caused an account of the Shekh's vision to be written, and copies of it spread abroad.

SECTION III.

THE war in Crete, an island nearly equal in population, and superior in fertility, to Peloponnesus, forms a sort of episode in the perplexed history of the Greek revolution.

Michael Comnenus Affendouli, chosen by its deputies Governor and Commander-in-Chief, having, on his arrival, published an eloquent and spirited proclamation (dated November the 15th, 1821), was received with enthusiasm by all classes, the Sfakiotes being the foremost to swear fidelity and obedience to his orders. Born in Muscovy, of Greek parents, and trained to Russian diplomacy, he, by the confession even of his enemies, was thought to possess very considerable administrative talents, but had no aptitude for military affairs, and therefore was not fitted to rule over the Cretans, who exclusively attached ideas of merit to strength, swiftness, and skill in handling the musket. Crete (as we have already observed) was in every respect, except natural fruitfulness, behind the rest of Greece; its Christian inhabitants had neither wealth nor knowledge ; its trade was in the hands of foreigners ; and the bulk of the people, destitute alike of schools and instructors, thought only of their vines and olive-trees. The Sfakiotes were, indeed, expert and intrepid soldiers ; but they deserve no other praise, being justly stigmatized with the vices of arrogance, treachery, and rapacity ; they despised the Katomerites (or dwellers in the low country), treating them as an inferior caste, making free with their property, and claiming authority for themselves alone. Affendouli wished to check this system ; but as he was unable to chastise the refractory Sfakiotes, his opposition tended to nothing, except to multiply his personal foes.

Various and weighty accusations were subsequently laid to the governor's charge; he was said to be blindly devoted to Russia, passionate, mistrustful, and too lightly swayed by the representations of those about him: his outward appearance was not more prepossessing than his mind was amiable, for, in addition to a short stature and a repulsive aspect, he laboured under the defects of a limping gait and a hoarse cracked voice.

During the winter there arrived at Loutro, from Malta, Leghorn, and Trieste, some necessary supplies of grain and ammunition, as well as a reinforcement of 500 Cretans, who, having been scattered about the Archipelago, were collected at Tinos, and embarked for their own isle. The brave Balesto likewise agreed to serve there, and in the month of February sent from Spezzia four European officers,* and fifty soldiers of his battalion, who voluntarily participated his lot; he intended to follow immediately, but a dangerous illness long detained him at Milo, where he had gone to meet his father. Hostilities recommenced with vigour in the very first days of the year: on the 5th of January there was fighting before the walls of Canea and Rhetymo, and in both actions the Turks were worsted, losing at Canea thirty-five killed, exclusive of their wounded. These defeats they avenged in their usual manner, by massacring twenty-five Christian peasants, who ventured, with regular passports, to carry into those two towns oil belonging to their Mohammedan Agas or landlords. In February and March, the insurgents, directing their principal efforts against Canea, blocked it on the land side, and advanced every day within cannon-shot of its ramparts: on the 17th of the former month, the Pasha marched out with a de-

---

* The captains Justin and Guilbert, the lieutenants Isolani and Rossi.

sign of penetrating to Rhetymo, but returned after a
vain attempt to force the passes.

The subjoined statement, derived from an authentic
source, will enable the reader to understand the strength
and position of the Christian troops in the island at the
opening of the second campaign. On the western side
General Papadaki, and his lieutenant, Captain Sify, commanded the division investing Canea, and some detachments guarding the defiles of Selino and Kissamo and
the environs of Suda, amounting altogether to 2400
men. In the centre, Rousso and seven other captains,
all of Sfakia, at the head of 3000 soldiers (Sfakiotes,
and levies of the province of Rhetymo), occupied the
passes of that Pashalik, save one road running along
the coast from Rhetymo to Candia. On the east, Antonio Melidori lurked near the foot of Mount Ida with
200 men, and occasionally could draw 1000 more from
the Christian villages in that part of Crete ; thus the
total Greek force did not exceed 6600 combatants.
The Turks, although suffering grievously from pestilence, were far more numerous, being reckoned by
some at 18,000, by others at 26,000 fighting men :
they were all under arms, while in many districts the
Rayahs had not yet made common cause with their
countrymen. The Mussulmans, too, had an immense
advantage in the possession of twenty-seven strongholds (including three fortified cities), and they were
well provided with artillery ; their adversaries, on the
contrary, had only a few old ship guns in the port of
Loutro.

Both officers and soldiers in the Greek camps showed
an anxious desire to see the governor : he was, however, in no hurry to take the field, and chose rather to
spend the winter at Loutro, receiving reports, drawing
up plans of organization, and writing proclamations,
for he was a man of the pen and not of the sword. At

length, on the 10th of March, he removed his head-
quarters to the monastery of Preveli, eight leagues
from Loutro. There he was met by Captain Justin,
whom he had sent on a tour of inspection through the
island, and who gave him correct information regarding the posture of affairs in its different provinces. In
the environs of Canea, the Greeks obtained daily successes in a series of small skirmishes, and precluded
the enemy from going beyond the range of their batteries: in the middle of March they again cut the
water pipes, and 1200 Turks, who sallied out to cover
a party of workmen employed in repairing them, were
driven in with a loss of thirty killed. That city was
full of anarchy, its usual population of 6000 or 7000
souls having been more than doubled by an influx of
Moslems from the country. On the 11th and 12th of
March, the garrison and populace, rising against the
Pasha, besieged him in his palace, and obliged him to
distribute money among the mutineers. The prospects
of the insurgents wore a less favourable aspect in the
Pashalik of Candia; the Ottomans, numerically stronger
there than in the other districts, had assumed the offensive, compelled Antonio Melidori to evacuate several posts, and began to intrench themselves at the village of Furfura. The tribe of Melebiotes prepared to
defend the important position of their native village
(the key of Sfakia on that side), but reinforcements
were absolutely necessary to stop the progress of the
Mohammedans, and repulse them to their fortress. It
was proposed that Affendouli should assemble his principal corps at the central point of Merona, whence he
could maintain his own communications with every
part of the island, and threaten those of the enemy;
but he was no warrior, and the Sfakiote primates,
afraid lest he should interfere in the disposal of the
flocks of sheep and other booty they were in the habit

of sharing among themselves, besought him not to expose his person. Yielding to their remonstrances, he fixed himself at the village of Rustika (near the mountains of Sfakia), where he loitered for a fortnight, and then, apprehending a sortie from Rhetymo, fell back two leagues farther to Samaropolis.

Meanwhile the Cretan chiefs, perceiving the necessity of dislodging the Turks from Furfura, collected almost all their troops in that quarter, and thereby so weakened the blockade of Rhetymo, that the garrison marched out and menaced their left flank. On the 24th of March the Greeks had the advantage in an action fought at Aposeti; but next day, want of concert caused the failure of a plan for attacking and turning Furfura; a column of 300 of them, which had got into the enemy's rear, was obliged to return for fear of being itself cut off. The two parties observed each other: however, Rousso's arrival having augmented the Christian forces to 4000, and Antonio Melidori having, at the village of Abadia, surprised in the night-time a convoy coming from Candia, killed many Turks, and captured their live cattle and thirty-six horse-loads of biscuit, the balance seemed to incline in favour of the Greeks, when the perfidious villainy of the Sfakiote chieftains gave a fatal turn to their affairs.

Antonio Melidori (whose brother was Affendouli's physician) had, by his patriotism and distinguished exploits, earned the good-will of the governor and the people's love: he was the terror of the Candiote Moslems, and had slain with his own hand some of their most renowned bravoes.* His well-merited reputation, and promotion to the rank of lieutenant-colonel, irri-

---

* In the Appendix to this chapter will be found a particular account of him, extracted from a short MS. work (by an anonymous author), containing the lives of several Greek worthies who figured in the Revolution.

tated the captains and primates of Sfakia, who appeared to look upon the war not as a grand national contest, but rather as a question, whether they or the Ottomans should tyrannize in Crete. They determined
to rid themselves of this rival, and accordingly a few
days after Melidori's late success, invited him to a ban-
quet, where Rousso in the basest manner assassinated
him with his dagger. The Turks, informed of Antonio's death, fired a feu-de-joie, while his friends and
followers, incensed at their leader's murder, quitted
the camp, and repairing to Samaropolis, declared to the
governor that they would no longer serve with such
traitors as the Sfakiotes. Affendouli felt the same indignation, without being able to bring the assassin to
condign punishment; all he could do was, to issue an
order of the day depriving him of his rank, and commanding him to retire to Sfakia. Rousso's relations
and adherents espousing his quarrel, departed with
him, and the army not being then strong enough to
make head against the enemy, the remaining chiefs
evacuated their camp, retreated to the mountains, and
thus abandoning the whole Pashalik of Candia, left
the communication free betwixt that fortress and Rhetymo.

Vexed and angry, the governor transferred his head-
quarters from Samaropolis to St George in the province
of Canea, where Papadaki and Sify maintained better
discipline among their troops. While on his way thither,
he received intelligence on the 2d of April, that Colonel
Balesto, with some officers and 300 Samian soldiers,
had landed at Loutro. Affendouli at first suspected
that Ypsilanti had sent Balesto to intrigue against him,
but his misgivings being set at rest, he ordered the
colonel to join him without delay. New measures were
then concerted betwixt them; the governor established
himself at the large village of Armenos (five leagues

from Canea, and a league and a half from Suda), whilst
Balesto went on the 7th to take the command of the
forces of the district of Rhetymo, which it was proposed to increase to the number of 6000, by drawing
levies from the country. Justin was appointed chief of
the colonel's staff, and Guilbert, named aide-de-camp to
the governor, remained with him to carry on his military correspondence. Balesto arriving on the 9th at Kog-
sarè, instead of the army that he expected, found but
800 men assembled in a state of total destitution. Reinforced by some detachments, he on the 11th occupied
Castello (two leagues from Rhetymo) with 1200 soldiers,
and pushed a reconnoissance towards the fortress ; but
on the following night, all the companies, except the
one which guarded his headquarters, fell back without
orders behind Castello.   As the season of Easter was
now approaching, he could not keep the Greeks to their
colours, each soldier wishing to pass the festival in his
native hamlet.   In the meantime the Turks of Candia
advanced to support those of Rhetymo, and encamped
apart and at a small distance from them, because they
dreaded the infection of the plague, which raged among
the latter.   On the 14th the colonel retired to the village of Kaloneti, leaving some troops at Castello; he
was joined the same day by the Sfakiote captain Protopapadaki, a faithless designing villain, and an accom-
plice in Melidori's murder.   That atrocity appeared to
be almost forgotten, and even Rousso himself was preparing at Loutro an expedition of 1000 men, to invade
the canton of Messara, in the east of Crete.   There
were not wanting, however, other sources of discord :
the primates of Sfakia had desired to have a governor,
hoping that he would be a phantom, and an instrument
to bring them aid from the mainland. Finding Affendouli a man of morose character, and divining his intention of strictly examining their accounts, and taking

from them the direction of affairs, they conspired to drive him from the island. As the magazines of Loutro were at their disposal, they could easily breed discontent amongst the troops by withholding supplies ; the Sfakiotes alone received bread and cartridges, the other contingents were left to penury and hunger. This difference of treatment naturally excited in the camp animosity and bloody quarrels. The primates then wrote to Protopapadaki to return to Sfakia with his soldiers ; Balesto's remonstrances prevented him indeed from immediately obeying the order, but it would have been better for the colonel that he had suffered those treacherous auxiliaries to march away. On the afternoon of the 20th, the Turks came down in force into the plain of Castello, and, after a smart skirmish, were repulsed to the heights of Rhetymo with the loss of twenty killed, twice as many wounded, and two standards taken. On the 24th, several vessels from Kassos sailed past the bay of Suda, and cast anchor at St Theodore, two leagues from Canea.

Aware that the scarcity of provisions would render it impossible for him to keep his army together much longer, Balesto resolved to hazard an attack, and therefore, on the 25th, commanded the captains to collect their companies next morning at Castello : his forces amounted to about 4000, for the Cretans were wont to assemble with rapidity, and disperse as suddenly. The Turks of Rhetymo (1500 strong) occupied an eminence, whose summit was defended by several pieces of cannon placed in the ruins of a burned house ; those of Candia, computed at between 2000 or 3000, were posted in a camp to the left of the former, and in a loftier position. On the morning of the 26th, the Greeks having rendezvoused at Castello, Balesto called together the principal officers and unfolded his plan ; he purposed to make a brisk assault in front, offering to march with his staff at the head of the column, while a detachment should turn the Ottomans and charge their rear : he had previously requested the Kasiotes to co-operate with him, by firing upon Rhetymo as soon as the action commenced. The Cretans thought his project too dangerous, and after a long discussion nothing was decided. During the conference it was reported to the colonel, that, excepting the Sfakiotes, his soldiers had only six cartridges per man ; he exclaimed that under such circumstances an offensive movement was impossible, and instantly despatched confidential officers to Sfakia and Armenos to demand ammunition and food. Hardly were they gone, when, at four hours after noon, the Turks unexpectedly quitted the heights, and descending into the plain, covered by the fire of their artillery, attacked the Greeks, who met them with resolution, and for three quarters of an hour the combat was maintained with spirit. Unfortunately a sudden panic, springing doubtless from treasonable malice on the part of the Sfakiotes, who had sworn Balesto's destruction, seized the insurgents, and they fled on all sides. The colonel endeavoured in vain to rally his troops : weakened by protracted illness, he threw himself on the ground, in a fit of despair, protesting that he preferred death to dishonour. Two captains carried him for some time, till, finding that the enemy pressed hard upon them, they concealed him among brushwood ;* but the Turks soon discovered and put him to death, cutting off his head and right arm. Lieutenant Kokini, a young Greek of Trieste, who had accompanied him from that city, exhibited on this occasion an instance of devoted attachment ; refusing to abandon the colonel, he sat down by him to share his fate, and was taken by the

---

* " Balesto (say the Cretans) was not a good soldier ; he could not run !"

Mussulmans, who, admiring his fidelity, spared his life. Thus fell the noble Balesto in the thirty-second year of his age : his mutilated remains were picked up next day, and interred at Rustika.

Disheartened by so signal a defeat, the insurgents sought shelter in the most inaccessible positions, and the Mohammedans wasted and burned at their pleasure the provinces of Rhetymo and Candia, although they dared not, for fear of ambuscades, penetrate into the high mountains. Before Canea, the Greeks were more successful: seconded by a disembarkation from the Kassiote vessels, they chased the Turks from the post of Galata, and established themselves in the village of Pyrghos Platania, thereby intercepting the road betwixt that fortress and the Mussulman districts of Selino and Kissamos, at the north-west point of the isle. The governor, who had, on the 13th of February, proclaimed in a state of blockade the ports and coasts of Crete, employed the squadron of Kassos to carry his decree into effect, agreeing to pay each sailor thirty piastres a month, and to allow them half the value of their prizes. In the beginning of May, several neutral merchantmen were captured in the waters of Canea, but their detention led to unpleasant altercations with the English and French, and at length the Fleur-de-lis, a frigate of the latter nation, arrested, and conducted to Milo, a Kassiote cruiser, which was finally sunk there.

Another event that occurred in the first week of the same month, and more sensibly affected Affendouli, was the arrival from the Morea of a deputy named Skilizzi Homerides, with full powers from the central government to investigate the condition of Crete, and unite it more closely to the rest of the confederacy. Nothing could be more galling to Michael Comnenus than this mission, so adverse to his scheme of erecting the island into a separate principality under Russian protection ; he nevertheless dissembled his chagrin, behaved with politeness to Skilizzi, and convoked at Armenos an assembly of Notables to deliberate on his proposals. A majority of Cretans, allured by promises of future support, showed an inclination to adhere to the Peloponnesian envoy ; each of the competitors laboured by clandestine manœuvres to undermine his rival's influence, and amidst these intrigues the war was neglected, although hostilities still went on around Canea. On the 27th the insurgents made a general attack, or rather demonstration of attack, by sea and land, and the engagement lasted from five o'clock in the morning till two in the afternoon. The Kassiote squadron interchanged a cannonade with the batteries, but at so respectful a distance that their vessels were not struck once, and only two of their shot fell in the town ; on land, the Turks, supported by a discharge of artillery from the walls, sallied out to encounter their foes ; the musketry fire was long and heavy, but neither party sustained much loss. As Homerides gained an ascendency in the convention of Armenos, brought over a great part of its members to his views, and succeeded in curtailing the governor's authority, and procuring the appointment of responsible ministers, Affendouli threatened to go away from the island, assigning as a reason, the constant anarchy that prevailed, and the excesses lately committed in two expeditions ; the first, under Rousso, against Messara, and the second, an incursion into the rich canton of Milopotamos (between Rhetymo and Candia), where, by putting all to fire and sword, the Greeks induced the Beylerbey to return into his own Pashalik. On the 9th and 10th of June, a violent storm hindered the governor from embarking in a Maltese vessel he had hired ; and next day, the 11th, his design of departing by sea was frustrated for the present by the appearance of a powerful Egyptian armament. This fleet, sent to the Sultan's assistance by the Viceroy, Mehemet Ali, left Alexandria on the 28th of May: it consisted of 106 sail of men-of-war and transports, and had on board 5000 troops, including 700 or 800 cavalry, and 2000 veteran Albanians, with a train of field-artillery; the whole commanded by Hassan Pasha.

The fleet coming to an anchor in the roads of Suda, a portion of the troops immediately landed, and advanced into the country; but the brave Sify, attacking them at the head of 1200 Cretans, forced them to retreat to the strand, where they formed a camp. As the Greeks were not numerous enough to cope with the Ottoman corps from Suda, Canea, Selino, and Kassamos, they withdrew from the low country, and, intrenching themselves at the strong position of Malaxa, among the White Mountains, waited for the enemy, who hesitated to assault them there. Several partial combats ended in favour of the insurgents, who from the heights rolled down large stones upon the Turks, until early in July, Hassan Pasha having animated his soldiers by promising a gratuity of 25,000 piastres to those who should be foremost in scaling the mountain, they, during the night, stormed Malaxa sword in hand, and to a certain distance cleared of rebels the environs of Canea.

In July, too, a fresh insurrection broke out in the eastern division of the island, and 2000 Greeks, approaching Candia, took post on the adjacent hills. The Ottomans made a sortie against them, but the Christians, profiting by the nature of the ground, avoided a decisive action, and, when the former fell back, pursued their rear, surrounded a corps of Albanians, who loitered in a village, shut them up in a convent, and setting fire to it, exterminated the whole body. About the same period, the Egyptian ships of war (forty-two

in number, of which three were frigates, and nine or
ten corvettes) sailed to join the Capitan Pasha in the
Archipelago ; operations then languished, and an expedition that menaced the Cretans with destruction had
very slender results.   The Egyptian general after his
victory wasted six weeks in inaction at Suda, and then,
accompanied by the Pasha of Canea, went to Rhetymo, and being there further reinforced by the Satrap
of that place with his troops, reached Candia on the
12th of September.   The four Pashas, thus united in
one point, boasted that they would invade Sfakia, and
conclude the war ; in reality, however, they did little
or nothing, and this campaign terminated like the former one, in the Moslems' confining themselves to their
camps and fortresses, where the plague did not cease to
thin their ranks.   Apprehension meanwhile allayed in
Crete the spirit of faction.   Homerides departed, and
Affendouli, who was residing in a tower near Sfakia,
regained his authority, and exercised it for some
months.   Although possessing the mountains, and
most of the interior, the Christians were in a very unhappy situation, and suffered from pernicious fevers ;
while the oppression and rapacity of the Sfakiotes became so intolerable, that (to borrow the expressions of
a Greek pamphlet on the affairs of Crete*) its inhabitants found themselves placed betwixt the tiger and the
panther, and knew not where to look for deliverance
from such confusion and misery.

* Published at Messalonghi in 1824.

APPENDIX TO BOOK II.—CHAP. VI.

Short Biography of ANTONIO MELIDORI.*

HAVING zealously dedicated himself to the service of his country, Antonio Melidori was sent into Asia, in the month of September 1820, for the purpose of communicating to the Greeks of those dis-tricts (with which he was well acquainted) the near approach and object of the revolution ; and in the space of five months he prepared the minds of 7000 individuals. From thence he passed over to Samos, and afterwards to Tinos, where meeting Theodore Negris and James Cornelius, he accompanied them to Hydra, with the intention of pro-curing ships in order to transport to Crete the Greeks who were assembled at Yeronda. He did not succeed at Hydra, and having no better fortune at Psarra, at length got a Kassiote vessel, and embark-ing 300 men, landed them in Sfakia. Encouraged by his arrival, the Sfakiotes refused to surrender their arms to the Turks, and joining the people of the village of Visiotti, began hostilities at Apokorona, a dependency of Canea. In this expedition, Captain Antonio marching with his soldiers by the village of Melidoni, and learning that there were Turks in it, drew near with a red flag, and speaking their lan-guage, deceived them, so that nine of them came out to him, whom he took and sent to Sfakia ; these were the first Turkish prisoners he made. He then went to a village called Hashi, and engaged its Mohammedan people ; when, during the combat, Captain Antonio entered it alone, and throwing himself into a house, fought till sunset : the other Greeks retired to a height at some distance. Finding him-self alone, he thought of escaping, but first proceeded to reload his musket, when the ball stuck in the barrel, and as he was endeavour-ing to ram it down, some Turks came into the court of the house, one of whom addressing him, asked if he was a Greek ? Antonio did not answer, but allowing his cap to fall off, stooped as though he would have picked it up ; at the same moment, laying his hand on his pistol, he shot dead the man who had spoken to him, and killed with his sabre another who attempted to seize him. Cutting his way through the Mussulmans, amidst a shower of balls, he outstripped his pursuers, although wounded in the thigh, and rejoined a party of his own men, who were lamenting his supposed death, and could hardly believe their senses when he appeared among them. They embraced him

* Although there is not perhaps in his life any thing particularly interesting, yet it may give an idea of the method of warfare in Crete, and the sort of ex-ploits performed there.

with tears of joy, but he told them that their abandoning him gave him more pain than his wound : he afterwards went to Sfakia to be cured.   A little later, the Turks of Candia and Rhetymo, having joined those of Canea, marched to invade Sfakia.   On hearing this, Captain Antonio instantly set out to place himself at the head of his corps, which was encamped at a village called Prosnero, whence they saw the enemy posted at the foot of a mountain.   Continuing their movement towards Sfakia, the Turks had to traverse a very dangerous pass ; nevertheless the Greeks quitted their position, regardless of the supplications of many unfortunate families thereby exposed to the enemy's inroad.   At that moment Antonio arrived, and putting himself at the head of his troops, commenced an action.   The Turks, unable to reach him with their muskets, fired a shell at him, crying aloud, " Art thou not yet fallen ?" " No !" replied he, " because ye are not able to overthrow me." The sight of Antonio animated his followers, who hindered the foe from advancing till night, when both parties retired.   During the darkness, Antonio heard the wailing of a child at some distance, and as his men all refused to go in the direction of the sound, for fear of the enemy, he went himself, and discovered an infant left by its mother in her flight, and laid on a cotton quilt ; he snatched it up, and rejoining the column, repaired to a neighbouring mountain.   Here he found a number of women and children flying from the fury of the Turks, and so extenuated by hunger that they could hardly move.   The captain halted, and desiring all those who were incapable of fighting, to gather wood and light a fire, ordered a female captive to be slain and roasted for food, while his soldiers, amounting to seventy, kept watch to prevent a surprise.   He then escorted the families to Sfakia, and immediately afterwards sailed to the Morea, with Nicholas Zenos, at the epoch of the siege of Tripolizza. Understanding that General Michael Affendouli was gone to Crete with full powers, he returned thither, and offered his services to him. Being despatched to besiege the village of Moni, and seeing that the soldiers neglected their duty, and gave themselves up to rapine, he proposed to the Turks (thirty in number) to capitulate on assurance of life and goods, and even put himself into their hands as a hostage : thus they surrendered their arms, and departed in safety.   On taking leave of them, Antonio said, " Oh Turks ! you see with what humanity we have treated you ; therefore, behave in the same way to any Greeks who submit." This noble conduct raised the envy of the other captains, who accused him of suffering himself to be bribed, and prevailed upon Affendouli to dismiss him, whereupon he withdrew with a resolution never to serve again.   In the month of December, 1821, while he was living in privacy, several soldiers told him that the Turks of Rhetymo had been enquiring whether he was yet alive ; on this he went forth once more, and collecting 200 men, marched close up to Rhetymo, and drove in the enemy. On this occasion, to show his courage, he went alone, with his sword in his hand, to drink at a fountain within musket-shot of the town. He likewise took in action a Mussulman of rank, and sent him to Sfakia, in obedience to a proclamation of Affendouli, commanding that prisoners of distinction should be transmitted to him. As the same proclamation called for the head of an Aga named Ghinid Ali, Antonio attacked, beat, chased him into a cavern, and seizing him there, cut off his head, and forwarded it to Affendouli, who in return wrote him a very flattering letter of thanks, dated January the 25th, 1822. Captain Antonio then drew together 500 troops, and continued his operations in the vicinity of Rhetymo, causing his followers to observe an exact discipline, and to respect the property of Christians; any disorder was severely punished, and the culprit driven out of his band; nevertheless, the soldiers were extremely attached to their chief. While he lay at the village of Tronkhidia, the monks of a convent, five miles distant, sent him word, that sixty Turks of Rhetymo, under a certain Garmeli, had a design of plundering their monastery. He instantly hastened thither with seventy men, and arriving in the night, found the enemy in possession, eating and drinking in the cells. Garmeli and his son were seated in that of the Sacristan, obliging the latter to hand them wine, and frightening him with terrible words. Antonio posted his party round the building, ordering them to remain quiet till daybreak, and then, after calling out once, " The Greeks are coming !" to hide themselves again. He conjectured that upon the alarm the Turks would all rush out, and that he might then destroy them; but one of his soldiers having fired a shot too soon, they retired back to the cells, and there defended themselves. Vexed at this disappointment, and afraid lest they should receive reinforcements, Captain Antonio unsheathed his sabre, burst open the door of the Sacristan's cell, wrested Garmeli's pistol from his grasp, laid his tremendous hand upon his breast, threw him down, and holding his sword over him, said, " Art thou really the bravest warrior in Rhetymo ?" Garmeli cried out for mercy, and Antonio telling him that he must turn Greek, he began to repeat the words, Kyrie eleison. Having forced him to give back fifty piastres he had taken from the Sacristan, Antonio decapitated him, and slew his son and all the other Turks. Some Sfakiotes belonging to Melidori's band having pillaged a poor old woman's house, the captain compelled them to refund; but on going away, they exclaimed, " that his tomb was open;" this circumstance he communicated to the governor, who, in reply, bade him be of good cheer and fear nothing.*

---

* The following is a copy of Affendouli's epistle :—" Brother and faithful patriot ! I have this instant read your letter with much pain. With respect to the tomb the robbers spoke of, fear nothing ; Providence will not abandon you, neither will I. He who lives in the fear of God, and sincerity of heart, need

At Monastrevo, Antonio, with no more than 260 men, insulted and defied a whole Turkish army in its camp; but being assailed with vigour, and overpowered with numbers, he extricated himself, and effected a skilful retreat. On the 1st of March O.S. he was joined by Captain Rousso, and his brother-in-law Anagnosti (both men of very bad character;) he received them with joy, not suspecting their sinister intentions towards him. Understanding that the Pasha of Candia was marching with 500 troops towards Furfura, and was to sleep at Abadia, he proposed to the Sfakiotes to surprise him there in the night; but they declined, and persuaded him to go on the expedition with his own troops, added to 100 from Sfakia. He set out accordingly with 300 men, half of whom deserted by the way: nevertheless, he entered Abadia, and, by speaking Turkish, deceived the inhabitants, and induced them to open their houses, pretending that the Greeks were coming to attack them. When once in, he exterminated the Mohammedans, capturing thirty-six horseloads of biscuit, twelve chests of silk, and all their cattle. With this booty he returned to Monastrevo, and even gave a share to the Sfakiotes who had left him on the road. Rousso and Anagnosti having sent Captain Antonio an invitation to feast with them, and accept their congratulations on his late victory, he went with a few of his followers. At table, Rousso began to pick a quarrel with him, and even said he would kill him, but Antonio answered him mildly. Presently after, while Melidori was amusing himself by fencing with one of his men, Rousso drew his sword and made at him; however, they were separated. Antonio then inveighing against the Sfakiotes, called for his horse and departed, but Anagnosti followed and begged him to return, assuring him Rousso was sorry for what had passed. Melidori assented to a reconciliation, when the traitor Rousso, in the act of embracing, plunged a dagger into his bosom. †

not dread devils, much less Turks and Sfakiotes; have patience, and every thing will go well. Be good and brave as you have ever been, and your country will honour you.   (Signed)   MICHAEL AFFENDOULIEFF.

" Perveli, February 11th, (O.S.) 1822."

† The MS. Memoirs of a Philhellene, then serving in Crete, give nearly the same account of Antonio's death.

END OF VOLUME FIRST.

EDINBURGH: PRINTED BY BALLANTYNE AND COMPANY.

London, January 1833,

PUBLISHED BY

JAMES DUNCAN,

37, PATERNOSTER ROW.

I. MEMORIALS of the PROFESSIONAL LIFE and
TIMES of Sir WILLIAM PENN, Knight, Admiral and General of the
Fleet during the Interregnum ; Admiral, and Commissioner of the Admiralty and Navy after the Restoration. From 1644 to 1670. By GRANVILLE
PENN, Esq. In Two Vols. 8vo. 1*l.* 16*s.*

Also, edited by the same Author,

THE CHARACTER of a TRIMMER. His Opinion of, 1. The Laws
and Government ; 2. Protestant Religion ; 3. The Papists ; 4. Foreign
Affairs. By the Honourable Sir WILLIAM COVENTRY, Knight. First
printed in 1687. 8vo, uniform with the above, 5*s.*

In Two Volumes 8vo., price 18*s. boards,*

II. THE YEAR of LIBERATION ; a Journal of the
Defence of Hamburgh against the French Army under Marshal Davoust,
in 1813, with Sketches of the Battles of Lutzen, Bautzen, &c. &c. By the
Author of " Salathiel."
" This is a work which compensates us for the perusal of a great deal of trash. Here are
truth, spirit, humour, and information combined on a subject of great and perpetual
interest."—*Spectator.*
" A book written with great spirit and talent, full of good sense and good feeling."—*Times.*

III. A SCRIPTURAL COMMENTARY on the BOOK of
GENESIS and the GOSPEL according to ST. MATTHEW ; comprising
the sacred Text of these Books, with most copious marginal References
annexed to each Clause of each Verse, in the Words of Scripture. By the
Rev. CHARLES LAMBERT COGHLAN, D.D. Vicar of Kilcaskin in the
Diocese of Ross. In Two Vols. 8vo, price 24*s.* boards.

IV. THE LAST DAYS of our LORD'S MINISTRY ; a
Course of Lectures delivered in Trinity Church, Coventry. By the Rev.
WALTER FARQUHAR HOOK, M.A. Prebendary of Lincoln, Vicar of the
Parish of the Holy Trinity, Coventry, and Chaplain in Ordinary to his
Majesty. In One Vol. 8vo, price 10*s.* 6*d.* boards.

V. HISTORY PHILOSOPHICALLY ILLUSTRATED,
from the Fall of the Roman Empire to the French Revolution. By
GEORGE MILLER, D.D. M.R.I.A., formerly Fellow of Trinity College,
Dublin. In Four Vols. 8vo, price 2*l.* 2*s.* boards.
" The general style of these volumes is honourable to the author's scholarship: it is
remarkably distinct, vigorous, and free from superfluous ornament; but in parts where the
subject admitted of the change, it becomes rich and eloquent. The brief sketch of Grattan's
oratory, towards the close of the fourth volume, is one of the happiest and most graphic
descriptions that we have ever seen of that singularly powerful speaker. On the whole, we
entirely congratulate the author and the public on the completion of this performance.
What Montesquieu accomplished for the laws of Europe, Dr. Miller has done for its history.
We know of no text-book which would be more essential to the college lecturer, no general
view of facts which is likely to be more valuable to the student, and no elucidation of the
mysterious ways of Providence which ought to be more gladly welcomed by the Christian."—
Literary Gazette, March 24, 1832,

VI. THE REMAINS of WILLIAM PHELAN, D.D.; with a Biographical Memoir. By JOHN, Bishop of Limerick, Ardfert, and Aghadoe. Second Edition. In Two Vols. 8vo, price 21s. boards.

VII. LIVES, CHARACTERS, and an ADDRESS to POSTERITY. By GILBERT BURNET, D.D., late Bishop of Sarum; edited, with an Introduction and Notes, by JOHN, Bishop of Limerick, Ardfert, and Aghadoe. In One Vol. 8vo, price 10s. 6d. boards.

VIII. PRACTICAL THEOLOGY; comprising Discourses on the Liturgy and Principles of the United Church of England and Ireland; critical and other Tracts; and a Speech delivered in the House of Peers in 1824. By JOHN JEBB, D.D. F.R.S., Bishop of Limerick, Ardfert, and Aghadoe. In Two Vols. 8vo, price 24s. boards.

"No work which has recently fallen into our hands more amply fulfils the promise of its title than that now before us."—*Quarterly Theolog. Review.*

IX. SACRED LITERATURE; comprising a Review of the Principles of Composition laid down by the late ROBERT LOWTH, D.D. Lord Bishop of London, in his Prælections, and Isaiah; and an application of the Principles so reviewed to the Illustration of the New Testament; in a Series of Critical Observations on the Style and Structure of that Sacred Volume. By JOHN JEBB, D.D. F.R.S. Bishop of Limerick, Ardfert, and Aghadoe. In One Vol. 8vo. New Edition, price 12s. boards.

X. SERMONS on Subjects chiefly Practical; with illustrative Notes, and an Appendix relating to the Character of the Church of England, as distinguished both from other Branches of the Reformation, and from the modern Church of Rome. By JOHN JEBB, F.R.S., Bishop of Limerick, Ardfert, and Aghadoe. Fourth Edition, corrected. In One Vol. 8vo, price 10s. 6d. boards.

XI. PIETY without ASCETICISM, or the PROTESTANT KEMPIS; a Manual of Christian Faith and Practice, selected from the Writings of Scougal, Charles How, and Cudworth; with Corrections and occasional Notes. By JOHN JEBB, D.D. F.R.S. Bishop of Limerick, Ardfert, and Aghadoe. In One Vol. 8vo, price 12s. boards.

XII. PASTORAL INSTRUCTIONS on the CHARACTER and PRINCIPLES of the CHURCH of ENGLAND, selected from his former Writings. By JOHN JEBB, D.D. F.R.S. Bishop of Limerick, Ardfert, and Aghadoe. In One Volume, price 7s. boards.

XIII. MAHOMETANISM UNVEILED; an Inquiry in which that Arch-Heresy, its Diffusion and Continuance, are examined on a new principle, tending to confirm the Evidences, and aid the Propagation of the Christian Faith. By the Rev. CHARLES FORSTER, B.D., Chancellor of Ardfert, and Examining Chaplain to the Lord Bishop of Limerick. In Two Vols. 8vo, 24s. boards.

"The reader will find the subject of the Ishmaelitish descent of the Arabian treated in a clear and convincing manner by Mr. Forster, in his learned and valuable work, Mahometanism Unveiled."—*Quarterly Review,* No. 83.

"From the novelty of the view which is thus given of Mahometanism, and the ability displayed by the author, we shall be greatly mistaken if a serious discussion of the whole subject be not revived among the learned men of the country."—*Monthly Review.*

XIV. THE LIFE and PONTIFICATE of SAINT PIUS the FIFTH.

Subjoined is a Re-impression of a Historic Deduction of the Episcopal Oath of Allegiance to the Pope in the Church of Rome. By the Rev. JOSEPH MENDHAM, M.A. In One Vol. 8vo, with Portrait, price 10s. 6d. boards.

" We recommend to our readers Mr. Mendham's interesting and ably executed volume, as exhibiting a faithful picture (the materials and colouring of which are derived from Popish authorities that cannot be rejected) of the papal constitution in church, state, and doctrine; and we shall rejoice to know that our pages have been instrumental in extending the utility of his truly valuable labours."—*Christian Remembrancer*, November 1832.

Also, by the same Author,

THE LITERARY POLICY of the CHURCH of ROME exhibited, in an Account of her Damnatory Catalogues or Indexes, both Prohibitory and Expurgatory, with various illustrative Extracts, Anecdotes, and Remarks. In One Vol. 8vo, price 10s. 6d. boards.

XV. AN ESSAY upon NATIONAL CHARACTER; being

an Inquiry into some of the principal Causes which contribute to form and modify the Character of Nations in the state of Civilization. By RICHARD CHENEVIX, Esq. F.R.S.L. and E.M.R.I.A. &c. In Two Vols. 8vo, price 28s. boards.

" What a noble legacy for a man to leave behind him! In these volumes are garnered the labours of a life—a life of profound investigation and of immense knowledge, digested by a singularly clear and contemplative mind. It is a work put forth too in the noblest spirit of literature—that which looks to the future, and builds up, not a palace for self to dwell in, but a noble and enduring monument for the instruction of ages yet to come."—*Literary Gazette*, January 14, 1832.

" We have not spoken of the author's style, which constitutes no small part of the attraction and charm of the work. Uniformly perspicuous, correct, and unaffected, it sometimes rises into eloquence. As the author's pride and vanity are now alike buried in the dust, our approbation or censure cannot affect him; but we have been not the less anxious to do justice to a work upon which have been bestowed the meditations of a life, and the best efforts of a mind of no ordinary endowments."—*Eclectic Review*, April 1832.

XVI. SIX SERMONS on the STUDY of the HOLY SCRIP-

TURES, their Nature, Interpretation, and some of their most important Doctrines, preached before the University of Cambridge in the years 1827–8. To which are annexed Two Dissertations; the first on the Reasonableness of the Orthodox Views of Christianity as opposed to the Rationalism of Germany; the second on the Interpretation of Prophecy generally, with an original Exposition of the Book of Revelation, shewing that the whole of that remarkable prophecy has long ago been fulfilled. By the Rev. S. LEE, B.D., D.D. of Halle, Prebendary of Bristol; Vicar of Banwell; and Regius Professor of Hebrew in the University of Cambridge, &c. &c. In One Vol. 8vo, price 14s. bds.

XVII. A SECOND COURSE of SERMONS for the YEAR;

containing Two for each Sunday, and one for each Holyday; abridged from the most eminent Divines of the Established Church, and adapted to the Service of the Day: intended for the Use of Families and Schools. Dedicated, by permission, to the Lord Bishop of London. By the Rev. J. R. PITMAN, A.M., alternate Morning Preacher of Belgrave and Berkeley Chapels. In Two Vols. 8vo, price 21s. boards.

" There is no question which the Clergy are more frequently asked, and to which they find it more difficult to give a satisfactory reply than this—What Sermons would they recommend for the use of a private family? There are so many circumstances which render the greater part of modern discourses totally unfit for the purposes of domestic instruction, and the old standards, unmodernised, are so little intelligible to common ears, that it is no easy matter to point out any set of discourses embracing a sufficient variety to excite attention, at the same time forcibly inculcating the pure doctrines and practical precepts of Christianity. We really think that Mr. Pitman's work bids fair to supply the deficiency which has been so much regretted."—*Quarterly Theolog. Review.*

*** A Third Edition, *revised throughout*, of the FIRST COURSE is just published, same size and price as above.

XVIII. The WHOLE WORKS of the Right Rev. JEREMY TAYLOR, D.D., Lord Bishop of Down, Connor, and Dromore, with a Life of the Author, and a Critical Examination of his Writings. By the Right Rev. REGINALD HEBER, D.D., late Lord Bishop of Calcutta. In 15 Volumes 8vo, new edition, price 9*l.* boards.

Also may be had separate, by the same Author,

1. HOLY LIVING and DYING. 8*vo.* price 12*s.* boards.
2. A COURSE of SERMONS for all the SUNDAYS of the YEAR. Two Vols. 8vo, price 24*s.* boards.
3. The LIFE of the Right Rev. JEREMY TAYLOR. In One Vol. 8vo, with a Portrait, price 10*s.* 6*d.* boards.

XIX. THE WHOLE WORKS of the Most Reverend Father in God, ROBERT LEIGHTON, D.D., Archbishop of Glasgow. To which is prefixed an entire new Life of the Author, by the Rev. J. N. PEARSON, M.A., of Trinity College, Cambridge, and Chaplain to the Most Noble the Marquess Wellesley. In Four Vols. 8vo, with a Portrait, price 36*s.* boards.

" We have placed a new edition of Archbishop Leighton's Works at the head of this article; and as Mr. Coleridge has neglected to furnish the biographical notice he had promised, we shall endeavour to supply its place by a few particulars of his life and writings, principally extracted from a spirited and eloquent Memoir prefixed to the new edition, by the Rev. Norman Pearson. It is a reproach to the present age, that his valuable writings, breathing as they do the sublimest and purest spirit of piety, rich in beautiful images and classical learning, throughout abounding in practical reflections, and all expressed with the sweetest and simplest eloquence, should have been neglected among us."—*British Critic.*

** The above may be had, printed in a small but neat type, and compressed into Two Volumes, price 21*s.* boards.

XX. A PRACTICAL COMMENTARY upon the FIRST EPISTLE of ST. PETER, and other Expository Works. By ROBERT LEIGHTON, D.D., Archbishop of Glasgow. To which is prefixed an entire new Life of the Author, by the Rev. J. N. PEARSON, M.A., Trinity College, Cambridge, &c. In Two Volumes 8vo., with Portrait, price 18*s.* boards.

** Compressed into One Volume, price 10*s.* 6*d.* boards.

XXI. The WORKS of the Right Rev. WILLIAM BEVE-RIDGE, D.D., Lord Bishop of St. Asaph, now first collected: with a Memoir of the Author, and a Critical Examination of his Writings, by the Rev. THOMAS HARTWELL HORNE, B.D., of St. John's College, Cambridge; Author of the " Introduction to the Holy Scriptures." In Nine Vols. 8vo, with a Portrait, uniform with the Works of Bishop Taylor, price 5*l.* 8*s.* boards.

XXII. The PRACTICAL WORKS of the REV. RICHARD BAXTER, with a Life of the Author, and a Critical Examination of his Writings. By the Rev. WILLIAM ORME. In Twenty-three Vols. 8vo, with finely engraved Portrait, price 12*l.* 12*s.* boards.

Also may be had separate,

The LIFE and TIMES of RICHARD BAXTER, with a Critical Examination of his Writings. By the Rev. WILLIAM ORME. In Two Vols. 8vo, with finely engraved Portrait, price 1*l.* 1*s.* boards.

XXIII. A THEOLOGICAL DICTIONARY; containing Definitions of all Religious Terms; a comprehensive View of every Article in the System of Divinity; an impartial Account of all the principal Denominations which have subsisted in the Religious World from the Birth of Christ to the present Day: together with an accurate Statement of the most remarkable Transactions and Events recorded in Ecclesiastical History. By the late Rev. CHARLES BUCK. Seventh Edition, corrected and greatly extended, by the Rev. E. HENDERSON, D.D., Professor of Divinity in Highbury College. In One very large Vol. 8vo. 18*s.*

** The number of additional articles in the present Edition amounts to nearly Five Hundred.—*Vide Preface.*

XXIV. A HISTORY of BRITISH ANIMALS, exhibiting the descriptive Characters and systematical Arrangement of the Genera and Species of Quadrupeds, Birds, Reptiles, Fishes, Mollusca, and Radiata, of the United Kingdom ; including the Indigenous, Extirpated, and Extinct Kinds ; together with Periodical and Occasional Visitants. By JOHN FLEMING, D.D., F.R.S.E., M.W.S., &c., and Author of the "Philosophy of Zoology." In One Vol. 8vo, price 18s. boards.

" This very important work, which has just appeared, we consider as infinitely superior to any Natural History of British Animals hitherto published. It will become the standard book on British Animals."—*Jamieson's Journal of Science.*

XXV. An INQUIRY into the MODERN PREVAILING NOTIONS respecting that FREEDOM of WILL which is supposed to be Essential to Moral Agency, Virtue and Vice, Reward and Punishment, Praise and Blame. By JONATHAN EDWARDS, A.M. With an Introductory Essay by the Author of "*Natural History of Enthusiasm.*" In One Vol. 8vo, price 12s. ; or in One Vol. 12mo, price 8s. 6d. boards.

" The author of *Natural History of Enthusiasm* has already taken his station among the most influential, as well as the most truly philosophical writers of the day ; and his present performance, whatever attention it may meet with, we cannot but regard as the most valuable service which he has yet rendered to the cause of truth and Scriptural piety."—*Eclectic Review,* October 1831.

" And now, having brought to a close our review of this very beautiful Essay, we cordially and confidently recommend it to our philosophical readers as an uncommonly able and eloquent performance."—*Presbyterian Review,* September 1831.

XXVI. CHRISTIAN RECORDS ; or, a Short and Plain History of the CHURCH of CHRIST : containing the Lives of the Apostles ; an Account of the Sufferings of Martyrs ; the Rise of the Reformation, and the present State of the Christian Church. By the Rev. THOMAS SIMS, M.A. Third Edition. In One Volume, 18mo, with a beautiful Frontispiece, price 3s. 6d. boards.

" Every Protestant child and young person should be generally acquainted with the outline of the history of the Church of Christ, and for this purpose we cannot recommend a better manual than that before us."—*Christian Observer,* January 1830.

*** This little Volume has been in part translated into the modern Greek and Chinese languages, by the Rev. Mr. JOWETT and Dr. MILNE.

XXVII. A SHORT HISTORY of the CHRISTIAN CHURCH, from its Erection at Jerusalem down to the Present Time. Designed for the Use of Schools, Families, &c. By the Rev. JOHN FRY, B.A., Rector of Desford, in Leicestershire. In One Vol. 8vo, 12s. boards.

" His matter is unquestionably selected with judgment, and luminously arranged ; his language is clear and concise, and not deficient in elegance ; and we rise from the perusal of his work with very favourable impressions of his character, with which otherwise we are unacquainted."—*Theological Review.*

" To such readers as wish for an Ecclesiastical History, written on the model of Milner's, and animated by the same spirit, Mr. F.'s work will be highly acceptable, particularly as it is complete, and comprised within a single volume."—*Eclectic Review.*

By the same Author,

1. A NEW TRANSLATION and EXPOSITION of the very Ancient BOOK OF JOB ; with Notes, explanatory and philological. In One Vol. 8vo, price 12s. boards.

2. LECTURES, Explanatory and Practical, on the EPISTLE of ST. PAUL to the ROMANS. Second Edition, in One Vol. 8vo, price 12s. boards.

3. CANTICLES ; or, SONG OF SOLOMON : a new Translation, with Notes, and an Attempt to interpret the Sacred Allegories contained in that Book ; to which is added, an Essay on the Name and Character of the Redeemer. In One Vol. 8vo. Second Edition, price 6s. boards.

XXVIII. A GREEK and ENGLISH LEXICON, for the
Greek Classics in general, but especially for the Septuagint, Apocrypha, and New Testament. By the Rev. GREVILLE EWING, Glasgow. In One large Vol. 8vo. Third Edition, price 24s. boards ; or the Lexicon may be had separate, price 18s.; the Grammar, 6s. boards.

" From its size, cheapness, and laudable brevity (in most respects), this book is capable of becoming generally useful."—*British Critic and Theological Review.*

" The student who is not neglectful of his own benefit in the most essential respects, will possess himself of the book, if in his power. Its cheapness is only equalled by the beauties and clearness of its typography ; and in the grand point of accuracy it is exemplary."—*Eclectic Review.*

XXIX. A MANUAL of RELIGIOUS INSTRUCTION for
the YOUNG. By the Rev. ROBERT SIMSON, M.A. Master of Colebrooke House Academy, Islington. In One Vol. 18mo, price 5s. boards.

" In presenting to the notice of our readers this interesting volume, our limits will scarcely allow us to do more than briefly to hint at the contents of this beautiful and valuable volume."—*Congregational Magazine.*

" This is a very comprehensive and useful little work."—*Evangelical Magazine.*

" Were all our British youth armed with as much religious knowledge as is contained in this book, infidelity could no longer stalk about our streets, or rear its hideous head in our land."—*Sunday School Teacher's Magazine.*

XXX. ELEMENTS of CONCHOLOGY, according to the
Linnæan System; illustrated by Twenty-eight Plates, drawn from Nature. By the Rev. E. I. BURROW, A.M., &c. Third Edition. In 8vo, price 16s. boards ; or beautifully coloured by Sowerby, price 1l. 11s. 6d. boards.

XXXI. BIBLIA HEBRAICA, Editio longè Accuratissima.
Ab EVERARDO VAN DER HOOGHT, V.D.M. In One large Vol. 8vo, (1200 pages) price 1l. 5s. boards.

It has been the particular object of the Publisher to offer to the Public a neat and correct copy of the Hebrew Scriptures at a moderate price ; and to ensure every attainable degree of accuracy, every page has been (independent of the care previously bestowed upon it) revised five times after the stereotype plates were cast, by persons familiar with the Hebrew language. The errors which have been discovered in the edition of Van der Hooght have in this been carefully corrected ; and the Publisher is determined to avail himself of that security which stereotype printing alone affords, to guard against their recurrence in future.

XXXII. A GRAMMAR of the HEBREW LANGUAGE;
comprised in a Series of Lectures, compiled from the best Authorities, and augmented with much Original Matter, drawn principally from Oriental Sources ; designed for the Use of Students in the Universities. By the Rev. S. LEE, B.D. ; D.D. of the University of Halle ; Honorary Member of the Asiatic Society of Paris ; Honorary Associate and F.R.S.L. and M.R.A.S. &c. &c. ; and Regius Professor of Hebrew in the University of Cambridge. Second Edition. In One Vol. 8vo, price 14s. boards.

*** Professor LEE is preparing for publication a HEBREW and ENGLISH DICTIONARY, in One large Vol. 8vo.

XXXIII. CORPUS POETARUM LATINORUM. Edited by
W. S. WALKER, Esq. Fellow of Trinity College, Cambridge. In One large Vol. 8vo, price 2l. 2s.

The authors comprised in this Volume constitute THE WHOLE OF THE CLASSICAL LATIN POETS, chronologically arranged, with brief notices of their Lives.

The Texts of the CORPUS POETARUM have not only been selected by the Editor from the best editions; but the Orthography and Punctuation have been by him reduced to a uniform Standard. The greatest care has been taken to ensure correctness in the Printing.

The peculiar advantages of this Edition are, its *portability* and its *cheapness*. The whole body of Latin Poetry may now lie *for reference on the table of the Student*, in a single Volume, printed in a type of great distinctness. The very lowest price of a pocket edition of those Authors, who are here given *entire, without the omission of a single line*, is about SIX GUINEAS. In the common Delphin Editions, they amount to EIGHT GUINEAS. The CORPUS POETARUM is thus *two-thirds cheaper* than any edition, even of the Text only, of the Latin Poets.

XXXIV. THE AJAX of SOPHOCLES, illustrated by English Notes. By the Rev. J. R. PITMAN, A.M. In One Vol. 8vo, price 9s. bds.

The Editor has endeavoured to comprise in the notes the most useful remarks of all the commentators on this play, and has made numerous references to the works of modern critics, by whom the force, either of single words or of idiomatical expressions, has been illustrated.

XXXV. TABLES of INTEREST, at 3, 4, 4½, and 5 per Cent, from 1*l.* to 10,000*l.*, and from 1 to 365 days, in a regular progression of single days; with Tables at all the above rates from 1 to 12 months, and from 1 to 10 years. By JOHN THOMSON, Accountant in Edinburgh. In One Volume, 12mo, Tenth Edition, price 8s. bound.

J. DUNCAN having purchased the whole remaining Copies of the under-mentioned Works, is enabled to offer them, for a limited time, at the low prices affixed.

1. PLATONIS OPERA OMNIA; recensuit et Commentariis Scholiisque illustravit IMMANUEL BEKKERUS. Accedunt Virorum Doctorum Heindorf, Wyttenbach, Ast, Buttmann, Gottleber, Pindeisen, Serrani, Routh, Stallbaum, Nitzch, Heusde, Fischer, Boeckh, Lange, Nurnburger, Stutzmann, F. A. Wolf, aliorumque Annotationes Textui subjectæ, Versio Latina, et Timæi Lexicon Vocum Platonicarum. In Eleven Vols. 8vo, price 7*l.* 14*s.*, or on large paper, royal octavo (of which only 150 copies are printed), price 11*l.* 11*s.* extra boards.

This beautiful Edition has received the highest encomiums from the late Professor Dobree, and many other eminent British and Continental Scholars, and is the only Variorum one hitherto published: it contains the whole of the Greek Text, revised and amended from manuscripts now first collated or used in any edition of Plato; the Latin Translation of Ficinus; the Greek Scholia; the Annotations, either entire or select, of the different Commentators on the Text of Plato, or the Works attributed to him; a Reprint of the Lexicon Platonicum of Timæus, as edited by Ruhnken; the whole preceded by Fischer's Literary Notice of the Life and Writings of Plato. Bekker's Text and Scholia are used, and such typographical errors are corrected as had escaped that Editor's vigilance.

The spirited Projector of this fine Classic intended to publish it at 10*l.* 10*s.* for the small, and 18*l.* 18*s.* for the large paper; but it is now offered at the above-mentioned reduced prices.

2. EURIPIDIS OPERA OMNIA. In Nine Vols. 8vo, small paper, 10*l.* 10*s.*, now offered for 6*l.* 6*s.*; large paper, 18*l.* 18*s.*, now offered for 10*l.* 10*s.*

3. THE WORKS of Dr. JOHN TILLOTSON, Archbishop of Canterbury, with LIFE. In Ten Vols. 8vo, 5*l.* 5*s.*, now offered for 3*l.* 10*s.*

4. PATRICK, LOWTH, and ARNOLD'S COMMENTARIES on the OLD and NEW TESTAMENTS. In Six Vols. royal 4to, price 12*l.* 12*s.*, now offered for 9*l.* 9*s.*

5. NOVUS THESAURUS PHILOLOGICO-CRITICUS; sive, Lexicon in LXX. et reliquos Interpretes Græcos, ac Scriptores Apocryphos Veteris Testamenti, congessit et edidit J. FREID. SCHLEUSNER. In Three thick Vols. 8vo, price 3*l.* 12*s.*, now offered for 2*l.* 2*s.*

" In this Edition many typographical errors have been corrected. Professor Schleusner's German explanations of particular words uniformly have English translations attached to them, and to the Third Volume there is appended an Index of all the Hebrew words occurring in the work; together with a Collection of verses and chapters, as set out respectively in the editions of the Greek Septuagint, by Wechel and Bos. This Appendix, which nearly fills 300 pages, is not to be found in the Leipsic edition."—HORNE's *Introduction to the Scriptures,* vol. ii. p. 72, Appendix.

6. SCHLEUSNER'S LEXICON to the NEW TESTAMENT. In Two very thick Vols. 8vo. price 3*l.*, now offered for 1*l.* 18*s.*

DEDICATED, BY PERMISSION, TO HIS MAJESTY.

*In Thirty Volumes 18mo, with numerous Maps and Engravings,
price 8l. 5s. bds.*

THE MODERN TRAVELLER;

CONTAINING

A Description, Geographical, Historical, and Topographical, of the Various
Countries of the Globe, compiled from the latest and best Authorities.

EDITED BY JOSIAH CONDER.

** The various Countries may be had separate, price 5s. 6d. per Vol., bds.

"We speak within the most cautious bounds when we say, that in any Volume of this
work the traveller will find more of the actual material of which he stands in need—the real
distinct matter-of-fact information—than in any ten voyages and travels to the same region.
No work can be found in our language, or any other, equal to supply the place of the
Modern Traveller."—*Literary Gazette.*

"Conder's Modern Traveller is worth all the Libraries taken together."—*Fraser's Mag.*
August 1831.

In Three Vols. 18mo, embellished with numerous Plates and Maps, 18s. bds,

ITALY.

By JOSIAH CONDER, Author of, "The Modern Traveller."
and in continuation of that Work.

"Conder's Italy will in future be the travelling companion of every man bent upon a
thorough investigation of that interesting land. He is the best compiler of the day;
and this is no small praise. Such compilation as Mr. Conder's requires industry of a
laborious nature, considerable knowledge, a methodical head, judgment, taste,—are these
qualities to be met with every where? Look at the manner in which compilations are
usually performed, and the question is answered. Mr. Conder is the compiler of the
Modern Traveller, the best and completest geographical and descriptive work in any
language. In the course of that work, the author, commencing anonymously, worked his
way up to distinction; and we pride ourselves on having taken every opportunity, public
and private, of pointing out the merits—modest, unpretending, but sterling merits—of the
book and the book-maker. Italy is on the plan; and, as we should conceive, a portion, of the
Modern Traveller detached, probably to attract the attention of persons who are solely
interested in that country. It contains the pith and marrow of all preceding travellers;
and Mr. Conder has shewn, that by staying at home, one may learn a great deal more about
a country than by running through it,—just as Mr. Mill has said, in his preface to the
British India, there was an advantage, in writing the history of a country, never to have
seen it. Three small volumes now contain the Italian traveller's library : with this work,
and a book of posts or roads, and a good map, the curious inquirer is completely set up;
he may throw Eustace overboard, surrender Lady Morgan to the Austrian douaniers, turn
his back on the Invalid, and cut the caustic Mr. Forsyth."—*Spectator*, April 23, 1831.

"We sincerely congratulate the public upon the appearance of a work which really is an
accurate and complete account of Modern Italy."—*Asiatic Journal,* May 1831.

LONDON:—J. MOYES, 28, CASTLE STREET, LEICESTER SQUARE.